Fodor's

GUATEMALA

2nd Edition

Where to Stay and Eat for All Budgets

Must-See Sights and Local Secrets

Ratings You Can Trust

Fodor's Travel Publications New York, Toronto, London, Sydney, Auckland
www.fodors.com

FODOR'S GUATEMALA

Editor: Molly Moker

Editorial Contributors: Joanna G. Cantor
Writers: Gerard Helferich, Teresa Nicholas, Lan Sluder, Jeffrey Van Fleet

Production Editor: Astrid deRidder
Maps & Illustrations: David Lindroth Inc.; Mark Stroud, Moon Street Cartography, *cartographers;* Bob Blake, Rebecca Baer, *map editors;* William Wu, *information graphics*
Design: Fabrizio La Rocca, *creative director;* Guido Caroti, Siobhan O'Hare, *art directors;* Tina Malaney, Chie Ushio, Ann McBride, Jessica Walsh, *designers;* Melanie Marin, *senior picture editor*
Cover Photo: (Hoku canoes on Lago Atitlan with San Pedro Volcano): Robert Leon/ www.robertleon.com
Production Manager: Angela McLean

COPYRIGHT

2nd Edition

ISBN 978-1-4000-0421-8

ISSN 1939-9901

SPECIAL SALES

This book is available at special discounts for bulk purchases for sales promotions or premiums. Special editions, including personalized covers, excerpts of existing books, and corporate imprints, can be created in large quantities for special needs. For more information, write to Special Markets/Premium Sales, 1745 Broadway, MD 6-2, New York, New York 10019, or e-mail specialmarkets@randomhouse.com.

AN IMPORTANT TIP & AN INVITATION

Although all prices, opening times, and other details in this book are based on information supplied to us at press time, changes occur all the time in the travel world, and Fodor's cannot accept responsibility for facts that become outdated or for inadvertent errors or omissions. So **always confirm information when it matters,** especially if you're making a detour to visit a specific place. Your experiences—positive and negative—matter to us. If we have missed or misstated something, **please write to us.** We follow up on all suggestions. Contact the Guatemala editor at editors@fodors.com or c/o Fodor's at 1745 Broadway, New York, NY 10019.

PRINTED IN THE UNITED STATES OF AMERICA

10 9 8 7 6 5 4 3 2 1

Be a Fodor's Correspondent

Your opinion matters. It matters to us. It matters to your fellow Fodor's travelers, too. And we'd like to hear it. In fact, we need to hear it.

When you share your experiences and opinions, you become an active member of the Fodor's community. That means we'll not only use your feedback to make our books better, but we'll publish your names and comments whenever possible. Throughout our guides, look for "Word of Mouth," excerpts of your unvarnished feedback.

Here's how you can help improve Fodor's for all of us.

Tell us when we're right. We rely on local writers to give you an insider's perspective. But our writers and staff editors—who are the best in the business—depend on you. Your positive feedback is a vote to renew our recommendations for the next edition.

Tell us when we're wrong. We're proud that we update most of our guides every year. But we're not perfect. Things change. Hotels cut services. Museums change hours. Charming cafés lose charm. If our writer didn't quite capture the essence of a place, tell us how you'd do it differently. If any of our descriptions are inaccurate or inadequate, we'll incorporate your changes in the next edition and will correct factual errors at fodors.com immediately.

Tell us what to include. You probably have had fantastic travel experiences that aren't yet in Fodor's. Why not share them with a community of like-minded travelers? Maybe you chanced upon a beach or bistro or B&B that you don't want to keep to yourself. Tell us why we should include it. And share your discoveries and experiences with everyone directly at fodors.com. Your input may lead us to add a new listing or highlight a place we cover with a "Highly Recommended" star or with our highest rating, "Fodor's Choice."

Give us your opinion instantly at our feedback center at www.fodors.com/feedback. You may also e-mail editors@fodors.com with the subject line "Guatemala Editor." Or send your nominations, comments, and complaints by mail to Guatemala Editor, Fodor's, 1745 Broadway, New York, NY 10019.

You and travelers like you are the heart of the Fodor's community. Make our community richer by sharing your experiences. Be a Fodor's correspondent.

¡Feliz viaje!

Tim Jarrell, Publisher

CONTENTS

MAPS

ABOUT THIS BOOK

Our Ratings

Sometimes you find terrific travel experiences and sometimes they just find you. But usually it's up to you to select the right combination of experiences. That's where our ratings come in.

As travelers we've all discovered a place so wonderful that its worthiness is obvious. And sometimes that place is so experiential that superlatives don't do it justice: you just have to be there to know. These sights, properties, and experiences get our highest rating, **Fodor's Choice,** indicated by orange stars throughout this book.

Black stars highlight sights and properties we deem **Highly Recommended,** places that our writers, editors, and readers praise again and again for consistency and excellence.

By default, there's another category: any place we include in this book is by definition worth your time, unless we say otherwise. And we will.

Disagree with any of our choices? Care to nominate a place or suggest that we rate one more highly? Visit our feedback center at www.fodors.com/feedback.

Budget Well

Hotel and restaurant price categories from ¢ to $$$$ are defined in the opening pages of each chapter. For attractions, we always give standard adult admission fees; reductions are usually available for children, students, and senior citizens. Want to pay with plastic? **AE, D, DC, MC, V** following restaurant and hotel listings indicates whether American Express, Discover, Diners Club, MasterCard, and Visa are accepted.

Restaurants

Unless we state otherwise, restaurants are open for lunch and dinner daily. We mention dress only when there's a specific requirement and reservations only when they're essential or not accepted—it's always best to book ahead.

Hotels

Hotels have private bath, phone, TV, and air-conditioning and operate on the European Plan (aka EP, meaning without meals), unless we specify that they use the Continental Plan (CP, with a continental breakfast), Breakfast Plan (BP, with a full breakfast), or Modified American Plan (MAP, with breakfast and dinner), or are all-inclusive (AI, including all meals and most activities). We always list facilities but not whether you'll be charged an extra fee to use them, so when pricing accommodations, find out what's included.

Many Listings

- ★ Fodor's Choice
- ★ Highly recommended
- ✉ Physical address
- ✣ Directions or Map coordinates
- ✉ Mailing address
- ☎ Telephone
- 🖷 Fax
- 🌐 On the Web
- ✉ E-mail
- 🎟 Admission fee
- ⏲ Open/closed times
- Ⓜ Metro stations
- 💳 Credit cards

Hotels & Restaurants

- 🏨 Hotel
- Number of rooms
- Facilities
- 🍽 Meal plans
- ✕ Restaurant
- Reservations
- Dress code
- Smoking
- BYOB

Outdoors

- ⛳ Golf
- ⛺ Camping

Other

- Family-friendly
- ⇨ See also
- ✉ Branch address
- ☞ Take note

Experience Guatemala

WORD OF MOUTH

"I've been to Antigua many times but this summer was the first time I'd visited the little indigenous villages surrounding it—lots of amazing museums, coffee farms, churches, convents, and cultural activities in places like Jocotenango, San Juan del Obispo, and San Antonion Aguas Calientes."

—hopefulist

"The highlight of my stay so far has been a guided hike with Roger's Tours. A short boat ride to San Marcos and then a three hour hike to Santa Cruz, stopping at the lovely Casa del Mundo for lunch. We had beautiful views of Lake Atitlan and the volcanoes the entire time."

—bar2150

www.fodors.com/community

WHAT'S WHERE

2 Guatemala City. The country's political, economic, and industrial capital is divided into 21 zonas, but you'll likely get to know only a few of them. Zona 1, its crowded heart with a few colonial monuments, is budget-travel central. The newer south-side zonas 9 and 10 have upscale hotels, restaurants, and shops.

3 Antigua. The colonial capital of Spanish Central America is continuously undergoing restoration of its centuries-old churches, convents, and palaces, but is just as content to leave some structures in ruins. Its proximity to Guatemala City means that you can fly in, get to Antigua in an hour, and never look back until it's time to go home.

4 The Highlands. Smoldering volcanoes, bustling markets, a shimmering lake, and a vibrant indigenous culture all lure visitors to the vast highlands that extend west from Antigua. The country's outposts on the Gringo Trail are all here: shop the twice-weekly market in Chichicastenango, study Spanish in Quetzaltenango, and swap travel stories with fellow visitors in Panajachel.

5 Las Verapaces. The Verapaces often get overlooked as an area to pass through rather than a destination. Don't make that mistake. The indigenous city of Cobán anchors this misty, ethereal cloud-forest region and Guatemala's ecotourism center. Partake of white-water sports, spelunking, and swimming.

6 Atlantic Lowlands. Wandering the streets of coastal Livingston will make you think you've detoured to Jamaica. The vibrant Garífuna culture, with roots in Africa and the Caribbean, gives a far different feel to this region. Then head inland via the magnificently canyoned Río Dulce, one of Guatemala's signature eco-excursions.

7 Pacific Lowlands. The lowland region sees few international visitors. The beach and water are written off as too rocky and rough, but a beach is a beach, and what's here is fun and funky, as evidenced by Monterrico, Guatemala's only community with a true beach-town vibe.

8 El Petén. The squared-off sector of northern Guatemala looks like the country's most inaccessible region, but is one of its most-visited ones. Credit Tikal, one of Mesoamerica's most famous Mayan ruins.

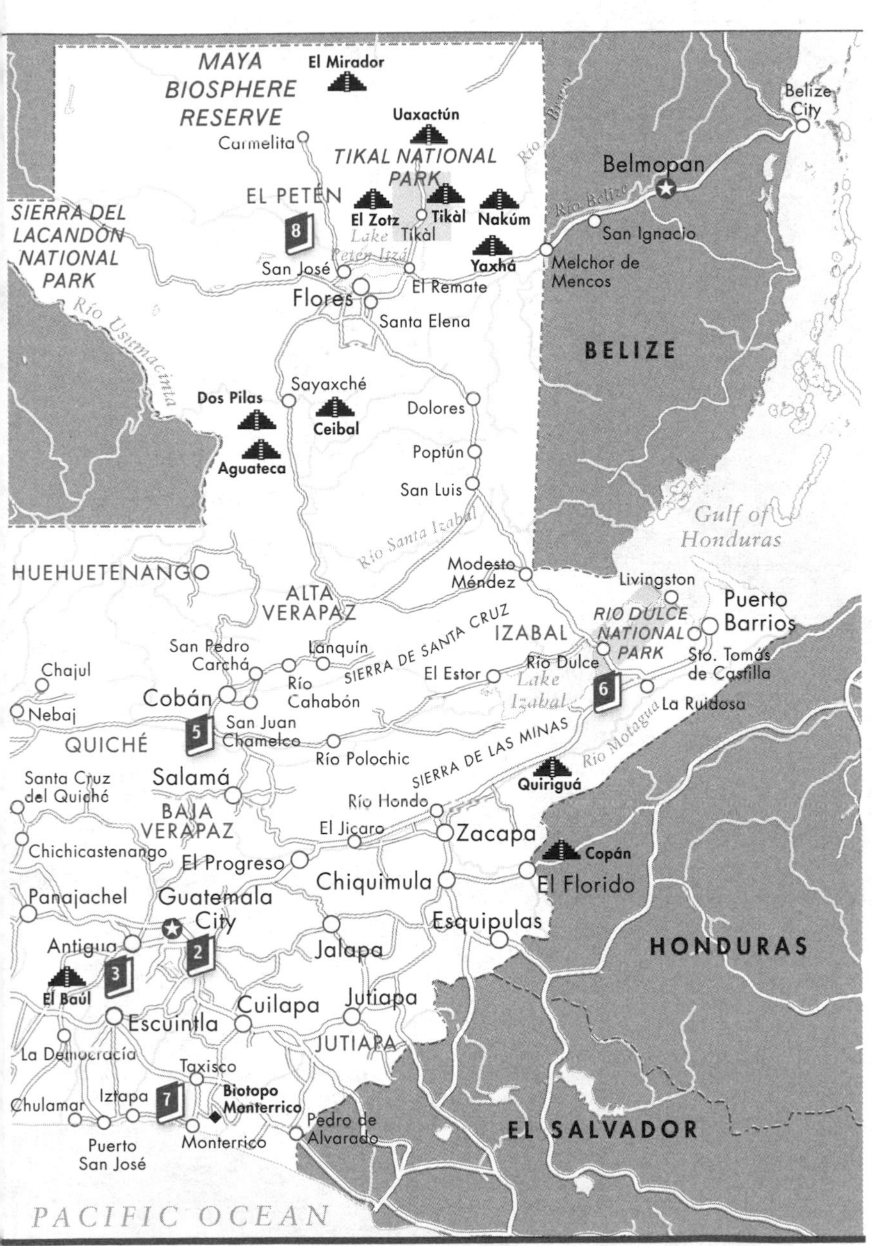
MAYA BIOSPHERE RESERVE
El Mirador
Uaxactún
Carmelita
TIKAL NATIONAL PARK
EL PETÉN
SIERRA DEL LACANDÓN NATIONAL PARK
El Zotz
Tikàl
Tikàl
Nakúm
Yaxhá
Lake Petén Itzá
San José
Flores
El Remate
Santa Elena
Río Usumacinta
Río Belize
Belize City
Belmopan
San Ignacio
Melchor de Mencos
BELIZE
Sayaxché
Dos Pilas
Ceibal
Aguateca
Dolores
Poptún
San Luis
Río Santa Izabal
Gulf of Honduras
HUEHUETENANGO
Modesto Méndez
Livingston
ALTA VERAPAZ
Puerto Barrios
RIO DULCE NATIONAL PARK
IZABAL
SIERRA DE SANTA CRUZ
San Pedro Carchá
Lanquín
Río Dulce
Sto. Tomás de Castilla
Chajul
Río Cahabón
El Estor
Lake Izabal
Cobán
La Ruidosa
Nebaj
San Juan Chamelco
QUICHÉ
Río Polochic
SIERRA DE LAS MINAS
Río Motagua
Santa Cruz del Quiché
Salamá
Quiriguá
BAJA VERAPAZ
Río Hondo
El Jícaro
Zacapa
Chichicastenango
El Progreso
Copán
Chiquimula
El Florido
Panajachel
Guatemala City
Esquipulas
HONDURAS
Antigua
Jalapa
El Baúl
Cuilapa
Jutiapa
Escuintla
JUTIAPA
La Democracía
Taxisco
Iztapa
Biotopo Monterrico
Chulamar
Pedro de Alvarado
Monterrico
EL SALVADOR
Puerto San José
PACIFIC OCEAN
1
2
3
5
6
7
8

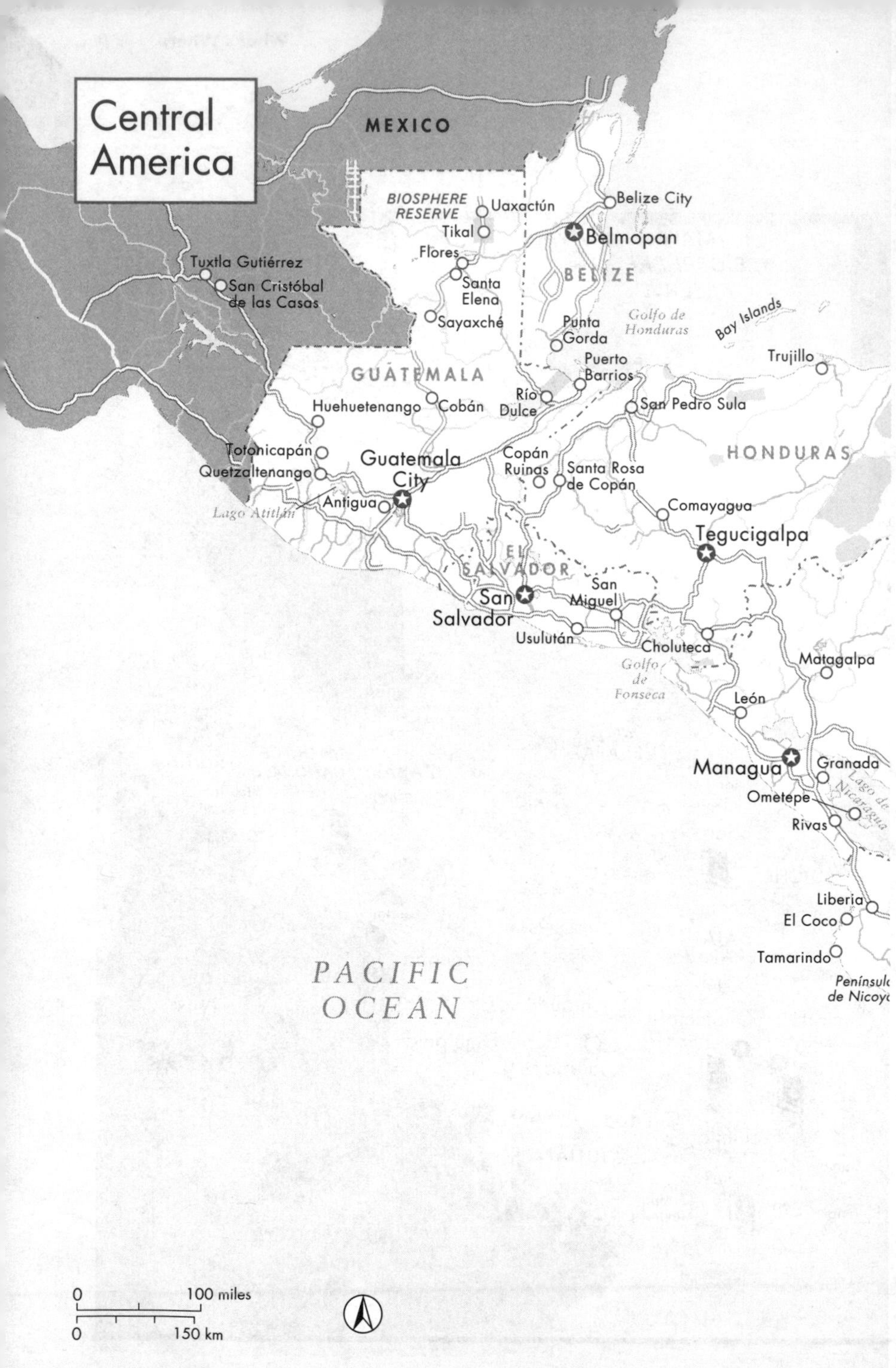

Central America

MEXICO
BIOSPHERE RESERVE
Uaxactún
Tikal
Belize City
Belmopan
Flores
Santa Elena
BELIZE
Tuxtla Gutiérrez
San Cristóbal de las Casas
Sayaxché
Punta Gorda
Golfo de Honduras
Bay Islands
Trujillo
Puerto Barrios
GUATEMALA
Río Dulce
Huehuetenango
Cobán
San Pedro Sula
Totonicapán
Quetzaltenango
Guatemala City
Copán Ruinas
Santa Rosa de Copán
HONDURAS
Lago Atitlán
Antigua
Comayagua
Tegucigalpa
EL SALVADOR
San Salvador
San Miguel
Usulután
Choluteca
Golfo de Fonseca
Matagalpa
León
Managua
Granada
Lago de Nicaragua
Ometepe
Rivas
Liberia
El Coco
Tamarindo
Península de Nicoya
PACIFIC OCEAN

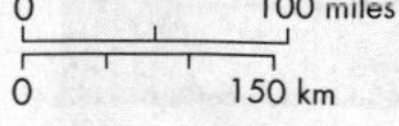

JAMAICA
Palacios
Puerto Lempira
Mosquitía
La Rosita
Puerto Cabezas
NICARAGUA
CARIBBEAN SEA
Laguna de Perkis
Isla de San Andrés
Rama
Bluefields
Islas del Maiz (Corn Islands)
Bahía Punta Gorda
COSTA RICA
Tortuguero
Turrialba
Limón
San José
Cartago
Golfo de Nicoya
Quepos
Bahía de Coronado
Bocas del Toro
San Blas Islands
El Porvenir
Panama Canal
Golfo de los Mosquitos
Panama City
Puerto Obaldia
Boquete
PANAMA
Bahía de Panamá
La Palma
Sirena
Matapalo
David
Península de Osa
Santiago
Chitré
Yaviza
Isla del Rey
Golfo de Chiriquí
Las Tablas
Golfo de Panamá
Isla de Coiba
COLOMBIA

GUATEMALA TODAY

. . . is modernizing its economy.
The cumbersome financial and economic systems of the past are no more. Recent administrations here have made a concerted effort to streamline Guatemala's economy, encourage foreign investment, and integrate the country into the modern world, as well as reduce its dependence on traditional agricultural crops (coffee, bananas, and sugar). Bulky, money-pit state enterprises have been privatized and made more efficient. Trade barriers have been reduced, as Guatemala has negotiated free-trade agreements with the United States, its Central American neighbors, and other countries. Much remains to be done, but infrastructure is improving, most notably in the transportation sector. Old Guatemala hands who remember a rickety primary-highway system will be pleasantly surprised to see how easy it is to get around between major cities, and the capital's La Aurora Airport, once one of the world's dreariest facilities, now gleams with space and efficiency following a 2007 makeover. There's always a "but" to these things, however: The new-found prosperity has not trickled down as much as the government has hoped. The richest 10 percent of the population still earn over half the country's income, and some 30 percent of Guatemalans live below the poverty line. A 30-percent illiteracy rate places limits on the marketability of the country's workforce to foreign firms. And the largest single contributor to the country's economy? It remains the remittances sent home by Guatemalans who live and work abroad—some estimates place the population of overseas Guatemalans at one million.

. . . is no-smoking.
One of the world's toughest no-smoking laws took effect in Guatemala in 2009, prohibiting lighting up in all public places. This includes stores, offices, public transportation terminals and vehicles, bars, restaurants, dance halls, and hotels. The prohibition even includes outdoor seating areas. The NO FUMAR signs are everywhere, and fines are heavy, both to the smoker (Q520, or $65) and to the business where the violation occurs (Q5,200, or $650).

. . . is religiously diverse.
Roman Catholicism, that historical bulwark of faith in Latin America, commands only a slight majority of believers in Guatemala. Evangelical and Pentecostal groups make up about one-third of the population, with mainline Protestants, Mormons, and Jehovah's Witnesses picking up most

WHAT'S HOT IN GUATEMALA NOW

The Mayan Calendar. The long-count indigenous calendar is coming to an end on December 21, 2012. Whether the date will mark the apocalypse or will merely reset the odometer to zero is hotly debated these days. Google MAYA CALENDAR 2012 to see what the fuss is about, and decide for yourself if you think the gods will grant another 5,126-year cycle.

Making a Difference.
Guatemala is secure, and long free from the iron grip of past military governments. It Is once again one of the Western Hemisphere's premier destinations for a volunteer vacation. (You can always pick them out: they'll be wearing group T-shirts.) Some trips are religious in nature, some travelers come down on their own and hook up with a Guatemala-based program, and still others

of the rest. You'll see a couple of Jewish synagogues, Islamic mosques, and Buddhist temples in the capital, too. As always in Guatemala, traditional Mayan beliefs overlay the system, especially among the sector of the indigenous population that professes Catholicism, as a visit to many small-town churches in the highlands will attest.

. . . is coming to terms with its past. A 36-year civil war (1960–96) took a heavy toll on Guatemala, but most of the population seems anxious to move on. To its great credit, the government has taken concrete steps to address past wrongs that came to the surface during the war. The army, once an institution feared by the average Guatemalan, has been stripped of its one-time internal-security role and has been replaced with a national civilian police force staffed by members of the communities in which they serve. The country now recognizes co-official status of 23 non-Spanish local languages, guaranteeing educational and administrative access for millions of citizens to the languages they speak at home. The government has devoted ever-increasing percentages of its budget to social programs that benefit the poor. The old adage about "taking one step forward and two steps backward" applies, though, and grievances still remain following a decade and a half of true peace. Downright baroque cases of scandal, graft, corruption, bribery, and even murder continue to plague the government. (None of these need interfere with your travels to Guatemala.) Not content with those aspects of the status quo, the population frequently mobilizes in opposition to government misdoings, these days with the 21st-century tools of YouTube, Facebook, and Twitter at its disposal.

. . . is no longer obsessed with Belize. Guatemala has renounced its long-standing territorial claims on its eastern neighbor that date from the 19th century, even if many maps here still show Belize as part of Guatemala, and the two countries now have diplomatic relations. Crossing borders between them is a cinch these days, although the Guatemalan government occasionally suspends flights between Flores, in El Petén, and Belize City if it decides to engage in a bit of posturing. Any lingering differences between Guatemala and Belize need not concern you as a visitor; it's easier than ever to combine both countries into one vacation.

---

who have done "Tourist Guatemala" have fallen in love with the country and look to return in a different capacity. Needs are great here, and the many programs offer you a chance to help and experience a new type of travel.

Ricardo Arjona. Guatemala's contribution to farándula—that's showbiz, Latin America style—is this one-time basketball player, two-time Grammy winner from Jocotenango, near Antigua. The musical style of singer-composer Arjona, born in 1964, is tough to pin down with an easy label, but think of him as a combination of Latin and rock, with social and political commentary, for which Guatemala and the region provide ample material.

QUINTESSENTIAL GUATEMALA

Religious Celebrations

Few countries wear the past on their collective sleeves quite the way Guatemala does. Devout Catholicism, a strong indigenous tradition, and a palpitating sense of history combine to pack the calendar with religious festivals. (The introductory pages to Guatemala City's telephone directory list them all. Take a look if you're in the capital.) Antigua's Holy Week processions, Chichicastenango's Santo Tomás celebrations, and various communities' Day of the Dead observances draw visitors from around the world. Other celebrations, while no less fervent, are purely local affairs, open to outside observers willing to maintain a certain unobtrusive distance. Part Christian, part Mayan, the observances, with their clanging bells, wafting incense, and impassioned chanting, are difficult to separate into their component parts.

Learning Spanish

Guatemalans will tell you that their careful pronunciation and lack of accent make for Latin America's purest Spanish. With more than 200 schools to choose from, a lower cost of living than in Spain, Mexico, or Costa Rica, and a geographic proximity to the United States, you have an ideal Spanish-study locale.

Morning might begin with you and your instructor, one-on-one—that's the structure for most beginning courses here—over a cup of coffee out on the school's patio, tackling conjugations with a few props to aid you. Bid farewell and move on to a café for the afternoon, notebook in hand to review your day's lessons. Evening means dinner with your host family and a chance to practice what you've learned. It's all about immersing yourself in the language.

The Lake

There's no need to specify *which* lake—or *lago* in Spanish—is being discussed. It's the shimmering blue Atitlán, billed as "the most beautiful lake in the world." British writer Aldous Huxley said so, and you'll likely agree. Ringed by three volcanoes, the lake provides what is arguably Guatemala's best-known postcard view.

Friendly old Panajachel, Guatemala's consummate, original expatriate hangout, sits on Atitlán's northeast shore. Ringing the rest of the lake are a dozen other villages whose names read like a litany of the saints—Peter, John, Mark, Catherine, Anthony, James, Luke—and are reachable via cross-lake ferries and water taxis. All retain their Mayan character, some more successfully than others, and different styles of indigenous dress are seen in each community. You may linger here longer than you intended, meeting fellow travelers, swapping stories, and getting advice.

A Colonial City

It's said that you can't throw a stone in Antigua without hitting an old church, convent, monastery, or palace (or the ruins of one). The Western Hemisphere's best preserved colonial city is Guatemala's top tourist attraction for a reason. Not only will Antigua's many sights transport you back to colonial times; your hotel, the restaurant where you linger over dinner, the shop where you pick out souvenirs, and the bank where you change money are all housed in structures from that era, too. (Or maybe they really are newly constructed, but strict building codes mean you can't always tell the difference.) If you're like most visitors, you won't want to be transported back to the modern world when it's time to leave.

TOP ATTRACTIONS

Antigua

For most travelers, Guatemala means Antigua. No place in the Western Hemisphere contains such a collection of colonial architecture, and strict standards mean that the city's priceless structures will never fall to the wrecking ball. A few did fall victim to long-ago earthquakes, and today sit majestically in ruins.

Chichicastenango

One of the world's most famous markets takes place twice weekly in this highland town. At first glance, the "Chichi" affair seems undeniably touristy, but walk a block or two away from the souvenir section, and let the sights, sounds, and smells of a highland bazaar take over.

Copán, Honduras

Don't tell Hondurans, but this just-over-the-border complex of Mayan ruins might as well be part of Guatemala . . . or at least part of any Guatemalan trip. Romantically billed as "the Paris of the Mayan world," Copán's intricately, artistically carved monuments and architecture really do live up to the hype.

Ixil Triangle

Beyond the tourism infrastructure of Chichicastenango lies this isolated region centering on the highland town of Nebaj and surrounded by an orbit of small villages. The region was hit hard by Guatemala's civil war, but indigenous tradition and language reign supreme here.

Lake Atitlán

A shimmering lake, ringed by three volcanoes and a dozen or so indigenous villages most easily reached by boat, and a polished tourism infrastructure translate into that archetypal place to hang out. Atitlán has changed many a vacationer's plans: "Maybe I could stay a few more days . . . or weeks . . . or months."

Quiriguá

This ruins complex in the Atlantic lowlands gets overshadowed by Tikal and Copán, but Quiriguá takes top place as the best-preserved, least-weathered Mayan site in Guatemala.

Río Dulce

One of Guatemala's most popular nature excursions takes you from the narrow mouth of Lago Izabal in the Atlantic lowlands to the Caribbean Sea at Livingston. The scant distance of 25 mi takes you past rain forests, jagged canyons, and hot springs. (All the tours stop for a soak.)

Semuc Champey

The tourist industry touts these limestone pools and waterfalls in the Verapaces as "the most beautiful spot in Guatemala." One visit and you just might agree. You are actually standing on a limestone bridge that spans the rushing Cahabón River that passes underneath and reemerges downstream.

Tikal

The Petén's top tourist draw (and one of Guatemala's, too) gets our vote for the country's most remarkable Mayan ruins. The structures themselves would be impressive enough on their own, but the lush rain-forest setting and abundant animal life create an otherworldly backdrop for a complex that once housed 100,000 people and wielded power over Mesoamerica.

Volcán Pacaya

This is your chance to get up close and personal with an active volcano. Pacaya has smoked, sizzled, and smoldered for nearly a half-century, and tours from either the capital or Antigua—you should go only with an escort—get you there to see the fiery evening spectacle.

GREAT ITINERARIES

Guatemala's small size—about the same as England or Louisiana—leads to the temptation to try to see it all during a short visit. This ignores the fact that it still takes time to get from one place to another. The country has a good primary highway system, but secondary and tertiary roads can be slower going. A rushed trip also overlooks the huge number of wonderful cultural and natural attractions in Guatemala.

In that vein, we present a first-timer's itinerary that takes in Guatemala's best-known highlights and can be fit into a week. Most of it is confined to a small geographical area; the one far-flung sight can be squeezed in only via a round-trip flight. We follow that with add-ons of one to three days each, which take in some lesser-known areas, useful to mix and match if you have a few more days, or to squeeze into a weeklong visit if you want a faster-paced trip.

THE GRINGO TRAIL

7 days

Days 1 and 2: Antigua

If you're a typical visitor, you'll fly into Guatemala City. Make a beeline out the airport door for one of the numerous minivan shuttles that meet each flight to take you to the old colonial capital of Antigua, less than an hour west. The city is compact and doable on your own, but if you like your sightseeing done efficiently, you can sign on to a walking tour. (Antigua is chock-full of churches, convents, monasteries, and palaces.) Any non-sightseeing time can be filled with shopping for handicrafts and jade, Antigua's signature souvenir, and dining at the best selection of restaurants outside the capital.

⇨ *Antigua in Chapter 3.*

Days 3 and 4: Lake Atitlán

A couple of hours west of Antigua takes you to Lake Atitlán, one of Guatemala's and the hemisphere's natural wonders. Look up "tourist friendly" in the dictionary, and you just might see a picture of the gleaming lake and its trademark trifecta of volcanoes. The area presents you with a choice of towns to see and in which to stay. Traditionally, visitors have opted for sociable Panajachel, Guatemala's consummate expat hangout, but nothing says you can't base yourself in any of the dozen towns ringing Atitlán. A system of ferries and water taxis makes it a breeze to get around.

⇨ *Panajachel and Lake Atitlán in Chapter 4.*

Day 5: Chichicastenango

Guatemala's most famous market takes place each Thursday and Sunday in the highland town whose name everyone shortens to "Chichi." Things get underway by mid-morning, and by 3 PM the market starts to wind down and the vendors pack up, anxious to get back home before dark. Though the Thursday market will not disappoint, come on Sunday if your schedule permits. This allows you to also take in mass in Chichi's Santo Tomás church and observe the ultimate blending of Maya and Catholic rituals.

⇨ *Chichicastenango in Chapter 4.*

Day 6 and 7: Tikal

It's back to Guatemala City for an early-morning flight to the country's most famous Mayan ruins. (The journey overland to the remote Petén region takes about 10 hours, so flying is vastly more efficient.) The hour-long flight deposits you outside the small town of Santa Elena, where you'll find lodging as well as in Flores, Santa Elena's pleasant twin "city." The ruins themselves lie about 64 km (40 mi)

north, and if you go on an organized tour, that transportation is taken care of. There are one-day tours to Tikal for those short on time, but an overnight trip gives you extra time to explore.

⇨ *Tikal in Chapter 8.*

Tips and Transportation

This itinerary may require some juggling to schedule your market trip to Chichicastenango on a Thursday or Sunday. Flights to Tikal leave early in the morning, so getting to La Aurora International Airport from Antigua is a far easier task. You may wish to insert your two days there between Antigua and Lake Atitlán. Unless you insist on absolute flexibility, your own vehicle is not necessary and is actually a bother for this itinerary. As two of the country's most popular travel destinations, Antigua and Panajachel have no shortage of shuttle services to take you anywhere in greater comfort than on a public bus, and at Lake Atitlán itself, water travel is the norm.

GUATEMALA CITY

1 day

Day 1: The Capital Circuit

Guatemala City suffers from bad public relations, and bad location: Antigua is so close, why not just go there? But the capital has at least a day's worth of sights in the Old City, its historic center, and several museums near the airport. Cap off your day with a scrumptious restaurant meal and a stay in one of the upscale hotels in the city's *Zona Viva.*

⇨ *Guatemala City in Chapter 2.*

Tips and Transportation

The capital's La Aurora International Airport lies within the city limits, some suggest too close for comfort, but you're just a few minutes' drive from the New City once you land. After you've checked in at your hotel, taxis are the easiest and safest way to get around.

THE VERAPACES VOYAGE

3 days

Day 1: Cobán

The hub of the Verapaces region lies a five-hour drive north of Guatemala City. An early-morning start still gives you an afternoon to explore the town. In particular, hike up to the Calvario shrine for the best views around, or grab a taxi for a short ride just out of town to the gardens at the Vivero Verapaz.

⇨ *Cobán in Chapter 5.*

Day 2: Biotopo Quetzal

To paraphrase Benjamin Franklin, early to bed and early to rise gives a man (and woman) the best chance of seeing the resplendent quetzal. Get an early-morning start to head about an hour south of Cobán to the nature reserve specifically dedicated to preserving Guatemala's national bird. Stop for lunch on the way back at any of the family-owned restaurants that line the highway.

⇨ *Biotopo Quetzal in Chapter 5.*

Day 3: Semuc Champey and Lanquín

The pools and water caverns of Semuc Champey, about a two-hour drive from Cobán, make a splendid place to cool off with a swim in the midday heat. (The site sits at a lower elevation than cool Cobán, so you will notice the warmth here.) Cap off the afternoon (and cool off some more) with a hike through the nearby caves of Lanquín.

⇨ *Semuc Champey and Lanquín in Chapter 5.*

Tips and Transportation

Having your own car is ideal for this region, but public bus service from Guatemala City is comfortable and convenient. Numerous minivan shuttles also connect Antigua with Cobán. Any of the Cobán–Guatemala City buses can drop you at the entrance to the Biotopo Quetzal. You'll need to wait for a return bus at the end of your visit. It's nearly impossible to do Semuc Champey and Lanquín via public transportation, but numerous Cobán outfitters include both as part of a daylong tour. Lanquín, in particular, is best done with a guide who knows the way through the caves; portions of the hike can be very tricky.

THE CARIBBEAN CORRIDOR

2 days

Day 1: Livingston and Siete Altares

Livingston, on the Caribbean coast, is the quintessential port city, more reminiscent of faraway Jamaica than of the rest of Guatemala. Here's the catch: no roads lead here. You'll need to take land transportation to nearby Puerto Barrios and connect with a ferry or water taxi across Amatique Bay. Near Livingston lie the beautiful waterfalls of Siete Altares.

⇨ *Livingston and Siete Altares in Chapter 6.*

Day 2: Río Dulce

The canyoned, forested river connecting Livingston with inland Lake Izabal is one of Guatemala's spectacular nature excursions, including a stop at the San Felipe fortress, constructed by the Spanish to thwart upriver attacks by pirates.

⇨ *Río Dulce in Chapter 6.*

Tips and Transportation

You can reach Puerto Barrios on the Atlantic coast easily by public transportation from Guatemala City or from Cobán, making the Caribbean a reasonable add-on following a visit to Las Verapaces. Only two public ferries per day connect Puerto Barrios with Livingston, but frequent water-taxi service fills in the gaps. You can also rearrange these days by starting your Río Dulce trip inland at the town of Fronteras, where the river meets Lake Izabal, then heading out to Livingston. The logistics of navigating Río Dulce make a tour worthwhile. Enough robberies have targeted people going to Siete Altares on their own that we recommend the security of a group tour.

A BEACH BREAK

2 days

Days 1 and 2: Monterrico

Guatemala really doesn't do the beach thing, but a quick two-hour jaunt to the enjoyable coastal town of Monterrico makes a pleasant break from the highlands. The undertow is rough, but you can spend your time on the beach rather than in the water.

⇨ *Monterrico in Chapter 7.*

Tips and Transportation

Shuttle transport is the easiest way to get to the coast, vans departing from Antigua. Make reservations if you're visiting on the weekend. During the week you can probably just show up and find ample places to stay.

IF YOU LIKE

Mayan Ruins

If you've come this far to see Mayan ruins, you're likely headed to Tikal. Good choice. But don't overlook the country's other important indigenous sites, some well known, others not. We also include a nod to a famous Mayan site just across the border in Honduras, an easy day trip for travelers to Guatemala.

Tikal, El Petén. Nothing surpasses the sight of Tikal's towering temples rising out of virgin rain forest. Adding to the mystique of the place is the fact that the site was virtually unknown to the outside world until the mid-1800s. Most visitors fly in and out on a day trip, but if you can overnight here, so much the better.

Yaxhá, El Petén. You've seen the ruins of Guatemala's third-largest Mayan city if you caught the 11th installment of megahit reality-TV series *Survivor,* which was set here in 2005. An in-person visit to this complex, still under excavation, and its shimmering green lake of the same name will be even more exciting.

Copán, Honduras, Atlantic Lowlands. The intricate art and detailed carvings on the structures here have earned Copán the moniker " Paris of the Mayan world." The ruins sit just across the border in Honduras, and have a tourist-friendly town right next door to boot.

Quiriguá, Atlantic Lowlands. The lowlands' most important Mayan city dwarfed the nearby site of Copán in size and importance, even if few people remember that today. Ease of access from many points around the country makes Quiriguá, arguably the best-preserved site in Guatemala, worth a visit.

Churches

Guatemalan churches cover the spectrum from strictly interpreted Catholic dogma to ancient Mayan rituals. The more isolated the area and the stronger the indigenous tradition, the more difficult to tell where one ends and the other begins. However, no matter what goes on inside them, many of Guatemala's churches are among the most beautiful in Central America.

La Merced, Antigua. The old colonial capital's brightly painted church with the wedding-cake exterior is a favorite. La Merced is so important to the history of Antigua that it's the usual starting point for the city's famous Holy Week processions.

Santo Tomás, Chichicastenango, Highlands. Everyone heads to the famous Sunday market in Chichicastenango, but make time for a far less touristed detour to the town's principal church. Inside, you'll get a primer on the blending of devout Catholicism with equally devout, and even older, Mayan tradition.

San Andrés Xecul, Highlands. Everyone refers to the structure in the small town of the same name near Quetzaltenango as the "iglesia amarilla" (yellow church), but that nickname doesn't do it justice. Yes, it is canary yellow, but a dazzling painted array of Catholic and Mayan iconography punctuates the facade.

Basilica of Esquipulas, Atlantic Lowlands. Numerous miracles have been attributed to the *Cristo Negro* (Black Christ) inside this 18th-century church, making it Guatemala's—some would argue Central America's—most important pilgrimage site. The precious object it houses is its most important object of veneration.

The Great Outdoors

It's not quite Chile or Costa Rica—not yet, at least—but Guatemala's outdoor offerings are gaining it a place on the Latin American–ecotourism circuit. You can go bird-watching, turtle-watching, biking, hiking, caving, climbing, rafting, fishing, and boating with a growing number of outfitters. The newest addition to the activities mix is the canopy tour, a zip line that lets you glide through the treetops courtesy of a helmet and a very secure harness.

Scaling Volcanoes, Antigua and Guatemala City. The proximity of the Pacaya, Agua, Fuego, and Acatenango volcanoes to two of the country's most-visited cities means you can hike (or sometimes bike) to their summits and be back in time to regale your dinner companions with tales of oozing lava.

Spelunking, Las Verapaces. Limestone caverns are said to perforate the entire underground of the Verapaces region. Lanquín and Candelaria are two of the most accessible caves, and remain sites of pilgrimage and observance of Mayan rituals.

Sportfishing, Pacific Lowlands. Guatemala's Pacific coast is the new kid on the block in sportfishing circles, and can satisfy dreams of reeling in a marlin or sailfish. Get in there before the rest of the world finds out.

Boating the Río Dulce, Atlantic Lowlands. Navigate the river passing through a narrow, forested canyon between the port town of Livingston and inland Lake Izabal. Pass by Afro-Caribbean Garífuna villages, hot springs, and a colonial-era fortress in the process.

Markets

No shortage of upscale tourist shops proffer their wares, but there's nothing like the sights, smells, and sounds of a real Guatemalan market. Every town holds one, usually one or two days a week. Some began life as local markets, but have morphed into largely tourist affairs. Others maintain their locals-only feel, although all are welcome. Sharpen your bargaining skills, but not too ruthlessly. Prices are already reasonable, and that difference of few quetzals means more to the vendor than to you.

Chichicastenango, Highlands. Thursday and Sunday market days in this highland town are Guatemala's most famous. We know travelers who dismiss the whole affair as "too touristy," but legions of visitors can't be *that* wrong. The Chichi outing is a fun way to spend a day.

Sololá, Highlands. This town near Lake Atitlán holds a large market each Tuesday and Friday, and provides you with an opportunity to see local-to-local sales in action. Browsing will turn up a few good buys in textiles, too.

Mercado Municipal, Antigua. Beyond the snazzy, gentrified face of Antigua, its municipal market, a few blocks west of the city center, buzzes with all the activity of a highland indigenous bazaar. This is the place where residents come to shop for daily supplies.

Mercado Central, Guatemala City. Smack-dab in the center of the city, behind the cathedral, sits the multistoried central market. It's primarily a local affair, but it's brimming with handicrafts for those with the patience to look. Just beware of pickpockets.

ECOTOURISM IN GUATEMALA

Nearby Costa Rica kicked off the eco-tourism trend in the early 1990s, and it arguably remains the Western Hemisphere's leader in the field. Guatemala's tourism has historically focused on indigenous culture, Mayan ruins, and colonial architecture, but with abundant swaths of nature in its territory, it now looks to a nascent ecotourism industry to round out offerings to its 1.7 million annual visitors.

Planning Your Trip

The "eco" trend is new to Guatemala, and the number of businesses practicing internationally recognized environmental standards remains small. Don't be afraid to ask tough questions about what your hotel or tour operator does to protect the environment and to benefit its local community.

You'll likely not get immediately satisfying answers to questions posed to your hotel about recycling, water conservation, and alternative-energy sources. Be realistic: Don't take too firm a stand. In today's Guatemala, you won't be left with many choices if you insist on only staying at hotels that recycle, for example. We're firm believers that if enough of us ask about such matters, we can help raise standards.

You will, however, be pleased to see that almost every accommodation in the country is well integrated into its local community. The almost total absence of chain hotels outside the capital means that nearly every lodging here is a smaller, locally owned enterprise that employs local people and pours its earnings back into the community. By visiting Guatemala, you are supporting those local communities, too.

Beyond Ecotourism to Sustainability

Ecotourism refers to travel in nature, to observe and learn about plant- and wildlife. It minimizes impact on the environment, and improves the lives of local people by strengthening conservation.

The buzz term these days is "sustainable tourism." This umbrella term takes in all that is good about ecotourism, but looks beyond the environment at long-term impacts on communities. Does tourism benefit or harm local people, their culture, and their economies, and, yes, their environment? In other words, is the enterprise "sustainable" long-term?

In this regard, Guatemala seems to do itself proud. Tourism is the second-largest contributor to the country's economy, and employs one in 15 members of the workforce here, a figure that is expected to increase over the next decade.

No doubt tourism has an impact on culture, and the jury is still out on its long-term effects on Guatemala's distinctive indigenous societies. A culture that survived colonial conquest and a long civil war and is still going gangbusters will likely survive tourism, too. Remember: Guatemala's unique Mayan styles and traditions have never existed for the benefit of us tourists. The country is still one of those wondrous places left that asks us to accept it on its terms, and not the other way around.

The Green Deal

No government entity in Guatemala is presently in the business of certifying ecotourism standards for hotels or tour operators. The decade-old, non-profit **Asociación Alianza Verde** (Green Alliance Association; 🌐 *www.alianzaverde.org*) works in conjunction with the Rainforest Alliance to promote environmentally conscious, low-impact, sustainable tourism in Guatemala. Since 2004 the association has evaluated tourism-related businesses. Those that meet environmental standards are awarded "Green Deal" certificates of sustainable tourism (🌐 *www.greendeal.org*). As evidenced by the Spanish-language Web site, numbers are still tiny: just 28 businesses have earned certificates. A perusal of the list turns up some interesting results, however. It is entirely predictable that Río Dulce's Hacienda Tijax, and the Verapaces' Ram Tzul, whose bread and butter are ecotourism, would gain certification. But awards have also gone to in-town Posada de Don José in the center of Retalhuleu in the Pacific lowlands for its efforts to recycle, as well as the restored, recently reopened Hotel Ajau, smack-dab in the center of Guatemala City's burgeoning Zona 1, for its historic preservation efforts.

What You Can Do

Don't litter. Sadly, garbage is a common sight in Guatemala. Dispose of your trash properly. You can also pay a little extra for biodegradable glass water bottles. If you plan to travel regularly in the developing world, consider buying a hand-pump water purifier, available at many sporting goods stores for around $25. You can make your own clean water wherever you go instead of generating a trail of disposable water bottles. Guatemala still lives in the era of returnable glass beverage bottles, too.

Don't disturb animal and plant life. When you're hiking, be as unobtrusive as possible. Don't remove plants for souvenirs, and don't feed animals, even if your guide says it's OK.

Volunteer if the spirit moves you. Guatemala is one of the Western Hemisphere's premier destinations for "voluntourism." Two large organizations serve as clearinghouses for a variety of volunteer organizations, and can work with you to find a nice fit. In Quetzaltenango, **Entre Mundos** (🌐 *www.entremundos.org*) works with about 150 such organizations, most of which are based in the highlands. **Proyecto Mosaïco Guatemala** (🌐 *www.alianzaverde.org*), based in Antigua, works with around 80 entities, many based in the capital. One volunteer organization here specifically deals in ecological concerns: **ProPetén** (🌐 *www.propeten.org*) recruits assistants with a good command of Spanish to work with biologists on research projects in the Petén.

FODOR'S CHOICE ECO LODGINGS

No entity in the country officially confers the eco-imprimatur on Guatemalan hostelries. Any list is, necessarily, completely subjective. Some of our choices for environmentally conscious lodgings are:

Chiminos Island Lodge (*Lake Petexbatún, El Petén ⇨ Chapter 8*)

Hacienda Tijax (*Río Dulce, Atlantic Lowlands ⇨ Chapter 6*)

Hotel Isla Verde (*Santa Cruz La Laguna, Highlands ⇨ Chapter 4*)

Ni'tun Ecolodge (*San Andrés/Flores, El Petén ⇨ Chapter 8*)

Posada Montaña del Quetzal (*Biotopo del Quetzal, Las Verapaces ⇨ Chapter 5*)

Ram Tzul (*Biotopo del Quetzal, Las Verapaces ⇨ Chapter 5*)

Takalik Maya Lodge (*Takalik Abaj, Pacific Lowlands ⇨ Chapter 7*)

GUATEMALAN ARTS AND CRAFTS

You won't waltz away with a souvenir ancient Mayan ceremonial headdress—it would be illegal to take such an item out of the country anyway—but Guatemala does have some unique answers to the "What did you bring me?" question you're sure to hear upon your return home. First-time visitor? You'll probably make it to the famous Thursday/Sunday market in Chichicastenango in the highlands, but don't forget about lesser-known weekly or twice-weekly markets around the country. And if you prefer your shopping inside walls and under a roof, fine shops abound in Antigua and Guatemala City. Although it may seem more authentic to buy items at their out-country source, any and all of Guatemala's best known souvenirs are available in Antigua and Guatemala City if you're pressed for time and need the efficiency of one-stop shopping. No matter where you make your purchase, quality is high, variety is amazing, and prices are reasonable.

Baskets

Palm, wicker, and bamboo get woven into simple or elaborate basketry in an age-old process that, unlike other artisan work, has never been industrialized. As with leather, think not just the primary basket-weaving materials, but frequently coverings or accents to the basket with woven yarn. Many small baskets purchased in souvenir shops give you a two-fer, and contain bags of coffee, spices, or yarn doll collections.

Blankets

Momostenango, in the highlands near Quetzaltenango, is Guatemala's center for traditional woolen blankets, but you'll find *momosteco* products sold in markets all over the country. It gets cold up here, and the town anchors a sheep- and goat-raising region. Their wool gets turned into *chamarras* (blankets) on foot looms, with or without designs.

Clothing

You'll have to decide how and whether a colorfully embroidered *huipil* and *corte* (blouse and skirt) worn by Mayan women might fit in back home. (The traditional clothing worn by indigenous men might look out of place on a street in the United States.) But many visitors do go home with traditional ponchos and caps and pashmina-like shawls. The tight weave on foot looms (for woolens) and back-strap looms (for cottons) gives clothing made here a fine, durable quality. A word of warning: indigenous people find it offensive when visitors go native. Try on your clothing purchase in the market or shop, and then pack it away and don't put it on again until you get back home.

Glass

Recycling is in its infancy in Guatemala, but several glassblowing cooperatives in and around Quetzaltenango happily collect discarded bottles and jars and turn them into decorative pieces, your purchase of which keeps glass out of landfills. Religious figures, vases, and goblets make up most of what is for sale here. Ornaments are a particular favorite, and make nice additions to your Christmas tree.

Jewelry

Guatemalan jewelry runs the gamut from inexpensive yarn bracelets and beaded necklaces—many of the pieces are quite decorative—to jade, mined in the eastern part of the country, and one of the signature souvenirs here. If you shop for the latter, the sky can be the limit in price, so stick to a reputable store that will guarantee your purchase is indeed jade. (The open-air markets sell some cheap knockoffs.) Antigua is Guatemala's jade central, with fine shops, many of which do the workmanship on-site.

Leather

Belts, sandals, handbags, and wallets are among the leather products prized by Guatemala visitors. Think not just leather, though, but leather combined with woven cotton. Fabric covers the leather—belts are a particular favorite that employ this technique—giving the same designs and colors unique to each community. Remote Todos Santos Cuchumatán is one of the country's premier leather-crafting centers. Fortunately, you can find such products all over Guatemala.

T-shirts

Though not usually lumped in under the "handicrafts" heading, Guatemala does produce T-shirts of fine quality. Two broad categories seem to predominate: shirts with decorative Mayan hieroglyphs are sure to please the history-minded traveler or person on your shopping list; and the ubiquitous Gallo beer–logo shirts are well constructed, but do include sayings in Spanish, frequently borderline bawdy. If you don't speak Spanish, ask for a translation before deciding whether you want to purchase one.

Textiles

The tight loom weave also imparts durability to non-clothing Guatemalan textiles. Colorful table settings are particular favorites, and a matching set of table runner, placemats, and napkins against a plain-color tablecloth adds pizzazz to any dinner party. Whimsical matching pot holders and oven mitts can spice up your kitchen. Wall hangings portraying Guatemalan scenes can adorn your home, although some of the scenes for sale look suspiciously Andean rather than Central American.

Toys

The highlands' Totonicapán is Guatemala's toy center, although they fall into more of the enjoy-as-a-work-of-art-while-it-sits-on-the-shelf category, rather than something a 4-year-old child will actually get down on the floor and play with. One toy-like item that's always a hit with kids and adults is the Mayan worry doll, tiny yarn figures, usually sold in a cloth sack in groups of six. Traditional belief holds that if you confide your concerns to the dolls before bedtime—keep it to one worry per doll—by morning, your cares will disappear.

Wood Carvings

Wood-carving workshops dot the country, but you'll find the most in the heavily forested Petén. That's where most of the wood comes from, too, and it gets turned into religious figures, Nativity scenes, and chess sets. Mahogany, walnut, the dense hardwood *cocobolo,* and the greenish-grayish *zircote* are favored woods used for carvings. Alas, all are becoming more scarce in Guatemala. Many of the carvers in El Remate tout that they use only wood from fallen trees, yet some debate whether or not *that* disturbs the ecosystem, too.

FLAVORS OF GUATEMALA

Guatemalan food will seem familiar to anyone who's been to Mexico—at least to a point. Like their neighbors to the north, Guatemalan cooks draw deeply on their indigenous origins. Maize has been the staple of the diet for millennia, and the Maya even believed that mankind was created from corn *masa,* or dough. Beans, tomatoes, *chiles,* squash, turkey, and tropical fruits are just a few of the other foods that trace their roots back to pre-Hispanic days.

As in Mexico, Guatemalan cooking also incorporates foods from Europe. Beef, pork, and chicken were all brought by the Spanish, and today these meats (along with the native turkey) are served in stews or grilled *a la plancha.* But in comparison to their Mexican counterparts, Guatemalan cooks tend to go much lighter on the *chile.* And if you order the Guatemalan version of Mexican standards like enchiladas and tacos, you may be surprised that they have little resemblance to their northern cousins (see descriptions below).

On menus you'll often see typical Guatemalan food referred to as *chapín.* It's slang for "Guatemalan," from a type of sandal once worn by indigenous peasants; originally pejorative, it's now been co-opted as a badge of national pride. A typical *chapín* breakfast, or *desayuno,* is a feast of eggs, refried black beans, cheese (another import from the Spanish), fried plantains, a mild tomato salsa called *chirmol,* and tortillas. Lunch, or *la comida,* is traditionally the heaviest meal of the day, and might consist of a soup followed by a meat dish, rice and beans, and dessert. Dinner, *la cena,* resembles lunch but tends to be more modest, with fewer courses and smaller portions.

Here are some classic Guatemalan dishes to try. You might also want to sample the tacos, which in Guatemala are doubled over and fried, like empanadas; enchiladas, which are crispy tortillas topped with chopped meat and vegetables; *gallo en chicha* (rooster cooked in a fermented corn drink); *puerco* (pork) marinated in a spicy *adobo* sauce; *sopa de tortuga* (turtle soup); or if you're feeling adventurous, maybe *tepescuintle,* a type of rodent from the rainforest. *¡Buen provecho!*

Chiles rellenos

Unlike their Mexican equivalents, Guatemalan stuffed peppers generally aren't made with the spicy *poblano chile* but with sweet bell peppers, filled with a mixture of chopped beef and vegetables. The peppers are then battered in egg and deep-fried, and often bathed in a mild tomato sauce.

Fiambre

Fiambre is a Guatemalan chef salad with up to fifty ingredients—cold cuts, sausage, cheese, carrots, corn, cabbage, cauliflower, beans, radishes, lettuce, boiled eggs, olives, and dozens of other vegetables and garnishes—all arranged on a festive platter and covered in a vinaigrette dressing.

Hilachas

The shredded meat in this mildly spicy beef stew is bathed in a sauce of tomatoes, tomatillos, and *chiles,* with potatoes and carrots generally included as well.

Jocón

A specialty of Antigua, *jocón* is a mild, slightly acidic green sauce prepared from tomatillos, cilantro, sesame, and pumpkin seeds, with soaked, ground tortillas used as a thickener. It's usually served over chicken, though pork or turkey is sometimes substituted.

Kaq-ik

Hailing from the area of Alta Verapaz, *kaq-ik* (seen with a variety of spellings, or known by its Spanish equivalent, *chunto de pavo*), is a savory turkey broth served with hunks of meat, often including a drumstick protruding Flintstone-like from the rim of the bowl. *-Ik* indicates that a dish includes *chile* peppers, but *kaq-ik* isn't particularly *picante*. Besides the *chiles,* the broth is flavored with tomatoes, tomatillos, onions, garlic, mint, cilantro, and other spices. *Kaq-ik* is generally served with white rice or occasionally with a plate of tamales.

Pepián

Also traditional around Antigua, Guatemalan *pepián* is a hearty stew. Pieces of chicken, potatoes, green beans, and carrots are served in a dense sauce of tomatoes, *chiles,* pumpkin seeds, sesame seeds, and other ingredients. Like Mexican *mole, pepián* comes in several varieties, ranging from *colorado* ("red") to *negro* ("black").

Pollo con loroco

From the eastern department of Jalapa, *pollo con loroco* is a stew, in this case chicken and vegetables served in a cream sauce seasoned with the flower that gives the dish its name. Native to central America and called *quilite* ("edible herb") in Mayan, *loroco* is a vine that produces flowers prized for their unique, pungent flavor.

Postres

The Spanish have exerted the strongest influence on Guatemalan cuisine in desserts, or *postres*. Some favorite ways to end a meal include: flan, or crème caramel; *buñuelos*, small balls of fried dough served with a sugar syrup seasoned with cinnamon and cloves; *pastel de tres leches* ("three-milks cake"), a wonderfully light, moist vanilla cake soaked in evaporated milk, condensed milk, and cream; and *torrejas*, a sort of "Spanish toast" made from sweet bread dipped in egg batter, then fried and served in a sugar syrup flavored with cinnamon.

Suban-ik

Originating around the town of San Martín Jilotepeque in the department of Chimaltenango, *saban-ik* is a mixture of chicken and pork (and sometimes beef), served in a delicious, complex tomato sauce seasoned with several different *chiles,* along with sweet peppers, tomatillos, and other condiments. Despite all the *chiles, suban-ik,* like *kak-iq,* isn't likely to trouble a delicate palate.

Tamales

Guatemalan tamales come in all shapes and sizes, including some you won't find anywhere else. They may be sweet or savory, stuffed with pork or chicken, flavored with seasonings such as *loroco* (a type of flower) or *chipilín* (an herb), and generally steamed in a banana leaf. *Chuchitos* ("little puppies") are small corn tamales filled with pork and wrapped in a cornhusk.

Tapado

Its name meaning "covered," *tapado* is a kind of tropical bouillabaisse from Guatemala's Caribbean coast. A specialty of the region's Garífuna population, descendants of African slaves, the dish is a seafood stew made with coconut milk, sweet peppers, and plantains. Other ingredients vary, but often include squid, crab, shrimp, snails, red snapper, and sea bass.

LODGING PLANNER

Good news: Lodging in Guatemala is affordable. Even five-star luxury doesn't cost an arm and a leg. *Hotel* isn't the only tag you'll find on accommodation: *hospedaje, hostal, pensión, casa de huespedes,* and *posada* also mean someplace to stay. Unfortunately, there are no hard and fast rules as to what each name means, though hotels and posadas tend to be higher-end places.

International-class Hotels

The big international chains are all in Guatemala City, but almost nowhere to be found outside the capital. Another group of hotels around the country may belong to a locally owned chain whose name you don't recognize, or may be single entities, but mimic the style and services of the big guys. Such accommodations have rooms and facilities equal to those back home, but usually lack atmosphere compared to other locally owned options. Their facilities and services make them popular with business travelers.

Inns

Guatemala truly shines in its selection of smaller, locally owned inns with 5–15 rooms each, and this is the type of accommodation most visitors associate with the country. (This is almost the only type of lodging found in Antigua.) Many are housed in colonial-era buildings, and those that are newly constructed make every effort to echo that same style with rooms arranged around a courtyard or garden. Antigua and Guatemala City have five-star guesthouses and boutique hotels that combine colonial class with modern amenities. At many Lake Atitlán hotels you get comfort and culture in utter isolation: hammocks with stunning views of the lake beat television sets every time.

Lodges

Lodges—both eco- and not-quite-so—are the thing in the Petén, near Tikal, and in remote sections of the Verapaces. Some are incredibly luxurious, others more back-to-nature; all are way off the beaten path, so plan on staying a few nights to offset travel time. If you're interested in sustainable accommodation, it pays to do your research. The *eco* term is used flexibly, sometimes simply to describe a property in a rural or jungle location, rather than a place that is truly ecologically friendly.

Budget Hotels

Guatemala has a good selection of cheap shared accommodation. Budget lodging terminology varies: hostel, *hostal,* and *la casa de* are commonplace names, and some places are just listed as a hotel or *pensión.* Staff in most Guatemalan hostels can often inform you about Spanish classes and excursions—many have in-house travel agencies. Hostels proper do tend to cater to party animals, so if you're traveling with kids, a family-run hotel might be quieter. While the country still offers a bed for the night in the $5 range, loosening the purse strings and spending $30–$40—still a bargain by any standard—buys much more comfort in terms of private room and bath.

House Rentals

Antigua and some of the smaller communities around Lake Atitlán offer you the option of a housekeeping holiday. Most are quite comfortable and run in the range of $1,000–$1,500 per week. (Few will touch rentals less than one week.) Expect most of the same standards as back home, but don't count on potable water or Internet access.

WHEN TO GO

Many countries make the claim, but in Guatemala it truly applies: You'll find no bad time to visit, although some seasons are more ideal than others. For near-perfect weather in the much-visited central part of the country (Guatemala City, Antigua, and the highlands), consider a trip during the November–April dry season. These are also the months when Guatemala's most famous religious festivals (the Day of the Dead, the Burning of the Devil, the Santo Tomás celebrations in Chichicastenango, Christmas, and Lent and Holy Week in Antigua) take place. However, don't feel the need to avoid the rainy season; rains rarely impede travel here, and will likely not interfere with your trip. Also, don't forget that the rest of the country (Las Verapaces, El Petén, and the Atlantic and Pacific lowlands) has a less distinct division between rainy and dry seasons.

Guatemala isn't a "fun in the sun" kind of destination, and there's little distinction between weather-based high and low seasons. Lodging and tour rates remain fairly constant year-round. (Some hotels at popular destinations such as Antigua and Lake Atitlán raise rates on weekends.) Two big exceptions to this rule are Christmas and Holy Week. Make reservations weeks or months in advance if you plan to travel during these times, and be willing, even then, to settle for alternate choices.

Climate

The high-elevation center of the country lives up to its self-described billing as "the land of eternal spring." Daytime temperatures reach 20°C to 25°C (68°F to 76°F) and may fall to 10°C (51°F) at night. The highest elevations of the western highlands see temperatures drop to freezing at night. This part of the country sees distinct rainy (May through October) and dry (November through April) seasons. Guatemalans confuse this situation by calling their dry season *verano* (summer) and wet season *invierno* (winter), although that conveys the opposite of the Northern Hemisphere's seasonal distinctions.

The rest of the country (the high-elevation Verapaces, low-elevation Petén, and Atlantic and Pacific coasts) sees less distinction between wet and dry seasons. Daytime temperatures in the lowlands reach 32°C (89°F), but occasionally soar to 40°C (104°F) during March and April, the hottest months of the year around the country. Although Guatemala has suffered occasional hurricane damage through the years—Mitch in 1998 and Stan in 2005—its short Caribbean coastline offers it greater protection than neighboring countries.

These charts list the average daily maximum and minimum temperatures for Guatemala City (representative of the highlands) and Flores (representative of the lowlands).

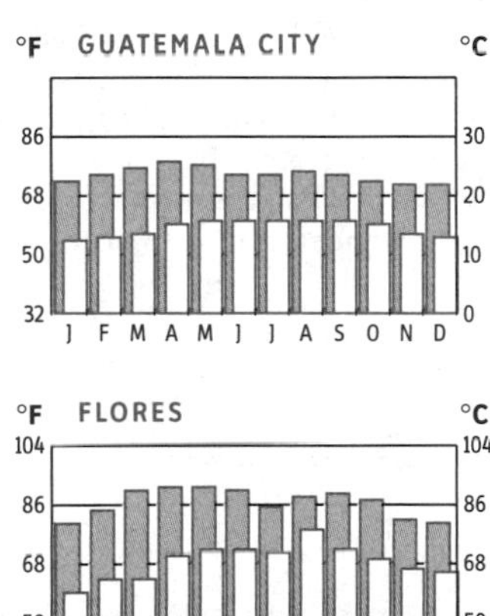

FAQ

Is it safe to visit Guatemala? Yes . . . mostly. This is probably the most frequently asked question about travel to Guatemala. We admit that the U.S. State Department information about the country sounds downright scary in places, but Guatemala is far safer than it was a decade ago. Much travel here entails standard, commonsense safeguards: leave the flashy jewelry and camera equipment at home; take taxis after dark; keep passport, credit cards, and cash well hidden. But Guatemala has a few unique "Never Do" precautions, too: don't hike volcanoes or the Cerro de la Cruz above Antigua or the remote reaches of Tikal on your own (go with an escorted group); don't ride the city buses in the capital; don't photograph children you do not know. Remember though: Most visitors have a safe and terrific trip.

My schedule will allow me to travel only during the rainy season. Will I regret that? Not at all. Guatemala's countryside is lush and green and the air is fresh during the May–October wet season. In a normal year, rain lasts an hour or two each afternoon or evening; make plans to be indoors at that time. Rains do become more prolonged in September and October—you might want to reconsider traveling then—but the standard North American summer vacation season makes a wonderful time to visit.

What's the best way to get around? You'll probably use a combination of transportation. We're big fans of the tourist shuttles, minivans seating 8–15 passengers that bop between tourist destinations. If your itinerary takes you on the standard Antigua–Lake Atitlán–Chichicastenango circuit, they'll serve you well. Make reservations at least a day in advance, and they will take you from hotel door to hotel door in far more comfort than a public bus. The buses are OK though. If you can, opt for the pullmans, the generic term Guatemalans use for Greyhound-style vehicles. You'll have more room and less commotion than on the smaller, much more crowded *camionetas*. Tikal, of course, is farther afield, so flying is the quickest way to get there. (It's about 10 hours overland from Guatemala City.) As it does anywhere, your own vehicle gives you maximum freedom, but it is entirely possible to visit Guatemala and never rent a car.

I've heard about Guatemala's chicken buses. Will I really be traveling with farm animals? The converted U.S. school buses, or camionetas, which generations of budget travelers have affectionately dubbed "chicken buses," will pack you in like livestock, but your fellow passengers will all be human.

Guatemala City

WORD OF MOUTH

"We visited the National Archeology and Ethnology Museum in Guatemala City. It has an amazing collection for anyone interested in Mayan history and art."

—vttraveler

"Against the repeated advice of the hotel and conference personnel, we ventured out, walked to a few nearby restaurants and shops, felt safe, and had no problems."

—kathleen

www.fodors.com/community

Updated by Gerard Helferich and Teresa Nicholas

Central America's largest metropolis has what you'd expect from an urban area of 2.5 million people—the best selection of hotels, restaurants, nightlife, and museums in the country. Yet most tourists come to Guatemala for ancient ruins, colonial towns, flamboyant markets, and spectacular volcanoes and lakes—not to explore a large, mostly modern city with a questionable reputation for security.

If time is tight, we certainly wouldn't recommend lingering in Guatemala City instead of, say, Lake Atitlán or Antigua. But if you have a couple of extra days, the capital, once known as "the Jewel of Latin America," does offer some unique attractions, all located within just a few of the city's 21 zones. Whereas the narrow streets of the Old City can be chaotic, the quieter, more polished streets of the New City, with their fine restaurants and comfortable hotels, can be a much-needed dose of civilization after hitting the country's more remote sights. Toss in visits to a couple of impressive museums, and Guatemala City might surprise you. Who knows, if you stay in the capital long enough, you just might start using the same affectionate name residents give to their city: "Guate."

ORIENTATION AND PLANNING

GETTING ORIENTED

Most Guatemalan cities are divided into numbered sectors. Guatemala City has 21 such *zonas*, although you will likely spend time in only five of them: Zonas 9 and 10, which make up the New City; Zona 1, which constitutes the Old City; the somewhat seedy Zona 4, which lies between the Old and New cities and contains many bus terminals; and Zona 13, where La Aurora International Airport and several fine museums are situated. The city's major arteries are 6 and 10 avenidas: 6 Avenida runs from Zona 1 to Zona 4 to Zona 9, passing three series of identically numbered calles; 10 Avenida runs through Zonas 1 and 4 before becoming the 10-lane Avenida La Reforma in Zona 10.

Numbered *avenidas* (avenues) run north–south, whereas *calles* (streets) run west–east. Addresses are given as a numbered avenida or calle followed by two numbers separated by a dash: the first number is the previous cross street or avenue and the second is a specific building. Building numbers increase as they approach the higher-numbered cross streets and then start over at the next block, so 9 Avenida 5–22 is on 9 Avenida near 5 Calle, and 9 Avenida 5–74 is on the same block, only closer to 6 Calle. Hit the pavement and you'll get the hang of it. A word of warning: make sure you're in the right zone. Each zone replicates the same grid system. In theory, the same address could appear 21 times throughout the city. Street signs always specify which zone you're in.

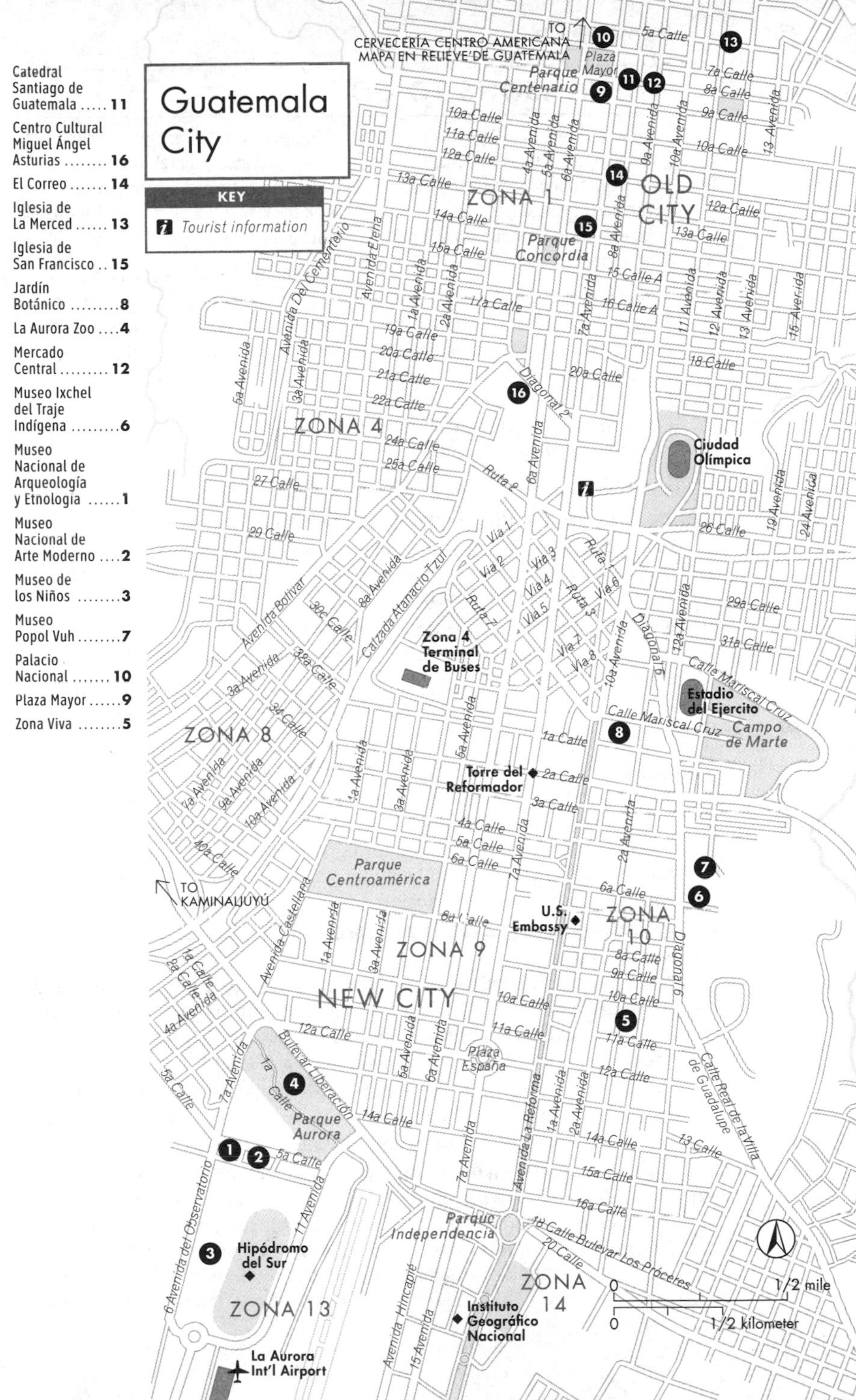
Catedral Santiago de Guatemala 11
Centro Cultural Miguel Ángel Asturias 16
El Correo 14
Iglesia de La Merced 13
Iglesia de San Francisco .. 15
Jardín Botánico 8
La Aurora Zoo 4
Mercado Central 12
Museo Ixchel del Traje Indígena 6
Museo Nacional de Arqueología y Etnologia 1
Museo Nacional de Arte Moderno 2
Museo de los Niños 3
Museo Popol Vuh 7
Palacio Nacional 10
Plaza Mayor 9
Zona Viva 5
Guatemala City
KEY
Tourist information
TO CERVECERÍA CENTRO AMERICANA
MAPA EN RELIEVE DE GUATEMALA
Plaza Mayor
Parque Centenario
ZONA 1
OLD CITY
Parque Concordia
ZONA 4
Ciudad Olímpica
Zona 4 Terminal de Buses
Estadio del Ejercito
Campo de Marte
ZONA 8
Torre del Reformador
Parque Centroamérica
TO KAMINALJUYÚ
U.S. Embassy
ZONA 10
ZONA 9
NEW CITY
Plaza España
Parque Aurora
Parque Independencia
Hipódromo del Sur
ZONA 13
ZONA 14
Instituto Geográfico Nacional
La Aurora Int'l Airport
0
1/2 mile
0
1/2 kilometer
Avenida La Reforma
Calzada Atanasio Tzul
Avenida Bolivar
Diagonal 6
Calle Mariscal Cruz
Bulevar Liberación
Avenida Castellana
Calle Real de la Villa de Guadalupe
18 Calle Bulevar Los Próceres
6 Avenida del Observatorio
Avenida Hincapié

TOP REASONS TO GO

Culture: Guatemala City boasts some impressive institutions, including the National Archaeology and Ethnology Museum, the Ixchel Museum of Indigenous Dress, and the Popol Vuh Museum.

Food and Drink: The capital has the country's highest concentration of fine restaurants, with an emphasis on international and fusion cuisine. There are also enough bars and clubs to keep the most ardent night owl busy for weeks.

R&R: After a week or two traveling in the provinces, there's no better place to check into a luxury hotel, kick back, and loll by the pool for a couple of days.

Shopping: If you're interested only in handicrafts, by all means head to Chichi; but if your tastes run toward fine art, antiques, and designer shops, Guate is the place to be.

The New City. On the south side of the capital, the New City takes in Zonas 9, 10, and more, and is home to most of Guatemala City's upscale lodgings, restaurants, shopping, and nightlife. This is where you'll want to stay if comfort is a priority.

The Old City. Zona 1, the Old City, encompasses the heart of the capital and contains most of its historic sights, budget lodgings, and bargain shopping.

PLANNING

WHEN TO GO

The capital has distinct rainy (May to October) and dry seasons (November to April). Being the center of business and politics, Guatemala City hosts more visitors during the week than on weekends. It's the obvious choice for the beginning or end of your Guatemala visit, since the country's major airport sits inside the city limits.

GETTING HERE AND AROUND

AIR TRAVEL

Most international flights into Guatemala head to the newly renovated Aeropuerto Internacional La Aurora (GUA). International airlines serving the airport are American, Continental, Copa, Cubana, Delta, Iberia, Mexicana, Spirit Air, Taca, United, and US Airways.

Domestic airlines Inter Regional (a division of Taca) and TAG fly between the capital and Aeropuerto Internacional Mundo Maya outside the twin towns of Flores and Santa Elena in El Petén.

TO AND FROM THE AIRPORT Less than a mile from the New City, Aeropuerto Internacional La Aurora is convenient if a bit too close. Make sure you negotiate a fare with the driver before getting into a taxi. A reasonable price from the airport to Zona 9 or 10 is about $10 (Q70 to Q80), but a driver could ask for as much as $30. Dollars are gladly accepted if you haven't had a chance to change money. Minivan shuttles to Antigua, less than one hour away, meet most flights, too. Upon leaving the country, you must pay a Q30 airport tax (also payable in dollars, with change returned in dollars).

BUS TRAVEL

TO AND FROM GUATEMALA CITY The *terminal de buses,* or main bus station, is in Zona 4. From here you can catch a bus to almost anywhere in the country. Fuente del Norte has service to the Atlantic lowlands, Las Verapaces, and El Petén. Trans Galgos travels to the highlands.

Some companies run small minivans, which are a much more comfortable way to travel. Atitrans, Autobuses de Oriente, Transportes Express, and Turansa offer shuttle service to most cities.

Information Atitrans (☎ *7832–3371* 🌐 *www.atitrans.com*). **Autobuses de Oriente** (☎ *2238–3894*). **Trans Galgos** (☎ *2232–3661*). **Transportes Express** (☎ *2431–5500* 🌐 *www.tourguatemala.net*). **Turansa** (☎ *2433–6080* 🌐 *www.turansa.com*).

WITHIN GUATEMALA CITY Guatemala's network of red public buses logs dozens of thefts (and a few armed robberies) each day. Your chances as an outsider of escaping unscathed are slim, so we advise against using the system. Taxis are plentiful and reasonably priced; take them instead. The exception to the "no bus" rule is the TransMetro, a system of green public buses that travel on special lanes and stop at fixed stations with ample security. The first line opened in 2007; however, it runs a route through Zonas 1, 3, 8, 11, and 12, where visitors are not likely to find themselves. More routes are in the works at this writing.

CAR TRAVEL

Driving in Guatemala City is a headache. You can expect narrow streets jammed with traffic at just about any time of day. Things get better once you move out of the center of the city and the narrow streets give way to broad boulevards. Drives to nearby destinations like Antigua, for example, can be more pleasant.

■ TIP→ Vehicle break-ins are common in the capital, so park in a guarded lot. All expensive and most moderate hotels have protected parking areas. Avoid leaving anything of value in the car.

CAR RENTAL If you're not intimidated by Guatemala's winding mountain roads, renting a car is a great way to see the countryside. There are several international agencies at Aeropuerto La Aurora and in the New City. Reputable local companies include Ahorrent, Tabarini, and Tikal.

Contacts Ahorrent (☎ *2383–2800* 🌐 *www.ahorrent.com*). **Avis** (☎ *2339–3249* 🌐 *www.avis.com*). **Budget** (☎ *2332–7744* 🌐 *www.budgetguatemala.com.gt*). **National** (☎ *2360–2030* 🌐 *www.nationalcar.com*). **Hertz** (☎ *2470–3700* 🌐 *www.hertz.com*). **Tabarini** (☎ *2362–2701* 🌐 *www.tabarini.com*). **Tikal** (☎ *2332–4721*).

TAXI TRAVEL

Taxis can be found waiting at hotels and intersections or can be flagged down on the street. Most do not have meters, so negotiate a price before getting in. Within a single zone a ride should cost Q20 to Q25; between zones expect to pay Q30 to Q50. We recommend having your hotel or restaurant call a taxi for you at night—establishments are happy to do it—and that you use the services of a cab even if you're only going a short distance.

Contacts **Amarillo Express** (☎ *2332–1515*). **Las Américas** (☎ *2362–0583*). **Verde Express** (☎ *2475–9595*). **Yellow-Car** (☎ *2437–4824*).

SAFETY AND PRECAUTIONS

Guatemala City has a bad reputation, and you do need to be careful, but it probably isn't more dangerous than any other large city in a developing country. Here are some tips to help you avoid being preyed upon by pickpockets and other unsavory characters:

Carry as little as possible. Leave expensive jewelry and watches at home, keep purses and cameras close to your body—or better yet, don't carry them at all. Use a money belt and put in your pocket only as much cash as you need. Carry a photocopy of your passport, leaving the original in your hotel safe.

Ask hotel personnel for the lay of the land. Get that invaluable where-to-go and where-not-to-go advice from the staff at your hotel. They know the neighborhood better than anybody.

Walk purposefully. Look like you know where you're going, even if you're hopelessly lost. Standing on a street corner with a puzzled look and your open *Fodor's* guide brands you as a tourist. Pop into a store or other public interior to get your bearings and ask for directions if you need to. Duck into a church, sit in a pew, and map out your route (and perhaps get a bit of divine guidance).

Take taxis. During the day, take taxis for longer distances, even if you would normally consider them walkable. At night stick to well-lighted areas and take taxis even for short trips. They're reasonably priced, and your hotel or restaurant will be happy to call one.

Watch out for motorcycles. Fast and nimble, they're the preferred get-away vehicle for thieves. Don't walk along the curb, where someone can snatch your bag or camera and be gone before you even realize what's happened.

Be careful crossing the street. Guatemala City drivers tend to drive fast whenever possible (maybe because the heavy traffic doesn't often give them the chance). They generally don't yield to pedestrians, so don't assume they will stop for you even at a crosswalk. Crossing the street can be particularly hazardous in the New City, where cars and motor-cycles tend to move more quickly than in the congested city center, and where there are few traffic lights.

EMERGENCIES

The ever-present Meykos chain has reputable pharmacies all over the city. Zuiva is another national chain, with some locations open 24 hours. Both Centro Médico and Hospital Herrera Llerandi have English-speaking staff and are accustomed to dealing with foreigners. The Red Cross (*Cruz Roja* in Spanish) serves as an ambulance and rescue service.

Emergency Services **Cruz Roja** (☎ *125*). **Fire** (☎ *122*). **Police** (☎ *120*).

Hospitals **Centro Médico** (✉ *6 Av. 3–47, Zona 10* ☎ *2279–4949*). **Hospital Herrera Llerandi** (✉ *6 Av. 8–71, Zona 10* ☎ *2384–5959* 🌐 *www.herrerallerandi.com*).

Pharmacies Meykos (✉ *18 Calle 25–76, Zona 10* ☎ *2363–5903* ✉ *6 Av. 5-01, Zona 9* ☎ *2385–1504*). **Zuiva** (✉ *Calzada San Juan 29– 93, Zona 7* ☎ *2433–2963*).

VISITOR INFORMATION AND TOURS

INGUAT, Guatemala's ever-helpful government tourism office, is open weekdays 8 to 4 and has an information desk in the lobby of its building in Zona 4. The airport office stays open daily 6 AM to midnight.

A number of reputable tour operators offer half- and full-day tours of the capital as well as day trips outside the city.

Information INGUAT (☎ *2421–2800*).

Tour Contacts Clark Tours (☎ *2412–4700* 🌐 *www.clarktours.com.gt*). **Guatemala Xpedition** (☎ *2385–2882*). **Maya Expeditions** (☎ *2363–4955* 🌐 *www.mayaexpeditions.com*). **Mayan World Vision** (☎ *5704-4069 or 5984–4121*). **Mayabalam** (☎ *5544–1141*). **STP Guatemala** (☎ *2223–5000* 🌐 *www.stpguatemala.com*). **Tropical Tours** (☎ *2339–3662* 🌐 *www.tropicaltoursoperador.com*). **Turansa** (☎ *2437–8182* 🌐 *www.turansa.com*). **Viguatur Guatemala** (☎ *2477–3752 or 5500–5595*).

GUATEMALA CITY TIPS

- All outlying distances in Guatemala are marked from the capital's Plaza Mayor.
- *Ciudad de Guatemala* is the Spanish translation of "Guatemala City," but it is hardly used. As you make your way to the capital, signs direct you simply to GUATEMALA.
- Guatemala City sits smack-dab in the center of the country, and Guatemalans refer to everyplace outside the capital as "the interior."
- We strongly recommend against using the public urinals scattered around the Old City.

EXPLORING GUATEMALA CITY

There's plenty in Guatemala City to occupy you for a couple of days. A textile and an anthropological museum will enhance your appreciation of ancient and indigenous cultures and get you ready to head into the highlands or El Petén. A pair of art museums display paintings and sculpture by Guatemalan masters; one focuses on the 20th century while the other goes back to colonial days. For families traveling with kids, there's a zoo and a children's museum. And if you're in town on a Sunday, you can stop by the Plaza Mayor, which explodes in a riot of music and color, with vendors selling handmade textiles and indigenous people wearing traditional dress. If you're lucky, you may even see one of Guatemala City's goatherds guiding his flock through the streets of the Old City and charging Q5 for a glass of fresh-squeezed milk.

TIMING In Guatemala on business? You'll likely spend time in the country's sprawling capital. Few other travelers do, instead making a beeline out-country after landing at La Aurora Airport, and not returning to Guatemala City until its time to fly home. (Antigua does lie so close, after all.) If you do choose to play tourist here, you'll experience enough in one day; two days is plenty.

THE NEW CITY

Whereas the Old City is the real Guatemala, the modern look and fast pace of the New City's Zonas 9 and 10 are reminiscent of upscale districts in other Latin American capitals. This is especially the case in Zona Viva, the posh center of Zona 10, where dozens of smart restaurants, bars, and clubs stay open long after the rest of the city goes to bed. During the day the New City's museums and cultural sites draw an equally affluent and savvy crowd.

Avenida La Reforma splits the New City down the middle, with Zona 9 to the west and Zona 10 to the east. ■**TIP→To save confusion, always check which zone your destination is in before heading there.**

TOP ATTRACTIONS

6 **Museo Ixchel del Traje Indígena.** The city's best museum, the Ixchel Museum of Indigenous Dress, focuses on textiles of Guatemala's indigenous community, with an impressive array of handwoven fabrics from 120 highland villages, some of which date from the 19th century. It will provide you with a good background in the regional differences among textiles before you head out to the highlands. You'll also find sculptures, photographs, and paintings, including works by Andres Curruchich, an influential Guatemalan folk painter. Multimedia and interactive weaving displays make the museum engaging for all ages—watch one of the short introductory videos describing the museum's holdings to get you grounded—and there's a café, a bookstore, and a terrific gift shop. The only drawback is its location—at the bottom of a long hill at the Universidad Francisco Marroquín. ✉ *End of 6 Calle at 6 Av., Zona 10* ☎ *2361–8081* 🌐 *www.museoixchel.org* 🎫 *Q35* ⏲ *Weekdays 9–5, Sat. 9–1.*

Fodor's Choice ★

1 **Museo Nacional de Arqueología y Etnología.** Dedicated to the history of the Maya, the National Museum of Archaeology and Ethnology has a large and excellent collection of Mayan pottery, jewelry, masks, and costumes, as well as models of the ancient cities. The jade exhibit, in particular, is stunning. The museum is a must for understanding the link between ancient and modern Mayan cultures, but the exhibits are labeled in Spanish only. ✉ *Edificio 5, La Aurora Park, 6 Calle and 7 Av., Zona 13* ☎ *2475–4399* 🎫 *Q60* ⏲ *Tues.–Fri. 9–4, weekends 9–12:30 and 1:30–4.*

7 **Museo Popol Vuh.** Religious figures, animals, and mythological half-animal–half-man creatures with stolid eyes, hawkish noses, and fierce poses inhabit this museum. Though much smaller than the city's other museums, Popol Vuh has an interesting display of well-preserved stone carvings from the Preclassic period, with the earliest pieces dating from 1500 BC. Some statues are quite large, all the more impressive given that they were each cut from a single stone. Also look for the "painted books," which were historical records kept by the Maya. The most famous is the museum's namesake, the *Popol Vuh,* otherwise known as the Mayan Bible, which was lost (and later recovered) after it was translated into Spanish. An ample collection of colonial artifacts and rotating special exhibits round out the museum's offerings. Monthly evening public lectures, in Spanish, deal with topics related to the institution's holdings.

✉ *Universidad Francisco Marroquín, End of 6 Calle, Zona 10* ☎ *2338–7896* 🌐 *www.popolvuh.ufm.edu.gt* 🎫 *Q35* ⏲ *Weekdays 9–5, Sat. 9–1.*

WORTH NOTING

8 **Jardín Botánico.** The small but lovely Botanical Garden at the northern end of Zona 10 contains an impressive collection of plants managed by the Universidad de San Carlos. Your ticket price also includes admission to a small, adjoining natural-history museum. ✉ *Calle Mariscal Cruz 1–56, near Av. La Reforma, Zona 10* ☎ *Gardens 2334–6065; museum 2334–6065* 🎫 *Q10* ⏲ *Tues.–Sat. 8:30–12:30.*

VIVE . . . GUATEMALA

At the intersection of 7 Avenida and 2 Calle stands the **Torre del Reformador** ("Tower of the Reformer"), a smaller version of the Eiffel Tower, topping out at 75 meters (245 feet). The tower came from the United States and was constructed in 1935 to mark the centennial of the birth of President Justo Rufino Barrios, known for implementing liberal reforms during his late-19th-century tenure. (Barrios's portrait adorns the Q5 bill.)

4 **La Aurora Zoo.** It's small, but the capital's zoo is well arranged and well maintained. The facility contains several exhibit areas, including the African savanna, the Asian subcontinent, the Mesoamerican tropics, and a down-home farm. You'll see everything from giraffes and elephants to cows and ducks. **■ TIP→ The zoo's proximity to the nearby Children's Museum makes a convenient outing for families with kids.** ✉ *La Aurora Park, Zona 13* ☎ *2475–0894* 🎫 *Q20;* ⏲ *Tues.–Sun. 9–5.*

2 **Museo Nacional de Arte Moderno.** Surrealism and multimedia works are among the wide range of styles represented at the National Museum of Modern Art. Some of the collection does go back to the early-19th-century independence period. Many of Guatemala's most distinguished 20th-century artists are represented here, including Efraín Recinos and Zipacna de León. Exhibits include works by other Latin American artists from similar periods. ✉ *Edificio 6, La Aurora Park, Zona 13* ☎ *2472–0467* 🎫 *Q50* ⏲ *Tues.–Fri. 9–4, weekends 9–noon and 1:30–4.*

3 **Museo de los Niños.** Via interactive exhibits, the capital's splendid Children's Museum takes the young and young-at-heart on a journey through space, the human body, a coffee plantation, and a giant Lego exhibit. Multiple tickets are available at a slight discount Friday afternoon and weekends. We recommend making a kids' day out by combining this museum with a visit to the nearby zoo. ✉ *La Aurora Park, 5 Calle 10–00, Zona 13* ☎ *2475–5076* 🎫 *Q35* ⏲ *Tues.–Fri. 8:30–noon and 1–4:30, weekends 9:30–1:30 and 2:30–6.*

NEED A BREAK?

Satisfy your sweet tooth on the porch of Café Zurich (✉ *6 Av. 12–52, Zona 10* ☎ *2334–2781*), a former colonial home. The menu has specialty coffees as well as chocolate, chocolate, and more chocolate.

5 **Zona Viva.** The so-called "lively zone" is undoubtedly the most cosmopolitan area of town. The daytime crowd is mostly business executives, but at night a more vivacious bunch takes over. The precise definition of the neighborhood differs depending on whom you talk to, but it roughly

A BIT OF HISTORY

Guatemala City exists only because of the 1773 earthquake that leveled nearby Antigua. Authorities decided once and for all to move their capital to supposedly safer ground after several such seismic events during colonial times. The new city broke ground three years later with the stately name *La Nueva Guatemala de la Asunción* ("The New Guatemala of the Assumption"), presiding over Spain's colony of Central America for nearly a half-century more before becoming the capital of an independent Guatemala.

The land wasn't empty pre-1776, however. The Maya had lived here for 2,500 years before the relocation of the colonial capital, as evidenced by the ruins of Kaminaljuyú, today nearly swallowed up by modern development in Zona 7. True to historical patterns in developing countries, waves of migration from poor rural areas have caused the capital to balloon in size, including country people who fled to the capital during Guatemala's long civil war, looking for safety when violence shook the highlands. Many shantytowns ring the city as a result.

That much-vaunted safety from seismic activity that led colonial authorities to set up shop here proved an illusion: three major earthquakes rocked Guatemala City in the 20th century, the most devastating in February 1976 killing 23,000 people. Small tremors remain a fact of life in the capital. With the government struggling to upgrade building codes, it is hoped that the next "big one" will cause less damage.

centers on the area from avenidas La Reforma and 4, and calles 12 and 14, fanning out from there. Streets accommodate pedestrians overflowing from the narrow sidewalks on which restaurants have introduced outdoor seating, and lines extend from bars. You won't find the boutiques that characterize most upscale neighborhoods; those that do exist are mostly inside the large, international chain hotels. An exception to this is Plaza Fontabella (4 Av. 12–59), an attractive outdoor mall with a variety of upscale shops selling everything from books to home decor to custom-made suits.

THE OLD CITY

Older and grittier than the New City, the Old City has the hustle and bustle of many Central American capitals. But walking around the area, especially around the Plaza Mayor, can be pleasant. The frenetic colors and sounds of the metropolis might be daunting at first, but with a little patience—and, of course, a well-hidden money pouch—the downtown experience can be both memorable and exhilarating. The Old City is also the best place in the capital to rub shoulders with everyday Guatemalans.

TOP ATTRACTIONS

12 **Mercado Central.** A seemingly endless maze of underground passages is home to the Mercado Central, where handicrafts from the highlands are hawked from overstocked stalls. It's not as appealing as the open-

CLOSE UP

Kaminaljuyú

Who says you can't find Mayan ruins in the metropolitan area? From 300 BC to AD 900, an early Mayan city of some 50,000 people flourished in what is now the heart of Zona 7 in one of Guatemala City's many gorges. What you can see today, about 100 mounds and platforms, is but a fraction of the original city, most of which is buried beneath today's urban sprawl. Excavation of this impressive site, which includes the bases of several pyramids, began in 1925, when a local soccer team dug into the ground to expand its practice field. Many of the figurines and artifacts originally unearthed were thought to be associated with burial, leading authorities to dub the site with its present name, a Quiché term meaning "hills of the dead." No one knows for sure what the city was originally called. Many of the objects found here are now on display at the Museo Popol Vuh.

air markets in Antigua or Chichicastenango, but the leather goods, wooden masks, and woolen blankets found here are often cheaper. There are skilled pickpockets in the market, so keep an eye on your belongings. ✉ *8 Calle and 8 Av., Zona 1* ☎ *No phone* ⊙ *Mon.–Sat. 8–6, closed Sun.*

10 **Palacio Nacional de la Cultura.** The grandiose National Palace was built between 1937 and 1943 to satisfy the monumental ego of President Jorge Ubico Castañeda. It once held the offices of the president and his ministers, but now many of its 320 rooms house a collection of paintings and sculptures by well-known Guatemalan artists from the colonial period to the present. Look for Alfredo Gálvez Suárez's murals illustrating the history of the city above the entry. The palace's ornate stairways and stained-glass windows are a pleasant contrast to the gritty city outside its walls. ■ **TIP→ You must visit with a guide, who will take you on a 30-minute highlights tour, which leaves every half hour throughout the day.** Your visit includes a stop at the presidential balcony off the banquet room. If the palace is a must on your itinerary, call ahead to confirm that it is open; the building occasionally closes for presidential functions. ✉ *6 Calle and 7 Av., Zona 1* ☎ *2230–1020* 💳 *Q40* ⊙ *Weekdays 9–4:30.*

9 **Plaza Mayor.** Some people refer to this expanse as the Parque Central, but, despite a few trees, it's more vast concrete plaza than park. Clustered around this historic square are landmarks that survived the 19th and 20th centuries' earthquakes. One original building did not get through the 1917 earthquake: the colonial-era Palacio del Gobierno, which once stood on the plaza's west side, was leveled and later cleared, adding a second city block to the expanse of the square. In the center of the plaza is a fountain where children sometimes splash while their parents relax on the nearby benches. Photographers set up shop here on weekends, putting up small backdrops of rural scenes—you can have your picture taken in front of them. On Sunday, the best day to go, the plaza is filled with vendors and families relaxing on their day off. ✉ *Between 6 and 8 calles and 6 and 7 Avs., Zona 1.*

WORTH NOTING

11 **Catedral Santiago de Guatemala.** Built between 1778 and 1867, Guatemala City's cathedral replaced the old Catedral de Santiago Apóstol in Antigua, destroyed in that city's 1773 earthquake. The structure is a rare example of colonial architecture in the Old City. Standing steadfast on the eastern end of the Plaza Mayor, it is one of the city's most enduring landmarks, having survived the capital's numerous 20th-century earthquakes. The ornate altars hold outstanding examples of colonial religious art, including an image of the Virgen de la Asunción, the city's patron saint. Off a courtyard on the cathedral's south side—enter through the church—stands the Museo de la Arquidiócesis de Santiago Guatemala, the archdiocesan museum with a small collection of colonial religious art and artifacts. ✉ *8 Calle and 7 Av., Zona 1* ☎ *2232–7621; museum, 2232–2527* 🌐 *www.catedraldeguatemala.org* 🎫 *Free, Q20 for museum* ⏲ *Cathedral: Mon.–Sat. 7–1 and 2–6, Sun. 7–6; museum: Mon.–Fri. 9–1 and 2–5, Sat. 9–1 and 2–4; closed Sun.*

16 **Centro Cultural Miguel Ángel Asturias.** The city's fine-arts complex consists of the imposing Teatro Nacional and the open-air Teatro del Aire Libre. Named for Guatemala's Nobel Prize–winning novelist who spent much of his life in exile for opposing Guatemala's dictatorship, the hilltop cluster of buildings overlooks the Old City. Check out the performance schedule while you're here and pick up a ticket if something strikes your fancy. Prices are far lower than what you'd pay at a comparable venue in Europe or North America. The only way to see the theater, other than attending a performance, is to take a 1½-hour tour. ✉ *24 Calle 3–81, Centro Cívico, Zona 1* ☎ *2232–4041* 🎫 *Q30* ⏲ *Weekdays 9–4.*

NEED A BREAK?

Satisfy your caffeine craving and sweet tooth at El Cafetalito (✉ *8 Av. 10–68, Zona 1* ☎ *2221–4696* 🌐 *www.elcafetalito.com*), a European-style café whose Swiss owners serve up sophisticated coffees and pastries to an appreciative clientele.

14 **El Correo.** You can mail packages from your hotel, but it's far more fun to come to the main post office, housed in a cantaloupe-color structure dating from the colonial era. ✉ *7 Av. 12–11,* ☎ *2413–0202* ⏲ *Weekdays 8:30–5:30, Sat. 9–12.*

13 **Iglesia de La Merced.** If religious iconography is your thing, step inside this lovely church dating from 1813 to see its baroque interior. Many of the elaborate paintings and sculptures originally adorned La Merced in Antigua, but were moved here after earthquakes devastated that city. The church also has two small museums. ✉ *5 Calle 11–67, Zona 1* ☎ *2232–0631* ⏲ *Daily 7–7.*

15 **Iglesia de San Francisco.** The Church of St. Francis, built by its namesake Franciscan order between 1800 and 1851, is known for its ornate wooden altar. A small museum explains the church's history. ✉ *13 Calle 6–34, Zona 1* ☎ *2232–3625* ⏲ *Daily 10:30–4.*

CLOSE UP

Mapa en Relieve

Mapa en Relieve. If you want to get the lay of the land before you head out to the country, this unusual relief map depicts Guatemala's precipitous topography. The layout is so immense—1,800 square meters, or 19,500 square feet—that your best view is from an observation tower. What makes it even more amazing is that it was completed in 1905, before satellite and aerial topography, and long before Google Earth. The flashy Spanish-language Web site focuses on the late-19th- and early-20th-century development and construction of the map, a labor of love of engineer (and amateur geographer) Francisco Vela (1859–1909). Altitudes are greatly exaggerated: horizontally, the map uses a 1:10,000 scale, but vertically, it's 1:2,000. The map lies several blocks north of the Old City, not far from the Cervecería Centroamericana and its brewery tour; a taxi is your best bet for getting here.

✉ *Parque Minerva, 6 Av. Norte final, Zona 2* ☎ *2254–1114* 🎫 *Q15* ⏲ *Daily 9–5.*

WHERE TO EAT

WHAT IT COSTS IN GUATEMALAN QUETZALES					
	¢	$	$$	$$$	$$$$
Restaurants	under Q40	Q40–Q70	Q70–Q100	Q100–Q130	over Q130

Restaurant prices are per person for a main course at dinner.

THE NEW CITY

Guatemala City has the varied cuisine you'd expect in a major city. Finer restaurants are clustered in the New City, and virtually every street in the Zona Viva has a selection of tempting restaurants. Some tried-and-true favorites are listed below. Fortunately, the Zona Viva is small enough that you can stroll around until you find that perfect place.

$$ LATIN AMERICAN ✕ **Casa Chapina.** For an around-Guatemala tour of the country's cuisine, we like this down-home New City restaurant with its bright yellow walls and colorful textiles hung from the ceiling. The emphasis is on meat, including typical national dishes such as *pollo loroco* (chicken-and-vegetables), *pepián* (chicken fricassee in pumpkin and sesame sauce), and *kaq'ik* (a turkey stew from Alta Verapaz). Be sure to accompany whatever you order with the restaurant's warm homemade tortillas. ✉ *1 Av. 13–42, Zona 10* ☎ *2367–6688* 💳 *AE, D, DC, MC, V.*

$$$ SPANISH ✕ **De Mario.** The menu here is one of the country's most original, combining flavors from both sides of the Atlantic: you can enjoy such Spanish traditions as paella and roast suckling pig or more local offerings like robalo with a mushroom sauce. During its 25-plus years in business, the restaurant has built a much-deserved reputation for impeccable

service. ✉ *1 Av. 12–98, Zona 10* ☎ *2339–2331* ▭ *AE, D, DC, MC, V* ⊙ *No dinner Sun.*

$$ LATIN AMERICAN ✕ **Hacienda de los Sánchez.** This Zona Viva steak house is known for its quality cuts of beef, yet the atmosphere has won over more than one vegetarian. The dining room calls to mind the American West, with such touches as sturdy wooden tables and old saddles. Eat inside or in the small garden. Grilled meats, chicken, and seafood dominate the menu, and there's a decent wine list. ✉ *5 Av. 14–38, Zona 10* ☎ *2360–5040* ▭ *AE, D, DC, MC, V.*

$$$ LATIN AMERICAN ★ ✕ **Hacienda Real.** This adobe building, set back from the street behind a high wall, is decorated in a Western theme, with tile floors and simple wooden furniture. There's also a pleasant central patio with a fountain and tables with umbrellas. Out front, away from the dining areas, is a small play area for kids. Specialties of the house include steak, ribs, pork, salmon, and robalo, all served with a variety of savory condiments like fresh salsa, pickled carrots, and jalapeños. The attentive, exuberant servers bring endless baskets of warm tortillas, but try not to fill up—the truly incomparable caramel flan shouldn't be missed. To top off the experience, a Latin trio strolls through in the evenings and at lunchtime on Fridays. ✉ *5 Av. 14–67, Zona 10* ☎ *2380–8383* 🌐 *www.hacienda-real.com* ▭ *AE, D, DC, MC, V.*

$$ CHINESE ✕ **J.K. Ming.** Located in the Plaza Fontabella shopping center, this upscale Chinese restaurant is decorated in a contemporary Asian theme, with slate floors, black booths, and painted murals. Through a picture window you can watch your food being prepared in the spotless, state-of-the-art kitchen. Or if you'd prefer to sit outside, there's a pleasant row of tables with the feeling of a sidewalk café. The menu is an eclectic mix of classics such as Peking duck and beef with ginger, as well as owner/chef Jake Denberg's special creations, like crab wontons and shrimp with chile sauce. The barbecue ribs make a great way to start the meal, and the fried plantains with homemade ice cream are the perfect ending. ✉ *4 Av. 12–59, Zona 10* ☎ *2385–4640* 🌐 *www.grupoculinario.com* ▭ *AE, D, DC, MC, V* ⊙ *No dinner Sun.*

$$$$ ECLECTIC Fodor's Choice ★ ✕ **Jake's.** If you only have one meal in Guatemala City, head to Jake Denburg's place. A New Jersey–bred painter-turned-restaurateur, Jake uses his creative talents on food, producing dishes ranging from osso buco to crab cakes with avocado-and-wasabi cream sauce. A long-time favorite is the *vaquero chino* (Chinese cowboy), a tenderloin steak served with a sweet soy, espresso, and star anise sauce. For dessert, the pudín de chocolate and cheesecake with crème brûlée are divine. The restaurant is in a beautiful converted farmhouse with hardwood ceilings, tile floors, an outdoor patio, and a sophisticated lounge. The wine list is quite possibly the best in Central America. ✉ *17 Calle 10–40, Zona 10* ☎ *2385–4615* 🌐 *www.grupoculinario.com* ▭ *AE, D, DC, MC, V* ⊙ *No dinner Sun.*

$$$$ FRENCH ★ ✕ **Jean François.** Set in a hacienda-style building, away from the bustle of the city, Jean François is one of the prettiest and most tranquil restaurants in town, with a lovely courtyard/garden and tables tucked under the surrounding arcades. If you prefer to sit inside, there's a charming dining room with floor-to-ceiling windows and a

cozy fireplace. The food is equally impressive, mostly French classics with an occasional New World touch. For an appetizer, try the warm shrimp mousse wrapped in spinach, and for your main course beef with béarnaise or Gorgonzola sauce, or maybe grilled robalo with fresh tomatoes and basil. The french fries are top-notch, and for dessert our favorite is the wonderful, light mousse *de chico* (a type of tropical fruit). ✉ *Diagonal 6 13–63, Zona 10* ☎ *2333–4785* 🌐 *www.grupoculinaro.com* 💳 *AE, DC, MC, V* ⏲ *No dinner Sun.*

COFFEE IN AN INSTANT

Historians credit one George Washington (not *that* George Washington), an Englishman living in Guatemala in the early 20th century, with the invention of instant coffee. A chemist by trade, Washington fiddled with the residue in his coffee pot to come up with a dried product to which hot water could be added for a quick cup. He patented his invention and marketed it here as "Red E Coffee."

2

$$$ LATIN AMERICAN ★ ✕ **Kacao.** Located in the heart of the Zona Viva, this popular eatery feels more like the beach, thanks to its setting in a huge palapa surrounded by tropical plants. At dinner the soft lighting and candles on the tables make for a romantic atmosphere. Although the menu includes a good selection of meat and fish, the specialties of the house are national dishes such as jocón and pepián; Kacao is also one of the best places in town to try an assortment of Guatemalan tamales. Waiters wear traditional dress, and to complete the effect, lively marimba music plays on the stereo. ✉ *2 Av. 13-44, Zona 10* ☎ *2337–4188* 🌐 *www.grupogastronomico.com.gt* 💳 *AE, D, DC, MC, V.*

$$$ LATIN AMERICAN ✕ **Los Ranchos.** A pretty white colonial facade with picture windows welcomes you to one of Guatemala's best steak houses. Most meats, including the rib eye and chateaubriand, come from the United States, including the specialty of the house, a skirt steak called the *churrasco los ranchos*. Ask your server to recommend one of the excellent wines from Argentina, Chile, Spain, or France. And save room for dessert, which ranges from tiramisu to *tres leches,* a type of cake soaked in condensed milk, evaporated milk, and cream. ✉ *14 Calle 1–42, Zona 10* ☎ *2367–6044* 🌐 *www.grupogastronomico.com.gt* 💳 *AE, D, DC, MC, V.*

$$$$ ECLECTIC Fodor'sChoice ★ ✕ **Tamarindos.** Asian and Italian tastes dominate at one of Guatemala City's best restaurants, Tamarindos, where Paris-trained chef Milly Bruderer serves up innovative, decidedly eclectic fare ranging from duck in tamarind sauce to Thai-style curries. Curlicue lamps and whimsical sofas that seem straight out of *Alice in Wonderland* bring a touch of postmodernism. It's an exhilarating destination for dinner, but the reasonably priced lunch menu also makes this an excellent choice during the day. The extensive wine list includes choices from around the globe. ✉ *11 Calle 2–19A, Zona 10* ☎ *2360–5630* 🌐 *www.tamarindos.com.gt* 💳 *AE, D, DC, MC, V* ⏲ *Closed Sun.*

$$ ITALIAN ✕ **Tre Fratelli.** This big, raucous restaurant/bar in the Plaza Fontabella shopping complex is the Guatemalan outpost of the popular American chain. As the name implies, the food is Italian, with favorites including *fettuccine frutti di mare* (with seafood), ravioli *alla Bolognese* (with a variety of meats), and the *quattro stagione* (four-season) pizza. Top it

A TOUR AND A BREW

The capital's **Cervecería Centroamericana** has brewed the majority of the beer sold in Guatemala since 1886. If you've been traveling around the country, you've seen (and likely sampled) Gallo, its ubiquitous flagship beer, pronounced *GAH-yo*. The *cervecería* manufactures a complete line of beverages, including Gallo Light, Victoria lager, the dark bock beer Moza, and Malta Gallo malt liquor. Gallo, incidentally, is marketed in the United States, but under the name "Famosa." (A certain California winery already holds the rights to the "Gallo" name there.)

The brewery offers fun, informative hour-long tours in Spanish and English of its installations several blocks north of the Old City each Monday to Thursday at 8, noon, and 3 PM. (A taxi is the best way to get here.) Reservations are necessary, and should be made at least a week in advance. Best of all, the whole thing is free, and the tour concludes with samples (also free) in the brewery café.

✉ *3 Av. Norte final, Zona 2* ☎ *2289–1555.*

all off with chocolate mousse, homemade ice cream, or a cappuccino or espresso brewed in an authentic Italian coffee machine. **■ TIP→ It's a good place to bring kids if you're looking for familiar cuisine and surroundings.** ✉ *4 Av. 12–59, Zona 10* ☎ *2320–0999* ▭ *AE, D, DC, MC, V.*

$$$$ ECLECTIC Fodor's Choice ★ **✕Zumo.** Occupying an elegant space in the heart of the Zona Viva, Zumo greets diners with simple modern decor, including a comfortable patio and a cozy downstairs bar. Chef Rodrigo Alvarado takes the often overused term "fusion cuisine" seriously, and mixes in-season Guatemalan ingredients with an around-the-world menu. We like the shrimp in mango sauce with avocado butter, the steak in tamarind sauce, and the pumpkin crème brûlée with amaretto ice cream. There's also an extensive wine list (one of the best in the capital, with 60 international offerings), and the service is impeccable. ✉ *1 Av. 12–16 , Zona 10* ☎ *2331–2895* 🌐 *www.zumo.com.gt* ▭ *AE, D, DC, MC, V* ⊙ *Closed Sun. No lunch Sat.*

THE OLD CITY

As the Zona Viva has become the hub of Guate nightlife, restaurants in the Old City have either moved out to where the action is or closed. There are only three establishments left in Zone 1 worthy of our recommendation—all popular establishments that will not disappoint.

$$ SPANISH Fodor's Choice ★ **✕Altuna.** Waiters in white jackets and ties move briskly around the pleasant covered courtyard that serves as the main dining room, once the home of Guatemala City's German Club. Founded in 1948, the restaurant is still serving classic Spanish and Basque dishes such as paella, *calamares en su tinta* (shrimp in their own ink), and for dessert wonderful *torrejas* (crusty bread soaked in whole milk, evaporated milk, and condensed milk with a touch of anise). A branch in the New City maintains the old style and impeccable service of the original city-center restaurant. ✉ *5 Av.*

12–31, Zona 1 ☎ *2253–6743* ✉ *10 Calle 0–45, Zona 10* ☎ *2332–6576* ▭ *AE, DC, MC, V* ⊙ *Closed Mon., no dinner Sun.*

$ LATIN AMERICAN ✕ **Arrin Cuan.** Ask locals to recommend a place to eat in the Old City, and chances are they'll send you to this spirited Guatemalan favorite. The decor couldn't be simpler—stone floor, small fountain, colorful fabrics, and vases of flowers on the tables. The flavorful cuisine, typical of the Cobán region, includes *kaq'ik* (a spicy turkey stew), *gallo en chicha* (chicken in a slightly sweet sauce), and *sopa de tortuga* (turtle soup). More adventurous types will want to sample the roasted tepezcuintle, a type of rodent. ■ **TIP➔ Everyday at lunch and on Friday and Saturday night live marimba music fills the restaurant.** There's a branch in the New City, which dishes up the same regional cuisine from Alta Verapaz. ✉ *5 Av. 3–27, Zona 1* ☎ *2238–0242* ✉ *16 Calle 4–32, Zona 10* ☎ *2366–2660* ▭ *AE, DC, MC, V.*

$$ INTERNATIONAL ✕ **Pan American.** A longtime Old City favorite, this courtyard dining room brims with the charm of another era, from the wooden balconies hung with colorful *huipiles* to the traditional highland dress worn by the waitstaff. The menu has an extensive selection of both international and Guatemalan fare, and among the desserts the coconut cream pie is a standout. On Sunday there is a brunch buffet with live marimba music. ✉ *9 Calle 5–63, Zona 1* ☎ *2232–6807* ▭ *AE, D, DC, MC, V.*

WHERE TO STAY

Guatemala City has the country's widest range of accommodations. Upscale hotels are found in the New City, while more moderately priced lodgings are clustered in the Old City.

WHAT IT COSTS IN GUATEMALAN QUETZALES					
	¢	$	$$	$$$	$$$$
Hotels	under Q160	Q160–Q360	Q360–Q560	Q560–Q760	over Q760

Hotel prices are for two people in a standard double room, including tax and service.

THE NEW CITY

$$$$ **Barceló.** Although its facade won't win any awards, the lovely lounge offers rest to the weary; relax with a cocktail in one of the comfortable armchairs as you listen to jazz. Or you can always head to the Health and Racquet Club, a spacious spa and sports facility. Rooms are nicely furnished, and each has a small balcony with a view of the city. **Pros:** chain amenities. **Cons:** several blocks to Zona Viva. ✉ *7 Av. 15–45, Zona 9* ☎ *2320–4000* ⊕ *www.barcelo.com* *38 rooms, 9 suites* *In-room: safe, Internet, Wi-Fi. In-hotel: 3 restaurants, room service, bar, pool, gym, spa, laundry service, Internet terminal, Wi-Fi, parking (paid), no smoking rooms* ▭ *AE, D, DC, MC, V* *EP.*

$$$ **Best Western Stofella.** For those who feel more at home in smaller hotels, Stofella is our pick in the mid-price category. A short staircase leads to a flower-filled reception area. Some of the guest rooms

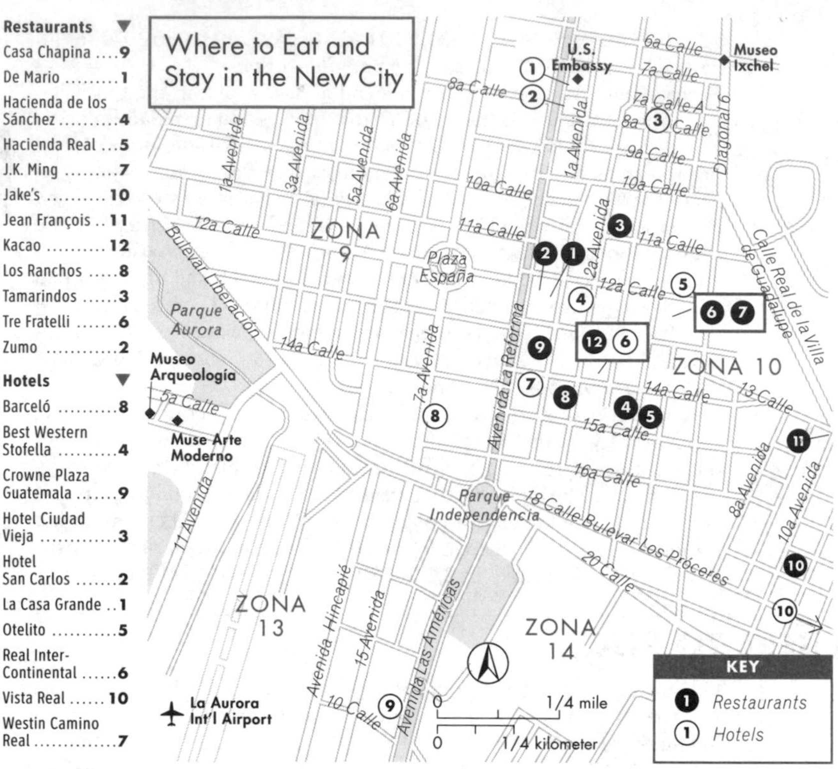

have small sitting areas. Ask for one in the original building, as those added during a recent renovation don't have the same character. If you're feeling social, join the other guests in the cozy bar. **Pros:** close to action, no high-rise feel, excellent value. **Cons:** lack of some amenities found in larger hotels. ✉ *2 Av. 12–28, Zona 10* ☏ *2410–8600* 🌐 *www.bestwestern.com* *82 rooms* *In-room: no a/c (some), safe, refrigerator (some), Internet (some), Wi-Fi. In-hotel: bar, gym, laundry service, Internet terminal, Wi-Fi, parking (paid), no-smoking rooms* ▭ *AE, D, DC, MC, V* *BP.*

$$$$ **Crowne Plaza Guatemala.** Giant glass elevators in the atrium-style lobby ascend to a dizzying view of the city. With 22 meeting rooms and 16 ballrooms, the hotel is designed to accommodate large conventions. Rooms on the south side have the most impressive views of the surrounding volcanoes—even the health club overlooks their peaks. The hotel is convenient to the airport, but it's quite a distance from the Zona Viva. **Pros:** chain amenities, close to airport, splendid views. **Cons:** far from the action, airport noise. ✉ *Av. Las Américas 9–08, Zona 13* ☏ *2422–5000* 🌐 *www.ichotelsgroup.com* *183 rooms, 8 suites* *In-room: safe, kitchen (some), refrigerator (some), Internet (some), Wi-Fi. In-hotel: restaurant, room service, bar, pool, gym, spa, laundry service, Internet terminal, Wi-Fi, parking (free), no-smoking rooms* ▭ *AE, DC, MC, V* *BP.*

$$$$ **Hotel Ciudad Vieja.** In a sector of the city with few mid priced lodgings, the Ciudad Vieja, a few blocks north of the Zona Viva, is a good bet. Two floors of rooms are arranged around an elongated garden, with a small restaurant situated at one end of the courtyard. Rooms are spacious and pleasantly—if a bit dowdily—furnished, most with two queen-size beds. **Pros:** good value, friendly staff. **Cons:** several blocks from Zona Viva, could use some redecorating. ✉ *8 Calle 3–67, Zona 10* ☎ *2331–9104* 🌐 *www.hotelciudadvieja.com* *26 rooms, 1 suite* *In-room: no a/c, Wi-Fi. In-hotel: restaurant, room service, bar, laundry service, Internet terminal, Wi-Fi, parking (free), no-smoking rooms* *AE, D, DC, MC, V* *BP.*

$$$$ **Hotel San Carlos.** This pretty colonial house puts a little space between you and the bustling Zona Viva. Floor-to-ceiling windows in the reception area look out onto a sunny courtyard dotted with statues. Sloping stairs lead up to the individually decorated rooms. Other rooms in an annex are newer, but they lack the charm of those in the main house. **Pros:** small hotel with big amenities, lovely rooms in main house. **Cons:** several blocks from Zona Viva, plain rooms in annex. ✉ *Av. La Reforma 7–89, Zona 10* ☎ *2362–9076* 🌐 *www.hsancarlos.com* *30 rooms, 1 suite* *In-room: no a/c, safe, kitchen (some), refrigerator (some), Wi-Fi. In-hotel: restaurant, room service, bar, pool, laundry service, Internet terminal, Wi-Fi, parking (free), some pets allowed, no-smoking rooms* *AE, D, DC, MC, V* *CP.*

$$$ **La Casa Grande.** You enter this stately hotel through iron gates, then step into a small reception area that leads to a comfortable lounge with a fireplace to keep out the chill. The restaurant spills out into the courtyard; its cast-iron chairs are surrounded by arches covered with dangling philodendrons. Traditional tile floors grace the rooms, which are furnished with antiques. Rooms in the front open onto a balcony, but those in the back are quieter. **Pros:** intimate feel. **Cons:** could use some redecorating, several blocks from Zona Viva. ✉ *Av. La Reforma 7–67, Zona 10* ☎ *2332–0914* 🌐 *www.casagrande-gua.com* *28 rooms, 1 suite* *In-room: no a/c (some), Internet, Wi-Fi. In-hotel: restaurant, room service, bar, laundry service, Internet terminal, Wi-Fi, parking (free), no-smoking rooms* *AE, D, DC, MC, V* *BP.*

$$$$ **Otelito.** This former colonial house has character that most other hotels can't match. Ivy-covered walls give way to a cozy reception area. Some rooms surround a breezy courtyard overflowing with potted plants, whereas others share a balcony reached by a spiral staircase. The softly lighted rooms have wooden paneling and tile floors. The Middle Eastern restaurant is an ideal lunch spot; take a table on the tranquil patio where hummingbirds surround a melodic fountain. **Pros:** close to action, upscale atmosphere, lively restaurant and hip bar. **Cons:** occasional noise from courtyard. ✉ *12 Calle 4–51, Zona 10* ☎ *2388–0500* 🌐 *www.otelito.com* *12 rooms, 1 suite* *In-room: safe (some), Wi-Fi. In-hotel: restaurant, room service, bar, laundry service, Internet terminal, Wi-Fi, parking (free), no-smoking rooms* *AE, D, DC, MC, V* *CP.*

$$$$ ★ **Real InterContinental.** The towering InterContinental, in the center of the Zona Viva, exudes a feeling of modernity and luxury throughout. The expansive lobby is graced with a monumental contemporary

sculpture and two sweeping staircases, and the large, comfortable rooms have modern art on the walls. The very good French restaurant imported its chef from Paris. Other restaurants, as well as shops and boutiques, are within walking distance. **Pros:** top-notch amenities and service, close to action. **Cons:** doesn't have the personal feeling of a smaller hotel. ✉ *14 Calle 2–51, Zona 10* ☎ *2379–4444* 🌐 *www.intercontinental.com* *234 rooms, 5 suites* *In-room: safe, refrigerator, Internet, Wi-Fi. In-hotel: 3 restaurants, room service, bar, pool, gym, laundry service, Internet terminal, Wi-Fi, parking (free), no-smoking rooms* 💳 *AE, D, DC, MC, V* *EP.*

$$$$ **Vista Real.** The colossal Vista Real has a neocolonial style—with vaulted ceilings and arabesque arches—and excellent views of the city and the neighboring volcanoes from its hilltop perch. A series of ponds and cascades play out below a covered bridge, which leads you to the main building. Suites are elegantly appointed with colonial art and sumptuously soft bedding. The only drawback is its location slightly outside the city. **Pros:** colonial decor, great views, good amenities. **Cons:** out-of-town location. ✉ *Prolongación Blvd. Los Próceres, Km 9, Zona 15* ☎ *2427–0000* 🌐 *www.vistareal.com* *123 suites* *In-room: safe, kitchen, Internet, Wi-Fi. In-hotel: restaurant, room service, bar, pool, gym, laundry service, Internet terminal, Wi-Fi, parking (free), no-smoking rooms* 💳 *AE, D, DC, MC, V* *EP.*

$$$$ ★ **Westin Camino Real.** With every imaginable amenity and a staff that aims to please, it isn't surprising that the immense Camino Real has hosted everyone from rock stars to heads of state. The spacious reception area lies just beyond a long foyer lined with overstuffed leather chairs. Stately rooms are furnished with carved French provincial–style pieces. Executive floors hold spacious suites with room for business travelers to spread out. French doors in the rooms on the executive floors provide views of the nearby volcanoes. **Pros:** close to action, excellent amenities, shopping arcade. **Cons:** large-hotel feel. ✉ *14 Calle and Av. La Reforma, Zona 10* ☎ *2333–3000* 🌐 *www.caminoreal.com.gt* *271 rooms, 19 suites* *In-room: safe, Internet, Wi-Fi. In-hotel: 3 restaurants, room service, bar, pool, gym, spa, laundry service, Internet terminal, Wi-Fi, parking (paid), no-smoking rooms* 💳 *AE, DC, MC, V* *EP.*

THE OLD CITY

$ **Chalet Suizo.** This quiet hotel has been popular with budget travelers for more than 40 years. An attractive, light-filled central courtyard behind the reception area is a nice place to relax. The rooms, all of which face the patio, are quite basic. The staff is friendly and will happily store your extra luggage while you travel around the country. **Pros:** knowledgeable staff, good value, great place to meet fellow travelers. **Cons:** small rooms, lack of decor. ✉ *7 Av. 14–34, Zona 1* ☎ *2251–3786* 🌐 *www.hotelchaletsuizo.com* *26 rooms, 15 with bath* *In-room: no a/c, no phone, no TV (some), Internet, Wi-Fi. In-hotel: restaurant, room service, gym, laundry service, Internet terminal, Wi-Fi, parking (free), some pets allowed, no-smoking rooms* 💳 *AE, D, DC, MC, V* *EP.*

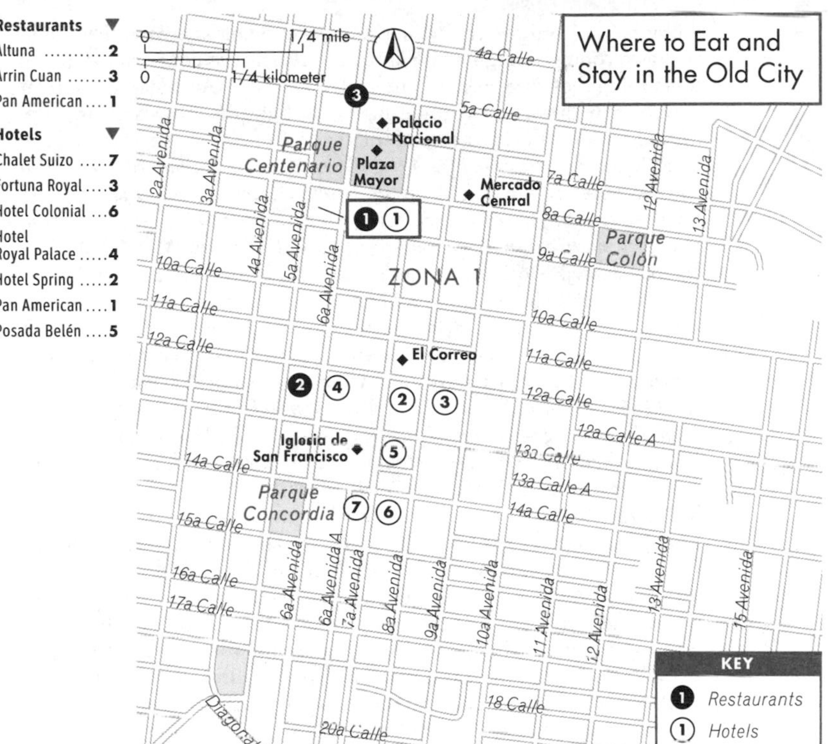

$ **Fortuna Royal.** This hotel has succeeded where few others have by offering comfortable accommodations for a reasonable rate, making it a favorite of Central American business travelers who don't have big expense accounts. From the small reception area you climb a steep staircase to the pleasant but plain rooms, which are fitted out with tile floors and pale-green bedspreads. **Pros:** good value. **Cons:** small rooms, could use some remodeling. ✉ *12 Calle 8–42, Zona 1* ☎ *2238–2484* *21 rooms* *In-room: no a/c, refrigerator (some). In-hotel: restaurant, room service, bar, Internet terminal, parking (free), no-smoking rooms* *AE, D, DC, MC, V* *EP.*

$ **Hotel Colonial.** It occupies a lovely 19th-century house, but this hotel isn't quite as charming inside. However, the reception area overlooks an enclosed patio overflowing with potted plants, and the lounge is furnished with reproductions of antiques. The rooms all have colonial-style furnishings; some of the larger ones have very nice views. **Pros:** lovely garden, quiet street. **Cons:** plainly decorated rooms could use remodeling. ✉ *7 Av. 14–19, Zona 1* ☎ *2232–6722* 🌐 *www.hotelcolonial.net* *42 rooms* *In-room: no a/c, no phone, Wi-Fi. In-hotel: restaurant, Internet terminal, Wi-Fi, parking (free), no-smoking rooms* *AE, D, DC, MC, V* *EP.*

$$ **Hotel Royal Palace.** In a lovely old building, this hotel is a welcome retreat from the frantic pace of the streets outside. The large, elegant

lobby has an antique chandelier and a sweeping staircase. The high-ceilinged rooms, though a bit plain, are nevertheless comfortable. If you don't mind the noise, ask for one with a view of 6 Avenida—it's a great way to view the action without having to fight the crowds. **Pros:** comfortable, good value, yesteryear ambience. **Cons:** some street noise. ✉ *6 Av. 12–66, Zona 1* ☎ *2416–4400* 🌐 *www.hotelroyalpalace.com* *75 rooms, 7 suites* *In-room: no a/c (some), Internet, Wi-Fi (some). In-hotel: restaurant, room service, bar, gym, laundry service, Internet terminal, parking (free), no-smoking rooms* 💳 *AE, D, DC, MC, V* *CP*

$ **Hotel Spring.** Most rooms here face a peaceful courtyard with cast-iron tables and chairs and lots of greenery. Several on the second floor share a balcony that overlooks the avenue. A small café behind the courtyard is a great place to relax after a day of exploring the city. **Pros:** pleasant courtyard, friendly café. **Cons:** street noise, basic decor. ✉ *8 Av. 12–65, Zona 1* ☎ *2230–2858* 🌐 *www.hotelspring.com* *39 rooms, 32 with bath* *In-room: no a/c, no phone, Wi-Fi. In-hotel: restaurant, laundry facilities, Internet terminal, Wi-Fi, parking (free), no-smoking rooms* 💳 *AE, D, DC, MC, V* *EP.*

$$ ★ **Pan American.** The grande dame of downtown hotels, the Pan American opened in 1942, and was for many years the most luxurious lodging in town. To step into the dark-wood lobby of this former mansion is to leave the confusion of the city behind. A covered courtyard with attractive wrought-iron chandeliers spills out from the restaurant, whose servers wear traditional highland dress. The rooms are small but attractive, with tile floors, handmade rugs and bedspreads, and walls adorned with traditional paintings. The restaurant, known for its brunches and its coconut cream pie, is one of the few dining options left in the Old City. **Pros:** lively restaurant, good value. **Cons:** small rooms, slight mustiness. ✉ *9 Calle 5–63, Zona 1* ☎ *2232–6807* 🌐 *www.hotelpanamerican.com.gt* *54 rooms* *In-room: no a/c (some), Wi-Fi (some). In-hotel: restaurant, room service, bar, laundry service, Internet terminal, Wi-Fi, parking (free), no-smoking rooms* 💳 *AE, D, DC, MC, V* *EP.*

$$ Fodor's Choice ★ **Posada Belén.** This little jewel of an inn on a quiet side street is exceptional, thanks to the couple that runs it. Built in 1873, the family's former home has been renovated just enough to combine quirky Old World charm with basic comforts. Rooms have tile floors, handwoven bedspreads, and walls decorated with Guatemalan paintings and weavings. Turtles roam the tiny garden, and a small but impressive collection of Mayan artifacts graces the dining room, where meals are served family style. The owners are also a great source of information about the city. **Pros:** knowledgeable staff, pretty garden, quiet street. **Cons:** some noise from courtyard, several blocks from the Plaza Mayor. ✉ *13 Calle A 10–30, Zona 1* ☎ *2253–4530* 🌐 *www.posadabelen.com* *10 rooms* *In-room: no a/c, no phone, safe, no TV, Wi-Fi. In-hotel: restaurant, laundry service, Internet terminal, Wi-Fi, parking (free), no-smoking rooms* 💳 *AE, DC, MC, V* *EP.*

2

NIGHTLIFE AND THE ARTS

The Guatemala City arts scene boasts three venues with extensive schedules of concerts, dance performances, and plays.

For those seeking a different kind of nocturnal adventure, the Zona Viva is the city's nightlife center, offering hosts of bars, clubs (sedate or lively), and discos. Expect lines at the most popular places. In the New City we recommend that you check out the Edificio Paseo Plaza, which offers half a dozen clubs in a single, relatively secure high-rise building.

> **STAY IN THE LOOP**
>
> Although published in Antigua, the free monthly English-language magazine *Revue* (🌐 *www.revuemag.com*) contains an ample section describing what's going on in the capital. The same company publishes the Spanish-language monthly *Recrearte* magazine (🌐 *www.revistarecrearte.com*) with a similar focus. Look for either at hotels and restaurants around the city.

Old City nightspots have more character, and many are conveniently clustered in two adjacent pedestrian walkways, the Pasaje Rubio and the Pasaje Aycinena. Like the Edificio Paseo Plaza in the New City, these two venues are the best bet for out-of-towners, for their convenience as well as relative safety.

Pick a place you want to visit, take a taxi there, and have your hotel or restaurant call one to take you back. Most clubs in both the Old and New cities are closed on Sunday and Monday nights, and the action often doesn't heat up until Thursday.

THE ARTS

As Spain is Guatemala's mother country, its **Centro Cultural de España** (✉ *Via 5 1–23, Zona 4* ☎ *2385–9066*) keeps up an active Spanish-language calendar of music, art, theater, and lectures, with something going on several nights a week.

The city's cultural venue par excellence, the **Centro Cultural Miguel Ángel Asturias** (✉ *24 Calle 3–81, Zona 1* ☎ *2232–4041*) has an active program of music, dance, and theater presentations by national and international groups. Most large shows are held at its Teatro Nacional; other presentations take place at the complex's smaller theaters. Loosely affiliated with the U.S. embassy, the **Instituto Guatemalteco Americano** (✉ *1 Ruta 4–05, Zona 4* ☎ *2422–5555* 🌐 *www.iga.edu*) presents an active calendar of cultural offerings by Guatemalan and international groups.

NIGHTLIFE

BARS AND CLUBS

THE NEW CITY Like its namesake 1980s television show, **Cheers** (✉ *13 Calle 0–40, Zona 10* ☎ *2368–2089*) draws a friendly crowd, mostly for the sporting events being shown on the big-screen TVs. **Edificio Paseo Plaza** (✉ *3 Av. 12–38, Zona 10*) makes club-hopping easy (and relatively safe) by offering half a dozen venues with differing personalities in the same building. A branch of the outlet by the same name in Antigua, **Frida's** (✉ *3 Av. 14–60, Zona 10* ☎ *2367–1611*) is a place to knock back a margarita with a few friends, with prints by Mexican artists Frida Kahlo and Diego Rivera as backdrop. **Giuseppe Verdi** (✉ *Westin Camino Real, 14 Calle at Av. La Reforma, Zona 10* ☎ *2333–3000*) is an upscale bar that caters mostly to tourists. **Jake's**(✉ *17 Calle 10–40, Zona 10* ☎ *2368–0351*), the popular restaurant, also has a sophisticated lounge perfect for a quiet drink in a grown-up atmosphere. We like **Kloster** (✉ *13 Calle 2–75, Zona 10* ☎ *2334–3882*), a German *oom-pah-pah* kind of place with a variety of fondues as well as tasty microbrews. **Otelito Season Lounge** (✉ *12 Calle 4–51, Zona 10* ☎ *2388–0500*), located in the Otelito hotel, offers an intimate, modern space where the color scheme changes with the calendar. Despite its name, **William Shakespeare Pub** (✉ *13 Calle and 1 Av., Zona 10* ☎ *2331–2641*) doesn't exactly evoke an English pub, but is a convivial place to stop for a drink.

THE OLD CITY **Blanco y Negro** (✉ *9 Calle 6–45, Zona 1*), located in the same block as the Pasaje Aycinena and the Pasaje Rubio, specializes in reggae. **Café & Bar Sabina** (✉ *8 Av. 12–21, Zona 1*) offers Trova, a kind of folk music that originated in Cuba. **Pasaje Aycinena** (✉ *9 Calle 6–47, Zona 1*), along the Pasaje Rubio, a convenient, relatively safe pedestrian zone, is the best bet for tourists. The atmosphere is "alternative," with lots of young people (including many Europeans). Among the establishments you'll find here are the venerable Cien Puertas (the oldest bar in the neighborhood), Bacabes (which features live rock music in Spanish and English), La Luna (Trova), and Capuccino (Spanish-language rock). **Pasaje Rubio** (✉ *9 Calle 6–25, Zona 1*), adjacent to the Pasaje Aycinena, is another popular pedestrian zone. It has a bohemian feel, with a variety of establishments for every personal and musical taste. A highlight is El Portalito, once the hangout of Guatemala's Noble Prize-winning author Miguel Ángel Asturias.

GAY AND LESBIAN

Guatemala City's same-sex scene is hidden, discreet, and changes frequently. Most venues are in the Old City. They're all frequented by an under-30 crowd.

THE NEW CITY **Frida's** (✉ *3 Av. 14–60, Zona 10* ☎ *2367–1611*) offers a gay night the last Friday of every month.

THE OLD CITY A lively young gay crowd frequents **Black & White** (✉ *11 Calle 2–54, Zona 1* ☎ *5904–1758*) Wednesday through Sunday night, and there always seem to be drink specials on tap. The mellow **Café del Arco** (✉ *12 Calle 8–52, Zona 1* ☎ *2232–5527*) serves light, café-style food to a mixed clientele, nightly except Sunday. A mixed crowd dances the night away at **Rouge** (✉ *4 Calle 5–30, Zona 1* ☎ *2253–4119*).

SHOPPING

> **GIMME A KISS**
>
> If you're here on an extended language-study trip, you might get a bit homesick. Tune in to Guatemala City's KISS-FM, which broadcasts in English and plays a steady diet of U.S. and British pop hits, present and past, at 97.7 FM.

With the exception of the Mercado Central in the Old City, shop hours are generally weekdays 9 to 1 and 3 to 7, Saturday 9 to 1. The midday break is gradually disappearing in the capital.

ART

THE NEW CITY **Carlos Woods** (✉ *10 Av. 5–49, Zona 14* ☎ *2366–6883*) has a nice collection of contemporary sculpture and paintings. Works by contemporary Guatemalan painters are on display at **El Ático** (✉ *4 Av. 15–45, Zona 14* ☎ *2368–0853*). **Galería Ríos** (✉ *2 Calle 0–96, Zona 9* ☎ *2331–7071*) has a wide selection of contemporary paintings. **Sol de Río** (✉ *14 Av. 15–56, Zona 10* ☎ *2368–0352*) is small, but well worth a visit.

BOOKS

THE NEW CITY At **Artemis Edinter** (✉ *12 Calle 1–25, Zona 10* ☎ *2335–2649*) you'll find works in Spanish and English, as well as coffee-table books on Guatemala and a nice selection of kids' books for that child on your list who is learning Spanish. The gift shop at **Museo Popol Vuh** (✉ *End of 6 Calle, Zona 10* ☎ *2338–7896* 🌐 *www.popolvuh.ufm.edu.gt*) has an interesting collection of books on art, archaeology, and history. In the Zona Viva, **Sophos** (✉ *4 Av. 12–59, in the Plaza Fontabella shopping center, Zona 10* ☎ *2419–70707*) is the largest general bookstore in the city, and one of the best places to find books in English. With its modern design and lots of natural light, it's a nice place to spend some time browsing. There's also a pleasant outdoor café.

HANDICRAFTS

■ TIP→ A number of stores east of Avenida La Reforma sell handmade goods.

THE NEW CITY **Algodones Mayas** (✉ *14 Calle 0–25, Zona 10* ☎ *2331–6311* 🌐 *www.algodonesmayas.com*) offers fine hand-woven cotton textiles in natural colors from all over Guatemala. The elegant **Casa Solares** (✉ *Av. La Reforma 11–07, Zona 10*) is pricey, but you can be certain that you are buying the best-quality goods. **Cerámicas Decorativas Artesanales** (✉ *1 Av. 12–41, Zona 10* ☎ *2334–1160*) sells hand-crafted tiles in colonial or contemporary style. In addition to *artesanía*, **Colección 21** (✉ *12 Calle 4–65, Zona 14* ☎ *2368–1659*) has an art gallery featuring works by local painters. **In-Nola** (✉ *18 Calle 21–31, Zona 10* ☎ *2367–2424* 🌐 *www.in-nola.com*) specializes in textiles, but you'll also find leather items. It's your best bet if you only have time to pop into one shop. Goods from highland artisans can be found at the **Mercado de Artesanías** (✉ *Blvd. Juan Pablo II, Zona 13* ☎ *2472–0208*). **Zuñil** (✉ *Westin Camino Real Hotel, 14 Calle 0–20, Zona 10* ☎ *2333–4633*) has a nice selection of handicrafts made specially for this shop, including high-quality textiles.

THE OLD CITY **Lin-Canola** (✉ *5 Calle 9–60, Zona 1* ☎ *2253–0138*) has an excellent selection with prices that are often inexpensive. If you're in the market for *típica*, roughly translated as "typical goods," head to the **Mercado Central** (✉ *8 Calle and 8 Av., Zona 1* ☎ *No phone*).

JEWELRY

THE NEW CITY In addition to jewelry, **Albuhi** (✉ *20 Calle 25–96, Zona 10* ☎ *2368–3842*) has a terrific selection of picture frames, plates, candlesticks, and religious articles crafted from Guatemalan pewter. **Coral y Plata** (✉ *4 Av. 12–59, in the Plaza Fontabella shopping center, Zona 10* ☎ *2336–7029*) has a good selection, including turquoise, jade, onyx, and fresh-water pearls. **Equinoccio Fine Art** (✉ *14 Calle 0–61, Zona 10* ☎ *2337–1384* 🌐 *www.equinocciofineart.com*) features high-quality, original works designed by the owner herself. **Jades** (✉ *Westin Camino Real, 14 Calle 0–20, Zona 10* ☎ *2368–3689* 🌐 *www.jademaya.com* ✉ *Barceló, 7 Av. 15–45, Zona 9* ☎ *2320–4000*), the well-known jewelry shop in Antigua, has two branches in the New City. **L'Elegance** (✉ *Westin Camino Real, 14 Calle 0–20, Zona 10* ☎ *2333–3000*) sells exquisitely crafted silver trays, vases, jewelry boxes, and place settings by the Italian Camusso family.

DAY TRIP FROM GUATEMALA CITY

The lovely colonial city of Antigua remains the most popular day excursion from Guatemala City for tourists and residents alike—the latter head out especially on weekends, many to attend weddings in Guatemala's most popular locale for tying the knot. (The majority of international visitors stay in Antigua and make the capital their day trip instead, if they go at all.) The Mayan ruins of Mixco Viejo lie 60 km (36 mi) north of the capital and make an easy do-it-yourself trip if you have a vehicle. Many operators also lead ascents to Volcán Pacaya south of the city. Although many people do this excursion on their own, we recommend going with an organized tour for safety reasons, both criminal and volcanic. *(See Antigua's Volcanoes box, in Chapter 3.)*

Tourist attractions around the country can be done as excursions, thanks to numerous tour operators who offer organized trips. Besides Antigua and Mixco Viejo, Lake Atitlán is also possible as a day trip. Chichicastenango appears on the tour lists on Thursday and Sunday market days. (Most Chichi trips include a stop at the lake.) Operators organize day excursions from the capital farther afield to the Mayan ruins at Copán, Honduras, or to Guatemala's own Tikal in El Petén. Flying is the only way to do Tikal in one day (although it's preferable to overnight at the ruins). The flight takes less than one hour, as compared to 10 hours overland.

MIXCO VIEJO

North of Guatemala City lie the 12th-century Mayan ruins of Mixco Viejo. The mountaintop site, thought to be largely ceremonial, was one of the last Mayan places to fall to Pedro de Alvarado and the conquistadors in 1525. Excavation began on the site's 120 structures in 1954.

Temples and palaces make up Mixco Viejo, but most notably it contains several ball courts used in the ballgame of *pitziil*, a game with many

LANGUAGE SCHOOLS IN GUATEMALA CITY

Guatemala City doesn't immediately leap to mind when contemplating Spanish instruction, but the city offers a number of fine language institutes. Reflecting the large number of business travelers who come to the capital, you'll see a higher percentage of such enrollees among the student population at schools here.

- **Academia Easy** (✉ *14 Av. 13–68, Zona 10* ☎ *2337–3970* 🌐 *www.easyfacilgt.com*).
- **Academia Europa** (✉ *15 Calle 2–64, Zona 10* ☎ *2363–5025* 🌐 *www.academia-europa.com*).
- **Berlitz** (✉ *Av. La Reforma 7–62, local #101, Zona 9* ☎ *2362–4444* 🌐 *www.berlitz-ca.net*).
- **Centro de Idiomas Oxford** (✉ *20 Calle 23–59, Zona 10* ☎ *2368–1332* 🌐 *www.olcenglish.com*).
- **Instituto Guatemalteco Americano** (✉ *Ruta 1 4–05, Zona 4* ☎ *2422–5555* 🌐 *www.iga.edu*).
- **Universidad de San Carlos** (✉ *Ciudad Universitaria, Zona 14* ☎ *2443–9500* 🌐 *www.usac.edu.gt*).

variations seen throughout pre-Columbian indigenous civilizations. (Historians today group the games under the general heading *ulama*, a Nahuatl word meaning simply "ballgame.") Objectively, it resembled a mix of soccer and volleyball, but for the Maya, pitziil transcended mere sport, providing a cosmic link between mortals and gods, between past and future.

Mixco Viejo is no Tikal or Quiriguá, but it's a favored destination for weekend visitors from the capital, who come for the splendid views of the surrounding countryside. A small museum documents the history of the site. ✉ *60 km (36 mi) north of Guatemala City* ☎ *No phone* 🎫 *Q20* ⏲ *Daily 7–4:30.*

Antigua

WORD OF MOUTH

"We were really surprised at all the ruins right in town amongst the quaint, colorfully painted houses and shops. It was amazing to see the remnants of the devastating earthquake of 1773. It was sad to see so many buildings that must have been magnificent in their days of glory, but seeing the crumbled remains really gave you a good idea of what it must have been like. We really did enjoy strolling through this lovely town."

—luv2globetrot

By Jeffrey Van Fleet

Filled with vestiges of its colonial past—cobblestone streets, enchanting squares, and deserted convents—Antigua, one of Latin America's loveliest cities, instantly transports you back hundreds of years to when the Spanish ruled this land. The city lost out on its role as colonial capital in the late 18th century, and yet with the reverence shown here to the past, you may think *Antigüeños* don't realize that era is over. No matter, La Antigua Guatemala ("the old Guatemala")—to use the city's official name—likely relishes its role as the capital of Guatemalan tourism far more.

At the height of its power, Antigua was home to 60,000 people and ruled Spanish Central America. Its enormous wealth was poured into the construction of churches, monasteries, convents, palaces, and mansions. Then came 1773: A massive earthquake damaged or destroyed some 3,000 of the city's structures, necessitating the move of the capital to what would become present-day Guatemala City. The poverty of the few who stayed behind meant over a century of stagnation and no funds to rebuild. Eventually, money did begin to flow back into the local economy, thanks to the lucrative coffee trade. Antigua's foundation of colonial architecture remained, and residents had no interest in tearing down the city's proud heritage. Power lines went underground, truck traffic was rerouted out of the city, and signage was greatly reduced. (McDonald's, Burger King, and Subway are all here, but you have to look to find them.) An active National Council for the Protection of Antigua Guatemala imposes stringent guidelines on the restoration of buildings, maintaining the colonial character of Antigua. History once dealt the city a severe blow, and yet without it, Antigua might today be—perish the thought—Guatemala City.

Antigua's mountainside community of about 35,000 people is vastly more pleasant than the capital. At a 1,530-meter (5,019-foot) altitude, its comfortable climate lives up to that oft-repeated boast that Guatemala is the land of eternal spring. Prices do tilt slightly higher here than in the rest of Guatemala, but walking and soaking up the atmosphere, Antigua's quintessential entertainment, are always free. An ever-increasing influx of visitors has brought in some of the country's finest hotels and restaurants, a collection of boutiques and galleries, and several dozen Spanish-language schools that attract students from all over the world. Yet as one member of the protection council once told us, Antigua was never created to be some vast indoor/outdoor museum. Increased tourism has been a nice side benefit, but the city's magnificent colonial architecture serves workaday purposes as hotels, restaurants, stores, homes, schools, barber shops, hardware stores, and everything in between.

TOP REASONS TO GO

Learn the native tongue: Antigua is one of the world's premier Spanish-study destinations. Just don't spend so much time hanging out with fellow English speakers that you forget to practice.

Witness a procession: Watch the faithful solemnly parade through Antigua's streets with incense and religious figures during Lent and Holy Week.

Experience the "Old" Guatemala: Antigua means "old" in the days gone by sense. An crafted an art of th of life. Join in.

Live like a noble: Every lodging here either dates from or is built to resemble one from colonial times. Play Spanish aristocrat...for a few days at least.

Play historian: The city is one of the hemisphere's great repositories of colonial architecture. For a sense of New World history, a visit to Antigua is a must.

ORIENTATION AND PLANNING

GETTING ORIENTED

Street naming in Antigua differs from that of other Guatemalan cities. *Avenidas* (avenues) run north–south, beginning with 1 Avenida in the east and increasing in number as you go west. *Calles* (streets) run east–west, beginning with 1 Calle in the north and increasing in number as you go south. Avenidas split into *norte* (north) and *sur* (south) at 5 Calle, the Palacio de Capitanes Generales side of the Parque Central. Calles split into *oriente* (east) and *poniente* (west) at 4 Avenida, the cathedral side of Parque Central. Building numbering begins at these points and continues sequentially without regard to blocks. Numbers on one side of the street increase independently of those on the opposite side, meaning that the 40s sequence might be across the street from the 20s. Take heart: the complex system does make some sense once you see it yourself.

PLANNING

WHEN TO GO

A distinct division between dry (November to April) and rainy (May to October) seasons makes winter and spring months the ideal time to be in Antigua. This is also prime time for Antigua's many religious observances, the most famous of which is Semana Santa (March or April). Holy Week brings a series of daylong vigils, processions, and reenactments of Christ's last days in Jerusalem. You'll see Roman centurions charging through the streets on horseback, boulevards carpeted with colored sawdust and flowers, and immense hand-carried floats winding their way through throngs of onlookers. **■TIP→Make reservations months in advance if you plan to be here for Semana Santa.**

A BIT OF HISTORY

Founded in 1543, the city was christened La Muy Noble y Muy Leal Ciudad de Santiago de los Caballeros de Goathemala ("The Very Noble and Very Loyal City of St. James of the Knights of Guatemala"), named for the apostle St. James, the patron saint of the conquistadors. For more than 200 years it administered a region that stretched from Mexico's Yucatán peninsula south to Costa Rica. Along with Lima and Mexico City, Antigua was one of the grandest cities of the Americas.

By the late 18th century the city had been decimated by earthquakes several times. Because it was a major political, religious, and intellectual center—it had 32 churches, 18 convents and monasteries, 7 colleges, 5 hospitals, and a university—it was always rebuilt. Powerful tremors struck again in late 1773, reducing much of the city's painstakingly restored elegance to rubble. The government reluctantly relocated to a supposedly safer site 45 km (28 mi) east, where Guatemala City now stands. The now-former capital became La Antigua Guatemala ("the old Guatemala"), still its official name.

Ironically, it is because Antigua was abandoned that it retains so much of its colonial character. Only the poorest inhabitants stayed put after the capital was moved, and being of limited means, they could only repair the old structures, not tear them down or build new ones. In the 1960s laws took effect that limited commercial development and required what development did occur to keep within the city's colonial character. The National Council for the Protection of Antigua Guatemala was formed in 1972 to restore the ruins, maintain the monuments, and rid the city of such modern intrusions as billboards and neon signs. Restoration projects, both private and public, have transformed Antigua into Guatemala's most popular tourist destination.

Antigua's tourist population increases dramatically on weekends, as Guatemala City residents head out from the capital to their favorite destination. The city fits nicely into the beginning or end of your trip. Its proximity to Guatemala City's La Aurora International Airport makes it a good first or last place to visit.

GETTING HERE AND AROUND

With limited parking and a majority of hotels, restaurants, and sights in a small area, Antigua is a quintessential walking city. If you have a vehicle, leave it in your hotel's parking lot (most upscale lodgings offer parking). We recommend taking a taxi after 9 PM. Have your hotel or restaurant call one for you at night.

AIR TRAVEL

The nearest airport is Guatemala City's Aeropuerto Internacional La Aurora, a little less than an hour's drive away. If your hotel does not offer a transfer from the airport, there are plenty of shuttle buses that run this route.

BUS AND SHUTTLE TRAVEL

Several companies run frequent shuttle buses between Guatemala City and Antigua. Adrenalina, Atitrans, and Turansa are all reputable companies. Call ahead for reservations. Public buses leave every 15 minutes from 18 Calle and 4 Avenida in Zona 1 in Guatemala City. They depart on a similar schedule from the bus station in Antigua.

Adrenalina, Atitrans, and Turansa also offer service to the highlands, with costs ranging from Q100 for Chichicastenango and Panajachel to Q200 for Quetzaltenango. You can also catch a public bus at the terminal, which is cheaper but much less comfortable. There are one or two direct buses to Panajachel and Quetzaltenango each day, as well as five or six bound for Chichicastenango. Tickets cost about Q16.

3

Shuttle Companies Adrenalina (☎ *7832–1108* 🌐 *www.adrenalinatours.com*). **Atitrans** (☎ *7832–3371* 🌐 *www.atitrans.com*). **Turansa** (☎ *7832–2928*).

Bus Station Terminal de Buses (✉ *Alameda Santa Lucía at 4 Calle Poniente*).

CAR TRAVEL

To reach Antigua, drive west out of Guatemala City via the Calzada Roosevelt, which becomes the Pan-American Highway. Signs direct you either to ANTIGUA or ANTIGUA GUATEMALA. At San Lucas Sacatepéquez, turn right off the highway and drive south to Antigua. The last several kilometers before Antigua have a steep descent. Note the FRENE CON MOTOR warnings ("engine brake")—use your lowest gear—and the RAMPA DE EMERGENCIA signs for the three emergency off-ramps for vehicles whose brakes give out. If you're coming from the highlands, head south near Chimaltenango.

All non-resident drivers must pay a daily Q10 fee to park on any city street. The permit takes the form of a tag (*marbete*) you hang from your rear-view mirror. They are sold at police checkpoints at the main entrances to town, or by officers roaming the streets wearing blue vests that say CONTROL DE ESTACIONAMIENTO (parking control). Tags change color each day; you must buy a new one. The rules are strictly enforced. We recommend avoiding the need for all this and leaving your vehicle in your hotel's lot. (Off-street parking is exempt from the daily fee.) Better yet, don't bring a vehicle into Antigua at all.

If you want to rent a car to explore Antigua, it's a good idea to do so in Guatemala City's Aeropuerto Internacional La Aurora. In Antigua, reputable local agencies are Ahorrent and Tabarini.

Local Car-Rental Agencies Ahorrent (☎ *2332–7744* 🌐 *www.ahorrent.com*). **Tabarini** (☎ *7832–8107* 🌐 *www.tabarini.com*).

TAXI TRAVEL

A taxi between Guatemala City and Antigua should cost about Q200. Many run between Aeropuerto Internacional La Aurora and Antigua. Taxis Antigua has a good reputation. Your hotel or restaurant can call a taxi for you after dark. Most Antigua taxis are three-wheeled Bajaj vehicles made in India. People here refer to them as "tuk-tuks."

Contact Taxis Antigua (☎ *7832–0479*).

HEALTH AND SAFETY

For all emergencies, call the municipal police department. Officers patrol most blocks downtown in male–female pairs. Look for them in white pullover shirts, dark trousers, and baseball caps. Contact the tourist police for free, regularly scheduled escorts to the Cerro de la Cruz, information, and minor matters. The office is near the market, and is open 24 hours.

Emergency Services **Police** (✉ *5 Calle Poniente, west end of Palacio del Capitánes* ☎ *7832–0251*). **Tourist police** (✉ *Across from market* ☎ *7968–5303*).

Hospitals **Hospital Privado Hermano Pedro** (✉ *Av. De la Recolección 4* ☎ *7832–1190*).

Pharmacy **Farmacia Fénix** (✉ *5 Calle Poniente 11C* ☎ *7832–0503*).

VISITOR INFORMATION AND TOURS

INGUAT, the national tourism office, has an office in the interior courtyard of the Casa Jaulón building on 4 Calle Oriente, one-half block east of Parque Central. It is open weekdays 8–5 and 9–1 and 2–5 on weekends. The office is slated to move to an as-yet-undetermined location sometime in 2010 or 2011. Directions will be posted at the current location when the move takes place.

A number of travel agencies can book you on trips around the region and throughout the country. Among the better known are Chiltepe Tours, Rainbow Travel Center, Vision Travel, and Turansa. One of the best is Antigua Tours, run by independent guide and longtime resident Elizabeth Bell. It offers all sorts of personalized trips, from walking tours of Antigua (daily except Sunday) to a tour of the traditional villages around Antigua, to excursions to Lake Atitlán, Chichicastenango, and Tikal. Guatemala Deaf Tours' name is self-explanatory: it conducts signed tours of the region for hearing-impaired visitors.

A number of *fincas* (farms) in the hills around Antigua offer tours. Finca Los Nietos and Finca Filadelfia, both coffee plantations, and Finca Valhalla, a macadamia farm, are southwest of the city.

Information **INGUAT** (✉ *4 Calle Oriente, interior of Casa Jaulón* ☎ *7832–0763*).

Tour companies **Adrenalina** (☎ *7832–1108* 🌐 *www.adrenalinatours.com*). **Antigua Tours** (☎ *7832–5821* 🌐 *www.antiguatours.net*). **Chiltepe Tours** (☎ *5709–0913*). **Guatemala Deaf Tours** (☎ *5186–1708 for text messages* 🌐 *www.guatemaladeaftours.com*). **Rainbow Travel Center** (☎ *7832–4202* 🌐 *www.rainbowtravelcenter.com*). **Turansa** (☎ *7832–4691* 🌐 *www.turansa.com*). **Vision Travel** (☎ *7832–3293* 🌐 *www.guatemalainfo.com*).

EXPLORING ANTIGUA

Few places in the Americas hold such a repository of colonial architecture. Some still serve their original purpose, whereas others have morphed into hotels, restaurants, and shops. Still others stand magnificently in ruins. If ever there were a place you could overdose on history, Antigua is it. Avoid the temptation to rush from church to convent to monastery to palace and off to another church, all in one morning. (You'll see dazed tour groups doing exactly that.) Build in some down

CLOSE UP

Something Old, Something New

Antigua's colonial magnificence disappeared in one day in 1773 following a massive earthquake. With the move of the capital to nearby Guatemala City, there was no need (and no money) to restore Antigua's treasures. Nearly two centuries of stagnation followed.

Things changed in the 1960s with a newfound interest among residents in preserving and restoring that former glory. The Guatemalan government had declared Antigua a national monument in 1944, a title largely ceremonial, but the Protective Law for the City of La Antigua Guatemala, enacted by the national government in 1969, would change the fortunes of the city forever.

Key to those newfound fortunes was the formation of an active Consejo Nacional para la Protección de La Antigua Guatemala (National Council for the Protection of Antigua Guatemala; ⊕ *www.cnpag.org*), whose efforts have focused on the rescue and restoration of some 50 monuments. That work comes at a price—money is scarce in Guatemala—but the governments of Spain, Japan, and Taiwan have chipped in to fund several projects. Guatemalan corporate sponsors—including cement manufacturer Cementos Progreso, Pepsi, chicken restaurant chain Pollo Campero, and national telephone company Telgua—have made generous donations, as well.

In a more general sense, beyond specific projects, the council actively spearheaded the elimination of street advertising from businesses. Walk down any Antigua street and you'll notice that signs are conspicuously and pleasantly discreet. Next on the council's wish list—it's a long shot to be sure—is the elimination of vehicular traffic from select downtown streets. You can get a taste of this on weekends, when Avenida 5 Norte, the street passing under the Santa Catalina arch, is closed to traffic.

An influx of visitors from around the world has nevertheless been an end result, but the restoration projects have always been undertaken as a matter of civic pride and not to create a vast outdoor museum.

Current and recent council projects include:

Convento de las Capuchinas: construction of colonial-art museum.

Iglesia de Nuestra Señora de La Merced: reinforcement of arcades in cloister and restoration of *Jesús Nazareno* figure.

Iglesia de San Cristóbal El Bajo: structural reinforcement of damage from 1976 earthquake and landscaping of plaza.

Iglesia de San Juan El Obispo: restoration of church bell.

Iglesia de Santa Inés: restoration of facade, remodeling of atrium, and exterior illumination.

Palacio de los Capitanes Generales: reinforcement of roof tiles, walls, and rotted wood.

Rescate del Color Antigüeño ("rescue of Antigua color"): ongoing campaign to repaint buildings in their original colors; most activity on 1 Avenida Norte, 2 Avenida Sur, 7 Avenida Norte, and 3 Calle Oriente.

San José Catedral: restoration of figures on cathedral facade damaged in 1976 earthquake.

time and delight in the small things (ice cream, music, or shoe shines) that make this one of the hemisphere's most special places. (*See the Antigua, Antigüeño Style box.*)

Nearly everything of interest (sights, restaurants, hotels, and services) sits in a 10-by-10-block grid in the center of the city, and you could possibly narrow that down even further by focusing on the immediate orbit of the central park. Most of the sights lie east, south, and north of the park.

SAFETY AND PRECAUTIONS Antigua is one of Guatemala's safest cities, and the streets around Parque Central are patrolled by the municipal and tourist police. Farther from the square you should walk in groups or take taxis after the sun goes down. Hotels and restaurants are always happy to call a taxi for you at night. Be careful in the countryside, where there have been some robberies. If you plan to tackle one of the nearby volcanoes, hire a reputable guide and ask what safety precautions the company takes. Under no circumstances should you hike the volcanoes without the safety of an escorted group tour.

TIMING A true aficionado of Spanish colonial America could spend a week in Antigua delving into all its history and architecture. If you're like most visitors, though, you can hit the highlights, catch some yummy restaurant dining, and take in some shopping in two or three days.

TOP ATTRACTIONS

10 **Arco de Santa Catalina.** The only remnant of the once-enormous Convent of St. Catherine is this beautiful orange-yellow arch that spans 5 Avenida Norte, a street locals call Calle del Arco. The convent was founded in 1613 with only four nuns, but by 1693 its growing numbers forced it to expand across the street. The arch was built to allow the sisters to pass from one side to the other unseen. The arch today serves as the iconic symbol of the city. ✉ *5 Av. Norte and 2 Calle Poniente* ☎ *7832–0184* 🎫 *Q30.*

13 **Casa del Tejido Antigüo.** This is the place to come for background information on the rainbow of textiles you'll see when you head out to the highlands. Exhibits present the utilitarian "how it's made" facts, delve into the cultural meaning of the patterns, and show how designs differ from region to region. Prices tend to be higher in the museum gift shop than other places around the country. It's near the central market, several blocks from the city center; call if you need transportation. ✉ *1 Calle Poniente 51* ☎ *7832–3169* 🎫 *Q5; under 12, free* ⏲ *Weekdays 9–5:30, weekends 9–5.*

4 **Catedral de Santiago Apóstol y San José Catedral.** Upon your first peek inside, you may wonder why the cathedral of Central America's preeminent colonial city seems so small. That's because what you see is one of only two remaining chapels in what was once the city's main house of worship. The lovely white cathedral (Santiago Apóstol) was completed in 1680 but destroyed in an earthquake less than 100 years later. Out back are the stark but magnificent ruins of the original cathedral—well worth a look for the nominal admission price. (Enter around the side on 5 Calle Oriente to visit the ruins.) Although restoration is underway, there are no plans to reopen the old cathedral as a house of worship. Today's smaller church (San José) is technically not a cathedral, but

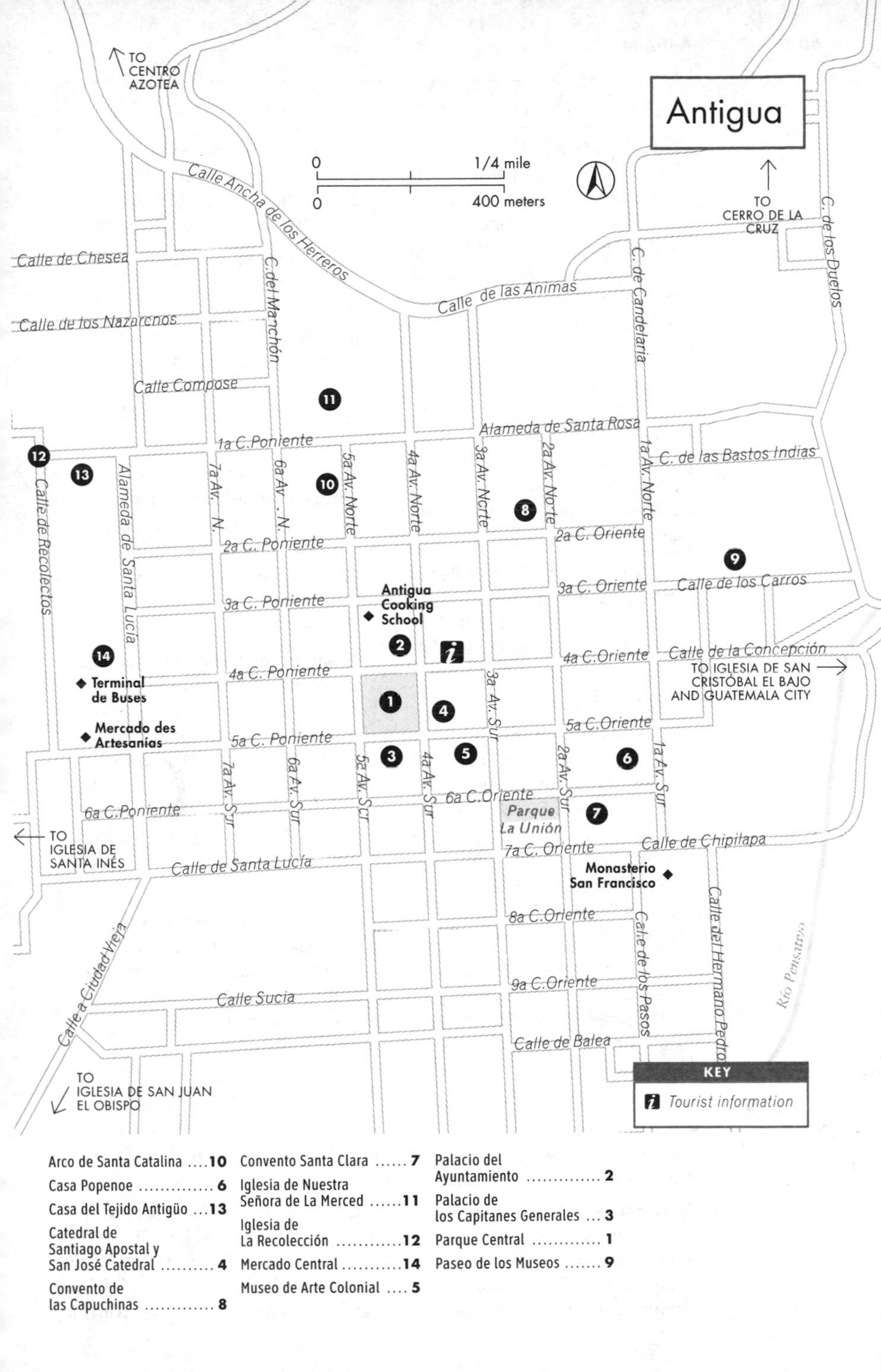
Antigua
TO CENTRO AZOTEA
TO CERRO DE LA CRUZ
0 1/4 mile
0 400 meters
Calle Ancha de los Herreros
Calle de Chesea
Calle de los Nazarenos
C. del Marchón
Calle de las Animas
C. de Candelaria
C. de los Duelos
Calle Compose
Alameda de Santa Rosa
1a C. Poniente
C. de las Bastos Indias
Calle de Recolectos
Alameda de Santa Lucía
7a Av. N.
6a Av. N.
5a Av. Norte
4a Av. Norte
3a Av. Norte
2a Av. Norte
1a Av. Norte
2a C. Poniente
2a C. Oriente
3a C. Poniente
3a C. Oriente
Calle de los Carros
Antigua Cooking School
4a C. Poniente
4a C. Oriente
Calle de la Concepción
TO IGLESIA DE SAN CRISTÓBAL EL BAJO AND GUATEMALA CITY
Terminal de Buses
Mercado des Artesanías
3a Av. Sur
5a C. Poniente
5a C. Oriente
7a Av. Sur
6a Av. Sur
5a Av. Sur
4a Av. Sur
2a Av. Sur
1a Av. Sur
6a C. Poniente
6a C. Oriente
Parque La Unión
TO IGLESIA DE SANTA INÉS
Calle de Santa Lucía
7a C. Oriente
Calle de Chipilapa
Monasterio San Francisco
Calle a Ciudad Vieja
8a C. Oriente
Calle de los Pasos
Calle del Hermano Pedro
Río Pensativo
Calle Sucia
9a C. Oriente
Calle de Balea
TO IGLESIA DE SAN JUAN EL OBISPO
KEY
Tourist information
Arco de Santa Catalina ... 10
Casa Popenoe ... 6
Casa del Tejido Antigüo ... 13
Catedral de Santiago Apostal y San José Catedral ... 4
Convento de las Capuchinas ... 8
Convento Santa Clara ... 7
Iglesia de Nuestra Señora de La Merced ... 11
Iglesia de La Recolección ... 12
Mercado Central ... 14
Museo de Arte Colonial ... 5
Palacio del Ayuntamiento ... 2
Palacio de los Capitanes Generales ... 3
Parque Central ... 1
Paseo de los Museos ... 9

ANTIGUA, ANTIGÜENO STYLE

The city packs a plethora of monuments into a compact area, but we recommend savoring it leisurely, the way locals do. (Don't take our suggestions below as a list of items you have to check off.) Remember that most sights close promptly at 5 PM, and that some ruins are closed on Sunday and Monday.

1. **Attend mass.** History and religion interlock in Antigua like nowhere else. The city's numerous churches hold mass several times a day, all week long. Even if you aren't Catholic, this is Antigua at its most devout, and well worth a look.

2. **Pay homage to Brother Pedro.** Pedro de San José Betancur, Guatemala's very own saint, is said to intercede on behalf of the faithful who pray at his tomb in the San Francisco Monastery.

3. **Take a horse-drawn carriage ride.** It's a wonderful way to see the city by day. Wagons congregate on the central park. Expect to pay Q200 per hour. Drivers are happy to give running commentary, but speak little English. If you want a tour in your own language, bring along your own guide.

4. **Jockey for the perfect photo position.** The Santa Catalina arch is the symbol of the city; and standing in front of it is the *de rigueur* photo. Your best chance of getting a clear shot is on weekends, when 5 Avenida Norte, the street running under the arch, is closed to traffic.

5. **Listen to the marimbas.** Music from the buzzing, xylophone-like marimba wafts from restaurants and hotel gardens, or out on the street as small ensembles spontaneously set up shop. Don't forget to leave a coin in their collection bowls for the entertainment.

6. **Scope out a bench in the Parque Central.** Antigua's tree-shaded central park is *the* people-watching venue in the city. You may have to circle benches like a vulture on Sunday when everybody else has the same idea.

7. **Get a shoe shine.** Locals pay Q5 to have their shoes polished to a brilliant shine. You'll likely be asked double that, but don't quibble over price with the kids who approach you in the central park. (They speak little English, but they do know the words "Shoe shine?") It's still a bargain, and your shoes will look like new again.

■ **TIP→ On the topic of shoes, flimsy soles mean you'll feel every cobblestone press through to the bottoms of your feet. Wear something sturdy and comfortable.**

instead a parish church, part of the Archdiocese of Guatemala City. It holds an honorary *catedral* designation in deference to Antigua's one-time role as capital on Central America. ✉ *4 Av. Sur, east side of Parque Central* ☎ *7832–0909* 🎫 *Ruins Q3* ⏲ *Daily 9–5.*

8 **Convento de las Capuchinas.** Antigua's largest convent was built by Capuchin nuns, whose number had swelled because they, unlike other sisterhoods, did not require young women to pay dowries to undertake the religious life. They constructed the mammoth structure in 1736, just a decade after the first of their order arrived from Madrid. The convent

3

was abandoned after the earthquake of 1773, even though damage to the structure was relatively light. In the 1940s the convent was restored and opened to the public. The ruins, which are quite well preserved, include several lovely courtyards and gardens, the former bathing halls, and a round tower lined with the nuns' cells—two of which illustrate cloistered life with rather eerie mannequins. Climb to the roof for a memorable view of the surrounding landscape. The building now houses the offices of the Consejo Nacional para la Protección de La Antigua Guatemala, the national council charged with preservation and restoration of the city. At this writing, a museum is under construction in the convent's interior, slated to open in late 2010. It will house colonial artifacts collected by the council. ✉ *2 Av. Norte at 2 Calle Oriente* ☎ *7872–4646* 🎫 *Q30* ⏲ *Daily 9–5.*

COOKING CLASSES

At the **Antigua Cooking School** (✉ *5 Av. Norte 25B* ☎ *5944–8568* 🌐 *www.antiguacookingschool.com*), each four-hour class includes English instruction for preparing three local dishes, plus tortillas and black beans (the requisite accompaniments to any Guatemalan meal). You'll get your hands dirty and help in the preparation and, of course, in the sampling after class. Lessons are Tuesday at 1 PM, and Monday, Wednesday, Thursday, and Friday at 10 AM. The per-person fee is Q500. Reserve a spot at least two days in advance. Instruction is for people 15 and older.

11 **Iglesia de Nuestra Señora de La Merced.** The Church of Our Lady of Mercy is one of Antigua's most eye-catching attractions, known for its fanciful yellow stucco facade that incorporates Mayan deities. The attached monastery, which has an immense stone fountain in the central courtyard, has excellent views of nearby volcanoes. The church was built in 1548, only to be destroyed by an earthquake in 1717. It was finally rebuilt in 1765, six years before a second massive earthquake forced the city to be abandoned. Architect Juan Luis de Dios Estrada wisely designed the church to be earthquake resistant. The squat shape, thick walls, and small, high windows are responsible for La Merced's surviving the 1773 quake with barely a crack. The church did suffer significant damage in the 1976 earthquake, but a massive restoration project reinforced the stone floor. ✉ *1 Calle Poniente and 6 Av. Norte* ☎ *7832–0559* 🎫 *Q5* ⏲ *Daily 8:30–6.*

1 **Parque Central.** Surrounded by old colonial buildings, this tree-lined square is the center of Antigua, and one of Latin America's most pleasant central parks. Residents and travelers alike pass quiet afternoons on shady benches listening to the trickling Fuente de las Sirenas ("fountain of the sirens"), conversing with neighbors, and getting their shoes shined under the jacaranda trees. Flowering *esquisúchil* (borage) trees accent the park; locals refer to them as *árboles de Hermano Pedro,* the tree of Pedro de San José Betancur, Guatemala's own saint. Legend holds that the flowers have curative powers for all manner of ailments. The park is a Wi-Fi hot spot, but we question the wisdom of taking out your laptop in such a public place. ✉ *Bounded by 4 and 5 calles and 4 and 5 Avs.*

WORTH NOTING

6 **Casa Popenoe.** A short loop through this beautifully restored colonial mansion takes you through courtyards and several rooms containing decorative objects, including original oil paintings, fine ceramic dishes, and other artifacts that have been in the house since its original construction in 1636. An English-speaking guide is usually available. Since this is a private home, hours are limited. ⊠ *1 Av. Sur 2* ☎ *7832–1767* 🎫 *Q10, under 10 free* 🕒 *Mon.–Sat. 2–4.*

7 **Convento Santa Clara.** Shortly after it was founded in 1699, the Convent of St. Clare grew to be a rather elaborate complex housing nearly 50 nuns. When it was destroyed by an earthquake in 1717, the sisters quickly rebuilt it. It was struck by violent tremors again in 1773, and the site was finally abandoned. The remaining arches and courtyards make a pleasant place to roam. Keep an eye out for hidden passages and underground rooms. Across the street is Parque La Unión, where, interestingly, you'll see several public washbasins where women do laundry. ⊠ *2 Av. Sur at 6 Calle Oriente* ☎ *7873–4646* 🎫 *Q30* 🕒 *Daily 9–5.*

12 **Iglesia de La Recolección.** Despite opposition from the city council, which felt the town already had plenty of monasteries, La Recolección was inaugurated in 1717, the same year it was destroyed by an earthquake. Like many others, it was quickly rebuilt but shaken to the ground again in 1773. A stone arch still graces the church stairway, but the ceiling did not fare so well—it lies in huge jumbled blocks within the nave's crumbling walls. The 1976 earthquake inflicted further damage. The monastery is in better shape though, with spacious courtyards lined with low arches. Enter by a small path to the left of the church. ⊠ *1 Calle Poniente at Calle de Recolectos* ☎ *7832–0743* 🎫 *Q30* 🕒 *Daily 9–5.*

14 **Mercado Central.** The smell of fresh fruits and vegetables will lead you to this unassuming market, the place where local residents come to shop for all manner of day-to-day goods. Women in colorful skirts sell huge piles of produce culled from their own gardens. Their husbands are nearby, chatting with friends or watching a soccer match. ⊠ *Between Alameda de Santa Lucía and Calle de Recolectos.*

5 **Museo de Arte Colonial.** After a year-long restoration and refurbishing, Antigua's Museum of Colonial Art gleams once again. On the former site of the University of San Carlos, the complex, its cloisters left largely intact through the shakier centuries, holds a collection of mostly 17th-century religious paintings and statues commissioned by the Castilians. There's also a display of photographs of Semana Santa celebrations. ⊠ *Calle de La Universidad and 4 Av. Sur* ☎ *7832–0429* 🎫 *Q25* 🕒 *Tues.–Fri. 9–4, weekends 9–noon and 2–4.*

NEED A BREAK?

Wander over to Cookies, Etc. (⊠ *4 Calle Oriente and 3 Av. Norte*), a 7-table café and pastry shop serving 15 kinds of homemade cookies filled with nuts, chocolate, coconut, oatmeal, and spices.

2 **Palacio del Ayuntamiento.** As in colonial times, the City Hall continues to serve as the seat of government. Today it also houses two museums, the **Museo de Santiago** (Museum of St. James) and **Museo del Libro Antiguo** (Museum of Antique Books). The former, which is housed in

CLOSE UP

A Bell-Ringing Saint

Guatemala points with pride and reverence to its very own saint, Pedro de San José Betancur (1626–67), a native of the Canary Islands who came to Central America at age 31. Hermano Pedro (Brother Pedrof), as he was known, became a familiar sight on the streets of Antigua, ringing a bell and collecting alms for the poor and homeless long before the Salvation Army came up with the idea. He wasn't actually a priest—try as he might, he couldn't master the studies necessary for ordination—but Rome conferred the title of a new religious order, the Bethlehemites, on Pedro and his associates in recognition of their charity. His good works led many to dub him the "St. Francis of the Americas."

Pedro is often credited with originating the custom of the *posada*, the pre-Christmas procession seen throughout Latin America, in which townspeople reenact Mary and Joseph's search for a room at the inn.

Pope John Paul II canonized Pedro in 2002, and his tomb at the **Monasterio San Francisco** is an important local landmark. Many miracles are ascribed to Hermano Pedro; according to tradition, a prayer and a gentle tap on his casket will send you help. His remains have since been moved to a more finely rendered receptacle to the left of the main altar. The remainder of the ruins, dating from 1579, house a small museum dedicated to Pedro's legacy. You can see his simple clothes and the knotted ropes he used for flagellation. The upper floor is worth a visit for the incredible views of the surrounding hinterland and volcanoes. Enter the ruins through a small path near the rear corner of the church.

✉ *7 Calle Oriente and 1 Av. Sur* ☎ *No phone* 🎫 *Ruins and museum Q3, church free* ⏲ *Church, daily 6:30–6:30; ruins and museum, daily 9–4:30.*

what was once the city jail, displays colonial art and artifacts; Central America's first printing press, dating from the late 17th century, is displayed in the latter, along with a collection of ancient manuscripts. Given the delicate nature of the collections in both museums, photography is forbidden. ✉ *4 Calle Poniente, north side of Parque Central* ☎ *7832–5511* 🎫 *Q10* ⏲ *Tues.–Fri. 9–4, weekends 9–noon and 2–4.*

3 **Palacio de los Capitanes Generales.** A long restoration project (primarily reinforcement of the walls) is currently underway at the Palace of the Captains General, easily recognized by its stately archways, and once the hub of Spanish colonial power in the region. It now houses police and governmental agencies. ✉ *5 Calle Poniente, south side of Parque Central*

9 **Paseo de los Museos.** The Casa Santo Domingo hotel complex contains several small museums that feature colonial and contemporary art, pharmacology, and archaeology from the pre-Columbian, colonial, and contemporary eras. There are also workshops where you can watch wax and ceramics being crafted. All are open to the public. ✉ *3 Calle Oriente 28* ☎ *7820–1220* 🌐 *www.casasantodomingo.com.gt* 🎫 *Q30* ⏲ *Daily 9–6.*

3

OUTSIDE TOWN **Centro Azotea.** Three modest museums make up this cultural center in the village of Jocotenango just outside Antigua. *K'ojom* means "music" in various Mayan languages, and **Casa K'ojom** highlights the musical traditions of Guatemala's vastly diverse indigenous population. An interesting 15-minute documentary film is a good introduction for the newcomer touring the collection of musical instruments and other artifacts. A gift shop sells locally made crafts, simple instruments, and recordings of Guatemalan music. While you're here, learn about harvesting and roasting coffee beans at the **Museo del Café,** on the adjacent coffee plantation, which has a working mill dating from 1883. The **Rincón de Sacatepéquez** contains dioramas exhibiting the dress of indigenous peoples in this part of Guatemala. The center also offers horseback riding around the farm on Tuesday and Thursday by advance arrangement. The fee is Q50. The museum is in the village of Jocotenango, 2 km (1 mi) from Antigua. Minivan shuttles (Q5, roundtrip) leave hourly from the south side of the Parque Central. Taxis from Antigua run Q20 to 25. ✉ *Calle del Cementerio Final, Jocotenango* ☎ *7831–1120* 🌐 *www.centroazotea.com* 🎫 *Q30* ⏲ *Weekdays 8:30–4, Sat. 8:30–2.*

Cerro de la Cruz. If the Santa Catalina arch is Antigua's iconic symbol, the view from this hillside perch north of the city, with its cross in the foreground, city rooftops and Volcán Agua in the background, is its best-known postcard vista. In person, the view is even better, but ⚠ **under no circumstances should you make the walk up the hill on your own.** Tales of robbery along the way are legion. Antigua's Tourist Police offer a free, armed, guided escort for walkers up the hill every day at 10 AM and 3 PM. Walks depart from the police offices near the market. Plan on a 45-minute walk one way, and bring a bottle of water. ✉ *1½ km (1 mi) north of Antigua on 1 Av. Norte* ☎ *Tourist police: 7832–0535* 🎫 *Free* ⏲ *Daily walks at 10 AM and 3 PM.*

WHERE TO EAT

Like Guatemala City, but on a smaller scale, Antigua assembles a mix of regional and international cuisines into its restaurant scene. Few other cities pack such a variety into a 10-block-by-10-block area. A good rule of thumb: more expensive restaurants line the streets east of the city's Parque Central. Less pricey options line those west of the park.

WHAT IT COSTS IN GUATEMALAN QUETZALES

	¢	$	$$	$$$	$$$$
RESTAURANTS	under Q40	Q40–Q70	Q70–Q100	Q100–Q130	over Q130

Restaurant prices are per person for a main course at dinner.

¢ CAFÉ ✕ **The Bagel Barn.** The name is apt. Anything and everything in the bagel realm makes up the bulk of the menu in this place just around the corner from the Parque Central. You'll find an equally wide variety of smoothie flavors here as well as decaf coffee (a real rarity in this country). Stop by at 4:15 or 7:15 PM for the nightly screenings of late-run Hollywood

CLOSE UP

Earthquake!

Throughout history, quakes large and small have ravaged Guatemala, a nation that forms part of the seismically active "Ring of Fire" encircling the Pacific Rim. Two major earthquakes rocked Antigua in colonial times, first in 1717, then again in 1773. (Several lesser ones also hit the city.) The latter event leveled many structures—contrary to popular belief, it did not completely destroy Antigua—and precipitated the transfer of the capital to supposedly safer ground in the nearby Ermita Valley, the site of present-day Guatemala City.

Folk wisdom held that the new capital's numerous ravines and gorges would absorb seismic shocks. Unfortunately, this was not so. Earthquakes caused significant damage and loss of life in Guatemala City in 1902, 1917, and 1918, but no one could begin to imagine the tragedy that would strike in February 1976, when a 7.5-magnitude quake hit the capital, killing 23,000 people and causing $1 billion in damage to the entire region.

Seismologists attribute the activity to the east–west Motagua fault, which separates the North American and Caribbean tectonic plates and slices through the center of Guatemala. The smaller Mixco fault runs perpendicular to the Motagua and passes between Antigua and Guatemala City.

In a perverse way, the earth's rumblings and grumblings have benefited Antigua. The ash spewed from nearby volcanoes fertilizes the soil, and has turned the countryside around the city into a lush, fertile agricultural region. Experts say that Guatemala Antigua, some of the world's finest coffee, owes its high quality to that fertile volcanic soil.

films on DVD; there's a huge selection of those, too. ✉ *5 Calle Poniente 2* ☎ *7832–1224* ▭ *AE, D, DC, MC, V.*

$$$ FRENCH ✕ **Bistrot Cinq.** Guatemalan colonial meets French country bistro at one of the city's newest eateries. Trout amandine, *pied de cochon*, and *steak frites* with béarnaise sauce are some of the French-themed highlights on the menu, along with an ample wine list that features mostly Chilean and Argentine vintages. You'll find a whimsical hog theme throughout, with pewter, ceramic, and wood pigs used to decorate the room with its dark wood and worn, exposed stucco walls. Lighting is low and romantic, with small spotlights and chandeliers made from frosted-white glass bottles. Jazz and blues provide the background music. ✉ *4 Calle Oriente 7* ☎ *7832–5510* 🌐 *www.bistrotcinq.com* ▭ *AE, D, DC, MC, V* ⏲ *No lunch Mon.–Thurs.*

$$ CAFÉ ✕ **Café Barista.** This one-time bank underwent a 2009 makeover, and now hustles and bustles with all the commotion of a big-city café. Coffees, teas, chai, and hot chocolate are on tap, along with a good variety of panini and salads. It can be difficult to find a table during the day, especially on weekends. If you're here with someone else, have one person in your party grab a table the minute one opens up, while another orders at the counter. Things thin out a bit after 8 PM. ✉ *4 Calle Poniente 12* ☎ *7832–2211* 🌐 *www.cafedeguatemala.com* ▭ *AE, D, DC, MC, V.*

3

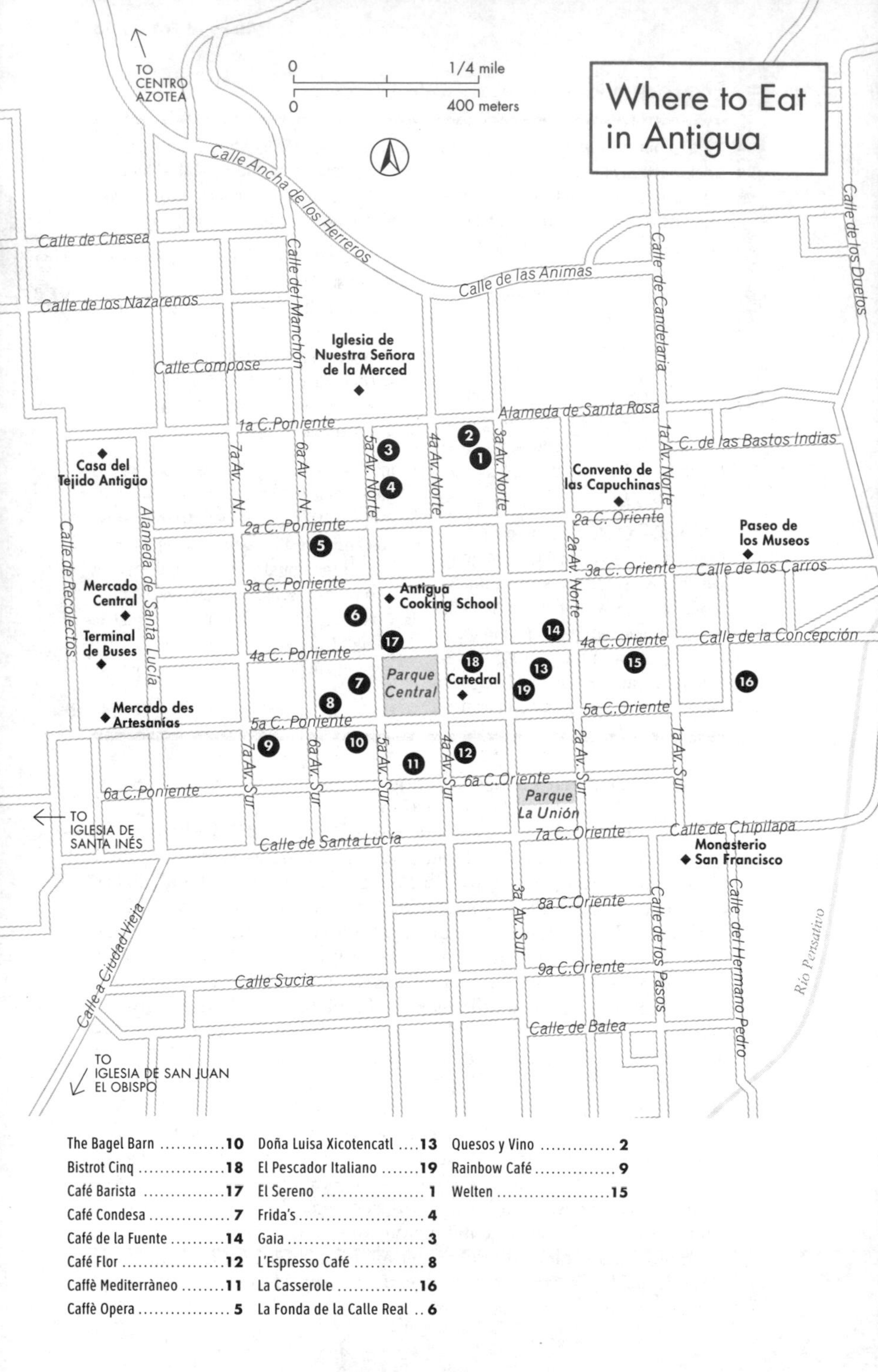
Where to Eat in Antigua
0
1/4 mile
0
400 meters
TO CENTRO AZOTEA
Calle Ancha de los Herreros
Calle de Chesea
Calle de los Nazarenos
Calle Compose
Calle del Manchón
Calle de las Animas
Calle de Candelaria
Calle de los Duelos
Iglesia de Nuestra Señora de la Merced
Alameda de Santa Rosa
1a C. Poniente
C. de las Bastos Indias
Casa del Tejido Antigüo
7a Av. N.
6a Av. N.
5a Av. Norte
4a Av. Norte
3a Av. Norte
1a Av. Norte
Convento de las Capuchinas
2a C. Oriente
2a C. Poniente
Paseo de los Museos
Calle de Recolectos
Alameda de Santa Lucía
2a Av. Norte
3a C. Oriente
Calle de los Carros
Mercado Central
3a C. Poniente
Antigua Cooking School
Terminal de Buses
4a C. Poniente
4a C. Oriente
Calle de la Concepción
Parque Central
Catedral
Mercado des Artesanías
5a C. Poniente
5a C. Oriente
7a Av. Sur
6a Av. Sur
5a Av. Sur
4a Av. Sur
2a Av. Sur
1a Av. Sur
6a C. Poniente
6a C. Oriente
Parque La Unión
TO IGLESIA DE SANTA INÉS
Calle de Santa Lucía
7a C. Oriente
Calle de Chipilapa
Monasterio San Francisco
Calle a Ciudad Vieja
3a Av. Sur
8a C. Oriente
Calle de los Pasos
Calle del Hermano Pedro
Río Pensativo
9a C. Oriente
Calle Sucia
Calle de Balea
TO IGLESIA DE SAN JUAN EL OBISPO
The Bagel Barn 10
Bistrot Cinq 18
Café Barista 17
Café Condesa 7
Café de la Fuente 14
Café Flor 12
Caffè Mediterràneo 11
Caffè Opera 5
Doña Luisa Xicotencatl 13
El Pescador Italiano 19
El Sereno 1
Frida's 4
Gaia 3
L'Espresso Café 8
La Casserole 16
La Fonda de la Calle Real .. 6
Quesos y Vino 2
Rainbow Café 9
Welten 15

¢ CAFÉ **Café Condesa.** Breakfast starts at 6:45 AM, and specials such as toast topped with strawberries, papaya, or mango, and omelets made with fresh vegetables will give you plenty of sightseeing fuel. (Breakfast is served all day if you like.) After such a big breakfast, don't count on eating much for the rest of the day. For lunch, try the quiche or the Brie plate; the homemade pies and pastries are also notable. You can eat in the café's airy dining room or grab a cappuccino and a sweet roll at Café Condesa Express next door. Either way, the location right on the Parque Central can't be beat. ✉ *5 Av. Norte, west side of Parque Central* ☎ *7832–0038* ▭ *AE, D, DC, MC, V.*

¢ CAFÉ **Café de la Fuente.** This popular eatery takes over the courtyard of La Fuente, a classy collection of shops in a renovated colonial estate. Classical music creates a peaceful atmosphere. The international breakfasts, served until 11 AM, are excellent, and the Mexican-style eggs *ranchero* are not to be missed. There are several vegetarian options. La Fuente also makes one of the best desserts in town—a decadently rich chocolate brownie topped with coffee ice cream and chocolate syrup. The Q20 daily lunch special is a good bet. ✉ *4 Calle Oriente 14, at 2 Av. Norte* ☎ *7832–4520* ▭ *AE, D, DC, MC, V.*

$ THAI **Café Flor.** The friendly proprietors serve a menu that includes Thai curries, Chinese noodles, and Indian vegetable dishes. Be careful—some of the dishes, especially the curries, are quite spicy. Asian food aficionados will find the food not at all like the real thing, but Antigua is, after all, about as far from the source as you can get. On weekends the restaurant is open until midnight. There's live piano music nightly. The restaurant is popular with the many students studying Spanish in Antigua. ✉ *4 Av. Sur 1* ☎ *7832–5274* ▭ *AE, D, DC, MC, V.*

$ ITALIAN ★ **Café Mediterráneo.** For Italian food in the city, this tiny restaurant can't be beat. Northern Italian specialties, delicious antipasti, and delicate homemade pastas are among the favorites. Wash it all down with a selection from the affordable wine list. The atmosphere and decor are low-key. Instead of giving out individual menus, waiters lug the menu board to your table to explain what's available. Hours can be a bit capricious; evening dining may begin at 6 or 7 PM, or whenever the restaurant opens, but the service is first-rate. Reservations are recommended. ✉ *6 Calle Poniente 6A* ☎ *7832–7180* ▭ *AE, D, DC, MC, V* ⏲ *Closed Tues.*

$$ ITALIAN **Café Opera.** You half expect Enrico Caruso to emerge from the shadows when you walk into this trattoria a couple of blocks from La Merced church. It's generally a bit cluttered and crowded, and it fills up quickly. You'll find overflow seating on the back patio, but sitting out there isn't nearly as atmospheric. For an Italian restaurant, the selection of pastas is small, but the café's signature plates are its various tenderloin dishes—we like the beef prepared with Gorgonzola cheese, nuts, and rosemary. Accompany your meal with a wide selection of panini and a gelato for dessert. ✉ *6 Av. Norte 17* ☎ *7832–0727* 🌐 *www.cafe-opera.com* ▭ *AE, D, DC, MC, V.*

¢ CAFE ★ **Doña Luisa Xicotencatl.** This restaurant—named after the mistress of Spanish conquistador Pedro de Alvarado—is something of a local institution; tables are scattered throughout a dozen rooms, but it's still not easy to get a seat. Early-morning specialties include fruit salad, pancakes, and very fresh bread (the bakery is right downstairs). Sandwiches and other light fare make for ample lunch and dinner options. The service can be slow, but the eclectic decor makes the wait pleasant. The bulletin board downstairs is an excellent source of information for travelers. ✉ *4 Calle Oriente 12 at 3 Av. Norte* ☎ *7832–2578* ▭ *AE, D, DC, MC, V.*

$$ ITALIAN ✕ **El Pescador Italiano.** This fun place behind the cathedral has quickly gained cachet with Antigua's foreign population, expat and tourist alike, who have made it one of the city's liveliest restaurants. You'll find a good selection of pizzas and pastas on the menu, along with less traditional dishes such as pan-fried salmon and grilled beef fillet with sautéed spinach. Italian music—it might be Sinatra, it might be Pavarotti—wafts through the three dark-wood rooms (one upstairs), along with convivial chatter from the spirited bar, making it an especially good place to eat if you're here with a group. ✉ *3 Av. Norte 1B* ☎ *7832–7328* ▭ *AE, D, DC, MC, V* ⏲ *Closed Wed.*

$$$$ LATIN AMERICAN ✕ **El Sereno.** One of Antigua's original elegant restaurants is in a 16th-century house near La Merced church a few blocks north of the Parque Central. The place is huge and does a brisk event business, but offers plenty of secluded tables for intimate, candlelight dinners. Lunch is served in the downstairs courtyard; dinner expands to the upstairs terrace with stupendous mountain and city views and gorgeous end-of-day sunsets. The menu changes every few months, but always consists of a mix of Guatemalan and international fare—perhaps a three-meat *pepián,* or a tarragon leg of lamb with a mango shrimp salad on the side. ✉ *4 Av. Norte 16* ☎ *7832–0501* 🌐 *www.elsereno.com.gt* ▭ *AE, D, DC, MC, V.*

$ MEXICAN ✕ **Frida's.** Looking for a place where you and your friends can knock back a few margaritas? At this festive cantina, a branch of a larger establishment in Guatemala City, the whole group can fill up on Mexican fare, including taquitos, enchiladas, and burros, the diminutive siblings of the American-style burrito. Things really get going when the mariachi band shows up. You can stop by Wednesday night for a free intro salsa lesson. Fans of Frida Kahlo and Diego Rivera will find a great selection of prints from these masters—the menu even bears Frida's signature portrait. ✉ *5 Av. Norte 29* ☎ *7832–1296* 🌐 *www.lasfridas.com* ▭ *AE, D, DC, MC, V.*

$$ MIDDLE EASTERN ✕ **Gaia.** Lebanon comes to Guatemala at this old favorite on busy Avenida 5 Norte. The fare is standard Middle Eastern: lamb or beef kebabs, couscous, tabouli, or *patush,* a Syrian salad. You have several seating choices here: you can sit on throw pillows at low tables in the front room or at one of the private booths out in the back courtyard. If you're so inclined, partake of an after-dinner flavored hookah in the front lounge. Come early to get a seat for the Thursday-evening belly-dancing show. It gets underway at 8:30 PM. ✉ *5 Av. Norte 35A* ☎ *7832–3670* ▭ *AE, D, DC, MC, V.*

$$$ FRENCH ✕ **La Casserole.** Classic French dishes incorporate subtle Guatemalan influences at La Casserole. Although the menu changes every week or so, there are a few constants—seafood bouillabaisse cooked in a slightly

CLOSE UP

Coffee? Macadamia Nuts?

The northern Las Verapaces is the part of the country most associated with coffee, historically and culturally (⇨ *See The Magic Bean box, in Chapter 5*), but Guatemala Antigua gets rave reviews as the country's best-known java ambassador to the world. Several *fincas* (plantations) lie near Antigua and offer tours. If your interests run more to macadamia nuts, one farm raises those, too. Make reservations at least one day in advance for any of the following options.

Finca Filadelfia (✉ *150 meters north of Iglesia de San Felipe de Jesús* ☎ *7831–1191* 🌐 *www.rdaltoncoffee.com*) offers coffee tours weekdays 10 AM and 2 PM, Sat. 10 AM. **Finca Los Nietos** (✉ *6 km [4 mi] from Antigua, San Lorenzo El Cubo* ☎ *7831–5438* 🌐 *www.fincalosnietos.com*) offers coffee tours weekdays 8:30 to 11 AM and 1:30 to 3 PM. Call in advance to arrange a tour in English. **Finca Valhalla** (✉ *7 km [4 mi] southwest of Antigua, ½ km [¼ mi] before San Miguel Dueñas* ☎ *7831–5799* 🌐 *www.exvalhalla.net*) has daily macadamia tours from 8 AM to 4:30 PM.

3

spicy tomato sauce and steak tenderloin with a salsa made from spicy *chiltepin* peppers are two standouts. The peach-and-gold walls of this restored colonial mansion are lined with rotating painting and photography exhibits. ✉ *Callejón de la Concepción 7* ☎ *7832–0219* 💳 *AE, D, DC, MC, V* ⊙ *Closed Mon. No dinner Sun.*

$ LATIN AMERICAN ✕ **La Fonda de la Calle Real.** An old Antigua favorite, this place has three locations serving the same Guatemalan and Mexican fare. The original restaurant, on 5 Avenida Norte near Parque Central, has pleasant views from the second floor. It tends to be a bit cramped, however. Newer spaces, across the street and around the corner on 3 Calle, are in colonial homes spacious enough to offer indoor and outdoor seating. Musicians stroll about on weekends. The menu includes *queso fundido* and the restaurant's famous *caldo real* (a hearty chicken soup). ✉ *3 Calle Poniente 7, at 5 Av. Norte* ☎ *7832–0507* 🌐 *www.lafondadelacallereal.com* ✉ *5 Av. Norte 5, at 4 Calle Poniente* 💳 *AE, D, DC, MC, V.*

¢ CAFE ✕ **L'Espresso Café.** Cabana-shirted waiters scurry around, serving up a delicious selection of light café fare, the foundation of which is various pastas and crepes. Accompany your meal with gourmet coffees or smoothies topped off with vanilla, mango, chocolate, or pistachio gelato. The decor is minimalist chic; there are brick walls and an exposed high-beam ceiling, and you're seated at a glass table on a stool covered with a burlap coffee sack. The view out the front door is the stark Compañía de Jesús, the colonial ruins of the Jesuit church, bathed in a soft, mysterious light each evening. ✉ *6 Av. Norte 4* ☎ *7832–0539* 💳 *AE, D, DC, MC, V.*

$ ITALIAN ✕ **Quesos y Vino.** One of Antigua's best small Italian restaurants serves up homemade pastas and pizzas from a wood-burning oven, and a variety of home-baked breads. Choose from an impressive selection of cheeses and wines sold by the bottle or glass. This is mostly a place to stop for a light bite, rather than a full meal. Most of the seating is outside, but you'll find plenty of covering to duck under on a rainy day. ✉ *1 Calle Poniente 1, near Arco de Santa Catalina* ☎ *7832–7785* ▭ *AE, D, DC, MC, V* ⊗ *Closed Tues.*

¢ CAFÉ ✕ **Rainbow Café.** We could picture Che Guevara plotting the revolution here at this café, a hangout of young expats in the heart of Antigua's language-school district. You'll find some meat on the menu, but vegetarian fare dominates. (We love the falafel and hummus dishes.) The place is immensely popular. Don't be afraid to ask if you can squeeze in if you see no available tables indoors or in the courtyard. There are lectures, in English, on some topic of political interest each Tuesday evening, and live music many other nights. ✉ *7 Av. Sur 8* ☎ *7832–4205* 🌐 *www.rainbowcafeantigua.com* ▭ *No credit cards.*

$$$$ ITALIAN Fodor's Choice ★ ✕ **Welten.** You'll feel like a guest in a private home when you arrive at this restaurant. Take your pick of tables, which are on a patio with cascading orchid plants, by a small pool, festooned with candles and flower petals, in the rear garden, or in one of the elegantly appointed dining rooms. The menu includes homemade pasta dishes, such as *anolini* served with a creamy pepper-and-cognac sauce, as well as fish and meat dishes served with a variety of sauces. All the vegetables are organic, and the bread is baked right on the premises. ✉ *4 Calle Oriente 21* ☎ *7832–0630* 🌐 *www.weltenrestaurant.com* ▭ *AE, D, DC, MC, V* ⊗ *Closed Tues.*

WHERE TO STAY

The old parlor game of guessing what lies behind Antigua's walls—buildings directly front sidewalks with nary a hint of what lies inside the gate—could apply to the city's hotels, too. (One of our favorite Antigua lodgings has a wooden gate in serious need of a coat of paint, but unimagined elegance lurks behind.) Inside all, you'll find rooms arranged around a central garden in the old colonial style. Most newly constructed hotels are also arranged thus. As with restaurants, more expensive hotels line the streets east of Parque Central. ■ **TIP→ Few lodgings offer air-conditioning, but you'll rarely miss it here.** Most hotels raise rates Friday and Saturday night, since Antigua is a popular weekend tourist destination for Guatemalans. Expect lodging rates to go up by 50% during Christmas and Holy Week. Most places also impose minimum lengths of stay during those weeks.

	WHAT IT COSTS IN GUATEMALAN QUETZALES				
	¢	$	$$	$$$	$$$$
HOTELS	under Q160	Q160–Q360	Q360–Q560	Q560–Q760	over Q760

Hotel prices are for two people in a standard double room, including tax and service.

$$$–$$$$ **Casa Azul.** Not many hotels have guest books filled with recommendations for specific rooms, but the ones on the second floor are so good that people want to be sure to share them with others. The upstairs rooms are more expensive, but they're larger and brighter and have views of the volcanoes; all rooms are painted in washes of red and,

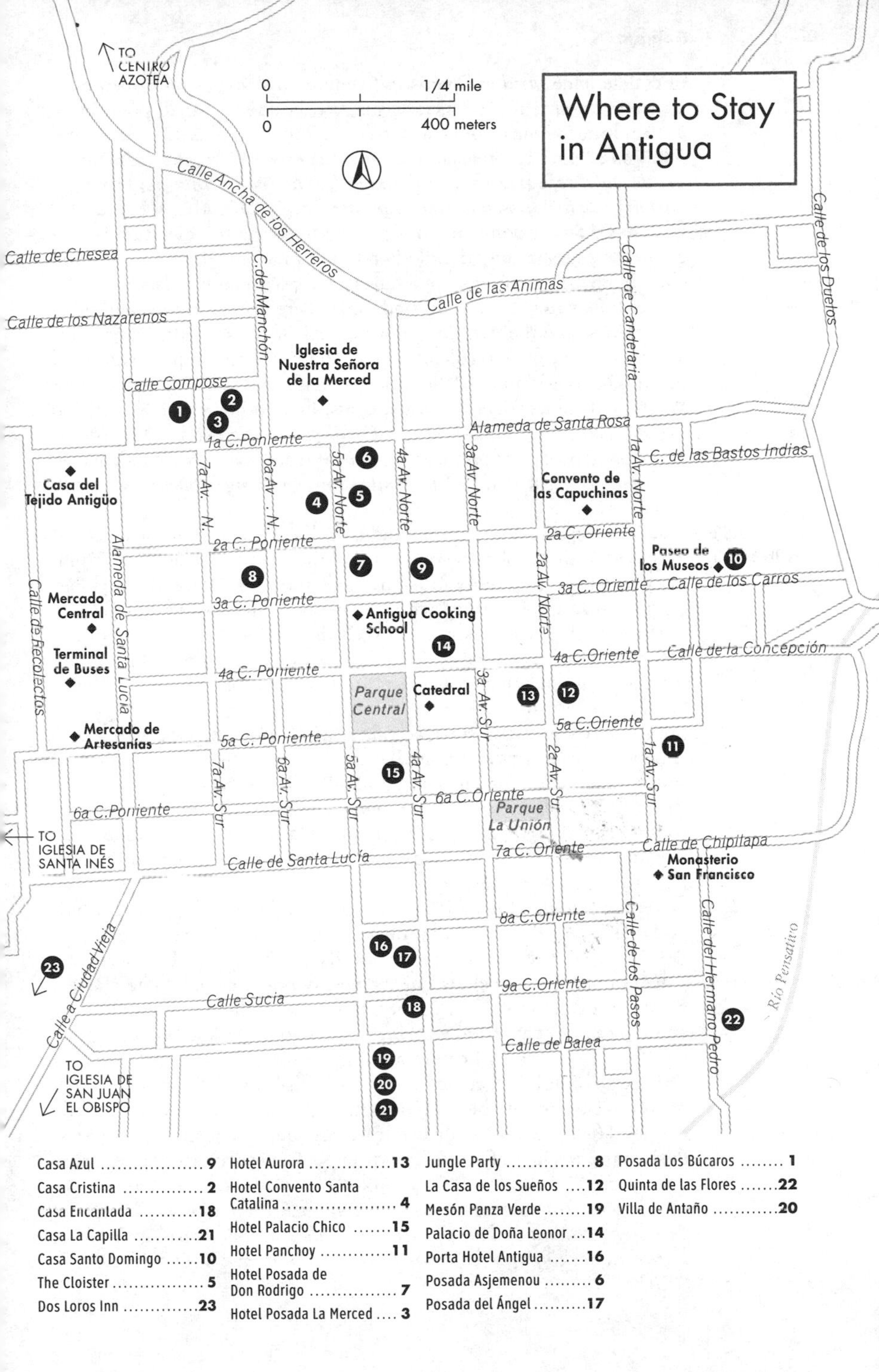
Where to Stay in Antigua
0 1/4 mile
0 400 meters
TO CENTRO AZOTEA
TO IGLESIA DE SANTA INÉS
TO IGLESIA DE SAN JUAN EL OBISPO
Calle Ancha de los Herreros
Calle de Chesea
Calle de los Nazarenos
C. del Manchón
Calle de las Animas
Calle de Candelaria
Calle de los Duelos
Iglesia de Nuestra Señora de la Merced
Calle Compose
Alameda de Santa Rosa
1a C. Poniente
C. de las Bastos Indias
Casa del Tejido Antigüo
7a Av. N.
6a Av. N.
5a Av. Norte
4a Av. Norte
3a Av. Norte
Convento de las Capuchinas
1a Av. Norte
2a C. Poniente
2a C. Oriente
Paseo de los Museos
Calle de los Carros
3a C. Oriente
2a Av. Norte
3a C. Poniente
Mercado Central
Alameda de Santa Lucía
Calle de Recolectos
Terminal de Buses
Antigua Cooking School
4a C. Poniente
4a C. Oriente
Calle de la Concepción
Parque Central
Catedral
3a Av. Sur
5a C. Oriente
Mercado de Artesanías
5a C. Poniente
7a Av. Sur
6a Av. Sur
5a Av. Sur
4a Av. Sur
2a Av. Sur
1a Av. Sur
6a C. Oriente
6a C. Poniente
Parque La Unión
Calle de Santa Lucía
7a C. Oriente
Calle de Chipilapa
Monasterio San Francisco
8a C. Oriente
Calle de los Pasos
Calle del Hermano Pedro
Río Pensativo
Calle a Ciudad Vieja
9a C. Oriente
Calle Sucia
Calle de Balea
Casa Azul 9
Casa Cristina 2
Casa Encantada 18
Casa La Capilla 21
Casa Santo Domingo 10
The Cloister 5
Dos Loros Inn 23
Hotel Aurora 13
Hotel Convento Santa Catalina 4
Hotel Palacio Chico 15
Hotel Panchoy 11
Hotel Posada de Don Rodrigo 7
Hotel Posada La Merced 3
Jungle Party 8
La Casa de los Sueños 12
Mesón Panza Verde 19
Palacio de Doña Leonor 14
Porta Hotel Antigua 16
Posada Asjemenou 6
Posada del Ángel 17
Posada Los Búcaros 1
Quinta de las Flores 22
Villa de Antaño 20

of course, blue (*azul* in Spanish). Communal sitting rooms open onto a pleasant courtyard; breakfast is served beside the small pool. **Pros:** central location, nice courtyard. **Cons:** dimly lit rooms. ✉ *4 Av. Norte 5* ☎ *7832–0961* 🌐 *www.casazul.guate.com* *14 rooms* *In-room: no a/c, safe, refrigerator. In-hotel: pool, no elevator, Internet terminal, parking (no fee), no-smoking rooms* *AE, D, DC, MC, V* *CP.*

$ **Casa Cristina.** Rooms acquire progressively more amenities as you go up the stairs in this friendly hotel on a small street near La Merced church. First-floor rooms are a tad spartan, with only beds and tables. By the time you get to the second floor, there are televisions and nicer furnishings, and the two third-floor rooms offer art on the stone walls and nice views of the Volcán Agua. The hot-water supply is limited here (5:30–10 AM and 6–10 PM, but all in all, this is a nice budget find. **Pros:** good value, friendly owner. **Cons:** limited hot water. ✉ *Callejón Camposeco 3A* ☎ *7832–0623* 🌐 *www.casa-cristina.com* *10 rooms* *In-room: no a/c, no phone, refrigerator (some), no TV (some), Wi-Fi. In-hotel: no elevator, Internet terminal, no-smoking rooms* *No credit cards* *CP.*

$$$$ Fodor's Choice ★ **Casa Encantada.** A twice-remodeled, half-century-old house designed in typical Antigua colonial style is one of the city's best small inns. You'll most remember the comfy four-post beds about this place: All are king- or queen-size and furnished with Italian linens and down pillows. Only one second-floor room contains two beds, making it the only option if you're not here as a couple. Getting to Room 7 requires a bit of sure footing: large stepping stones lead to its door over a small pond with floating votive candles. An amply sized rooftop suite has its own private hot tub. **Pros:** attentive staff, terrific service, romantic vibe. **Cons:** several blocks from city center, small rooms, more oriented to couples than singles. ✉ *9 Calle Poniente 1* ☎ *7832–7903, 866/837–8900 in North America* 🌐 *www.casaencantada-antigua.com* *9 rooms, 1 suite* *In-room: no a/c, no phone, safe, refrigerator, Wi-Fi. In-hotel: restaurant, bar, laundry service, no elevator, Internet terminal, parking (fee)* *AE, D, DC, MC, V* *BP.*

$$$$ **Casa La Capilla.** *Capilla* means "chapel" in Spanish and, indeed, you'll find one here in the middle of this lodging's requisite fine colonial garden, the site of occasional weddings and church services. But sacred the place is not. The chapel also hosts weekly poker games, yoga classes, or corporate dinners. Next to the chapel is a log-fire sauna, perfect for warming away aches from walking up and down Antigua's cobblestone streets. There's a fun vibe here amid the colonial elegance. Rooms are arranged around the garden, and have high-beam ceilings, lime-wash walls, and plenty of colonial-era art, and guests get personal mobile phones. Huge breakfasts consist of freshly squeezed juices and pastries. **Pros:** many activities, friendly atmosphere. **Cons:** occasional noise from courtyard. ✉ *5 Av. Sur 21* ☎ *7832–0182* 🌐 *www.casalacapilla.com* *6 rooms, 1 apartment* *In-room: no a/c, no phone, DVD, Wi-Fi. In-hotel: restaurant, bar, pool, no elevator, laundry service, Internet terminal, parking (no fee), no-smoking rooms* *AE, D, DC, MC, V* *BP.*

$$$$ **Casa Santo Domingo.** This elegant hotel was built around the ruins of the ancient Monasterio Santo Domingo, taking advantage of its long passageways and snug little courtyards. Dark carved-wood furniture, yellow stucco walls, and iron sconces preserve the monastic atmosphere, but luxurious amenities abound. Unfortunately, the food at the restaurant is considerably less inspiring than the rest of the package. **■ TIP→ The hotel serves as a tourist attraction in its own right—do visit its museums and grounds—but for guests here, the outside visitors occasionally translate into a lack of intimacy.** **Pros:** historic setting, lovely gardens. **Cons:** several blocks from city center, many outside visitors to hotel. ✉ *3 Calle Oriente 28* ☎ *7832–1220* 🌐 *www.casasantodomingo.com.gt* *128 rooms* *In-room: no a/c, safe, refrigerator. In-hotel: restaurant, room service, bar, pool, spa, concierge, laundry service, airport shuttle, parking (no fee), no-smoking rooms* ▭ *AE, D, DC, MC, V* 🍴 *EP.*

$$$$ **The Cloister.** This aptly named hotel began life as a cloistered convent near the Santa Catalina arch that dates from about 1700. We imagine that its original inhabitants never experienced such luxury. Rooms are arranged around a beautiful garden that has a bubbling fountain and wrought-iron patio furniture for enjoying a lovely Antigua afternoon. Each room comes with fireplace, library, terra-cotta floors, oak furnishings, and exposed high-beam ceilings. You enter some rooms via Dutch-style half-doors. Two have a sleeping loft. Many comparable lodgings in the city charge much more, so you're looking at good value. Traveler's checks are accepted as payment. **Pros:** historic setting, lovely garden, good value. **Cons:** some street noise in front rooms. ✉ *5 Av. Norte 23* ☎ *7832–0712* 🌐 *www.thecloister.com* *7 rooms* *In-room: no a/c, no phone, no TV, Wi-Fi. In-hotel: restaurant, parking (no fee), no-smoking rooms* ▭ *No credit cards* 🍴 *BP.*

$$ Fodor's Choice ★ **Dos Loros Inn.** If you have a car, or don't mind an occasional taxi ride, this hotel on the west edge of town is a terrific find. The place is simply immaculate, with blinding white walls and bright Guatemalan bedspreads and drapes in all rooms. On the subject of the rooms, they're huge, as are the bathrooms. Each comes with one queen and one twin bed. You have access to shared kitchen facilities if you don't feel like going out to eat. **Pros:** huge rooms, attentive staff, great value. **Cons:** far from city center, no sign in front. ✉ *Calle San Luquitas 20* ☎ *5348–7867, 800/234–2705 in North America* 🌐 *www.doslorosinn.com* *4 rooms* *In-room: no a/c, no phone, Wi-Fi. In-hotel: Internet terminal, parking (no fee)* ▭ *AE, D, DC, MC, V* 🍴 *CP.*

$$ **Hotel Aurora.** This genteel inn, Antigua's oldest and still run by the same family that opened it in 1923, has an unbeatable location in the heart of the city. The dimly lighted colonial-style rooms face a beautifully tended garden. You can relax in a tiled portico strewn with plenty of comfortable rattan chairs. Rooms have wooden furniture and old-fashioned armoires. **Pros:** lovely garden. **Cons:** dimly lit rooms. ✉ *4 Calle Oriente 16* ☎ *7832–0217* 🌐 *www.hotelauroraantigua.com* *17 rooms* *In-room: no a/c, Wi-Fi. In-hotel: laundry service, Internet terminal, parking (no fee), no-smoking rooms* ▭ *AE, D, DC, MC, V* 🍴 *BP.*

$$$ **Hotel Convento Santa Catalina.** This hotel was built amid the ruins of an old convent of which only the often-photographed Arco de Santa Catalina

remains. The spacious rooms, all a bit dimly lighted, are tastefully decorated with handicrafts and handwoven bedspreads. Most face a verdant courtyard, where a smattering of tables and chairs encourages you to settle in with a good book. The modern rooms in the annex are brighter and have kitchenettes. **Pros:** central location, historic setting. **Cons:** dimly lit rooms, occasional street noise in front rooms. ✉ *5 Av. Norte 28* ☎ *7832–3080* 🌐 *www.conventohotel.com* *16 rooms* *In-room: no a/c (some), kitchen (some), safe. In-hotel: restaurant, laundry service, public Wi-Fi, Internet terminal, parking (fee), no-smoking rooms* *AE, D, DC, MC, V* *BP.*

SPAAAAH

Antigua Spa Resort. Massages, facials, and a variety of other treatments are available at this spa (aka Jardines del Spa), roughly 3 km (2 mi) from Antigua in the village of San Pedro El Panorama. Free transportation to and from Antigua is provided when you book an appointment. ✉ *3 Av. 8–66, Zona 14* ☎ *7832–3960 or 2333–4620* *7832–3968.*

$$ **Hotel Palacio Chico.** The so-named "Little Palace" formed part of the original Palacio de los Capitanes Generales complex, and so sits at a prime location just around the corner from the Parque Central. Rooms vary in size, so look at a few before you decide. All contain terra-cotta floors and colonial-style furnishings. The hotel serves a full breakfast on Sunday, but goes continental the other six days of the week. **Pros:** central location. **Cons:** small rooms. ✉ *4 Av. Sur 4* ☎ *7832–7137* *7 rooms* *In-room: no a/c, no phone. In-hotel: laundry service, parking (no fee), no-smoking rooms* *V* *BP, CP.*

$$ **Hotel Panchoy.** The Panchoy sits behind a gate in an odd complex of three separate hotels. It's the bright yellow one, and the only one of the three we recommend. Carpeted rooms are simply furnished with beds, tables, tile floors, and a private patio or balcony. **Pros:** good budget value. **Cons:** spartan furnishings, several blocks from city center. ✉ *1 Av. Norte 5A* ☎ *7832–1020* 🌐 *www.hotelpanchoy.com* *21 rooms* *In-room: no a/c, no phone, safe, refrigerator, Wi-Fi. In-hotel: no elevator, laundry facilities, parking (no fee), no-smoking rooms* *AE, D, DC, MC, V* *BP.*

$$$$ **Hotel Posada de Don Rodrigo.** A night in this restored colonial mansion is a journey back in time. All rooms have soaring ceilings and gorgeous tile floors, and are set around two large courtyards and several smaller gardens. A tile fountain trickles in the dining room, which is on a garden terrace; to the side, a woman prepares tortillas on a piping-hot grill. Indulge in a serving of Antigua flan, a dessert layered with figs and sweet potatoes. Light sleepers, beware: the lively marimba band can sometimes play long into the night. The lodging is part of a two-hotel chain, with another branch in Panajachel; a stay at both places in a single trip gets you a 10% discount off the rates. **Pros:** historic setting, lively evening entertainment. **Cons:** some noise from garden. ✉ *5 Av. Norte 17* ☎ *7832–0387* 🌐 *www.posadadedonrodrigo.com* *41 rooms* *In-room: no a/c, Wi-Fi. In-hotel: restaurant, bar, laundry service, Internet terminal, parking (no fee), no-smoking rooms* *AE, D, DC, MC, V* *CP.*

$–$$ **Hotel Posada La Merced.** A pair of conjoined colonial homes—leading to a pair of two colonial garden courtyards—makes up this friendly lodging a block from its namesake church. Rooms are simply furnished with wood furniture and colonial-style art. A few of the larger rooms have their own kitchen and are large enough to accommodate a family. Elsewhere in the hotel, you'll have access to shared kitchen facilities. The hotel offers discounts for long-term stays, as well as baggage storage if you plan to travel elsewhere around Guatemala. **Pros:** friendly owners, family friendly. **Cons:** small rooms. ✉ *7 Av. Norte 43 A* ☎ *7832–3197* 🌐 *www.merced-landivar.com* *23 rooms, 21 with bath, 1 apartment* *In-room: no a/c, no phone, kitchen (some), no TV, Wi-Fi. In-hotel: no elevator, laundry service, no-smoking rooms* *V* *EP.*

¢ **Jungle Party.** The cleanest, cheapest, and friendliest budget hostel in Antigua, Jungle Party is the place for backpackers and bargain hunters who enjoy its little touches like nightly happy hours and Saturday-evening barbecues. The simple, shared rooms with bunk beds are spotless, and the showers have plenty of hot water. The pleasant courtyard restaurant has funky orange and yellow mushroom-shaped chairs and swinging hammocks for lounging. Salvadoran owner Mónica is happy to help with travel arrangements. They also serve some of the best smoothies Antigua has to offer. **Pros:** friendly atmosphere, many activities. **Cons:** occasional noise from courtyard. ✉ *6 Av. Norte 20* ☎ *7832–0463* 🌐 *www.junglepartyhostal.com* *35 beds in 6 dormitories* *In-room: no a/c, no phone, no TV. In-hotel: restaurant, bar, laundry service, public Wi-Fi, Internet terminal, airport shuttle, no-smoking rooms* *AE, DC, MC, V* *BP.*

$$$$ **La Casa de Los Sueños.** This stunning colonial mansion, converted into an elegant bed-and-breakfast, may truly be the house of your dreams, as the name implies. A lovely patio is covered on all sides by hanging plants. A joyful antique hobbyhorse and a square grand piano reside in the sitting room. Tastefully decorated with antiques, the rooms are painted the washed-out hues that typify Antigua. **Pros:** historic setting. **Cons:** several blocks from city center. ✉ *1 Av. Norte 1* ☎ *7832–9897* 🌐 *www.lacasadelossuenos.com* *8 rooms* *In-room: no a/c. In-hotel: restaurant, pool, parking (no fee), no-smoking rooms* *AE, D, DC, MC, V* *BP.*

$$$–$$$$ **Fodor's Choice** ★ **Mesón Panza Verde.** A beautiful courtyard with a fountain and colorful gardens welcomes you to this retreat. The elegant rooms downstairs open onto small gardens, whereas the romantic suites upstairs have four-poster beds piled high with down comforters and terraces where hammocks swing in the breeze. The rooftop patio is wonderful in late afternoon or early morning, and the restaurant is one of the best in town. The meat dishes are particularly good, such as the *lomito* (pork) bourguignonne with escargots. ■ **TIP→ The hotel and restaurant maintain an active evening cultural-events program open to the public.** **Pros:** good views, great restaurant, active cultural program. **Cons:** small rooms downstairs. ✉ *5 Av. Sur 19* ☎ *7832–1745* 🌐 *www.panzaverde.com* *3 rooms, 9 suites* *In-room: no a/c, safe, Wi-Fi. In-hotel: restaurant, bar, laundry service, parking (no fee), Internet terminal, no elevator, no kids under 15, no-smoking rooms* *AE, D, DC, MC, V* *CP.*

$$$$ **Palacio Doña Leonor.** The one-time palace of Leonor de Alvarado de Cueva, the daughter of Spanish conquistador Pedro de Alvarado, today serves as a lovely hotel and gives Casa Santo Domingo a run for its money in Antigua's top-notch sweepstakes. Just half a block off the Parque Central, it's the most centrally located hotel in the city. The large, flat-screen televisions in each room are a nice touch—one almost never seen in Guatemala—but look a bit out of place among the colonial elegance of canopied beds, period art, fireplaces, stone-tile floors, and garden. Descending the beautiful grand staircase will make you look just as grand as we assume Doña Leonor did. **Pros:** central location, historic setting, many amenities. **Cons:** some street noise in front rooms. ✉ *4 Calle Oriente 8* ☎ *7832–2281* 🌐 *www.palaciodeleonor.com* *12 rooms* *In-room: no a/c, safe, Wi-Fi. In-hotel: restaurant, bar, pool, spa, no elevator, laundry service, Internet terminal, parking (no fee), no-smoking rooms* 💳 *AE, D, DC, MC, V* *BP.*

$$$$ **Porta Hotel Antigua.** As a tasteful combination of colonial elegance and modern comfort, Porta Hotel Antigua, part of a small Guatemalan chain, is one of the city's most popular lodgings. The sparkling pool, set amid lush gardens, is a treat after a day exploring the dusty city streets. Standard rooms have plenty of space for two, whereas one- and two-level suites can house a whole family quite comfortably. The oldest part of the hotel is a colonial-style building with a restaurant, bar, and a beautiful sitting room. A newer annex building is connected by tunnel under the street, and, although constructed in the old colonial style, contains more modern rooms. Although this is now the city's largest lodging, nothing is overpowering about the place. Weddings are sometimes held in a sunny esplanade overlooking the ruins of Iglesia de San José. **Pros:** chain amenities with individualized decor. **Cons:** several blocks from city center. ✉ *8 Calle Poniente 1* ☎ *7832–2801, 888/790–5264 in North America* 🌐 *www.portahotels.com* *107 rooms, 8 suites* *In-room: no a/c, safe, Wi-Fi. In-hotel: 2 restaurants, room service, bar, pools, laundry service, Internet terminal, parking (no fee), no-smoking rooms* 💳 *AE, D, DC, MC, V* *BP.*

¢–$ **Posada Asjemenou.** There are plenty of charming hotels in colonial mansions, but you won't pay through the nose at this one. The rooms are clean and comfortable, although a bit dark—door panels serve as their only windows—and the staff is friendly and eager. The small café serves breakfast and snacks. Lots of good bagels are on the menu. If you're hankering for more substantial fare, head to the nearby pizzeria run by the same family. You get a 10% discount on the hotel rate if you pay in cash. **Pros:** good value, lively café. **Cons:** no outside windows, occasional noise from courtyard. ✉ *5 Av. Norte 31* ☎ *7832–2670* *asjemenouantigua@hotmail.com* *12 rooms, 9 with bath, 3 with shared bath* *In-room: no a/c, no phone, no TV. In-hotel: restaurant, bar, no-smoking rooms* 💳 *V* *CP.*

$$$$ **Posada del Ángel.** You'd never know from the unassuming, borderline-rickety wooden gate that you're at the threshold of Antigua's most beautiful lodging. It's all part of the ruse at this truly angelic inn. Large corner fireplaces warm the rooms, each of which is decorated with well-chosen antiques. Those on the main floor look out onto a plant-filled

Fodor's Choice ★

CLOSE UP

Holy Week in Antigua

Much of Latin America flees to the beach or the mountains for seven days of vacation during Holy Week (*Semana Santa*), the week preceding Easter, and the most sacred week in the Christian calendar. But if you want to observe this part of the world at its most devout, the Western Hemisphere has no place during Holy Week like Antigua.

The entire week in Antigua, but especially Good Friday, seems one long procession with enormous floats (*andas*), some weighing three tons, depicting Christ, the Virgin Mary, and various saints, emerging from palls of incense. Cadres of robe-clad men known as *cucuruchos* bear the constructions on their shoulders, swaying side to side in time to the brass-band funeral dirges. Floats depicting female saints weigh less and are always borne by women.

Integral to the Good Friday processions are the elaborate *alfombras*, street carpets made of flowers, colored sawdust, and, sometimes, fruit, arranged in intricate designs that take hours to create. "Ephemeral" doesn't begin to describe these works, but the designs will be trampled by the bearers of the Christ figure. Don't bother asking residents why they would spend so much time creating a work of art only to have it obliterated in a matter of seconds. Many will tell you that they create and assemble the carpets in gratitude for some grace bestowed upon them.

Your window for experiencing Antigua's annual pageantry isn't as small as you might think. The city does the entire Lenten season (*Cuaresma*) up big, with elaborate processions each Wednesday, Friday and Sunday during the six weeks preceding Easter. They become bigger and grander as Holy Week approaches. Nor is your window limited geographically: If you don't feel like braving the Semana Santa crowds in Antigua, most towns and cities hold some variation on religious processions, but on a smaller scale. Fine observances take place in the highlands in Quetzaltenango and Santiago Atitlán.

In thoughtfulness to residents and visitors alike, for all the processions, Lenten or Holy Week, you can pick up a leaflet (Spanish only) at various booths around Antigua listing their schedules and arrival points. Processions are measured in hours—the Good Friday doings get underway at 3 AM—and you'll appreciate knowing where to position yourself for the best view.

Longtime resident Elizabeth Bell of Antigua Tours presents a Wednesday-evening slideshow on the topic each week during the Lenten season. (*See* The Arts *in* Nightlife and the Arts.)

A couple of words of warning: The sanctity of the observances doesn't prevent the city from worshiping the almighty tourist dollar, as lodgings raise rates by 50 to 100 percent during Holy Week. (Reserve months in advance if you plan to be in town for the week. Remember also that many lodgings impose minimum stays during the week. You can't necessarily breeze in Thursday night, watch Friday's processions, and head back out that afternoon.) And pickpockets are out in force working the crowds. Attend the processions with a photocopy of your passport—keep the original locked away if you can—and minimal cash.

courtyard, and the large suite on the second floor has a private rooftop terrace. The staff has catered to presidents and prime ministers—former U.S. president Bill Clinton, who stayed in the upstairs suite, is the most famous guest on the register—but you'll receive the same fine service. **Pros:** attentive service, lovely courtyard. **Cons:** several blocks from city center. ✉ *4 Av. Sur 24A* ☎ *7832–0260, 305/677—2382 in North America* 🌐 *www.posadadelangel.com* *5 rooms, 2 suites* *In-room: no a/c, no phone. In-hotel: room service, bar, pool, concierge, airport shuttle, parking (no fee), no elevator, no-smoking rooms* 💳 *AE, D, DC, MC, V* 🍽 *BP.*

$$ **Posada Los Búcaros.** The pretty fountain that gives this hotel its name—*búcaro* refers to a water jar—set against a wall in the courtyard, is just one of the little touches that make this hotel special. The rooms have red-tile floors and wrought-iron furnishings. The owner and staff are extremely friendly. **Pros:** friendly owners, good value. **Cons:** several blocks from city center. ✉ *7 Av. Norte 94* ☎ *7832–2346* *15 rooms* *In-room: no a/c. In-hotel: parking (no fee), no-smoking rooms* 💳 *No credit cards.*

$$$–$$$$ **Quinta de las Flores.** Several blocks southeast of the city center, Quinta de las Flores has plenty of peace and quiet along with views of three volcanoes from the well-tended gardens and the open-air dining room. This 19th-century hacienda combines colonial comfort with a sense of whimsy—the decor includes modern takes on traditional crafts. All rooms have fireplaces to keep you cozy on chilly evenings. The quaint bungalows, which sleep as many as five, even have small kitchenettes. **Pros:** quiet atmosphere, lovely gardens. **Cons:** several blocks from city center. ✉ *Calle del Hermano Pedro 6* ☎ *7832–3721* 🌐 *www.quintadelasflores.com* *14 rooms, 5 bungalows* *In-room: no a/c, no phone, kitchen (some), refrigerator. In-hotel: restaurant, bar, pool, no elevator, laundry service, Internet terminal, no-smoking rooms* 💳 *AE, D, DC, MC, V* 🍽 *EP.*

$$$–$$$$ Fodor's Choice ★ **Villa de Antaño.** Your first just-inside-the-gate glance here is the parking lot. Keep your disappointment in check, however. Loveliness lurks behind this rambling, ochre-colored building's front door. The six room offerings are a mix-and-match affair, and each is decorated differently. The largest contains a fireplace, whirlpool tub, glassed-in shower and huge walk-in closet. The two smaller suites have their own patios, and the sole second-floor room comes equipped with kitchen and private dining balcony; the volcano views are stupendous. Common to all are colonial paintings, cedar beds, tables, and marble or stone-and-bronze floors, all set between elegant common areas such as the three sitting rooms (each with fireplace) and a rushing fountain in a beautiful garden. **Pros:** great views, many amenities. **Cons:** several blocks from city center. ✉ *5 Av. Sur 31* ☎ *7832–9539* 🌐 *www.villadeantano.com* *1 room, 4 suites, 1 villa* *In-room: no a/c, kitchen (some), refrigerator (some), Wi-Fi. In-hotel: restaurant, bar, laundry service, Internet terminal, parking (no fee), no-smoking rooms* 💳 *AE, D, DC, MC, V* 🍽 *BP.*

NIGHTLIFE AND THE ARTS

Nightlife, Antigua style, offers you the chance to flex your cultural knowledge, or to flex your arm hoisting a few with friends. The city is filled with watering holes. Many of the spots within a few blocks of the Parque Central are favored by people studying Spanish at one of the many language schools. Don't forget, either, that lingering over dinner is a time-honored way to pass an Antigua evening.

Your best source for upcoming events is the monthly English-language *Revue* magazine (🌐 *www.revuemag.com*). Pick up a free copy in hotels and restaurants around town, or check out its Web site for complete reproduction in PDF format.

THE ARTS

Numerous cultural events sprinkle Antigua's evening calendar, including two regularly scheduled weekly lecture series in English, both of which, unfortunately, take place on Tuesday evenings.

Antigua Tours' Elizabeth Bell presents a slide show called **Antigua: Behind the Walls** each Tuesday evening at 6 PM at the **Centro Cultural El Sitio** (✉ *5 Calle Poniente 1* ☎ *7832–5821*). She has assembled her vast collection of images during her almost four decades in Antigua. Admission is Q30, and proceeds go to buy textbooks for area elementary schools. Bell supplements her weekly offerings on Wednesday during the six weeks of Lent with a slide presentation devoted to Antigua's Semana Santa processions, also 6 PM, at the same place.

Weekly lectures in English with a political or social bent on some topic related to Guatemala get underway on the patio at the **Rainbow Café** (✉ *7 Av. Sur 8* ☎ *7832–4205* 🌐 *www.rainbowcafeantigua.com*) each Tuesday evening at 5:30 PM. Come early. Seats fill up quickly, but don't be afraid to grab a chair at a partially occupied table. Admission is Q25, with proceeds going to a charitable cause.

The city's most active cultural venue is the **Centro Cultural El Sitio** (✉ *5 Calle Poniente 1* ☎ *7832–3037* 🌐 *www.elsitiocultural.org*), which presents concerts, films, and lectures (almost always in Spanish) several nights a week.

The **Mesón Panza Verde** (✉ *5 Av. Sur 19* ☎ *7832–1745* 🌐 *www.panzaverde.com*) hotel and restaurant is known for its weekly Art Flicks and Dharma Flicks film series—most films are in English—as well as the occasional concert.

The Spanish government funds the **Centro Cultural de España** (✉ *6 Av. Norte between 3 and 4 calles poniente* ☎ *7832–1276*), as it does with similar institutions all over Latin America. Something is going on, whether a film, lecture, or concert, a couple of nights a week. All presentations are in Spanish.

NIGHTLIFE

BARS

Down a beer with proudly bohemian friends at **Café No Sé** (☒ *1 Av. Sur 11C* ☎ *5242–3574*). Stop by **Café Sky** (☒ *1 Av. Sur 15* ☎ *7832–7300*), whose rooftop terrace offers the best volcano and sunset views to accompany a drink. Unpretentious **El Muro** (☒ *3 Calle Oriente 19D* ☎ *7832–8849*) variously has classic-rock nights, darts nights, and just all-around good times and good conversation. If you're homesick for a pub, head to **Reilly's** (☒ *5 Av. Norte 31*), where pub grub and Guinness are served in a relaxed atmosphere. Its Sunday-night pub quiz is an Antigua institution. Upstairs from Frida's is **El Ático** (☒ *5 Av. Norte 29* ☎ *7832–1296*), a popular local hangout. The pool table is free as long as you're drinking. You're a long way from the Caribbean coast, but **El Pelícano Dorado** (☒ *Calzada Santa Lucía 7* ☎ *7832–7232*) presents Garífuna music Thursday through Sunday evenings.

Guatemalans and foreigners alike enjoy the contemporary elegance of **La Sala** (☒ *6 Calle Poniente 9* ☎ *7832–9524*). Tuesday is movie night, live music is on tap Thursday to Saturday nights, and Sunday is salsa night. They close their doors around midnight, but the party continues on inside until the wee hours of the morning. Feast on pub grub with a friendly expat crowd at **Micho's Pub** (☒ *4 Calle Oriente 10* ☎ *7832–5680*), either in the tiny indoor area or the back patio.

Root for your favorite team at **Monoloco** (☒ *5 Av. Sur 6* ☎ *7832–4235*), where soccer matches are always on the television. Wash down one of the giant burritos with a pint of one of the microbrews. **Sabor Cubano** (☒ *4 Calle Oriente 3A* ☎ *7832–4137*) dishes up music and food Cuban-style evenings Thursday through Sunday. **Sangre** (☒ *5 Av. Norte 33A* ☎ *5656–7618*) serves wine and *bocas* (appetizers) for your noshing pleasure each evening.

DANCE CLUBS

You can dance Wednesday through Sunday night at **La Casbah** (☒ *5 Av. Norte 30* ☎ *7832–2640* 🌐 *www.lacasbahantigua.com*). Latin rhythms make the place popular. No cover is charged on Wednesday's '80s Nights. A packed salsa club with a gin-and-tonic, 1920s speakeasy feel, **La Sin Ventura** (☒ *5 Av. Sur 8* ☎ *7832–4884*) frequently has live bands on the weekends. A 20-something crowd heads to **Torero's** (☒ *Av. Los Recolectos 6* ☎ *7832–5141*) Thursday to Saturday nights, out near the Central Market.

LIVE MUSIC

The conversation is convivial and the cocktails are inexpensive at **Riki's** (☒ *4 Av. Norte 4* ☎ *No phone*). Live music is yours seven nights a week, with jazz on Wednesday, Saturday, and Sunday. **La Cueva** (☒ *5 Av. Sur 19* ☎ *7832–2925* 🌐 *www.panzaverde.com*), in the Hotel Mezón Panza Verde, gets jazzy, bluesy, or Latin-y nightly except Sunday. **La Peña de Sol Latino** (☒ *5 Calle Poniente 15C* ☎ *7832–4468* 🌐 *www.lapenadesollatino.com*) has Andean music nightly beginning at 7:30 PM. Monday is open-mike night. Show off your talents if you're feeling adventurous.

LANGUAGE SCHOOLS

Antigua ranks second to Quetzaltenango in sheer number of Spanish schools within its city limits. Its desirability as a place to live means that tuition and living costs skew slightly higher. The city's huge international population (resident, student, and tourist) leads to an oft-stated disadvantage to studying here: it becomes distressingly easy to spend all your out-of-class time with other English speakers. Don't succumb, and you can learn as much Spanish here as you can anywhere.

Academia Colonial (✉ *7 Calle Poniente 11* ☎ *7882–4244* 🌐 *www.academiacolonial.com*).

Academia de Español Guatemala (✉ *7 Calle Oriente 15* ☎ *7832–5057* 🌐 *www.learnspanishguatemala.com*).

Academia de Español Intercontinental (✉ *7 Av. Norte 56* ☎ *7832–5147* 🌐 *www.spanishantigua.com*).

Academia de Español Probigua (✉ *6 Av. Norte 41B* ☎ *7832–2998* 🌐 *www.probigua.org*).

Academia de Español Tecún Umán (✉ *6 Calle Poinente34A 15* ☎ *7832–2792* 🌐 *www.tecunuman.centroamerica.com*).

APPE (✉ *1 Calle Oriente 15* ☎ *7832–2552* 🌐 *www.appeschool.com*).

Casa de Lenguas (✉ *6 Av. Norte 40* ☎ *7832–4846* 🌐 *www.casadelenguas.com*).

Centro América Spanish Academy (✉ *Callejón Santa Ana* ☎ *7832–5147* 🌐 *www.guacalling.com/ca*).

Centro de Aprendizaje de Español Universal (✉ *2 Av. Sur 34* ☎ *5508–5999* 🌐 *www.universalspanishschool.com*).

Centro Lingüístico Internacional (✉ *Av. del Espiritú Santo 6* ☎ *7832–1039* 🌐 *www.spanishcontact.com*).

Centro Lingüístico La Unión (✉ *1 Av. Sur 21* ☎ *7832–7337* 🌐 *www.launion.edu.gt*).

Centro Lingüístico Maya (✉ *5 Calle Poniente 20* ☎ *7832–0656* 🌐 *www.clmmaya.com*).

Cooperación Spanish School (✉ *7 Av. Norte 15B* ☎ *5812–2482* 🌐 *www.spanishschoolcooperacion.com*).

CSA (✉ *6 Av. Norte 15* ☎ *7832–3922* 🌐 *www.learncsa.com*).

Don Pedro de Alvarado Escuela de Español (✉ *1 Calle Poniente No. 39* ☎ *7832–6645* 🌐 *www.donpedrospanishschool.com*).

Dos Loros Spanish Immersion School (✉ *Calle San Luquitas 20* ☎ *5348–7867* 🌐 *www.doslorosinn.com*).

Fundación Proyecto Lingüístico Francisco Marroquín (✉ *7 Calle Poniente 31* ☎ *7832–1422* 🌐 *www.spanishschoolplfm.com*).

Ixchel Spanish School (✉ *7 Calle Poniente 15* ☎ *7832–0364* 🌐 *www.ixchelschool.com*).

Spanish Academy Antigüeña (✉ *7 Calle Oriente 15* ☎ *7832–5057* 🌐 *www.acad.conexion.com*).

Spanish Academy Sevilla (✉ *1 Av. Sur 8* ☎ *7832–5101* 🌐 *www.sevillantigua.com*).

Spanish Language Center (✉ *6 Av. Norte 16A* ☎ *7832–6608* 🌐 *www.bestspanishlesson.com*).

Zamora Academia (✉ *9 Calle Poniente 7* ☎ *7832–7670* 🌐 *www.learnspanish-guatemala.com*).

3

OUTDOOR ACTIVITIES

BIKING

The rolling hills that surround Antigua make for great mountain biking. Local agencies rent bikes as well as equipment like helmets and water bottles. **Mayan Bike Tours** (✉ *1 Av. Sur 15* ☎ *7832–3383* 🌐 *www.guatemalaventures.com*) offers trips ranging from easy rides in a morning or afternoon to more challenging treks taking in the highlands and lasting several days. **Old Town Outfitters** (✉ *5 Av. Sur 12* ☎ *7832–4171* 🌐 *www.adventureguatemala.com*) caters to a backpacker crowd, but its trips are suitable for people of all ages. It also offers volcano hikes and rock-climbing excursions.

HIKING

Antigua's best volcano expeditions are offered by **Eco-Tours Chejos** (✉ *3 Calle Poniente 24* ☎ *7832–2657*), whose friendly owner has climbed Volcán Pacaya more than 1,800 times. The prices are higher than most, but there are usually fewer people in each group. **Sin Fronteras** (✉ *5 Av. Norte 15A* ☎ *7832–1017* 🌐 *www.sinfront.com*) will take you on a one-day trip to Pacayá or a two-day trip to Fuego or Acatenango. **Voyageur** (✉ *4 Calle Oriente 14* ☎ *7832–4237*) is a reputable outfitter with excursions to Pacaya. **Adrenalina** (✉ *5 Av. Norte 31* ☎ *7832–1108* 🌐 *www.adrenalinatours.com*) also leads daily guided hikes to all four volcanoes.

ZIP-LINE TOURS

The so-called "canopy tour," which zips you via a series of cables and secure harness from platform to platform in the forest canopy, is taking hold in Guatemala. The folks at **Antigua Canopy Tours** (✉ *500 m. north of church, San Felipe de Jesús* ☎ *4010–6592*) give you the choice of their **Forest Express** tour, six zip lines and a rappel to wind things up, or the **Canyon Express**, two cables at an astounding 1,700 feet length each and 500 feet above the ground. Each excursion is $50, or $75 for both. If you're not feeling so adventurous, a hike through the **Forest Trail** ($15) keeps both your feet on the ground. Tours begin at 9 and 11 AM and 2 PM, and include free round-trip transportation from in front of Antigua's cathedral.

SHOPPING

Stroll down any street and you'll find boutiques selling everything from finely embroidered blouses to beautiful ceramics.The single largest concentration of shops—more than 400—can be found in the **Mercado de Artesanías** (✉ *4 Calle Poniente and Alameda de Santa Lucía*). The complex has its own parking lot, too.

BOOKS

Thanks to its sizable expatriate population, Antigua has Guatemala's best selection of English-language reading material. Facing Parque Central, **La Casa del Conde** (✉ *5 Av. Norte 4* ☎ *7832–3322*) has a good selection of books. Along with new and used books, **Hamlin & White** (✉ *4 Calle Oriente 12A* ☎ *7832–7075*) sells newspapers and magazines. Hamlin & White's sister store, **Tiempo Libre** (✉ *5 Av. Norte 25B* ☎ *7832–1816*), stocks an equally good selection of books. **Librería del**

CLOSE UP

Antigua's Volcanoes

Four volcanoes make up this region's sector of a seismic spine that runs the width of Guatemala from the Mexican to Salvadoran borders, forming a ridge between the highlands and the Pacific lowlands. Three of these masses are directly visible from Antigua. Two of the volcanoes make for popular ascents if you are in reasonable shape; the others require considerable climbing experience. Don't wear sandals to climb any of these monoliths; the volcanic rock can be razor sharp.

The volcanoes' popularity and proximity to the metropolitan area have translated into safety issues, criminal in addition to volcanic. The worst of the problems took place over a decade ago, and since then, security has been beefed up, and crime on the volcanoes' slopes is at its lowest in years. The risk is still there, however; and you should make the ascent only as part of an organized excursion.

Volcán Agua: Agua is the nearly perfectly conical mass that looms 10 km (6 mi) directly south of Antigua and forms its postcard backdrop. The 3,760-meter (12,335-foot) mountain was named "water" by Spanish colonists who saw the volcano spew rivers of water and rock over their original capital at nearby Ciudad Vieja in 1541. That is the last time Agua erupted, although vulcanologists say that the volcano will always pose some risk to Antigua. Agua offers the easiest ascent of the four regional volcanoes, but its lack of activity means you go for the views and little else. Excursions depart from the nearby village of Santa María de Jesús.

Volcán Acatenango and **Volcán Fuego:** It's impossible not to discuss these two volcanoes together, joined at the hip as they are by a high ridge. Area residents refer to the massif, 19 km (11½ mi) southwest of Antigua, as the *camellón* ("the big camel"). Acatenango itself is two summits, the 3,976-meter (13,044-foot) Pico Mayor and the 3,880-meter (12,729-foot) Yepocapa. Acatenango blew its top several times in the 1920s, and again in 1972, but has been dormant for more than three decades. However, sulfur gases fizz up through its fumaroles. The same is not true for the continuously active 3,763-meter (12,345-foot) Fuego, whose name means "fire" in Spanish. The name is apt, low-level though its activity may normally be, although the volcano did erupt most recently in 2007. Climbing Fuego and Acatenango is for experts only.

Volcán Pacaya: The area's most popular volcano ascent is to Pacaya, not visible from Antigua itself and most associated with Guatemala City. The 2,252-meter (7,388-foot) peak sits 25 km (15½ mi) southeast of Antigua, and the same distance south of the capital's La Aurora International Airport. Pacaya's popularity stems from its activity. It has logged 23 major eruptions since the 16th century—the last in 2005—and near constant displays of smoke and lava since 1965. Eruptions in 1998 and 2000 blanketed much of the region with ash and closed the airport for several days each. Excursions to Pacaya leave from either Antigua or Guatemala City. Most depart in the early afternoon to get you to the summit in time for the early-evening spectacle. The vapors smell terrible, so bring a handkerchief to cover your nose. You'll also want a sweater as the sun begins to set.

Pensativo (✉ *5 Av. Norte 29* ☎ *7832–0729*) has a huge selection of used books. **Un Poco de Todo** (✉ *5 Av. Norte 10* ☎ *7832–4676*) is a good fall-back for a decent selection of English titles.

CLOTHING AND TEXTILES

The **Central American Art Gallery** (✉ *1 Av. Norte 10* ☎ *7832–0618*) offers a contemporary-patterned twist on the standard Mayan textile fare. **Colibrí** (✉ *4 Calle Oriente 3B* ☎ *7832–6404*) sells traditional back-strap-loom textiles prepared by a local women's cooperative. **El Telar** (✉ *5 Av. Sur 7* ☎ *7832–3179*) has a good selection of high-quality handwoven tablecloths, wall hangings, and rugs. **Katún** (✉ *5 Calle Poniente 2* ☎ *7832–6601*) crafts a nice selection of cotton T-shirts with exclusive designs that make a nice change from the ubiquitous Gallo beer wear. **Nativo's** (✉ *5 Av. Norte 25B* ☎ *7832–6556*) carries a great selection of shawls, sashes, and blouses in traditional design. **Nim Po't** (✉ *5 Av. Norte 29* ☎ *7832–2681*) is a self-proclaimed *centro de textiles tradicionales*. Here you'll find a large selection of fabrics from a few dozen neighboring villages. **Pues Si Tú** (✉ *4 Calle Poniente 30* ☎ *7832–7837*) is a little shop that carries a variety of clothing in traditional patterns.

A 10-minute drive southwest of Antigua brings you to San Antonio Aguas Calientes, a dusty little village built around a hot springs. It's worth a special trip here to visit **Artesanías Unidas** (✉ *San Antonio Aguas Calientes* ☎ *7831–5950*), known for its incomparable selection of handwoven fabrics.

GALLERIES

Centro de Arte Popular Galería (✉ *3 Av. Norte 10* ☎ *7832–6634*) is a small gallery that features works by contemporary Guatemalan artists. An excellent selection of primitivist paintings is on display at **Wer Art Gallery** (✉ *4 Calle Oriente 27* ☎ *7832–7161*).

La Antigua Galería de Arte (✉ *4 Calle Oriente 15* ☎ *7832–2124* 🌐 *www.artintheamericas.com*) features works from the 19th and 20th centuries. The **Mesón Panza Verde** (✉ *5 Av. Sur 19* ☎ *7832–1745*) hotel and restaurant has a small collection of rotating exhibits.

Centro Cultural El Sitio (✉ *5 Calle Poniente 15* ☎ *7832–3037*) screens many films and hosts concerts in addition to maintaining a small gallery.

HANDICRAFTS

With a wide selection of wood figures and carvings and jewelry, **Casa de Artes** (✉ *4 Av. Sur 11* ☎ *7832–0792* 🌐 *www.casadeartes.com.gt*) is a nice place to browse. **Casa de los Gigantes** (✉ *7 Calle Oriente 18* ☎ *7832–4656*) has a good selection of quality goods, including genuine antique festival masks. **El Mercadito** is a warren of vendors' stalls (✉ *5 Av. Norte 4A* ☎ *No phone*) that offers standard souvenir fare. **La Casa de Angelina** (✉ *4 Calle Oriente 22* ☎ *7832–0203*) sells surreal items made

WORD OF MOUTH

"On the central park in Antigua there's a little row of shops. In the middle there's a bookstore. If you go in . . . and . . . wander out through the back door you will have a surprise: a darling garden/fountain area with . . . a great little café. Antigua is full of these beautiful little hidden gardens." —Suzie2

CLOSE UP

All That Glitters

Several jade shops and factories dot the streets east of Antigua's Parque Central. Although Guatemala's best-known gem is extracted in the eastern part of the country near Zacapa, jade is inexorably linked with Antigua, where the processing and polishing goes on. Much of the work is done by hand, and most shops have an affiliated factory, sometimes at another location, sometimes out in back, open to guided tours.

The umbrella term "jade" technically encompasses two types of silicate stone: nephrite and jadeite. Nephrite is mined in East Asia, giving rise to its sometimes name "Chinese jade." It's less durable and less valuable than the rarer jadeite, which is found only in Guatemala, Russia, and Myanmar. High content of sodium, aluminum, iron, cobalt, and nickel give jadeite its distinctive durability and brilliance. Though green is the color usually associated with jadeite—experts recognize 25 tones of green—black, white, and lavender also make up its spectrum.

Olmec, Mayan, and Aztec peoples in pre-Columbian Mesoamerica highly prized the stone. In fact, the Olmec established lucrative jade trade routes throughout the region. The Spanish observed the Maya using the mineral to cure various loin and kidney ailments, and so gave it the name *piedra de ijada* (stone of loin), from which the English word jade was taken. Jade became so integral a part of Mayan funeral masks that it was deemed to be a passport to the afterlife. Indeed, one of the requisite items for sale in most shops here, among the standard jewelry offerings, is an entirely jade reproduction of the famous sixth-century Tikal funeral mask unearthed in 1963.

TIPS:

Some advice regarding jade shopping: First, a lot of the "jade" floating around Antigua (and in the market in Chichicastenango) isn't jade at all. Don't buy from the vendors who sidle up to you on the street here and say, "Jade, mister?" Their wares *are* dirt cheap, but who knows what you're actually getting? It's possibly quartz. Make your purchases from a reputable shop in Antigua or Guatemala City, one that can certify that you have purchased true jadeite. Such an establishment is not going to gamble its reputation on a knock-off stone.

The pronunciation of the word in Spanish, where *J* is always rendered with an *H*-sound, is *HAH-day.*

3

of carved wood. For hand-painted pottery by local artisans, try **Topis Diseños** (✉ *5 Av. Norte 20B* ☎ *7832–2429*).

JEWELRY

Jade is mined in the eastern part of the country, but it is fashioned into jewelry almost exclusively in Antigua. Most of the jade shops offer free tours of their facilities, so you can see how the stones are selected, cut, and polished. The craftsmanship is beautiful, and many pieces are quite affordable by U.S. standards. **El Reino de Jade** (✉ *5 Av. Norte 28* ☎ *7832–1597*) offers on-site tours of its workshop. **La Casa del Jade** (✉ *4 Calle Oriente 10* ☎ *7832–3974* 🌐 *www.lacasadeljade.com*) is small but nice. Perhaps the best place to watch artisans carving the green stone is at **Jades** (✉ *4 Calle Oriente 34* ☎ *7832–3841* 🌐 *www.jademaya.com*). Former U.S. president Bill Clinton bought a necklace here for daughter Chelsea, his photo greets you as you walk in. With a small in-house workshop, **Jades Imperio Maya** (✉ *5 Calle Oriente 2* ☎ *7832–0927* ✉ *4 Calle Poniente 16B* ☎ *7832–0699* 🌐 *www.jadesimperiomaya.com*) has an extremely friendly staff.

Tired of green stones? **Joyería del Angel** (✉ *4 Calle Oriente 5A* ☎ *7832–3189* 🌐 *www.delangel.com*) has a fine selection of 100% jade-free jewelry. **Platería Típica Maya** (✉ *7 Calle Oriente 9* ☎ *7832–2883*) is a top-notch silver retailer.

SIDE TRIPS

As in Guatemala City, Antigua's numerous tour operators can take you out to much of the country on a day trip. Guatemala City lies less than one hour away, as do several volcanoes in the immediate region (⇨ *See the Antigua's Volcanoes box, above*). Panajachel and Lake Atitlán are about two hours west of town. The famous Thursday and Sunday markets in Chichicastenango are a must. The famous Maya ruins at Copán, Honduras, lie a few hours away (⇨ *See Chapter 6*), as does Guatemala's own claim to fame in the Mayan world, Tikal in El Petén. That last one, if done as a day trip, entails a flight from Guatemala City.

The Highlands

4

WORD OF MOUTH

"Pana was lovely, but more interesting with Spanish classes. Loved the used Mayan clothing sale in front of the fire station on Thursdays, great food in the market, and incredible views of the volcanoes. Did a home stay and learned a lot about the people and the culture."

—zedlanier

"We went to Chichi the day before the market so we could watch them set up. I was really glad that we did this."

—ttraveler

www.fodors.com/community

By Jeffrey Van Fleet

The region that locals call the Occidente (west) or the Altiplano (high plain) is the Guatemala that everyone comes to see. The highlands begin near the colonial capital of Antigua and run all the way to the border of Mexico, in a spectacular stretch of territory where grumbling volcanoes rise above broad alpine lakes, narrow river ravines, subtropical valleys, misty cloud forests, and pastoral plains.

The highlands are an ideal place for outdoor activities, but for most visitors they offer the country's ultimate cultural experience as well, and in that regard, the Guatemala of the postcards and tourist brochures does not disappoint. The highlands what-to-do list grows out of its position as the bridge between pre- and post-Columbian Mesoamerica. The region is home to the majority of Guatemala's indigenous people, most of whom live in small villages nestled in the valleys and perched on the hillsides. Village life consists of backbreaking work in the fields. Most survive on subsistence farming, selling what little is left over. Entire families pack fruits, vegetables, and whatever else they have onto their backs and head to market. Highland markets were once a local affair, but in the past decade or so they have begun to attract the attention of the rest of the world. Market day, held at least once a week in most communities, is as much a social gathering as anything else. Activity starts in the wee hours, when there is still a chill in the air. Bargaining and selling are carried out in hushed, amicable tones. The momentum wanes around late afternoon as the crowds depart, eager to head home before the sun sinks behind the mountains.

No region suffered the pain and tragedy of Guatemala's 36-year civil war as much as the highlands did, but everybody is anxious to move on once again. During those terrible years, Mayan dress and language branded certain groups targets for the army and paramilitary units. Some 15 years of peace have now, thankfully, taken hold, and you'll sense the pride and renaissance of indigenous culture. It's all here for you to enjoy and observe, "observe" being the operative term. Here is one of those rare, refreshing tourist destinations that have maintained a strong, vibrant, authentic culture and defended it from outside influences.

This combination of natural and cultural beauty leads us to describe the highlands with an oft-overused term: the region is Guatemala at its most fabulous. Experience the hubbub of weekly markets, the drifting incense, the exploding fireworks, the rumbling volcanoes, and a morning boat ride zipping across Lake Atitlán. We wager you'll agree.

TOP REASONS TO GO

Blending the old and the new: The highlands mix the best of Mayan and European cultures. Although Christianity has been practiced here for 500 years, it still has seemingly only a tentative hold. You'll get the feeling Western influence still hasn't quite caught on, and possibly never will.

Enjoying the outdoors: Volcanoes, forests, and one spectacular lake afford many opportunities for day hikes, riding, and mountain biking, but always best as part of an organized tour.

Celebrating festivals: There's always a celebration going on somewhere. Holy Week (March or April) and Day of the Dead (November) observances dot this region, but every town celebrates the feast day of its patron saint.

Shopping 'til you drop: Whether you find that perfect souvenir, or decide simply to take in the cacophony, the highlands are the pageantry of traditional markets. Chichicastenango is the country's most famous affair, but every town holds a market once or twice a week.

Pitching In: The majority of Guatemala's development projects are headquartered here in the highlands. You can make a difference and have a different type of travel experience.

4

ORIENTATION AND PLANNING

GETTING ORIENTED

Envision this immense region as four clusters. Panajachel and Lake Atitlán lie at the southeastern corner of the region, and are most visitors' first encounter with the highlands. Chichicastenango and the El Quiché heartland are to the north, although most visitors don't make it past Chichi to Santa Cruz del Quiché and Nebaj farther north. Quetzaltenango, the country's second largest city, and its orbit of mountain-market towns form a third bunch of places to visit. Off toward the Mexican border, Huehuetenango and Todos Santos Cuchumatán are the final, less-visited cluster and the heart of the country's Mam culture.

Lago Atitlán. A ring of indigenous communities around an easily accessible, gleaming lake watched over by three volcanoes has drawn visitors for more than four decades. One visit and you'll understand why.

Chichicastenango. The center of Mayan Quiché culture reveres the rituals of the past, but manages to worship commerce too with its world-famous, twice-weekly, you-gotta-see-it market. Less-visited towns to the north of Chichi let you delve further into Quiché tradition.

Quetzaltenango. Hip, educated Quetzaltenango might be Guatemala's second-largest city, but its proud residents concede second place to no one. The real attraction of "Xela," to use the city's beloved original name, is its orbit of communities where indigenous tradition rules.

Huehuetanango. The less-visited region just east of the Mexican border is anchored by the easy-to-reach, medium-size city that everyone calls "Huehue." Todos Santos Cuchumatán, one of the country's most fascinating indigenous communities, is worth the time if you're up to a rugged trip.

PLANNING

> **PACKING TIP**
>
> Guatemala has been dubbed the "land of eternal spring," and this region's warm afternoons and cool evenings fit the bill. But Quetzaltenango and other high-altitude towns can get downright cold at night, especially in the winter. There's no need to overpack, but a sweater or jacket is essential.

WHEN TO GO

The highlands have distinct rainy (May–October) and dry (November–April) seasons, the latter of which offers the best weather conditions for outdoor-market shopping, lake boating, and volcano hiking. Travel during the rainy season is rarely a hardship; it usually rains just for a couple of hours in the afternoon. Evenings get chilly enough for a jacket, and can get downright cold the farther west you travel. In December and January, temperatures drop to near freezing at higher elevations. That said, the highlands have no weather-based high and low seasons per se. The region does see a greater number of visitors in July and August, and during Christmas and Holy Week.

TIMING

A first-timer's visit to the highlands should include three or four days at Lake Atitlán, with a one-day visit to the market in Chichicastenango, which needs to be a Thursday or Sunday. Other destinations can add days or weeks onto that time. A visit here combines nicely with Antigua or Guatemala City (two or three hours from Lake Atitlán, respectively), or the Pacific lowlands (an hour from the lake or Quetzaltenango).

GETTING HERE AND AROUND

AIR TRAVEL

There is no scheduled air service to the highlands. The Guatemalan government is retooling dormant airfields in Quetzaltenango (AAE) and Huehuetenango (HUG) at this writing, with plans to restore one-time domestic-air routes from Guatemala City. No date has been announced for resumption of such service. For now, Adrenalina Tours in Quetzatenango and Antigua charters air service between Guatemala City and Quetzaltenango.

Air Services **Adrenalina Tours** (☎ *7761–4509 in Quetzaltenango, 7832–1108 in Antigua* 🌐 *www.adrenalinatours.com*).

BOAT AND FERRY TRAVEL

With the exception of the service between Panajachel and Santiago Atitlán, Lago Atitlán's public ferries have been replaced by private water taxis. Although they don't follow a schedule, the private boats are much faster and cost about the same, provided there are other passengers with whom to share the ride.

BUS AND SHUTTLE TRAVEL

Large Greyhound-style buses (*pullmans* in local parlance) connect Guatemala City with Panajachel, Quetzaltenango, and Huehuetenango. Beyond that, the infamous cramped "chicken buses" form the backbone of the transportation network here. If you're on a truly barebones, adventure budget, pickup trucks are also a time-honored mode

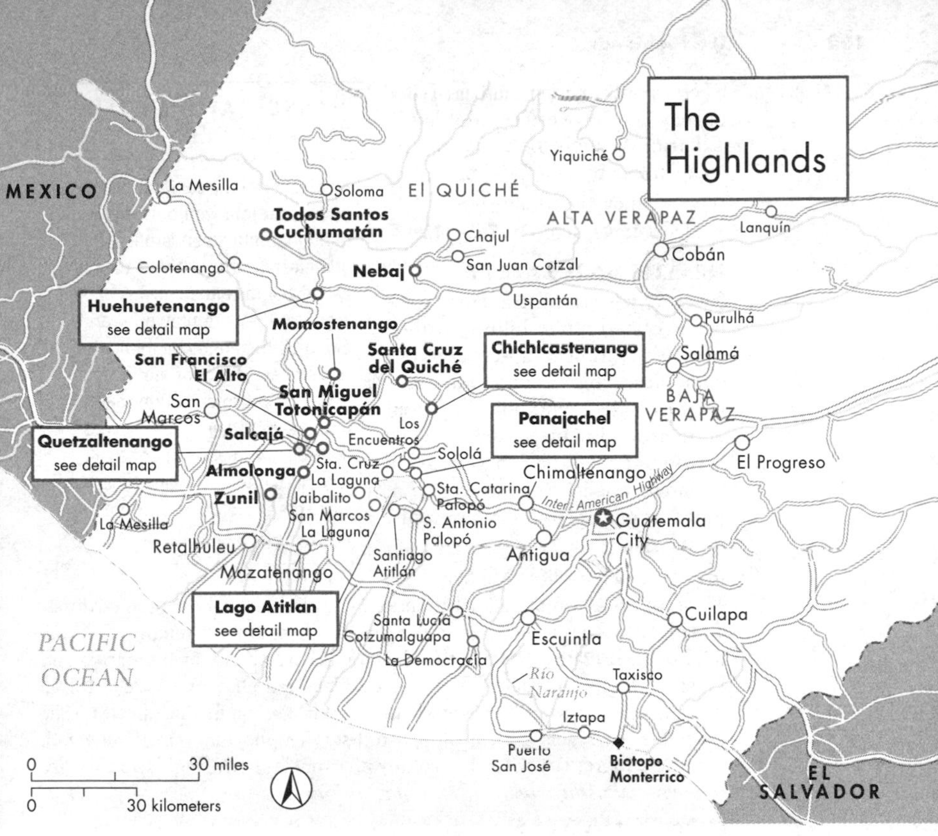

of transport. (You ride in back.) Most visitors opt for the comfort of scheduled minivan tourist shuttles to get from the capital and Antigua to Panajachel, Chichicastenango, and Quetzaltenango.

Atitrans and Turansa have shuttle minivans that travel from Antigua to towns in the Western Highlands. You can also catch a public bus at the terminal, which is cheaper but much less comfortable. There are one or two direct buses to Panajachel and Quetzaltenango each day, as well as five or six bound for Chichicastenango.

Shuttle Contacts **Atitrans** (☎ *7762–2246*). **Turansa** (☎ *7879–9370*).

CAR TRAVEL

Although mountainous, Guatemala's highlands are not the Andes, so driving isn't too treacherous, and primary and most secondary roads are in decent shape. The Pan-American Highway (CA-1) heads northwest out of Guatemala City, where it is called the Calzada Roosevelt. It bypasses Antigua and passes through Chimaltenango before reaching the highlands. The highway, being expanded to four lanes in many sectors, forms the transportation spine of this region, although most of what you'll want to see lies off the highway. (The northern hub city of Huehuetenango and the market town of Salcajá are the only two sights we list that actually sit on the highway.) North of Huehuetenango and Nebaj, roads deteriorate to dirt or gravel.

CAR RENTAL There is only one national car-rental agency in the western highlands, Tabarini. It might be easier to rent a car in Guatemala City instead.

Local Agency Tabarini (✉ *9 Calle 9–21, Quetzaltenango* ☎ *7763–0418*).

A FASCINATION WITH FIRECRACKERS

First, rest reassured: that loud boom that jolts you out of your early-morning sleep is not a gun, and, despite the fact that they are called *bombas* in Spanish, is not a bomb. They are fireworks, and along with *cohetes* (homemade rockets) are a fact of life in Guatemala, set off to celebrate market day, a saint's day, a special mass, an ordinary mass, someone's wedding. Any observance that warrants celebration, warrants firecrackers.

HEALTH AND SAFETY

Several groups of travelers have been robbed while hiking around the Lago Atitlán area. It is always a good idea to hire a guide, especially when you are not familiar with your destination. In Quetzaltenango and Chichicastenango it is best to avoid the areas outside the city center at night, as gang activity is reportedly on the rise.

In Panajachel, Clínicas Médicas Pana Medic offers 24-hour medical attention. The physicians, Francisco Ordoñez and his wife Zulma Buitrago both speak English. Quetzaltenango is home to two fine private hospitals, the Hospital Privado de Quetzaltenango and Hospital La Democracia. The Hospital Nacional Dr. Jorge Vides Molina in Huehuetenango and Hospital Nacional in Panajachel are both public hospitals. Farmacia La Unión is a full-service pharmacy in Panajachel. Farmacia Batres is a chain with many pharmacies in the highlands. (⇨ *See the regional listings below for contact information.*)

MONEY MATTERS

All the larger towns in the western highlands have ATMs where you can use your bank card. Bancared has branches in Panajachel, Chichicastenango, Quetzaltenango, and Huehuetenango. In deference to market day, banks in Chichicastenango keep all-day hours on Sundays, but close on Tuesdays.

RESTAURANTS

You'll find a few international restaurants in Quetzaltenango (by virtue of its being a large city) and in Panajachel (due to its concentration of tourists), but local cuisine in the highlands echoes the land itself: hearty, filling, and substantial. A few signature highland dishes appear on the menus of most local restaurants. Chicken *pepián* (a fricassee in pumpkin and sesame sauce), *chile relleno* (a stuffed bell pepper), and *arroz con pollo* (chicken with rice) all make use of abundant regional ingredients. Accompanying them might be *frijoles* (black beans, usually mashed up with a bit of onion and tomato sauce), corn tortillas, and a caramel-custard flan for dessert. Lunch is the big meal of the day in small-town eateries. Lighter fare is served for dinner in this early-to-bed, early-to-rise region.

A BIT OF HISTORY

Following the decline of lowland Mayan society in Guatemala's northern Petén region, beginning around AD 500, subsequent generations began to seek refuge in the adjoining highlands, carving out livelihoods of agriculture and commerce for themselves. Although we tend to think of "Maya" as a monolithic concept, these were several distinct peoples, speaking different languages, who saw little in common with their compatriots in the next valley. Alone, each group proved no match for Pedro de Alvarado and the Spanish conquistadors, who were able to employ a divide-and-conquer strategy to subjugate most of them.

Much of the country's 1960 to 1996 civil war was fought in the highlands. During the "scorched earth" campaigns of the early 1980s, entire towns were burned to the ground and tens of thousands of people were tortured and killed by paramilitary forces. The violence was designed to terrify the indigenous people into refusing to assist the rebel guerrillas. Thousands fled into the mountains or across the border into Mexico or Belize.

Although many issues remain unresolved, the people of the highlands are now weary of fighting, and most, regardless of their wartime sympathies, say that they simply are grateful for the peace that resulted from the 1996 accords. The army is gone, thankfully stripped of its internal-security role, and has been replaced by civilian police, whose members come from their local communities. Problems remain, and grievances are numerous, but everyone seems interested in moving on and putting the past behind them.

HOTELS

International hotel chains are nowhere to be found in this region, and aside from a couple of resort-type accommodations on Lake Atitlán, the highlands remain the province of smaller lodgings, most with fewer than 30 rooms each. That makes reservations a good idea any time of year, but especially on weekends. Air-conditioning is unheard of in this part of the country, but you won't miss it at these altitudes. The chill is a far more pressing concern, especially the farther west you travel, where the nighttime temperatures get colder. Many lodgings contain *chimineas,* or fireplaces, in their rooms. If not, don't be afraid to ask for an extra blanket.

WHAT IT COSTS IN GUATEMALAN QUETZALES

	¢	$	$$	$$$	$$$$
Restaurants	under Q40	Q40–Q70	Q70–Q100	Q100–Q130	over Q130
Hotels	under Q160	Q160–Q360	Q360–Q560	Q560–Q760	over Q760

Restaurant prices are based on the median main course price at dinner. Hotel prices are for two people in a standard double room in high season, including tax and service

CLOSE UP

Weaving Culture, Weaving History

It is said that the Mayan goddess Ixchel gave the art of weaving to her people. Today's Maya descendents still make fervent use of that gift in generating the riot of bold, cultural color that punctuates the muted green and brown natural tones of the highlands.

Key to the taut weave of Guatemalan textiles is the back-strap loom, a technique peculiar to this part of the world. Characteristics always identify the wearer with a specific town, a salient feature of indigenous Guatemalan clothing. Although today's Maya-descended peoples proudly wear their attire as a badge of where they live, the classification actually began as a dress code implemented by Spanish colonial officials. They wanted to be able to identify their subjects by community of origin for tax-collection purposes. The system took on a far darker side during Guatemala's civil war, when the government used clothing to identify and target specific indigenous communities.

A brief visit to the highlands will let you scratch the surface in identifying community differences: you'll begin to recognize the bright turquoises and bold geometric patterns of Santa Catarina Palopó; the tight embroidery of Nebaj, the showy, embroidered flowers and birds of Santiago Atitlán, or the knot tie-dyes of Salcajá.

A bit of vocabulary: a *huipil,* sometimes spelled *guipil,* is a woman's blouse. Structurally, it is little more than two pieces of cloth sewn together, but what a huipil lacks in tailoring, it more than makes up for in elaborate design. Equally simple in fit is her *corte,* a wraparound skirt, also woven with complex patterns. In some communities women wear a *tocoyal,* a piece of cloth wrapped tightly and worn as a circular headdress. (Alternately, this headgear is called a *cinta* [ribbon], but foreigners often refer to it simply as a "halo.") What about traditional menswear? You won't see much of that, period—you'll come to that realization after a short time in the highlands—except in a few isolated communities such as Sololá or Todos Santos Cuchumatán, where men still don a traditional woven shirt (*camisa*) and knee-length trousers (*calzoncillos*). Those trousers may be covered by an apron-like *sobrepantalón,* and a belt or sash (*faja*) might accent the ensemble.

The market for Guatemalan textiles has grown by leaps and bounds, and many villages have benefited, but, alas, many of the finer points of the weaving tradition are being left by the wayside to accommodate the frenzied shoppers. The traditional back-strap looms are speedily being replaced with gleaming sewing machines so garments can be churned out faster. The patterns that once relayed information about the wearer's town are now abandoned for those favored by visitors. Even garments worn by local peoples have undergone change. The explosion of vendors selling *ropa americana*—literally "American clothing," but a generic term referring to secondhand clothes—means that a pair of jeans or a sweater can be had for a fraction of the cost (and time) it takes to produce a huipil and corte.

VISITOR INFORMATION

The Guatemala government tourism office INGUAT has branches in Panajachel, open daily 9 to 5, and in Quetzaltenango, open weekdays 9 to 5 and Saturday 9 to 1. The staff at the office in Panajachel is particularly helpful. An Internet café does double duty as Chichicastenango's tourist office, and is open Monday, Wednesday, Friday, and Saturday 10–noon and 2–6; Thursday 8–noon and 2–6; and Sunday 8–2.

To minimize risks to you, both natural and manmade, any nature-related excursion should be undertaken with an organized tour operator who knows the region and takes proper security precautions.

A QUESTION OF TERMINOLOGY

Stick to the term "indigenous" (*indígena*) to describe Guatemala's Maya-descended peoples. Although you'll hear the term used, "Indian" (*indio*) is considered pejorative here. We don't use the word in this book (except to describe an Indian restaurant). Likewise, among Guatemalans, "native" (*nativo*) and "tribe" (*tribú*) conjure up images best left to old Tarzan movies.

Information INGUAT (✉ *Edificio San Rafael, C. Santander, Panajachel* ☎ *7762–1106* ✉ *Casa de la Cultura, Parque Centro América, 7 Calle 11–35, Quetzaltenango* ☎ *7761–4931*). **Oficina de Información Turística** (✉ *7 Calle at 5 Av. Chichicastenango* ☎ *7756–0222*).

LAGO ATITLÁN

Postcard-perfect Lago Atitlán lies at the foot of three massive dormant volcanoes—San Pedro (3,023 meters/9,920 feet), Tolimán (3,152 meters/10,340 feet), and Atitlán (3,523 meters/11,560 feet). Early in the morning and on calm nights the lake's water is as smooth as glass, capturing the huge volcanic cones in its reflection. You'll see why this is arguably the loveliest spot in Guatemala, and why British writer Aldous Huxley dubbed Atitlán "the most beautiful lake in the world."

Most visitors find a place to stay, park for the duration, and make cross-lake day trips (⇨ *See Lake Savvy box, below*). A dozen or so communities ring Atitlán; each has its own personality, and you should be able to find one that matches yours. Panajachel anchors the lake at its one o'clock position, and offers the most polished infrastructure for visitors. Continuing clockwise, intensely traditional Santa Catarina Palopó, and even more traditional San Antonio Palopó lie on Atitlán's eastern shore. Traditional, workaday market town San Lucas Tolimán lies just south. Across the lake from Panajachel, Santiago Atitlán welcomes visitors to enjoy its rich culture, tradition, and history—but on its terms. Just northeast lies youthful, party-hearty San Pedro La Laguna, the hot new destination on the budget-travel circuit. Next door is indigenous, environmentally minded San Juan La Laguna. New Age devotees dock at San Marcos La Laguna. Beyond lies tiny Jaibalito, so small that it doesn't appear on some maps, and, almost completing the loop around the lake, Santa Cruz La Laguna captures that middle ground if you want to kick back and relax without too much fuss.

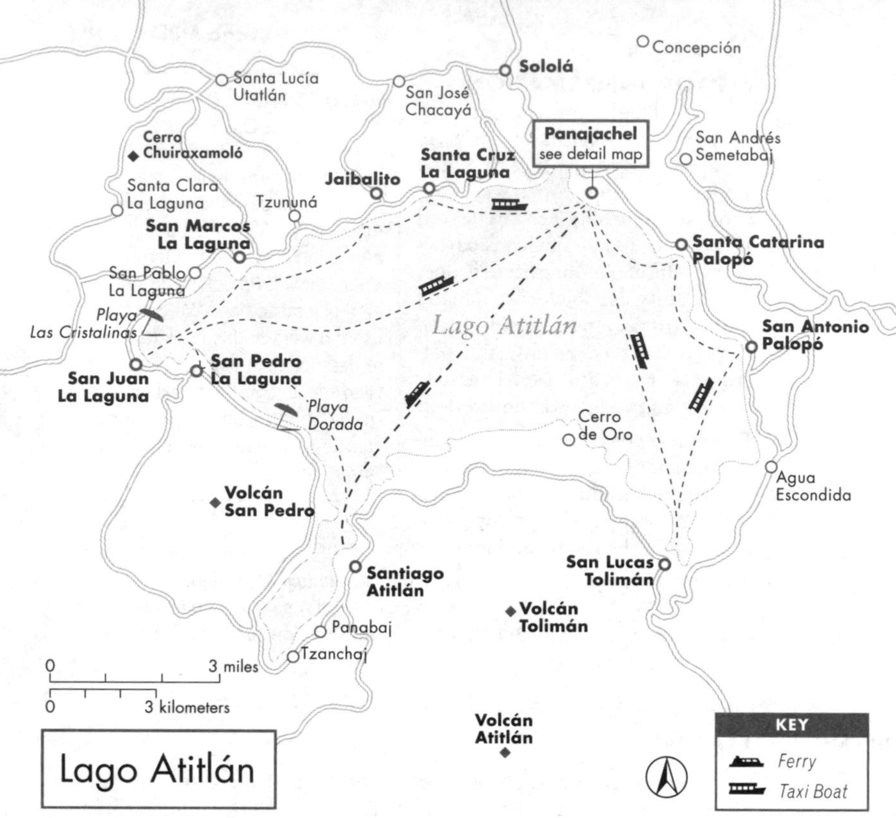

PANAJACHEL

110 km (68 mi) northwest of Antigua.

The quiet Cakchiquel village of Panajachel on the northern shore of Lago Atitlán began welcoming international visitors during the heady, hippie 1960s, and never looked back. This is still Guatemala's consummate hangout, a place where many end up staying longer than planned. And who can blame them? With a view of three volcanoes that drop off into the crystalline waters of Lago Atitlán, Panajachel's setting could hardly be more dramatic. For better or for worse, though, the '60s are over and the "Pana" of old has been tamed. Once exclusively the province of bare-bones lodging for backpackers with bare-bones resources, the town has matured in its middle age and today welcomes visitors and foreign residents of all stripes and budgets. It remains as fun as ever, and counts an ever-increasing number of activities to keep you occupied. There may still be a few dead heads floating around, but today's Panajachel is a place you would be proud to take your parents.

GETTING HERE AND AROUND

The classic route to Panajachel takes you from Guatemala City past Chimaltenango. Just beyond the Encuentros crossroads that leads north to Chichicastenango, follow the signs that direct you south to Panajachel through Sololá. An alternate route turns southwest beyond

LAKE SAVVY

Regularly scheduled passenger ferries ply the route between Panajachel and Santiago Atitlán during daylight hours. Boats depart from the dock at the foot of Calle Rancho Grande in Panajachel at 6:30, 9, 9:30, and 10:30 AM, and 1, 3, 4:30, and 5 PM, with return trips from Santiago at 6, 7, 11:45 AM, and 12:30, 1:30, and 4:30 PM. You'll pay Q20, and the journey takes just under an hour. Private boat taxis supplement service on this route—they slice the Pana–Santiago ferry time in half. Other boat taxis fill in the gaps to and between other lake towns, departing from the foot of Panajachel's Calle del Embarcadero, two blocks from the ferry dock. Taxi service is collective: the driver departs after the boat fills up—the wait is never more than 30 minutes—and makes stops at towns along the shore. If you wish to hire a boat for yourself, expect to pay Q200 for the ride. During the slower tourist seasons of Easter–June and September–November, you may need to do just that if you are traveling to less popular towns outside the Panajachel–Santiago–San Pedro circuit. You can negotiate the price of the entire boat for very short distances, say Panajachel to Santa Cruz La Laguna.

■ **TIP→ If you are prone to motion sickness, make your cross-lake jaunt in the morning, when the water surface is usually calm.** By early afternoon, a wind that locals call the *xocomil* picks up, making for a choppy ride. Sitting near the back of the boat will be a bit less bumpy. In any case, try to be on the final boat of the day heading back to Panajachel by 4 PM, after which selection thins out as drivers make plans to be back home before dark.

In theory, you can circumnavigate the lake's perimeter on land, although most of your trip takes you inland, rather than hugging the lakeshore. In practice, you'll find a gap between Santiago Atitlán and San Pedro La Laguna. Only 4x4 vehicles can navigate that rough sector. More crucial, land travel between those two towns is crime-ridden and dangerous, and should not be attempted. Even public transportation avoids that road segment. (Fill in that gap by boat.) Networks of chicken buses and pickup trucks (*peek-oops*) ply the rest of the loop. If you're game, sure-footed, adventurous, and don't mind sharing the back of a truck with several other people, the latter is a dirt-cheap way to get from town to town.

Chimaltenango to Patzún, then to Panajachel. This isolated route fell into disuse for many years because of numerous robberies. The problem seems to have abated. Most transport uses the Sololá route, which is smoother and more convenient.

The Transportes Rébuli public busses travel from Guatemala City to Panajachel hourly from 5 AM to 4 PM daily. Buses bound for Guatemala City leave Panajachel hourly from 6 AM to 3 PM daily. The 6 AM and 3 PM Greyhound-style buses are more expensive than Rébuli's chicken-bus service, but they're also much more comfortable. Count on a four-hour trip.

Two reputable tour companies, Atitrans and Union Travel, are based in Panajachel and offer tours to just about everywhere in the region.

THE LAKE, LONG-TERM

It's not all about staying in a hotel at the lake. This is a part of Guatemala where people can rent a house or flat for a few days and chill out. What's available reflects each community's demographics. Panajachel's mostly year-round population rarely leaves long enough to rent places out. If they do, it's through an informal process that short-term visitors can rarely take advantage of. The same holds true in Santiago Atitlán and San Pedro La Laguna.

Smaller lake communities with substantial numbers of seasonal residents are a good bet. Property-management firms rent out homes during owners' absences. Santa Catarina Palopó and, to a lesser extent, San Antonio Palopó contain many exclusive homes whose owners live in Guatemala City much of the year. Housing is a tad more modest, though still quite comfy, in San Marcos La Laguna, Santa Cruz La Laguna, and Jaibalito, all of which have numerous seasonal residents.

The longer you stay, the lower your cost per day turns out to be. Most management firms won't handle stays of less than a week. Although $1,000 per week for a two-bedroom house sounds expensive, split among four people, the price compares to that of an upscale hotel here. It's impossible to find rental properties on the lake around Christmastime. A rental for Holy Week should be arranged far in advance, but is not as difficult. Some properties come with options for a cook and cleaning staff. Don't expect Internet access or potable water—stock up on bottled water from local stores, and boat into Panajachel, Santiago, or San Pedro to check e-mail.

Your other long-term option here is a homestay in conjunction with Spanish study. Both Panajachel and San Pedro La Laguna have language schools that can arrange boarding with local families. Expect housing to be modest.

In Panajachel, both **Atitlán Solutions** (☎ *7762–0959* 🌐 *www.realestateatitlan.com*) and **Terra-X** (☎ *7762–1229* 🌐 *www.terraxatitlan.com*) handle real estate and property management.

Panajachel has two primary docks, one at the end of Calle del Embarcadero and one at the end of Calle Rancho Grande. The first is for private boats on the San Pedro route, stopping at Santa Cruz, Jaibalito, San Marcos, Santa Clara, and San Pedro. It's about Q15, no matter where you get off.

The other dock is for hour-long journeys to Santiago, with departures at 6, 8:30, 9, 9:30, and 10:30 AM, and 1, 3, 4:30, and 5 PM, and return trips at 6, 7, and 11:45 AM, and 12:30, 1:30, and 4:30 PM. The cost is about Q10. Private boats occasionally take passengers to Santiago in about half the time.

ESSENTIALS

Bank **Bancared** (✉ *Calle Principal 0–78, , Panajachel*).

Bus Contact **Transportes Rébuli** (✉ *Calle Principal and Calle Santander, Panajachel* ☎ *2230–2748*).

Emergencies Ambulance (☎ *7762-4121*). Police (☎ *7762-1120*).

Medical Assistance Clínicas Médicas Pana Medic (✉ *Calle Principal 0-72, Panajachel* ☎ *7762-2174*). Farmacia La Unión (✉ *Calle Santander near Calle Principal, Panajachel* ☎ *7762-1138*).

Visitor and Tour Info Atitrans (✉ *Calle Santander, Panajachel* ☎ *7762-2246*). INGUAT (✉ *Edificio San Rafael, Calle Santander, Panajachel* ☎ *7762-1106*). Union Travel (✉ *In Los Pinos, Av. Santander, Zona 2, Panajachel* ☎ *7762-1392*).

THE PLACE OF THE GRINGO

The *-tenango* suffix in many Guatemalan place names (Quetzaltenango, Chichicastenango, Huehuetenango) means "the place of." Panajachel, with its large international population, long ago acquired the nickname "Gringotenango" among travelers.

4

EXPLORING

The tourist's Panajachel centers on seven-block Calle Santander, which connects the lakefront with the fringes of the original village, and typifies the main drag of a resort town; open-air restaurants, bars, and vendors' stalls line the street, giving you a front-row seat to observe the passing parade of pedestrians, vendors, dogs, and tuk-tuks, the three-wheel motorized Bajaj taxis made in India, common here and elsewhere in Guatemala. We hear different takes on Calle Santander: Some tire of the sellers who wander into cafés to sell their wares—times are tough and the vendors are trying to eke out a living—or the street dogs who beg for a morsel; others relish the commotion of tourist town in a developing country. You'll have to decide. The inland end of Calle Santander hooks up with Calle Principal, the highway leading north and east out of town. Avenida de los Árboles climbs the hill to the old part of town. You'd never know you were in a tourist mecca when you stand on the small plaza in front of the town's lovely church. Especially on its Thursday market day, Panajachel looks pretty much like any other highland village.

For a brief history of the lake and its people, head to the **Museo Lacustre de Atitlán.** Here you'll find a handful of informative displays tracing the history of the region back to precolonial times. ✉ *End of Calle Santander, in the Hotel Posada de Don Rodrigo* ☎ *7762-2326* *Q35* ⊙ *Daily 8-6.*

The **Reserva Natural Atitlán** has a walking trail that loops through a small river canyon, crossing suspension bridges and passing a butterfly atrium and enclosures of spider monkeys and coatimundis. If you feel like playing Tarzan, the complex contains a zip-line tour (Q150), where you glide through the forest canopy courtesy of a series of cables, a helmet, and a very secure harness. There's also a private beach for a bit of post-educational relaxation. Campsites are available in the park, or if you'd like a bit more luxury, cabins ($$), albeit spartan ones, are also available. ✉ *2 km [1 mi] west of Panajachel* ☎ *7762-2565* ⊕ *www.atitlanreserva.com* ⊙ *Daily 8-4* *Q50*

Restaurants

Café Bombay 4
Casablanca 1
El Bistro 6
El Patio 2
El Tocoyal 7
Guajimbo's 3
Pájaro Azul 5

Hotels

Cacique Inn 10
Hotel Atitlán 8
Hotel Dos Mundos 3
Hotel Posada de Don Rodrigo 7
Hotel Primavera . 2
Hotel San Buenaventura ... 9
Hotel Utz Rajil ... 5
Porta Hotel del Lago 6
Posada de los Volcanes 4
Rancho Grande Inn 1

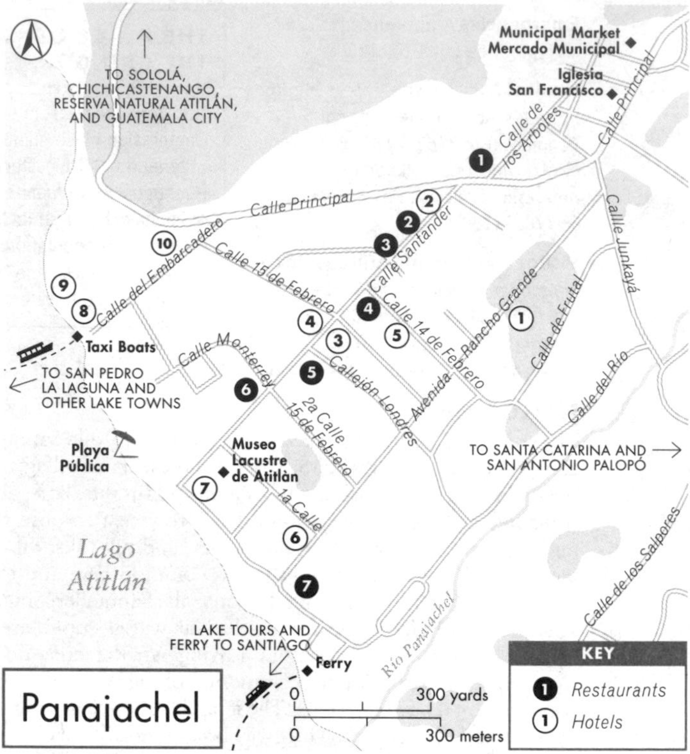

Municipal Market Mercado Municipal
Iglesia San Francisco
TO SOLOLÁ, CHICHICASTENANGO, RESERVA NATURAL ATITLÁN, AND GUATEMALA CITY
Calle Principal
Calle de los Árboles
Calle Santander
Calle del Embarcadero
Calle 15 de Febrero
Calle 14 de Febrero
Avenida Rancho Grande
Calle de Frutal
Calle Junkayá
Calle del Río
Calle Monterrey
Callejón Londres
2a Calle 15 de Febrero
1a Calle
Taxi Boats
TO SAN PEDRO LA LAGUNA AND OTHER LAKE TOWNS
Playa Pública
Museo Lacustre de Atitlàn
TO SANTA CATARINA AND SAN ANTONIO PALOPÓ
Calle de los Salpores
Lago Atitlán
Río Panajachel
LAKE TOURS AND FERRY TO SANTIAGO
Ferry
0 300 yards
0 300 meters

KEY
Restaurants
Hotels

Panajachel

WHERE TO EAT

$ VEGETARIAN

✕ **Café Bombay.** Despite the name, you'll find very little that is Indian about the cuisine here. The menu is a real catch-all, and "vegetarian" or "macrobiotic" are better descriptions to describe the falafel, pita, pad thai, burritos, lasagna, and key lime pie. Dine inside, or grab one of the two umbrella-covered tables on the front deck and survey the action on Calle Santander. ✉ *Calle Santander* ☎ *7762–0611* ▭ *No credit cards* ⊙ *Closed Tues.*

$$$ SEAFOOD

✕ **Casablanca.** Panajachel's most elegant restaurant, Casablanca has a white-walled dining room with windows overlooking the main street. The handful of tables on the upper level is much more intimate. The menu is ample, if a bit overpriced, and includes a few seafood and fish standouts such as lobster and black lake bass, as well as tenderloin in a green-pepper sauce. Musicians occasionally entertain. ✉ *Calle Principal 0–93, at Calle Santander* ☎ *7762–1390* ▭ *AE, D, DC, MC, V.*

$ ECLECTIC Fodor's Choice ★

✕ **El Bistro.** Hummingbirds dart among flowering vines at this romantic eatery just up the street from the lake. Enter through an iron gate that leads into a garden hidden behind a low wall. There are outside tables and a pair of intimate dining rooms. All the delicious Italian food, from the tasty bread to the fresh pasta, is homemade. Two standout specialties are the fettuccine *arrabiata* (with a slightly spicy tomato sauce), and the steak au poivre (cooked in a wine sauce and black pepper) served with fresh vegetables. ✉ *End of Calle Santander* ☎ *7762–0508* ▭ *AE, D, DC, MC, V.*

CLOSE UP

I, Rigoberta Menchú . . . Mostly

In 1992 the Nobel Peace Prize was awarded to Guatemalan writer Rigoberta Menchú, raised in the tiny highland village of San Miguel Uspantán. Menchú was born in 1959, just before a string of military dictators usurped control of Guatemala for 36 war-filled years. She grew up as dozens of opposition and guerrilla groups rose to resist them. Along with many of her family members, Menchú opposed the dictatorship with peaceful demonstrations that included peasants from various regions. When she was eventually forced into exile, she continued her opposition to Guatemala's military rule by drawing international attention to the repressive regime.

In 1983 she published her testimonial, *I, Rigoberta Menchú: An Indian Woman in Guatemala,* and the plight of Guatemala's indigenous people—and the brutality of the military regime—was revealed in wrenching detail. In her book Menchú described losing two brothers to malnutrition on a coffee plantation and the razing of her village by wealthy land prospectors. Most disturbingly, Menchú related the story of a third brother, who was kidnapped by the army, tortured, and then burned alive.

In 1999 American anthropologist David Stoll challenged Menchú's account with the publication of *Rigoberta Menchú and the Story of All Poor Guatemalans.* His research suggested that the conflict over the lands of Menchú's village was actually a long-running dispute between her father and his in-laws, and that although Menchú's brother was unquestionably kidnapped, tortured, and murdered by the military, it was probably not carried out in the manner that Menchú had suggested. Although still a potent symbol of indigenous rights, Menchú is now viewed by some with incredulity.

Whether or not Menchú personally witnessed the events she describes, it is indisputable that hundreds of indigenous workers, particularly children, died of disease, malnutrition, or outright abuse on the plantations. It is also clear that the military committed innumerable acts of brutality, including public executions, in villages all across the country. In 1998 the Guatemalan Truth Commission sponsored by the United Nations denounced the military's actions during the civil war as genocide. Some argue that if Menchú's account wasn't wholly her own, but included incidents suffered by other indigenous men and women, it doesn't detract from the horror of what occurred. If she included the experiences of others to draw attention to a conflict the international community had ignored for more than 20 years, they argue, can anyone really blame her?

Stoll himself admits that Menchú is fundamentally right about the army's brutality, though he downplays it considerably, no doubt to bolster his own book's more dubious claim: that it was the guerrillas, not the ruling generals, who were responsible for igniting political violence in the highlands. But it is the debunking of Rigoberta Menchú that he will be remembered for, and that will forever endear him to Guatemala's war criminals, many of whom remain in public life.

—Gary Chandler

$ LATIN AMERICAN **El Patio.** Although it's known by the outdoor patio with umbrella-covered tables that gives the place its name, most of the restaurant's tables are inside a large dining room decorated with lots of palms and ferns, and a few indigenous drawings on the wall. Nevertheless, the lunch and dinner menus offer great variety, including such choices as pepper steak, roast pork, and chicken à la king. It's also a popular spot for breakfast. You'll find a couple of Internet computers to log on to after you eat. *Calle Santander 7762–2041 AE, D, DC, MC, V.*

$$ LATIN AMERICAN ★ **El Tocoyal.** Our favorite in-town lakefront restaurant, with great views from its picture window, takes its name from the tightly wrapped cloth worn as a headdress by Tzutuhil women in the area. This is about as elegant as Panajachel gets: waiters in white shirts and bow ties scurry around and serve pepián or chile relleno on the local side of the menu, or a good steak if you're looking for something international. This is still Pana, though, so you don't need to dress up. *Calle del Lago 7762–1555 AE, D, DC, MC, V No dinner Sun.–Thurs.*

$ AMERICAN Fodor's Choice ★ **Guajimbo's.** The Uruguayan and American owners contribute to the live acoustic music many evenings here at one of Calle Santander's liveliest restaurants and a favorite with Pana's expat community. Grab a seat in this semi-open-air place, enjoy the entertainment, and survey all the action on the main drag. Uruguayan-style beef tenderloin rules, as do *churtos* (beef cutlets prepared variously with mozzarella cheese, ham, bacon, peppers, or olives). *Calle Santander 7762–0063 AE, D, DC, MC, V Closed Thurs.*

¢ FRENCH ★ **Pájaro Azul.** Tired of frijoles? There isn't a single bean to be found at this café, which serves up outstanding crepes. Choose from a small but creative menu of savory dinner crepes—fill them with vegetables, tofu, chicken, or pork—and sweet dessert crepes—we like the banana–brown sugar–yogurt Jamaica one—or pick and choose among your favorite ingredients. While you wait, you can thumb through a pile of back-issue magazines (including, oddly enough, the *New Yorker*). *Calle Santander, next to the post office 7762–2596 No credit cards Closed Thurs.*

WHERE TO STAY

TIP→ If you stay on Calle Santander, ask for rooms that don't face the street, and consequently don't get the street noise.

$$ **Cacique Inn.** This inn is a collection of little buildings about a block from the main street. Spacious, if sparsely furnished, rooms have sliding-glass doors that open onto the lovely garden. The rooms may seem a bit cool because of the tile floors, but they have fireplaces that warm you up in a snap. The grounds are surrounded by a wall, which makes the terraces by the pool a private place to sunbathe. The restaurant is one of the best in town, serving a wide selection of Guatemalan dishes. The agreeable chefs will sometimes even prepare dishes to order. You receive a 5% discount off the room rates if you pay in cash. **Pros:** quiet street; good restaurant. **Cons:** basic rooms; can be chilly at times. *Calle del Embarcadero, near Calle Principal 7762–1205 7762–2053 34 rooms In-room: no a/c. In-hotel: restaurant, room service, bar, pool, parking (no fee), no-smoking rooms AE, D, DC, MC, V EP.*

$$$$ Fodor's Choice ★ **Hotel Atitlán.** Keep any disappointment in check until you arrive. You turn into a quiet cove northwest of Panajachel, and will spot an ugly high-rise building. That isn't this hotel. This Spanish-style inn consists of a main building flanked by two-story wings that surround a pool. The extensive grounds border on a long stretch of shoreline and the Reserva Natural Atitlán, a wooded reserve crossed by footpaths and hanging bridges. The rooms, each with tile floor, carved wooden furniture, and handwoven bedspreads, have balconies overlooking the gardens or the lake. Even if you don't stay here, stop by for views of the lake at sunset. The restaurant is reliable, if a bit overpriced. The hotel also offers weekly rates, which include all meals if you like. **Pros:** terrific views; wooded setting. **Cons:** far removed from town. ✉ *2 km (1 mi) northwest of Panajachel* ☎ *7762–1441, 2334–0641 in Guatemala City* 🌐 *www.hotelatitlan.com* *63 rooms, 6 suites* *In-room: no a/c, Wi-Fi. In-hotel: restaurant, bar, tennis court, pool, beachfront, no elevator, laundry service, public Internet, parking (no fee), no-smoking rooms* 💳 *AE, D, DC, MC, V* *EP, FAP.*

HURRICANE STAN

In October 2005 Hurricane Stan, the 18th named tropical storm of a record season, made landfall on Mexico's Yucatán peninsula. It brought torrential rains that drenched the entire region. Lake Atitlán was hit especially hard by landslides as a direct result of the rains Stan spawned. An estimated 1,500 people died, many in Santiago Atitlán. Coming in the aftermath of catastrophic Hurricanes Katrina and Rita, Stan received limited attention from the U.S. news media.

$$ **Hotel Dos Mundos.** Set amid colorful gardens, this hotel gives you comfortable accommodations without the hefty price tag of more deluxe digs. The medium-size rooms are simply and tastefully furnished. Most open onto the pool area—these are set way back from the street, giving you no sense of being smack-dab in the center of town—where you can spend your afternoon on a lounge chair with a cocktail. The restaurant has a certain elegance, with tables set beneath a soaring thatch roof. The menu includes well-made pasta dishes and lots of wine. **Pros:** good value; right in town, but most rooms set back from street noise; park-like setting. **Cons:** rooms closer to street still get some noise. ✉ *Calle Santander 4–72* ☎ *7762–2078* 🌐 *www.hoteldosmundos.com* *22 rooms* *In-room: no a/c, no phone, safe, Wi-Fi. In-hotel: restaurant, room service, bar, pool, no elevator, Internet terminal, parking (no fee), no-smoking rooms* 💳 *AE, D, DC, MC, V* *BP.*

$$$$ **Hotel Posada de Don Rodrigo.** At the end of Calle Santander, this excellent hotel—there's a branch by the same name in Antigua, and a stay at both branches in one trip gets you a 10-percent discount on the rates—has some of the best views of the lake. The rooms make use of handwoven fabrics from the local communities. Ask for one of the newer beachfront rooms with slightly more modern amenities and better views. Relax by the pool or in one of the hammocks hung along a breezy corridor. There's a small on-site museum that gives insight into the history of the Maya. **Pros:** close to lake, some rooms have good lake views. **Cons:** a bit removed from action. ✉ *End of Calle Santander*

VOLCANO VIEWS

From left to right, the three volcanoes you see that make that oh-so-perfect backdrop across Lake Atitlán from Panajachel are: partially obscured **Volcán Atitlán** (3,523 meters/11,560 feet), **Volcán Tolimán** (3,151 meters/10,340 feet), and **Volcán San Pedro** (3,023 meters/9,920 feet). All are dormant. San Pedro is logistically the easiest of the three to climb—access is via San Pedro La Laguna—but "easy" is relative here. The ascent is steep, and that makes for a steep descent, too. The trail gets slippery in sections, even during the dry season, and rarely levels off to allow you to catch your breath. Your reward for the grueling hike? The views of the entire lake region are stunning. Atitlán and Tolimán have been ascended, but their remoteness relative to San Pedro has meant occasional robberies. (San Pedro has suffered that problem, too.) No matter which one of the three lake volcanoes you attempt, for safety reasons we recommend you climb with an organized excursion.

The 3,772-meter (12,375-foot) **Volcán Santa María** keeps watch over Quetzaltenango. Santa María last erupted in 1902. It and accompanying earthquakes caused widespread damage to the city and to the slopes heading down to the Pacific coast, and killed an estimated 1,500 people. The eruption was said to spew ash as far away as San Francisco, California, and decimated the region's coffee industry, but paradoxically, Santa María's volcanic ash provided a much-needed fertilizing boost to the countryside near Antigua, allowing that city to take the lead in coffee production. If you can handle the altitude, the dormant volcano is a reasonable day-trip ascent, with stupendous views east as far as Volcán Pacaya south of Guatemala City, and as far west as far as Mexico. The real treat is the view of the nearby 3,500-meter (11,482-foot) **Volcán Santiaguito,** which hatched through the earth during the 1902 eruption of Santa María. Santiaguito, continuously active since then, is too dangerous to climb. Clouds move in and obscure the views by late morning, making a very early morning start essential. Although safety is far less a concern here than for the volcanoes close to the capital or Atitlán, a few robberies of solo hikers have occurred. We recommend that you take the trip with an organized tour.

Guatemala's highest peak, the 4,220-meter (13,845-foot) **Volcán Tajumulco,** sits outside the small city of San Marcos, 48 km (29 mi) northeast of Quetzaltenango, and a scant 15 km (9 mi) from the Mexican border. As with Santa María, if you can handle the altitude—gauge your abilities carefully—the ascent itself is reasonable. Numerous Quetzaltenango outfitters organize two-day, one-night Tajumulco trips.

Adrenalina Tours (✉ *Quetzaltenango* ☎ *7761–4509* 🌐 *www.adrenalinatours.com*) leads excursions up the Santa María and Tajumulco volcanoes.

Atitrans (✉ *Panajachel* ☎ *7762–2246* 🌐 *www.atitrans.com*) leads ascents up the San Pedro volcano.

Quetzaltrekkers (✉ *Quetzaltenango* ☎ *7765–5895* 🌐 *www.quetzaltrekkers.com*) leads trips up the Santa María and Tajumulco volcanoes.

☎ 7762–2326 🌐 www.posadadedonrodrigo.com ⇨ 39 rooms ♖ In-room: no a/c (some), Wi-Fi. In-hotel: restaurant, room service, pool, laundry service, public Internet, parking (no fee), no-smoking rooms ▭ AE, D, DC, MC, V 🍽 EP.

$ **Hotel Primavera.** Friendly owners are a nice plus at this budget find with mostly second-floor rooms in the center of town. Of the hotels we recommend in Panajachel, this one is closest to the bar action on Calle Santander. The noise is really only a problem on weekends, but rooms 1, 8, and 9 do not face the street and make for quieter evenings. Their bay windows face a center courtyard occupied by the sedate restaurant downstairs. Those three rooms are larger than the others and have fireplaces, too. We like Room 9 in particular; it has its own interior balcony. **Pros:** friendly owners, closest hotel to action. **Cons:** front rooms get street noise. ✉ *Calle Santander ☎ 7762–2052 🌐 www.primaveraatitlan.com ⇨ 10 rooms ♖ In-room: no a/c, no phone. In-hotel: restaurant, no elevator, laundry service, public Internet, no-smoking rooms ▭ AE, D, DC, MC, V 🍽 EP.*

$$$$ **Hotel San Buenaventura.** The well-manicured gardens of this small complex lead down past a shallow pool, bricked Mayan sauna, and Jacuzzi to a private beach. Although many of the condos lack good views of the lake, their barrel-roof brick ceilings and understated Moorish design more than make up for it. This is a great place for groups or families—each bungalow can sleep six, and has a separate living area, fully outfitted kitchen, and private terrace. The San Buenaventura sits in the same cove as the Hotel Atitlán, above. **Pros:** secluded wooded setting, great for families or groups. **Cons:** far removed from town, few rooms have lake views. ✉ *2 km (1 mi) west of Panajachel ☎ 7762–2559, 2337–0461 in Guatemala City 🌐 www.hotelsanbuenaventura.net ⇨ 10 bungalows ♖ In-room: no a/c, kitchen. In-hotel: restaurant, bar, pool, beachfront, bicycles, public Wi-Fi, parking (no fee), no-smoking rooms ▭ AE, D, DC, MC, V 🍽 BP.*

$ **Hotel Utz Rajil.** This three-floor lodging sits on a quiet street, just one-half block off Calle Santander. Rooms come with cabinet, bed, and table—not much else—but the place is a good, peaceful budget find. **Pros:** good budget value, quiet street. **Cons:** simple rooms, owners have dogs. ✉ *Calle 14 de Febrero ☎ 7762–0303 📠 7762–1496 ⇨ 16 rooms ♖ In-room: no a/c, no phone. In-hotel: no elevator, no-smoking rooms ▭ No credit cards 🍽 EP.*

$$$ **Porta Hotel del Lago.** At six stories high, Panajachel's biggest in-town hotel is a veritable skyscraper, and also has the most amenities. Although it lacks the character of smaller hotels, it's comfortable and convenient and has top-notch service. Rooms have balconies overlooking the public beach on Lago Atitlán. The huge restaurant next door, which looks out onto the pool, is for guests only. **Pros:** good value, huge number of activities, always something going on. **Cons:** always something going on, so not ideal if you want seclusion. ✉ *End of Calle Rancho Grande at Calle Buenas Nuevas ☎ 7762–1555, 2361–9683 in Guatemala City 🌐 www.portahotels.com ⇨ 90 rooms, 10 suites ♖ In-room: no a/c, safe (some). In-hotel: 2 restaurants, room service, bar, pool, gym, laundry service, parking (no fee), no-smoking rooms ▭ AE, D, DC, MC, V.*

$ **Posada de los Volcanes.** The friendly owners here operate their own small tour company, and are likely to be your guide or driver if you use their services. The layout isn't complicated: four levels, three rooms, and a communal veranda on each level. Those at the top have great views of the lake. Rooms are bright, colorful, and simply furnished. Although it's on Calle Santander, the place is far enough removed from the string of bars and restaurants to feel quiet and secluded, but still within walking distance of the action. **Pros:** friendly owners and staff, removed enough from street noise. **Cons:** simple rooms, long climb to top-floor rooms if you don't like stairs. ✉ *Across from post office, Calle Santander 5–51* ☎ *7762–0244* 🌐 *www.posadadelosvolcanes.com* *12 rooms* *In-room: no a/c, no phone, Wi-Fi. In-hotel: no elevator, Internet terminal, parking (no fee), no-smoking rooms* *AE, D, DC, MC, V* *EP.*

$$ **Rancho Grande Inn.** A German immigrant by the name of Milly Schleisier opened this string of bungalows back in the 1940s. In so doing, she created what is still one of the most charming of Panajachel's accommodations, melding the designs of country houses in her homeland with the colorful culture of her adopted country. Each of the rooms is unique; the large bungalow, which can sleep up to five, has a fireplace. Breakfast is served family-style every morning. **Pros:** quiet street, friendly staff. **Cons:** a bit removed from action. ✉ *Calle Rancho Grande* ☎ *7762–2255* 🌐 *www.ranchograndeinn.com* *15 rooms, 1 bungalow* *In-room: no a/c, Wi-Fi. In-hotel: restaurant, pool, Internet terminal, parking (no fee), no-smoking rooms* *AE, D, DC, MC, V* *BP.*

NIGHTLIFE

As a resort town, Panajachel has some of the liveliest nightlife in the highlands. Calle Santander is *the* place to see and be seen. Stroll the street, look for a bar, café, or restaurant to park yourself, and watch the parade go by. Many other bars cluster near the intersection of Avenida de los Arboles and Calle Principal on the fringes of the Old Town.

The dimly lighted **Chapiteau Disco** (✉ *Av. de los Arboles* ☎ *7762–0374*) plays mostly rock, Wednesday through Saturday. The **Circus Bar** (✉ *Av. de los Arboles* ☎ *7762–2056* 🌐 *www.panajachel.com/circusbar*) is a popular spot for locals and travelers alike, and has live Latin music most nights. Up above the fray of Calle Santander, **La Terraza** (✉ *Calle Santander, near Av. de Los Arboles* ☎ *7762–0041*) has an open-air, casual elegance perfect for early-evening cocktails. They also have a good menu focusing on continental favorites like rabbit and fondue Bourguignonne. The **Pana Rock Café** (✉ *Calle Santander* ☎ *7762–2194*) has live music many nights, and wins Panajachel's loudest-bar award. **Solomon's Porchá** (✉ *Calle Principal* ☎ *7723–0751*) screens films several nights a week. You can enjoy good Mexican food at the aptly named **Sunset Café** (✉ *Calle Santander*). There's live music almost every night.

OUTDOOR ACTIVITIES

BIKING For exploring the countryside you can rent a mountain bike at **Moto Servicio Quiché** (✉ *Av. de los Arboles at Calle Principal*) and pedal over to nearby villages.

WATER SPORTS Water sports are becoming more popular at Lago Atitlán, giving the lake a Club Med feel. You can rent a canoe from **Diversiones Acuáticas Balom** (✉ *On the public beach near ferry terminals* ☎ *7762–2242*). It's best to get out early and be back by noon, as the afternoon winds can be fierce. The company also offers tours of the lake.

LANGUAGE SCHOOLS IN PANAJACHEL

Pana's diverse international population makes it one of Guatemala's hot places to be. Don't spend so much time with your fellow foreigners, however, that you neglect to practice Spanish outside the classroom.

Jabel Tinamit (✉ *Calle Santander* ☎ *7762–0238* 🌐 *www.jabeltinamit.com*).

Jardín de América (✉ *Calle 14 de Febrero 4–44* ☎ *7762–2637* 🌐 *www.jardindeamerica.com*).

SHOPPING

Panajachel's weekly Thursday market (mostly fruits, vegetables, and animals) takes place in the old town near the church. Calle Santander is one long open-air souvenir market, lined on both sides with vendors who hang their wares from fences and makeshift stalls. Examine the items carefully, as goods purchased here are often not the best quality.

An outdoor market called **Tinamit Maya** (✉ *Calle Santander*) is easily the best place for reasonably priced *artesanía*.

Named for its location, the **Bus Stop Bookshop** (✉ *Calle Principal at Calle Santander* ☎ *No phone*) has many used books in English.

El Guipil (✉ *Calle Santander*) is a large boutique with a varied selection of handmade items from highland villages.

Ojalá Antiques (✉ *Av. de los Arboles*) has a small but excellent selection of antiques.

SANTA CATARINA PALOPÓ

4 km (2½ mi) southeast of Panajachel.

Santa Catarina Palopó provides an odd mix of deep-seated Cakchiquel tradition and sumptuous luxury in the vacation homes outsiders have built on the fringes of this small town. You'll be surrounded by the brilliant blues and greens of huipils worn by local women as you walk down the cobblestone streets of this picturesque town. (Interestingly enough, the women used to wear predominantly red huipils, but an influx of tourists in the 1960s requesting turquoise blouses caused the local women to change their traditional dress and adopt the gringafied turquoise color scheme.) This is one of the few places in the highlands where men retain traditional dress; their clothing echoes the geometric designs seen in women's huipils. From here you'll be treated to magical views of the trio of volcanoes that loom over the lake. In Santa Catarina you'll see ramshackle homes standing within sight of luxury chalets whose owners arrive as often by helicopter as they do by car.

GETTING HERE AND AROUND

Chicken buses and pickup trucks leave throughout the day from Calle Principal and Calle Santander in Panajachel. Taxi boats leave from the docks in Panajachel.

WHERE TO STAY

$$$$ Fodor's Choice ★ **Casa Palopó.** By far the best B&B on the lake, and one of the country's loveliest hotels, luxurious Casa Palopó has an almost mystical atmosphere. Each of the seven rooms in the main house, decorated with religious-theme artworks from around the world, offers incredible views of the volcanoes. Muted blues run throughout this former villa, mirroring the colors of the lake. Most baths have giant tubs perfect for prolonged soaks. Just down the road, an annex offers two equally sumptuous suites, each with its own pool and hot tub. **Pros:** refined elegance, attentive staff. **Cons:** ideally, need car to stay here. ✉ *Km 6.8, Santa Catarina Palopó* ☎ *7762–2270* 🌐 *www.casapalopo.com* *7 rooms, 2 suites* *In-room: no a/c, kitchen (some), no phone, refrigerator, no TV, Wi-Fi. In-hotel: restaurant, room service, bar, pool, gym, beachfront, no elevator, public Internet, public Wi-Fi, parking (no fee), no kids under 15, no-smoking rooms* ▭ *AE, D, DC, MC, V.*

$$$ **Villa Santa Catarina.** Villa Santa Catarina has outstanding views. The long yellow building with an adobe-tile roof has small rooms, each with a private balcony overlooking the lake. The restaurant serves international fare including pastas, sandwiches, and chicken. You can relax in the pool or head to a series of natural hot springs that are only a few hundred feet away. **Pros:** good value, good restaurant. **Cons:** small rooms. ✉ *Calle de la Playa* ☎ *7762–1291, 2334–8136 in Guatemala City* 🌐 *www.villasdeguatemala.com* *36 rooms* *In-room: no a/c. In-hotel: restaurant, room service, bar, pool, no elevator, laundry service, public Internet, public Wi-Fi, parking (no fee), no-smoking rooms* ▭ *AE, D, DC, MC, V* *EP.*

SAN ANTONIO PALOPÓ

6½ km (4 mi) southeast of Santa Catarina Palopó, 11 km (6½ mi) southeast of Panajachel.

San Antonio Palopó is a quiet farming town, larger, but much less known, than neighboring Santa Catarina Palopó. Most people have plots of land on terraced gardens where they grow green onions, which you may see them cleaning down by the lake. This is one of only a handful of regions in Latin America where men still dress in traditional costumes on a daily basis. Their pants have geometric motifs and calf-length woolen wraparounds fastened by leather belts or red sashes. Women go about their business wearing white blouses with red stripes.

GETTING HERE AND AROUND

Chicken buses and pickup trucks leave throughout the day from Calle Principal and Calle Santander in Panajachel. Taxi boats leave from the docks in Panajachel.

EXPLORING

The beautiful adobe **Iglesia de San Antonio Palopó** stands in a stone plaza that marks the center of town. The interior is particularly peaceful. During the day the steps are a meeting place where all passersby are sure to stop for a while.

WHERE TO STAY

$ **Terrazas del Lago.** This charming hotel overlooking the lake is notable for its floral-pattern stone tiles. Simply decorated rooms have wooden tables and iron candlesticks. Those in front have patios with great vistas. A small restaurant serves simple meals, while several terraces are perfect for a quiet cup of afternoon tea. **Pros:** good value, friendly owners. **Cons:** small rooms. ✉ *CAlle de la Playa* ☎ *7762–0157* 🌐 *www.hotelterrazasdellago.com* *12 rooms* *In-room: no a/c, no phone, no TV. In-hotel: restaurant, parking (no fee), no-smoking rooms* 💳 *No credit cards.*

SHOPPING

On the main street, not far from the church, is an excellent women's textile cooperative, where you see master weavers in action. The process is fascinating to watch, and the finished fabrics are stunning. There's a small shop on-site where the proceeds help sustain the cooperative.

4

SAN LUCAS TOLIMÁN

11 km (7 mi) south of San Antonio Palopó.

San Lucas Tolimán, in the shadow of the Tolimán volcano, is the first town you encounter if approaching Lake Atitlán from the south. (It lies a mere 50 km (30 mi) north of Highway CA-2, which runs through the Pacific lowlands.) San Lucas hosts a Tuesday and Friday market with some decent buys on textiles and baskets. It is also home to one of the lake's nicest lodgings. Several private nature reserves dot the area just outside of town. The folks at the Hotel Tolimán can hook you up with a guided tour.

GETTING HERE AND AROUND

Chicken buses and pickup trucks leave throughout the day from Calle Principal and Calle Santander in Panajachel. Taxi boats leave from the docks in Panajachel.

WHERE TO STAY

$$ **Hotel Tolimán.** Any lodging with its own heliport must cater to an affluent clientele, right? Yet rates are very reasonable here. Opt, if you can, for one of the 14 rooms across the street from the reception. They are scattered throughout a pleasant garden. With their stucco walls, big wooden doors, armoires, antique furniture, tile floors, and hammocks in the breezeways (and some rooms with fireplaces), they echo an old Guatemalan hacienda. Eight other rooms sit either above the reception area or near the parking lot. Beef is the specialty in the restaurant ($–$$), along with great lake views. **Pros:** friendly staff, terrific value, beautiful garden. **Cons:** town is not as interesting as some other lake towns, rooms around parking lot are smaller. ✉ *End of Calle Principal* ☎ *7722–0033* *21 rooms, 1 suite* *In-room: no a/c, no phone, kitchen (some), refrigerator (some), Wi-Fi. In-hotel: restaurant, room*

service, bar, pool, no elevator, laundry service, Internet terminal, parking (no fee), no-smoking rooms ▭ *AE, D, DC, MC, V* 🍽 *BP.*

SANTIAGO ATITLÁN

18 km (11 mi) west of San Lucas Tolimán

★ Across the lake from Panajachel lies its rival in size, Santiago Atitlán, a small city with a fascinating, tragic history. With a population of about 48,000, this capital of the proud and independent Tzutuhil people is one of the largest indigenous communities in Guatemala. It bravely resisted political domination during the country's civil war, which meant that many residents were murdered by the military. After a 1990 massacre in which 11 unarmed people were killed, the villagers protested the presence of the army in their town. To everyone's surprise, the army actually left, and Santiago Atitlán became a model for other highland towns fighting governmental oppression.

A road that leads up from the dock is lined on both sides with shops selling *artesanía*—take a good look at the huipils embroidered with elaborate depictions of fruits, birds, and spirits, Santiago's signature designs. Many local women wear a *tocoyal,* which is a 12-yard-long band wrapped around their forehead. Older men also wear traditional dress, black-and-white-stripe calf-length pants with detailed embroidery below the knee. As happens so many other places in Guatemala, younger men have latched onto Western-style clothing.

GETTING HERE AND AROUND

Chicken buses and pickup trucks leave throughout the day from the intersection of Calle Principal and Calle Santander in Panajachel. Because of robbery—on occasion violent—along the road, there is no overland public transportation between Santiago Atitlán and San Pedro La Laguna. You should not attempt the route either. Ferries (60 minutes) and taxi boats (30 minutes) leave from the docks in Panajachel.

EXPLORING

The main road leads to the squat white 1547 **Iglesia de Santiago Apóstol,** the church dedicated to town patron, St. James the Apostle, but where Tzutuhil deities can be seen in the woodwork around the pulpit. Fondly remembered onetime American parish priest Father Stanley Rother was assassinated in the church rectory by right-wing death squads in 1981 for his outspoken support of the Tzutuhil cause.

On the road west to San Pedro, **Parque de la Paz** commemorates 11 Tzutuhil people, including several children, who were killed when the army open fired on a peaceful demonstration that protested the military presence here. The memorial is a sober reminder of Guatemala's tortured past.

WHERE TO EAT AND STAY

$$ SPANISH ✕ **Bambú.** One of the lake's most popular restaurants is affiliated with the hotel of the same name. Look for the A-frame, thatch-roof structure right by the dock as your taxi boat is pulling in. (Many diners arrive that way, although the virtual absence of lake transport at night makes Bambú a better lunch option, unless you're based in Santiago Atitlán.) Spanish cuisine dominates here, corvina and garlic chicken

CLOSE UP

The Heroes of Santiago Atitlán

In this *American Idol*-ized world, a visit to Santiago Atitlán puts renown and heroism into true perspective.

Oklahoma native Father Stanley Rother (1935–81) arrived as a missionary in Santiago Atitlán in 1968. During his 13 years here, he translated the New Testament into and celebrated mass in the local Tzutuhil language. As time went on, he began to decry the treatment of Guatemala's indigenous peoples at the hands of the army and paramilitary forces. On July 28, 1981, the priest was murdered, presumably by paramilitaries, in the rectory adjoining the parish church. Although Rother is buried in Oklahoma, his heart is interred in the church here. A nascent movement to have Rother beatified and eventually canonized has been undertaken by officials of the Archdiocese of Oklahoma City (🌐 *www.catharchdioceseokc.org*). Click on the site's CAUSE FOR BEATIFICATION link for information. Rother's writings were compiled posthumously and published in a book, *The Shepherd Cannot Run: Letters of Stanley Rother.*

Turn the clock ahead to December 1, 1990, when, by all accounts, a night of drunken revelry on the part of soldiers posted near Santiago turned tragic. Townspeople assembled just outside of town after midnight December 2 to discuss what could be done about harassment from army forces. They had witnessed the deaths of hundreds of their fellow citizens throughout the war. When soldiers appeared to break up the meeting, members of the assemblage began to hurl stones. Soldiers fired into the crowd, killing 11, many of them children, and injuring 40. The massacre drew national outrage, and townspeople petitioned to have the military forces removed from the town. President Serrano Elías himself apologized and complied. To this day, the Guatemalan army, whose internal security role was eliminated with the 1996 peace accords, does not set foot in Santiago Atitlán.

4

being particular favorites. Fruits, vegetables, and herbs are grown in the on-site hotel garden. A crackling fireplace keeps you warm on chilly evenings, of which there are many here. ✉ *1 km (½ mi) east of town* ☎ *7721–7332* 💳 *AE, D, DC, MC, V.*

$$ 🏨 **Bambú.** On the beautifully tended grounds at the dock entrance to Santiago Atitlán is a string of rooms with private patios overlooking the lake. Stone pathways loop through a series of taxonomically arranged gardens (cacti in one, flowers in the next, and so on)—and most of the hotel's restaurant's fruits, vegetables, and herbs are cultivated out back. Canoes are available for paddling around the lake. **Pros:** top-notch restaurant; beautiful grounds; close to docks. **Cons:** some small rooms. ✉ *1 km (½ mi) east of town* ☎ *7721–7332* 🌐 *www.ecobambu.com* *11 rooms* *In-room: no a/c, no TV, Wi-Fi. In-hotel: restaurant, bar, pool, parking (no fee), no-smoking rooms* 💳 *AE, D, DC, MC, V* 🍴 *CP.*

$$–$$$ Fodor's Choice ★ 🏨 **Posada de Santiago.** This longtime favorite has deluxe accommodations in private stone-wall bungalows with volcano views, as well as a few rooms and suites in the main building. Pass through the carved-wood doors of your bungalow and you'll find a fireplace and thick wool

CLOSE UP

Drinking and Smoking with the Saints

Arguably Guatemala's most curious object of veneration is the cigar-smoking, rum-swilling deity Maximón. He is still actively idolized a few places in the highlands, most notably in Santiago Atitlán, and in the small town of Zunil, near Quetzaltenango, where he is known by his alternate name, San Simón.

Scholars debate just what Maximón (whose name is pronounced *Mah-shee-MOHN*) is supposed to represent. His cult likely descended from worship of the Mayan god Mam, but the Catholic church holds that he is the apostle Peter. (Peter's original name was Simon, of course.) Some suggest that Maximón is really Judas Iscariot, the betrayer of Jesus. Others liken him to Spanish conquistador Pedro de Alvarado. In any case, according to tradition, he is more a malevolent than benevolent being, and it's best to stay on his good side with offerings.

As you get off the boat here in Santiago, small children may offer to lead you to the **Casa de Maximón,** the local home housing his figure, in exchange for a few quetzals. (Five will suffice.) You will need their guidance, for Maximón's guardianship changes each year during an elaborate Holy Week observance, a different member of the local *cofrade* (religious society) taking charge of the wooden idol and accommodating his many faithful followers. When the children bring you to the house, you'll be ushered inside to see the shrine. Maximón's stern figure is dressed much like a 19th-century Spanish nobleman, and is said to like cigars and rum. (He apparently still smokes in spite of Guatemala's strict no-smoking laws.) If you haven't brought such items to leave in the collection plate, another Q5 bill will do just fine. (Make it Q10 if you plan to take a photo.) Maximón is reputed to have proffered myriad favors, from curing illnesses to helping the faithful get a bigger house. We can't vouch for your success.

blankets piled high on the bed. The restaurant (¢–$) serves exquisite food, such as smoked chicken píbil in a tangy red sauce and Thai coconut shrimp. The wine list is surprisingly extensive. On the premises is a small store where you can rent canoes and mountain bikes. **Pros:** attentive staff, good restaurant. **Cons:** far from center of town. ✉ *1 km (½ mi) south of town* ☎ *7721–7366* 🌐 *www.posadadesantiago.com* *9 rooms, 3 suites, 7 bungalows* *In-room: no a/c, no TV (some). In-hotel: restaurant, bar, pool, bicycles, Internet terminal, no-smoking rooms* 💳 *AE, D, DC, MC, V.*

SAN PEDRO LA LAGUNA

10 km (6 mi) northeast of Santiago Atitlán.

"It's the new Pana," proclaim its growing number of fans. Indeed, as Panajachel and its international population have matured—a few wags would say "gentrified"—the young and the restless have crossed the lake and set up shop in burgeoning San Pedro La Laguna. This traditional Tzutuhil fishing village knows it is on the cusp of something, but what that "something" will be can only be revealed in someone's crystal ball. This is still proudly budget-travel territory. For now, lodgings and facilities fall into the "as long as you're not too fussy" category, but all offer good value for very little money. That will no doubt change as the world begins to discover San Pedro.

GETTING HERE AND AROUND

Chicken buses and pickup trucks leave throughout the day from Calle Principal and Calle Santander in Panajachel. Because of robbery—on occasion violent—along the road, there is no overland public transportation between Santiago Atitlán and San Pedro. You should not attempt the route either. For San Pedro and all lake towns to the east, overland public transportation goes counter-clockwise around the lake to avoid the dangerous section of road. Taxi boats leave from the docks in Panajachel and Santiago Atitlán.

4

WHERE TO STAY

¢ **Hotel Mansión del Lago.** Rooms are simple here—expect tiled floors and two beds each—but the hillside location just above the dock gives you the best views in town, especially if you lodge on the top floor. All guests have access to the rooftop terrace. **Pros:** good budget value, immaculate rooms. **Cons:** rooms are simply furnished. ✉ *4 Av. and 8 Calle* ☎ *7721–8041* 🌐 *www.hotelmansiondellago.com* *18 rooms, 16 with bath* *In-room: no a/c, no phone, no TV (some). In hotel: no elevator, public Internet, laundry service, parking (no fee), no-smoking rooms* 💳 *V* 🍽 *EP.*

¢ **Hotel Nahual Maya.** Make this your first choice in San Pedro. It costs no more than the other budget options, and provides you with a big step up in quality. Rooms are on two floors—those on the top floor have good views—and are bright and cheery, with either a double or a pair of twin beds. **Pros:** good budget value, top floor has good lake views. **Cons:** rooms are simply furnished. ✉ *100 meters from dock* ☎ *7721–8158* *16 rooms* *In-room: no a/c, no phone, no TV (some). In-hotel: no elevator, parking (no fee), no-smoking rooms* 💳 *No credit cards* 🍽 *EP.*

SAN JUAN LA LAGUNA

3 km (1½ mi) north of San Pedro La Laguna.

The tiny, one-hotel village of San Juan La Laguna bills itself as "the cleanest town in Guatemala," and it lives up to its claim. San Juan is a great place to get away from the crowds and get a more authentic look at indigenous life on the lake.

GETTING HERE AND AROUND

To get here, take a water taxi from any lake town and ask the driver to drop you at the Muelle Uxlabil, the Ecohotel Uxlabil's own dock. The boat ride from San Pedro La Laguna takes five minutes.

Chicken buses and pickup trucks leave throughout the day from Calle Principal and Calle Santander in Panajachel.

EXPLORING

There are several artisan collectives in the town's center. **Lema** (✉ *San Juan La Laguna* ☎ *5967–7747*) is an association of local weavers who use environmentally friendly dyes in their work. **Artesanos de San Juan** (✉ *San Juan La Laguna* ☎ *5849–6434*) is a cooperative of 58 artisans who weave textiles and sell from their showroom just north of the dock. Atitlán is known for its fair-trade coffee, and a local 140-member cooperative, **La Voz que Clama en el Desierto** (✉ *San Juan La Laguna* ☎ *7723–2301*) —that translates as "The voice that cries in the desert"—offers tours of its coffee-processing facilities and artisan shop. Call to arrange a visit.

LANGUAGE SCHOOLS IN SAN PEDRO LA LAGUNA

Arguably Guatemala's hippest locale for studying Spanish means a large, young foreign population has the same idea. Interact with local people, rather than fellow students if you expect your language skills to progress.

Casa Rosario Spanish School (✉ *Cantón Sanjay* ☎ *7613–6401* 🌐 *www.casarosario.com*).

Corazón Maya Spanish School (✉ *Playa Dorada* ☎ *7721–8160* 🌐 *www.corazonmaya.com*).

San Pedro Spanish School (✉ *7 Av. 2–20* ☎ *7721–8176* 🌐 *www.sanpedrospanishschool.com*).

WHERE TO STAY

$ **Ecohotel Uxlabil.** San Juan La Laguna's best (and only) lodging option, the Uxlabil has its own thatched dock and extensive grounds with a medicinal herb garden, Mayan sauna, and Jacuzzi. The simple rooms have textured walls reminiscent of beach sand, rather hard beds, and traditional-textile bedclothes. **Pros:** good budget value; nice garden. **Cons:** phone number at hotel difficult to contact; basic rooms; hard mattresses. ✉ *San Juan La Laguna, Muelle Uxlabil* ☎ *5990–6016, 2366–9555 in Guatemala City* 🌐 *www.uxlabil.com* *10 rooms, 2 bungalows* *In-room: no a/c, kitchen (some), no TV. In-hotel: restaurant, bar, no-smoking rooms* *AE, D, DC, MC, V* *BP.*

SAN MARCOS LA LAGUNA

15 min by boat from Panajachel.

San Marcos has acquired fame as a center of New Age devotion, thanks to the presence of the Pirámides del Ka meditation center/lodge. The tiny village does cater mostly to tourists of all stripes, however, and even those whose vacation schedule is not "Yoga at 9, meditation at 10" will find their own bliss here. (San Marcos is home to a couple of our favorite Guatemalan hotels.) From the dock you can reach the center of the village by walking uphill along a narrow cobblestone path. The village itself has one or two stores and a restaurant around the central square. **■ TIP→ If you plan on staying in San Marcos, you should remember to bring a flashlight, as much of the town lacks electricity. Also, lodgings here can be difficult to contact by phone at times. Keep trying.**

GETTING HERE AND AROUND

Chicken buses and pickup trucks leave throughout the day from Calle Principal and Calle Santander in Panajachel.

WHERE TO EAT AND STAY

¢ ITALIAN **Il Giardino.** An open-air restaurant centered around a bamboo hut and a fire pit, this little Italian eatery offers such continental favorites as fondue and spaghetti, and also has a good selection of vegetarian entrées. There's live music from time to time, making this one of San Marcos's social hubs. Be sure to leave room for the delicious tiramisu. *San Marcos La Laguna 5891–0482 No credit cards.*

$ Fodor's Choice ★ **Hotel Jinava.** This small hotel is in a secluded cove, and each of its stone-floor, stucco bungalows is shaded by avocado and papaya trees. Ask the friendly German owner to make you a tropical drink, one of his favorite pastimes. If piña coladas aren't your thing, request a massage—he is rumored to be the best masseur on the lake. The restaurant serves up great curries and other international dishes. **Pros:** good value; beautiful, secluded setting; friendly staff. **Cons:** steep climb from pier. *San Marcos La Laguna 5406–5986 www.hoteljinava.com 5 bungalows In-room: no a/c, no phone, no TV. In-hotel: restaurant, bar, no elevator, no-smoking rooms No credit cards.*

$ **Las Pirámides del Ka.** Here is the place that gives San Marcos its New Age-y reputation. The tranquillity of the lake provides the perfect setting for this yoga retreat, which offers day-, week-, and month-long courses. Pyramid-shaped cabins concentrate energies for spiritualists seeking that elusive transcendence. The reasonable price includes accommodations, classes, and use of the sauna and other facilities. You stay here, you're expected to participate. (Guests staying at other lodgings are welcome to enroll in courses, too.) As they are fond of saying here: This isn't a hotel. **Pros:** many activities; perfect for New Age devotees. **Cons:** basic accommodation; difficult to make advance reservations. *San Marcos La Laguna 5205–7151 www.laspiramidesdelka.com 5 rooms In-room: no a/c, no phone, no TV. In-hotel: restaurant, no-smoking rooms No credit cards.*

$–$$ **Posada Schumann.** Full of old-fashioned charm, this little inn has bungalows set along a narrow swath of garden stretching down to the lake. Exposed stonework and unfinished wood paneling lend the place a slightly rustic feel, but the rooms are enlivened by the festive colors from local textiles. The hot water can be unreliable. You'll get a 10% discount if you pay in cash rather than with a credit card. **Pros:** friendly staff; beautiful woodwork. **Cons:** erratic hot-water supply; can be difficult to contact by phone. *San Marcos La Laguna 5202–2216 6 rooms, 2 rooms without bath, 4 bungalows In-room: no a/c, no phone, safe, kitchen (some), refrigerator (some), no TV. In-hotel: restaurant, laundry, no-smoking rooms AE, D, DC, MC, V.*

JAIBALITO

10-min boat trip west of Panajachel.

So small that it rarely appears on maps of the region, Jaibalito is the most undisturbed of the villages surrounding Lago Atitlán. Santa Cruz La Laguna is a short walk away, but otherwise Jaibalito is quite isolated. There is no boat service after 6 PM, so this village is only for travelers seeking peace and quiet. ■ **TIP→ Lodgings here can be difficult to contact by phone at times. Keep trying.**

GETTING HERE AND AROUND

Chicken buses and pickup trucks leave throughout the day from Calle Principal and Calle Santander in Panajachel. Taxi boats leave from the docks in Panajachel.

WHERE TO STAY

$$–$$$ **La Casa del Mundo.** Built atop a cliff overlooking the azure waters, this gorgeous inn unquestionably has a great vantage point for gazing at Lago Atitlán. All the rooms have views, but those from Number 1 and Number 3 are the most breathtaking. If you can tear yourself away from the windows, you'll notice that the beautifully decorated rooms have wood-beam ceilings, red-tile floors, and stucco-and-stone walls hung with local handicrafts. If you want to get a closer look at the lake, kayaks are available. Meals are served family style in the cozy restaurant (¢–$). **Pros:** terrific views; friendly staff. **Cons:** some rooms are steep climb from pier. *Jaibalito dock 5218–5332 www.lacasadelmundo.com 12 rooms, 8 with bath In-room: no a/c, no phone, no TV. In-hotel: restaurant, no elevator, no-smoking rooms No credit cards.*

$$$ **Lomas de Tzununá.** Our nod for the best views on the lake goes to this cliffside hotel just outside Jaibalito near the tiny village of Tzununá. All rooms and the restaurant and pool share the same amazing vista. The payback for those views is the 100-meter (330-foot) climb up from the dock via hundreds of steps to reach the place. (Better to make advance arrangements with the hotel to have someone meet you in Tzununá and transport you here via Jeep.) No matter how you get here, lodging is in ample-size stone and wood bungalows with tile floors and bright drapes and spreads. The restaurant ($$) serves local and international cuisine, with seafood the specialty. **Pros:** best views on the lake; friendly staff. **Cons:** long climb up from dock. *Tzununá 5201–8272 www.lomasdetzununa.com 10 rooms In-room: no a/c, no phone, no TV. In-hotel: restaurant, room service, bar, pool, water sports, laundry service, Internet terminal, no-smoking rooms AE, D, DC, MC, V BP.*

$ **Vulcano Lodge.** This lodge amidst a coffee plantation has well-tended gardens strung with hammocks for afternoon naps. The tastefully decorated rooms are on the small side, but they all have private terraces. Alas, there are no views of the lake. The restaurant (¢–$) serves up international favorites. **Pros:** good budget value; beautiful garden. **Cons:** small rooms; no lake views; long walk from pier. *Jaibalito 5410–2237 www.atitlan.com/vulcano.htm 8 rooms, 1 suite In-room: no a/c, no phone, no TV. In-hotel: restaurant, no elevator, no-smoking rooms AE, D, DC, MC, V.*

SANTA CRUZ LA LAGUNA

10-min boat ride west of Panajachel.

Your first view of Santa Cruz La Laguna is the hubbub of a couple of hotels and a few vendors who hang around the dock. (A boat is realistically the only way to get here.) It's a steep walk up to the hillside village itself, but the hale and hearty are rewarded with a stroll through a Tzutuhil community that most travelers overlook. The square adobe houses are positioned precariously on the slopes, looking as if they might be washed away by the next heavy rain. A highlight of this little village is a squat adobe church, the **Iglesia de Santa Cruz,** in the main plaza. Make sure to look inside at where the walls are lined with carved wooden saints.

■TIP➜ Lodgings here can be difficult to contact by phone at times. Keep trying.

DECEMBER 29, 1996

Guatemala has just over a decade of peace under its belt, a fact you'll be reminded of each time you pick up a one-quetzal coin. PAZ FIRME Y DURADERA (FIRM AND LASTING PEACE) reads the inscription, along with the date the peace accords were signed ending the 36-year civil war. On the center of the coin, the word *paz* (peace) flows into a stylized illustration of a dove.

GETTING HERE AND AROUND

Chicken buses and pickup trucks leave throughout the day from Calle Principal and Calle Santander in Panajachel. Taxi boats leave from the docks in Panajachel.

WHERE TO STAY

$ **Arca de Noé.** Magnificent views are the big draw at this rustic retreat. Rooms, in several wood-and-stone bungalows, are small but neat. The delicious home cooking is served family style in the main building, which resembles a New England farmhouse. The menu ($) changes constantly, but each meal comes with fresh vegetables and bread hot out of the oven. Electricity is solar-generated, with gas used to fuel the supply of hot water. **Pros:** good budget value; solar-powered electricity. **Cons:** electricity can be erratic at times; rustic rooms. ✉ *Santa Cruz La Laguna* ☎ *5515–3712* ✉ *arcasantacruz@yahoo.com* *10 rooms, 5 with bath, 5 bungalows* *In-room: no a/c, no phone, no TV. In-hotel: restaurant, no-smoking rooms* ▭ *No credit cards.*

$–$$ **Hotel Isla Verde.** A series of A-frame cabins climb the hillside garden here up from the hotel's private dock. (The views are lovely, but the walk can be bracing.) Inside the cabins, expect rustic wood and blindingly white walls decorated with primitivist art. We like the whimsical, partially open bathrooms. (A hummingbird might be your companion in the shower.) You'll receive a 10-percent discount if you pay in cash. Thursday evenings this becomes one of Santa Cruz's places to hang out. The folks here present a weekly documentary film. The Q20 admission includes the price of one beer or herbal tea. **Pros:** good value; friendly owners; lovely garden setting. **Cons:** some rooms are a steep climb up from reception; some shared bathrooms reached only from outside. ✉ *Santa Cruz La Laguna* ☎ *5760–2648* ⊕ *www.islaverdeatitlan.com* *9 rooms, 6 with bath* *In-room: no a/c no phone, no TV. In-hotel: restaurant, bar, pool, laundry service, Internet terminal, Wi-Fi, no-smoking rooms* ▭ *AE, D, DC, MC, V* *EP.*

$ **La Iguana Perdida.** The traditionally backpacker-oriented "Lost Iguana" is part hotel and part summer camp. It hasn't forgotten its roots, but has upgraded some of its offerings, which range from simple to splendid. The restaurant ($) serves up good family-style meals, and the dormitory rooms can hold up to eight of your traveling companions. For a bit more privacy, choose one of the stone-floor, thatch-roof bungalows—each has its own balcony—lit with kerosene lamps. (Even the nicer rooms are a good value.) Guests tend to be fairly young—most come for scuba-diving courses. You can also choose between Spanish, art, or weaving classes, too. **■TIP➔ Stop by for the Saturday-night barbecue, even if you aren't staying here.** **Pros:** good value; lots of activity. **Cons:** young vibe; difficult to find space on weekends. ✉ *Santa Cruz La Laguna* ☎ *5706–4117, 7762–2621 in Panajachel* 🌐 *www.laiguanaperdida.com* *14 rooms, 3 cabins, 2 dormitory rooms* *In-room: no a/c, no phone, no TV. In-hotel: restaurant, bar, diving, no elevator, public Internet, no-smoking rooms* *No credit cards.*

OUTDOOR ACTIVITIES

There are plenty of opportunities for hiking in the hills around Santa Cruz. It is the starting point of a scenic four-hour walk to San Marcos La Laguna. The trail passes through several tiny villages and over gusty bluffs overlooking the lake.

Lago Atitlán's wealth of underwater wonders draws divers from around the world. **ATI Divers** (✉ *Iguana Perdida* ☎ *5706–4117* ✉ *C. Santander, Panajachel* ☎ *7762–2621*) is a certified diving school that offers courses for all levels, from basic certification to dive master.

SOLOLÁ

5 km (3 mi) north of Panajachel.

The Atitlán area's "metropolis" of Sololá is the region's administrative capital. Sololá lies a steep, 20-minute climb up from Panajachel and offers stunning mountainside views of the lake. You'll find one of Guatemala's largest markets here. Something goes on, on a smaller scale, every weekday, but Friday is the principal market day, with produce and a decent selection of souvenirs for sale. Sololá remains one of the few places in the highlands where men wear traditional dress, in particular, gold-embroidered jackets distinctive to the town. Sololá's symbol of pride is its 1914 clock tower, still ticking despite damage in Guatemala's 1976 earthquake.

GETTING HERE AND AROUND

Sololá lies about 20 minutes north (and a steep uphill) from Panajachel. Chicken buses and pickup trucks leave throughout the day from Calle Principal and Calle Santander in Panajachel.

ESSENTIALS

Medical Assistance **Farmacia Batres** (✉ *Calle Principal 0–32, Zona 2Zona 2, Sololá* ☎ *7762–1485*). **Hosptial Nacional** (✉ *Calzada Venancio Barrios, Sololá* ☎ *7762–4122*).

EN ROUTE

A crossroads called Los Encuentros marks the turnoff on the Pan-American Highway for Chichicastenango. Just north of the junction, you'll pass through a mandatory vehicle inspection. El Quiché, the region Chichicastenango is in, is a protected agricultural zone. Officials need to determine that you aren't bringing in any outside produce with attendant pests who have hitched a ride.

CHICHICASTENANGO

Fodor'sChoice ★ *37 km (23 mi) north of Panajachel, 108 km (67 mi) northwest of Antigua, 144 km (86 mi) northwest of Guatemala City, 94 km (56 mi) northeast of Quetzaltenango.*

Perched on a hillside, Chichicastenango ("the place of the nettles") is in many ways a typical highland town. The narrow cobblestone streets converge on a wide plaza where most days you'll find a few old men passing the time. You'd hardly recognize the place Thursday and Sunday, the two days a week on which one of the world's most famous markets takes place, when row after row of colorful stalls fill the square and overflow into the adjoining alleys. There's a dizzying array of handmade items, from wooden masks to woolen blankets to woven baskets. Much of the *artesanía* is produced for tourists, but walk a few blocks in any direction and you'll find where the locals do their shopping. South of the square is a narrow street where women sell chickens. To the east you might run across a family trying to coax a just-purchased pig up a rather steep hill.

Believe it or not, Chichicastenango does not disappear the other five days a week; if you come here on, say, a Tuesday, you'll have the place to yourself. Few tourists actually do that. At just an hour from Panajachel, two hours from Antigua or Quetzaltenango, or three hours from the capital, Chichicastenango will always be Guatemala's consummate day trip for most. But a visit here on a *non*-market day gives you a chance to see "Chichi"—few people ever bother to wrap their tongues around the entire six-syllable name—the spiritual center of Quiché Mayan culture, at its most serene.

GETTING HERE AND AROUND

The Pan-American Highway (CA-1) reaches a crossroads called Los Encuentros, from where you head north to Chichicastenango and beyond.

Veloz Quichelense has public chicken buses that leave Guatemala City on the half hour between 5 AM and 6 PM and return on a similar schedule. Chichi has no central terminal; buses congregate near the corner of 5 Avenida and 5 Calle.

Every tour operator in Guatemala City, Antigua, Panajachel, and Quetzaltenango can arrange round-trip minivan transportation to Chichi on Thursday and Sunday market days. Options are fewer other days of the week. Chichicastenango's only tour company, Chichi Turkaj–Tours, is wellregarded, and arranges transportation around the region.

ESSENTIALS

Bank **Bancared** (✉ *5 Av. and 6 Calle, Chichicastenango*).

Bus Contacts **Veloz Quichelense** (✉ *Terminal de Buses, Zona 4, Guatemala City* ☎ *No phone*).

Emergencies **Police** (☎ *7756–1365*).

Medical Assistance **Farmacia Batres** (✉ *6 Av. 6–05, Chichicastenango* ☎ *7756–1029*).

Tours **Chichi Turkaj–Tours** (✉ *5 Calle 4–42, Zona 1, Chichicastenango* ☎ *7756–2111*).

Visitor and Tour Info Oficina de Información Turística (✉ *7 Calle at 5 Av., Zona 1, Chichicastenango* ☎ *7756–0222*).

EXPLORING

Chichicastenango does offer more than its market, and a break from shopping to see the town's sights is essential if you want some insight into Quiché culture. On market days a small cadre of guides certified by INGUAT, the national tourist office, meets the tour buses. (Look for them in their red vests and with INGUAT badges.) They speak Spanish and English, and can rustle up colleagues who speak French, German, Dutch, or Italian if need be. On many levels, we recommend their services. They can provide insight into the sights that you'll never get on your own. They are also protection insurance: there have been a few robberies of tourists visiting the cemetery and the Pascual Abaj shrine. Guides charge Q300 for a half-day tour, or Q100 for an hour-long abbreviated circuit. ■ **TIP→ Wear sturdy shoes. Chichi's rough stone streets are murder on the feet if you don't.**

TOP ATTRACTIONS

2 **Iglesia de Santo Tomás.** Standing watch over the square is this gleaming white Dominican church, Guatemala's most intriguing, busy with worshippers all day and late into the night. The structure dates from 1540, built on the site of an ancient temple, and locals say a block of stone near the massive front doors is all that remains of the altar. The Quiché people still consider Chichicastenango their spiritual city. Perhaps no church in the country better represents the concept of syncretism, the blending of theologies, than does Santo Tomás. Church officials look the other way as Mayan ceremonies are still practiced here today. In fact, once the daily 9 AM mass ends, the rest of the day and evening are given over to indigenous rituals conducted by shamans (*curanderos* in Spanish, or *chuchkajaues* in Quiché), who wave around pungent incense during the day, and at night toss rose petals and pine needles into a raging fire right on the steps of the church as part of purification rituals. ■ **TIP→ Take care: If you are at all sensitive to heavy fragrance, the incense aroma can be overpowering.** The age-old ritual has darkened the once-white steps—18 steps correspond to the months in the Mayan calendar—leading to the church entrance. ■ **TIP→ Outsiders should not pass through the front doors. Instead, enter through the door via the courtyard on the building's right side. Also, under no circumstances should you take photos inside the church.** Inside, candles are affixed to 12 tablets embedded in the floor, four each representing sun, moon, and rain. Curanderos place conjoined candles there on behalf of married couples, solitary candles on behalf of single people. Yellow candles represent entreaties for business affairs; blue, for rain; green, for agriculture; and white, for health. ✉ *East end of Parque Central*

Fodor's Choice ★

1 **Parque Central.** As in most colonial villages, the heart of Chichicastenango is its central square, and any tour begins here. It's pretty tranquil here when the market isn't open, but not on Thursday and Sunday when hundreds of vendors (and buyers) arrive from near and far. The market long ago outgrew this square, and spills onto adjoining streets. All the major sights

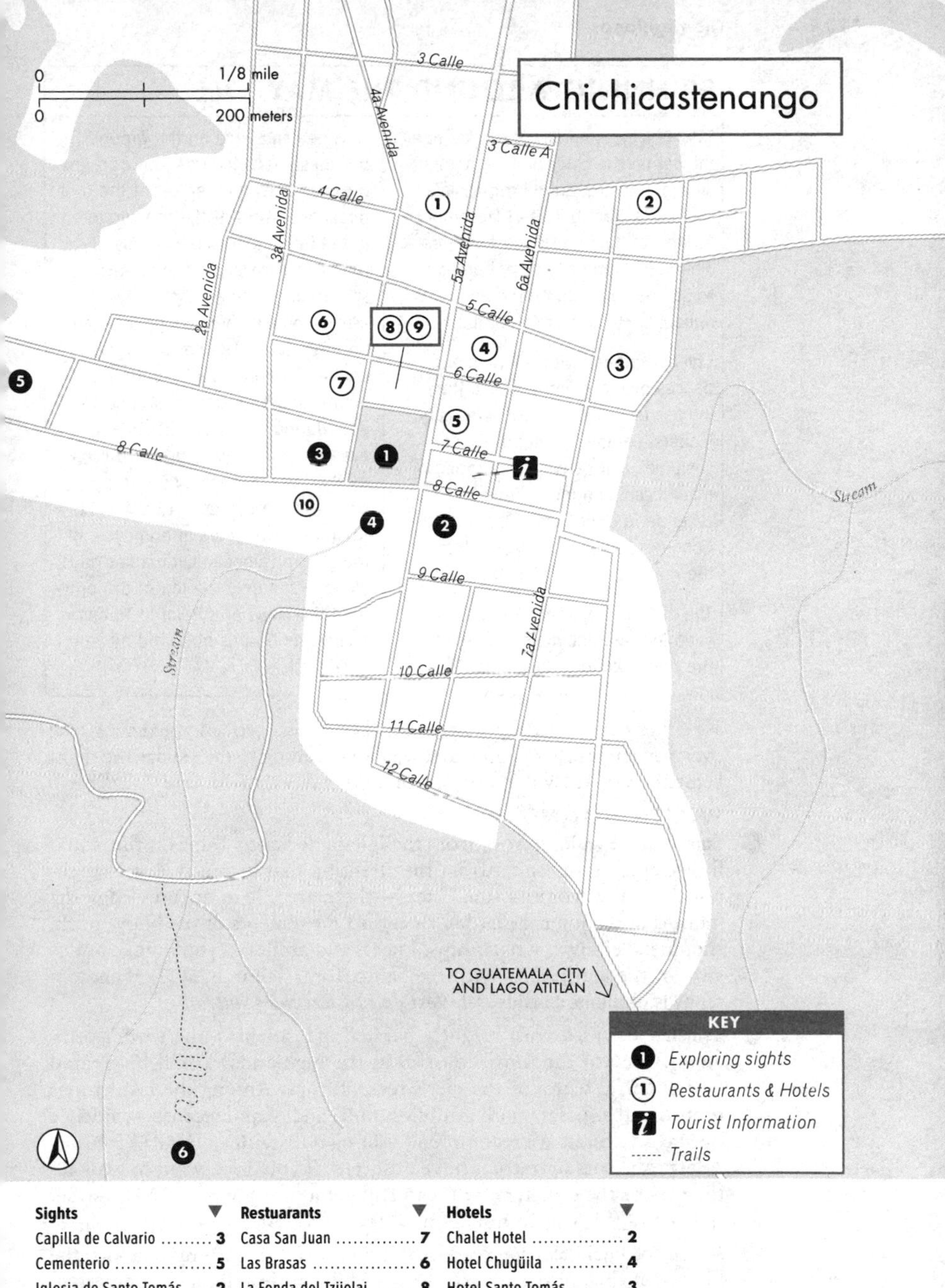

Sights		Restuarants		Hotels	
Capilla de Calvario	3	Casa San Juan	7	Chalet Hotel	2
Cementerio	5	Las Brasas	6	Hotel Chugüila	4
Iglesia de Santo Tomás	2	La Fonda del Tzijolaj	8	Hotel Santo Tomás	3
Museo Regional	4	La Villa de los Cofrades	9	Mayan Inn	10
Parque Central	1	Tu Café	5	Posada El Arco	1
Pascual Abaj	6				

SPINNING AROUND THE MAYPOLE

Take Chichicastenango's market and ratchet up the color and excitement several notches. Sound impossible? Just come here between December 13 and 21, and you'll see how possible it is as the city pays homage to St. Thomas, its patron saint, in its annual Santo Tomás celebrations.

Chichi explodes with parades and dances over the entire week. During the festivities the *cofrades* (city leaders) parade in elegant silver costumes and carry staffs topped by magnificent sun medallions. In the *Baile de la Conquista* ("Dance of the Conquest," masked dancers reenact the meeting of Old and New Worlds.

The highlight of Santo Tomás is a variation on a maypole dance, called the *palo volador* ("flyer's pole"). Anyone can dance on the ground, but these participants—four of them dress as birds and represent the four directions—start at the top, wrapped in their own individual strands of rope and unravel a bit with each spin through the air until they arrive, completely unwrapped, safely on the ground. The dance requires elaborate choreography, with dancers making 13 rotations around the pole during their descent. As with everything in Mayan culture, there's method to the math (and in this case, to the madness): 13 x 4 = 52, the number of years in one cycle of the Mayan calendar. On market day you can see only the top of the pole from the steps of the Santo Tomás church. Its base is obscured by vendors' stalls.

are either here or nearby. Three blocks north is Arco Gucumatz, an arch over 5 Avenida where you watch vendors heading to the square the night before or *very* early the morning of market day. ✉ *5 Av. and 7 Calle.*

WORTH NOTING

3 **Capilla de Calvario.** Across from the Iglesia de Santo Tomás is this squat little chapel. It doesn't attract the attention that its much larger neighbor does, but from its steep steps—there are 13, to acknowledge the months in the lunar calendar, or the 13 movements of the body (neck, shoulders, elbows, wrists, hips, knees, and ankles)—you'll have a nice view of the market. As with the Santo Tomás church, ■ **TIP→ photography is prohibited inside.** ✉ *West end of Parque Cantral.*

5 **Cementerio.** Filled with brightly painted mausoleums, the town's cemetery is one of the most colorful in the highlands. You'll be treated to wonderful views of the city's red rooftops. Among the headstones topped with crosses you'll doubtless find candles and incense—evidence of Mayan rituals. We recommend visiting only with an INGUAT guide. A few robberies of tourists have occurred. If you don't want to walk all the way to the cemetery, you can still get a nice photo from the street in front of the Mayan Inn. ✉ *West end of 8 Calle.*

4 **Museo Regional Colección Rossbach.** If you want to learn more about the history of Chichicastenango, check out this little colonial-era building, which displays pre-Columbian artifacts that came from the private collection of a local priest. Painted scenes depicting Mayan history adorn the front of the building. ✉ *Next to Iglesia de Santo Tomás* ⏲ *Sun. 8–2; Tues.–Wed., Fri.–Sat. 8–12:30 and 2–4:30; Thurs. 8–4* 🎫 *Q5.*

WATCH YOUR CAMERA

Photography is a touchy subject in what is arguably Guatemala's most photogenic city. It is prohibited outright inside the Santo Tomás and Calvario churches on the main plaza. Snapping away outdoors at people observing rituals in the cemetery or at the Pascual Abaj shrine is also considered intrusive. As always in Guatemala, fears of child abduction among many local people mean that you should not photograph children you do not know or show any undue interest in them.

❻ **Pascual Abaj.** Local shamans lead villagers in special rites at this site whose name translates as "stone of sacrifice" perched on a hilltop south of town. The shrine is dedicated to Huyup Tak'ah, the Mayan god of the earth, who receives offerings of flowers, incense, liquor, and, occasionally, slaughtered chickens. Because it's one of the most accessible of the highland shrines, Pascual Abaj often attracts travelers eager to see these rituals firsthand. Be as unobtrusive as possible, and always ask permission before taking photos. (The answer will almost always be no, though.) To see the shrine, follow 9 Calle until you see the signs for the narrow footpath up the hill. Boys hanging around the Parque Central will offer to guide you to the shrine for a small fee, and can tell you when the rituals will take place. Robberies of tourists have occurred along the route, so we recommend using the services of the official red-vested INGUAT guides instead. There is a mask factory on-site. ✉ *South of Chichicastenango.*

4

NEED A BREAK?

Chichi's best selection of hot beverages is served up at Tzigan Tinamit, a small café that sits on the corner of 5 Avenida and 6 Calle, the street you are likely to walk between your minivan shuttle and the market. These folks brew up all manner of cappuccinos, espressos, mochas, and hot chocolate, all perfect to wrap your hands around on a chilly day, of which there are many here. Not that you're likely to be lugging your laptop here on market day, but you'll find Wi-Fi access, too. ✉ *5 Av. 5–67* ☎ *7756–1144*.

WHERE TO EAT

Chichicastenango's eateries do a brisk business on market day. No matter where you eat lunch on Thursday and Sunday, expect a few vendors to stroll in and show you their wares, even if you dine on the second floor. Proprietors don't seem too anxious to shoo them away, but a simple "*No, gracias*" from you is all it takes for them to leave.

$ LATIN AMERICAN

✕ **Casa San Juan.** Though smack-dab in the middle of the market hubbub, this peaceful second-floor restaurant, with its wrought-iron chairs and wood tables, offers a reasonably quiet respite from the activity below. These folks dish up their signature *pollo estilo San Juan* (chicken breast in tomato sauce), with guacamole salad and rice on the side. The menu makes a big deal of specifying that the chile relleno is "not spicy." It's actually a beef and vegetable-filled bell pepper, a signature highland dish. Whatever your main dish, be sure to accompany it with the warm homemade tortillas. Sunday market-day lunch gives way to

CLOSE UP

Market Days in the Highlands

Believe it or not, highland markets mean more than Thursday and Sunday in Chichicastenango. Most towns hold a market one or two days a week, drawing buyers and sellers from miles around. None are as famous to the outside world as Chichi's, but you'll feel like a real insider, for example, knowing that the twice-weekly market in Momostenango is *the* place to go for good buys on blankets. Others have nothing you'd be interested in buying; colorful though Nebaj's Thursday affair is, you'll likely not want to cart a hen home, even if she is a prolific egg layer. Vendors at lesser-known markets rarely see outsiders; all will be amused to welcome an obvious visitor. Show an interest, strike up a conversation, make a new friend or two, and always ask permission before you take photos of individuals.

Almolonga: produce. *Wednesday, Saturday*

Chajul: produce, some textiles. *Tuesday, Friday*

Chichicastenango: souvenirs, textiles, produce, livestock. *Thursday, Sunday*

Chimaltenango: souvenirs, textiles, produce. *Monday, Friday*

Comalapa: textiles, produce, livestock. *Tuesday*

Huehuetenango: textiles, produce, livestock. *Wednesday*

Momostenango: woolens, blankets, produce, livestock. *Wednesday, Sunday*

Nebaj: produce, livestock. *Thursday, Sunday*

Olintepeque: livestock. *Tuesday*

Panajachel: produce, livestock. *Thursday*

Patzún: textiles, produce, livestock. *Tuesday, Sunday*

Quetzaltenango: produce, livestock, some textiles. *First Sunday of month*

Sacapulas: produce, livestock, some textiles. *Thursday*

Salcajá: textiles, produce, livestock. *Tuesday*

San Andrés Xecul: produce, livestock. *Thursday*

San Francisco El Alto: produce, livestock, some textiles. *Friday*

San Lucas Tolimán: textiles, baskets. *Tuesday, Friday*

Santa Clara La Laguna: textiles, produce. *Sunday*

Santa Cruz del Quiché: produce, livestock. *Thursday*

Santiago Atitlán: textiles. *Friday*

Sololá: produce, some textiles. *Friday*

Tecpán: textiles, produce. *Wednesday, Sunday*

Todos Santos Cuchumatán: produce. *Thursday, Saturday*

Totonicapán: toys, ceramics, produce, livestock. *Tuesday, Thursday, Saturday*

Zacualpa: produce. *Thursday, Sunday*

Zunil: textiles. *Monday*

a sumptuous buffet. ✉ *4 Av. 6–58* ☎ *7756–2086* ▭ *AE, D, DC, MC, V* ⊗ *Closed Mon. Breakfast served Thurs. and Sun.*

$ LATIN AMERICAN ✕ **La Fonda del Tzijolaj.** This restaurant's second-story balcony overlooking Plaza Mayor is a great place to watch the vendors set up on the eve of the market. The *pollo chimichurri* (chicken in an herb sauce) is one of the best choices from the mostly traditional menu. There are also a few surprises, such as pizza and pasta. ✉ *7 Calle and 4 Av., Centro Comercial Santo Tomás 30* ☎ *7756–1013* ▭ *AE, D, DC, MC, V.*

$ LATIN AMERICAN ✕ **La Villa de los Cofrades.** With two locations within a block of each other, it's hard to miss this longtime favorite. The smaller of the two has patio seating right on the Parque Central, where you can watch the vendors setting up their stalls while you feast on Belgian waffles or sip one of the finest cappuccinos in the country. If you're in a hurry to get to the market, remember that the service here can be miserably slow. The other location, called simply Los Cofrades, a block away on 5 Calle, has a less hectic atmosphere on a second floor that lets you survey the fringes of the market. ✉ *6 Calle and 5 Av.14006* ✉ *Centro Comercial Santo Tomás 11* ☎ *7756–1643* ▭ *AE, D, DC, MC, V* ⊗ *Closed Mon. and Tues.*

$ ECLECTIC ✕ **Las Brasas.** An eclectic collection of local handicrafts brightens the walls of this excellent second-floor steak house. The chef, formerly of the Hotel Santo Tomás, grills up a great steak, but there are plenty of other options, including a delicious *longaniza* (a spicy sausage similar to chorizo). Music and a full bar keep things lively, but not intrusively so. ✉ *6 Calle 4–52, 2nd level* ☎ *7756–2226* ▭ *AE, D, DC, MC, V.*

¢ LATIN AMERICAN ✕ **Tu Café.** Take a break from shopping at this tiny eatery—you'll find just 10 tables here—with plain decor on the corner of the Parque Central. This place offers a huge selection of sandwiches—choose from chicken, various cheeses, ham, roast beef, or club—or opt for the daily lunch special, with a main course, usually chicken-based—perhaps a *pepián,* with a side of rice and vegetables—for Q25. You can fortify yourself early in the day, too, with a breakfast of omelets or pancakes. ✉ *5 Av. 6–44* ☎ *7756–1448* ▭ *No credit cards.*

WHERE TO STAY

Lodgings in town raise their rates on Wednesday–Thursday and Saturday–Sunday. There aren't that many hotels in Chichi, so make reservations if you plan to be in town on any of those nights. Stay here on a Monday, Tuesday, or Friday night and you'll pay a lot less.

$ **Chalet Hotel.** The Alps are nowhere to be seen, but at the very least, the sun-splashed breakfast room at this cozy little hotel does the name justice. The rooms are smallish but not cramped. Wooden masks and other handicrafts adorn the walls. A pleasant terrace is a great place for relaxing after a taxing day of roaming the markets. The hotel is down a small unpaved road near 7 Avenida, and removed from the cacophony of market central. **Pros:** friendly owners; removed from market hubbub. **Cons:** small rooms; not close to market. ✉ *3 Calle 7–44* ☎ *7756–2286* *9 rooms* *In-room: no a/c, no phone, no TV. In-hotel: no elevator, no-smoking rooms* ▭ *No credit cards.*

4

$ **Hotel Chugüila.** This hotel in an older building a few blocks north of the plaza has a variety of rooms facing a cobblestone courtyard. The plant-filled portico leading to most rooms is scattered with inviting chairs and tables. Rooms are simply furnished, and a few have fireplaces. The hotel even offers its own rooftop market with 45 vendors on Thursday and Sunday market days. **Pros:** close to market; hotel has own market on Thursday and Sunday. **Cons:** basic rooms, can be noisy on market days. ✉ *5 Av. 5–24* ☎ *7756–1134* 📠 *7759–9412* *15 rooms* *In-room: no a/c, no phone, Wi-Fi. In-hotel: restaurant, no elevator, public Internet, parking, no-smoking rooms* *No credit cards.*

$$$$ Fodor'sChoice ★ **Hotel Santo Tomás.** Built in the Spanish style around a central courtyard, Hotel Santo Tomás is one of the town's best lodgings. Breezy passageways in which hundreds of plants spring from rustic clay pots lead past two trickling fountains. Spacious rooms are decorated with traditional textiles and antique reproductions. Each has a fireplace to warm you when the sun goes down. The back of the hotel is quieter, and has views of the surrounding countryside. The large restaurant ($$) is a quiet lunch refuge from the market cacophony. **Pros:** good restaurant; mostly removed from market hubbub. **Cons:** many visitors on market day compromise intimacy of hotel. ✉ *7 Av. 5–32* ☎ *7756–1061* 🌐 *www.paginasamarillas.com/hotelsantotomas.htm* *76 rooms* *In-room: no a/c, no phone, no TV. In-hotel: restaurant, bar, pool, gym, no elevator, parking (no fee), no-smoking rooms* *AE, D, DC, MC, V.*

$$$$ **Mayan Inn.** Long regarded as Chichicastenango's "second hotel" (after the Santo Tomás), the Mayan Inn was actually the first lodging to set up shop here. (It dates from the 1930s, and is one of the country's best-known hotels.) Rooms have corner fireplaces, and surround a series of beautifully maintained garden courtyards. Most have wide windows overlooking the pine-covered hills. The service is as impeccable as always—an attendant in traditional costume is assigned to each room. **Pros:** close to market, attentive service. **Cons:** room doors lock only from inside (but are guarded by attendant when you're out of room). ✉ *3 Av. at 8 Calle, behind El Calvario church* ☎ *7756–1176, 2412–4753 in Guatemala City* *30 rooms* *In-room: no a/c, no phone, no TV. In-hotel: restaurant, bar, laundry service, parking (no fee), no-smoking rooms* *AE, D, DC, MC, V.*

$ **Posada El Arco.** This small hotel has a distinctly homey feel. The spacious rooms are clean, if a tad musty, and tastefully decorated with *típica*. All rooms have fireplaces for the chilly evenings. To get here, climb up the stairs to the top of the arch that crosses 5 Avenida and turn left. **Pros:** good budget value. **Cons:** spartan rooms; can smell a bit musty at times. ✉ *4 Calle 4–36* ☎ *7756–1255* *8 rooms* *In-room: no a/c, no phone, no TV. In-hotel: no elevator, laundry facilities, parking (no fee), no-smoking rooms* *No credit cards.*

SHOPPING

Although the market is paramount, Chichicastenango has a decent selection of fixed shops selling high-quality souvenirs and artisan work. Many are on 6 Calle, the street you're likely to walk between your tour

MARKET DAY IN CHICHICASTENANGO

Chichicastenango's famous Thursday and Sunday market is also one of Guatemala's top-notch fun things to do. Although a Thursday visit won't disappoint, come here for the Sunday market if your schedule permits. During your shopping breaks, you can observe the fascinating rituals on the steps of the Santo Tomás church; they mix Mayan and Catholic, and the boundary is never clear.

At dawn, mist swirls around the vendors as they set up shop. Firecrackers go off and smoky incense wafts from the steps of the church in anticipation and celebration of the ritual of market day. (Lodging here the night before market day lets you take in that part of the spectacle before the day-trippers arrive.)

Credit one Alfred Clark with bringing Chichi's market to the attention of the outside world. Clark founded the Mayan Inn, the town's first lodging, in 1932. (Newspaper accounts at the time described the "*gringo loco*" who had opened a hotel in such a remote locale.) Clark needed to attract guests, so he encouraged area makers of textiles, pottery, and carvings to bring their wares to Chichi's longstanding twice-weekly market. The rest is history.

Tours depart on market days from many places around the country. (Cruise ships that dock at Puerto Quetzal on the Pacific coast on Thursday or Sunday also offer their passengers optional shore excursions to Chichi; at four hours one-way from the cruise docks, it makes for a long day.) Some include only transport and "Be back at the van at 2 PM and we'll head home" instructions from your driver. (On that topic, we recommend jotting down the license-plate number of your van. Vehicles have a strange way of all looking the same when you return at the end of your shopping day.) Other excursions may include a lunch voucher, often at the Hotel Santo Tomás. As far as we know, not even "fully escorted tours" include shopping guides.

Things begin to wind down by mid-afternoon, as the shoppers head out, and vendors, anxious to get home before dark, start to pack up. Here's another advantage to lodging in Chichicastenango: Savvy market shoppers know that this is the hour for the best bargains, as sellers are frequently willing to give discounts so they won't have to lug everything home.

We hear complaints about the market: "There are too many tourists." "The walkways between vendors' stalls are too narrow." "I see too many things I don't want to buy." Yes. Yes. And, yes. It gets crowded, but that's part of the fun. (On that note of crowding, do watch your things. The market is generally safe, but a few wallet-snatchers prey on unsuspecting shoppers.) Despite all appearances to the contrary, this age-old spectacle is not really staged for us visitors. Chichicastenango has been a center of trade since pre-Columbian times. Many vendors' stalls burst at the seams with souvenirs these days, but the real focus of Chichi's market are fruits, vegetables, and poultry—all the day-to-day goods that sustain the families who come here twice a week. Always has been. Always will be.

van and the market and back. Here's the kicker: Most of them open only on Thursday and Sunday market days.

Casa Maya (✉ *6 CAlle* ☎ *7756–1349*) has a distinctive array of quality T-shirts. **Típica Maya** (✉ *6 Calle 6–35* ☎ *5910–1424*) offers a good selection of women's clothing—in particular, woven huipils and cortes.

Galería de Artes Pintores de Chichicastenango (✉ *6 Calle* ☎ *5443–0074*) exhibits primitivist paintings created by a cooperative of 12 local artists. We especially like the hand-painted Nativity scenes at **Tashe Artesanía** (✉ *6 Calle 6–13* ☎ *7756–1622*) among all the other ceramics for sale.

Bucking the trend and staying open every day of the week, **De Colores** (✉ *6 Calle 6–21* ☎ *7756–1027*) deals in woven and embroidered textiles, sweaters, and blouses. Check out the selection of cute oven mitts and pot holders.

You'll find the best selection of traditional handmade masks at **Casa de Máscaras Santo Tomás** (✉ *9 Calle 4–54* ☎ *7756–1882*) just down the street from the Santo Tomás church. These folks stay open every day of the week.

NIGHTLIFE AND THE ARTS

"In Chichicastenango, they never dance the tango," crooned Xavier Cugat with his orchestra during the Big Band era of the 1940s. Nightlife is limited in hard-working Chichi. Linger over a restaurant meal or have a drink at a hotel bar. That's about it. Do not stray from the city center at night, as there have been occasional attacks by *maras* (gangs).

EL QUICHÉ

It doesn't get much traffic, but adventurous travelers may want to continue north from Chichicastenango for further glimpses of the region called El Quiché, where you'll find traditional villages on pine-covered hills. Although Chichi remains the ceremonial center of the Quiché people, its heavy tourist overlay can be an impediment to seeing real Quiché culture. For a far more authentic view, head north to this region.

SANTA CRUZ DEL QUICHÉ

19 km (12 mi) north of Chichicastenango.

A half-hour north of Chichicastenango lies the provincial capital of Santa Cruz del Quiché, which serves as a base for exploring the area. Quiché, as the town is commonly called, is known for its pretty white church on the east side of the Parque Central. It was built from the stones taken from a Mayan temple destroyed by the Spanish.

GETTING HERE AND AROUND

Veloz Quichelense buses travel to and from Guatemala City on the half-hour between 5 AM and 6 PM. Plan on 30–45 minutes of travel, depending on the number of stops the bus makes, and a fare of Q10.

ESSENTIALS

EmergenciesPolice (☎ *7755–1325*).

Medical Assistance Farmacia Batres (✉ *2 Av. 6–13, Zona 1, Santa Cruz del Quiché* ☎ *7755–3700*).

EXPLORING

North of town is **K'umarcaaj,** the ancient capital of the Quiché kingdom. This once-magnificent site was destroyed by Spanish conquistadors in 1524. The ruins haven't been restored, but they are frequently used for Mayan rituals. A taxi to and from the ruins should cost less than Q60. You can also walk the pleasant 3-km (2-mi) route without much difficulty. Follow 10 Calle out of town, where it becomes a dirt road. A tight S curve is the halfway point. The road forks at the bottom of a hill; take the road to the right.

4

WHERE TO EAT AND STAY

¢ LATIN AMERICAN **Comedor Flipper.** A cage of lively birds lends a cheerful atmosphere to this small eatery, which serves good Guatemalan fare. The *avena* (a warm oat beverage) is delicious, especially on a cold morning. There is no sign of the restaurant's trusty namesake, though a ceramic sailfish atop the refrigerator comes close. ✉ *1 Av. 7–31, around the corner from Hotel San Pasqual* ☎ *No phone* ▭ *No credit cards.*

¢–$ **Hotel San Pasqual.** This little hotel has a definite charm, most of it emanating from the engaging couple that runs it. The simple rooms, with handwoven bedspreads, surround a sunny courtyard. Clotheslines full of the day's laundry stretch to the roof next door. The shared baths are clean, but hot water is available only in the morning. **Pros:** friendly owners, good budget value. **Cons:** basic rooms. ✉ *7 Calle 0–43, Zona 1* ☎ *7755–1107* *37 rooms, 11 with bath* *In-room: no a/c, no phone, no TV. In-hotel: parking (no fee), no-smoking rooms* ▭ *No credit cards.*

NEBAJ

95 km (59 mi) north of Santa Cruz del Quiché.

A fascinating part of the highlands, although one of Guatemala's most inaccessible regions, is the so-called Ixil Triangle. It's home to the indigenous Ixiles, who speak a unique Mam-based language, different from the Quiché spoken in the surrounding area. Isolation has meant that the people here have been able to preserve a rich culture; you'll have some trouble finding fluent Spanish speakers here. Women wear bright-red cortes with green or yellow huipils; men have mostly abandoned traditional wear, but retain colorful sashes, which may decorate an otherwise Western outfit of jeans and sweater. For many years, traditional Ixil wear meant doom for the people here; the war hit this region hard, as the Ixiles were specifically targeted for elimination. Out of fear for their own safety, many people here abandoned their *traditional* costume, and have only begun to don it again since the signing of the peace accords.

The main town in this region is Nebaj, where cobblestone streets lead to a central plaza with a large colonial church. On Thursday and Sunday the town swells with people who come from the surrounding villages to sell their distinctive weavings. Besides shopping, hiking in the surrounding mountains is the main draw for tourists.

CLOSE UP

Dancing with the Dead

Colorful cemeteries, with their turquoises and pinks, mauves and sky blues, play an integral part in the living fabric of contemporary Guatemalan society. It's not uncommon to see entire families visiting their deceased relatives on Sundays. But a visit to the cemetery need not be mournful, and they often bring a bottle of alcohol to share, occasionally tipping the bottle to the earth, so that their dead relatives also get their share. Incense is burned and shamans perform ancient rites alongside Catholic and evangelical clergy. The November 2 observance of the Day of the Dead gives family members their greatest chance to celebrate and honor their deceased relatives with music, dance, song, festivals and, yes, much drinking and merriment.

Celebrating the dead rather than mourning their passing is a Mayan tradition that reaches back to pre-Columbian times. The *Popol Vuh* or Mayan Bible as it's sometimes referred to, looks toward an active relationship with deceased friends and relatives. "Remember us after we have gone. Don't forget us," reads the *Popul Vuh.* "Conjure up our faces and our words. Our image will be as dew in the hearts of those who want to remember us." It is unknown who authored the *Popol Vuh,* which was translated into Spanish in the early 18th century by Father Francisco Ximénez, but the practices and myths of the sacred book of the Maya still make their way into the Day of the Dead celebrations across Guatemala.

The country's two most fascinating Day of the Dead celebrations take place in Santiago Sacatepéquez and Todos Santos Chuchumatán on November 1. In Santiago Sacatepéquez, a Cakchiquel town located 30 km (19 mi) from Antigua, villagers gather in the early morning hours and file through the narrow streets to the cemetery. Once there, they take part in what is one of Guatemala's most resplendent ceremonies, flying giant kites of up to 2 meters (6½ feet) in diameter to communicate with those who have passed away. The villagers tie messages to the kite tails to let the dead know how they are doing and to ask God for special favors. The colorful celebration is finished with a lunch feast of *fiambre,* a traditional dish of cold cuts, boiled eggs, vegetables, olives, and other delicacies. The so-called "drunken horse race" in the remote mountain village of Todos Santos Cuchumatán, near Huehuetenango—the riders get plastered, not the horses—is not to everyone's taste, but is an integral part of that town's Day of the Dead celebration.

The color scheme of the cemeteries is more than just decorative: turquoise and green tombs signify that an adult member of the family was recently interred in the above-ground crypts, whites and yellows indicate the passing of an elderly family member, and pinks and blues are reserved for deceased children.

Just remember that although foreigners are welcome in the cemeteries, it's important to respect the traditions and dignity of those visiting deceased relatives—tread softly and leave your camera behind.

—Gregory Benchwick

GETTING HERE AND AROUND

The drive north from Santa Cruz del Quiché takes about 90 minutes over a precipitously curving road at stretches. Eight buses daily connect Nebaj with Santa Cruz del Quiché. The trip takes two hours, or more if the bus makes a lot of stops. The fare is Q10.

LANGUAGE SCHOOL IN NEBAJ

Almost no one here speaks anything but Spanish and Ixil—you can study the latter, too, if you like—so learning the language in such a remote location virtually eliminates the temptation to lapse into English outside the classroom.

Nebaj Language School (✉ *Nebaj* ☎ *7832–6345 in Antigua* 🌐 *www.nebajlanguageschool.com*).

WHERE TO STAY

¢ **Hotel Ixil.** Nebaj doesn't have much in the way of lodging; the best bet is this friendly whitewashed hotel set around two courtyards. Some of the basic but spacious rooms overlook the garden. A few rooms in an annex next door have nicer furnishings and even toss in cable TV. **Pros:** good budget value, pretty garden, only option in town. **Cons:** basic furnishings, remote location. ✉ *Nebaj* ☎ *7755–1091* *12 rooms* *In-room: no a/c, no phone, no TV (some). In-hotel: parking (no fee), no-smoking rooms* *No credit cards.*

QUETZALTENANGO (XELAJÚ)

91 km (56 mi) southwest of Chichicastenango, 201 km (121 mi) northwest of Guatemala City.

Guatemala's second-largest city might seem quite provincial if you've first visited the capital. But we'll take friendly, old Quetzaltenango any day. Historically, the city never entirely warmed to the idea of authority from far-away Guatemala City, and, in fact, was a hotbed of separatist sentiment during the 19th century. Those dreams have long faded, but you'll see Quetzaltenango's blue-white-red regional flag flying far more frequently here than the blue-white-blue national flag.

The first attraction of the place is the city itself. You won't find many must-see sights here, but Quetzaltenango's large student population gives it a cosmopolitan, politically astute, slightly bohemian feel, with a good selection of restaurants, cafés, and nightlife. It's no wonder that the city has become such a choice place to study Spanish.

The city anchors a valley guarded by the Volcán Santa María, with an economy based on agriculture. The rolling hills, enriched by fertile volcanic soil, are particularly good for growing coffee. The area attracts travelers who come here to purchase the intricate weavings from the surrounding villages. The first Sunday of each month is the main market day in Quetzaltenango itself, and the central square is filled with women selling their wares. Many days a week, towns in the Quetzaltenango orbit play host to their own markets, and are well worth their easy day trips.

Streets in Quetzaltenango vaguely follow the Guatemala City organizational model. The city is divided into 11 zones, although nearly everything you need is in Zona 1. Avenidas run north–south; calles,

4

east–west. Outside the very heart of the city, hills interrupt the regular grid system, and many streets need to be designated as *Diagonal*.

GETTING HERE AND AROUND

Beyond the turnoffs to Panajachel and Lake Atitlán, the Pan-American Highway continues over some impressive ridges and then descends to a crossroads called Cuatro Caminos, about 200 km (124 mi) from Guatemala City. The road to Quetzaltenango heads off to the south from here.

Quetzaltenango-bound Galgos buses leave Guatemala City at 5:30, 8:30, and 11 AM, and 12:45, 2:30, 5, 6:30, and 7 PM. They depart from Quetzaltenango at 4, 5, 8:15, 9:45, and 11:45 AM, and 2:45 and 4:45 PM. The trip takes four hours, and the fare is Q50.

In Quetzaltenango, Quetzaltrekkers supports social-service programs in the area. Adrenalina Tours in Quetzaltenango and a branch in Antigua lead trips to area volcanoes and surrounding towns on their market days.

ESSENTIALS

Banks Bancared (✉ *4 Av. 17–40, Zona 3, Quetzaltenango*).

Bus Contact Galgos (✉ *21 Calle 0–14, Zona 1, Quetzaltenango* ☎ *7761–2248* 🌐 *www.transgalgosinter.com*).

Emergencies Ambulance (☎ *7761–2746*). **Police** (☎ *7761–4990*).

Medical Assistance Farmacia Batres (✉ *10 Av. and 6 Calle, Zona 1, Quetzaltenango* ☎ *7761–4531*). **Hospital La Democracia** (✉ *13 Av. 6–51, Zona 3Quetzaltenango* ☎ *7763–6760*). **Hospital Privado de Quetzaltenango** (✉ *5 Calle 12–44, Zona 3, Quetzaltenango* ☎ *7763–4381*).

Visitor and Tour Info Adrenalina Tours (✉ *12 Av. 4–25, Zona 1, Quetzaltenango* ☎ *7761–4509* 🌐 *www.adrenalinatours.com*). **INGUAT** (✉ *Casa de la Cultura, Parque Centro América, 7 Calle 11–35, Zona 1Quetzaltenango* ☎ *7761–4931*). **Kaqchiquel Tours** (✉ *7 Calle 15–20, Zona 1, Quetzaltenango* ☎ *5294–8828* ✉ *kaqchikeltours@hotmail.com*). **Quetzaltrekkers** (✉ *Casa Argentina, Diagonal 12 8–67, Zona 1, Quetzaltenango* ☎ *7765–5895* 🌐 *www.quetzaltrekkers.com*).

EXPLORING

❷ **Catedral del Espíritu Santo/Catedral de los Altos.** On the southeastern corner of Parque Centro América, this cathedral dates from 1535. All that remains of the original building (Espíritu Santo) is the facade, which features life-size saints that look down upon worshippers headed here to pray and is offset to the left of the newer cathedral (Los Altos), with its own front, constructed in 1899. ✉ *11 Av. and 7 Calle, Zona 1.*

❺ **Iglesia de San Nicolás.** This bluish church on the east side of Parque Benito Juárez is known for its unusual baroque design. Although lovely, it looks a bit out of place in the town's mix of Greek Revival and colonial structures. ✉ *15 Av. and 3 C., Zona 3.*

❸ **Museo de Historia Natural.** In the Casa de la Cultura on the south side of Parque Centro América, the Museum of Natural History is interesting mainly for its neoclassical flourishes. Inside are some examples of pre-Columbian pottery. Your ticket also includes admission to the so-called

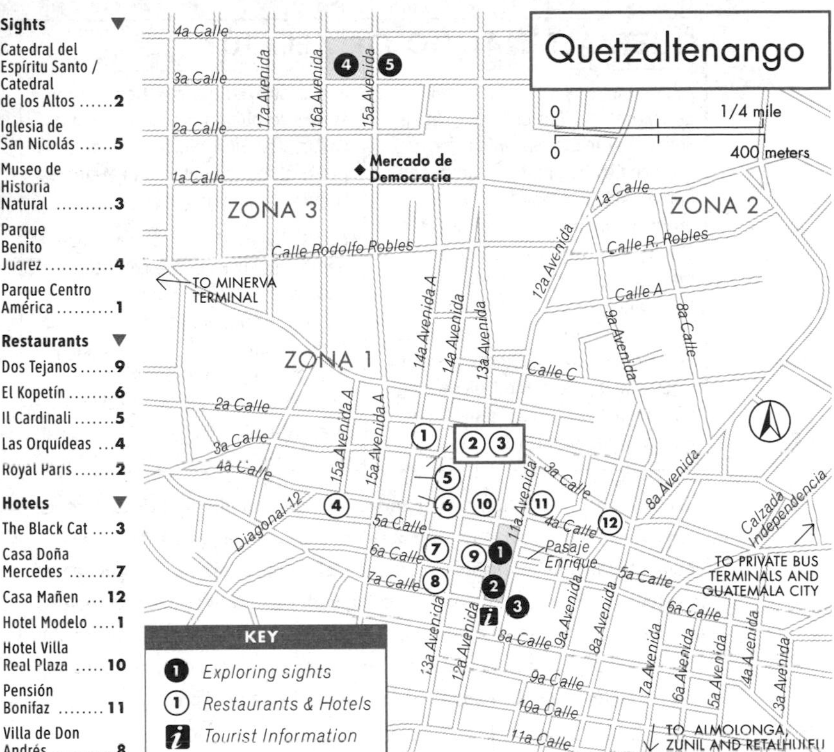

Museo de la Marimba, which, despite its name, has little to do with marimbas, and is more a hodgepodge collection of Quetzaltenango artifacts. It's a must only if you're a true aficionado of regional history. ✉ *7 Calle and 11 Av., Zona 1* ☎ *7761–6427* *Q10.*

4 **Parque Benito Juárez.** About 10 blocks north of Parque Centro América is this palm-lined park where many families spend their Sunday afternoons. Ice-cream stands are in glorious abundance. ✉ *15 Av. and 3 Calle, Zona 3* *Q6.*

1 **Parque Centro América.** The city's central plaza, ablaze with pepper trees, is one of the most beautiful in Central America. It is surrounded by neoclassical architectural masterpieces, most of which date from the early 20th century (earthquakes took their toll on older colonial structures), such as the magnificent building called Pasaje Enríquez, built in 1900 in the style of a center-city European shopping arcade. Bees buzz around the park's numerous flower beds. Be careful if you're susceptible to harm from their stings. ✉ *12 Av. and 4 C., Zona 1.*

NEED A BREAK?

Anyone can buy a huipil as a souvenir of Guatemala. How about coming home with a few flashy moves that will wow your friends on the dance floor? The Salsa Rosa dance studio (✉ *Diagonal 11 7–79, Zona 1* ☎ *5204–0404*) gives group salsa lessons each weeknight at 6 PM, and the cost is a bargain

QUETZALTENANGO OR XELAJÚ?

All the highway signs direct you to QUETZALTENANGO, but once you arrive, you'll hear most residents refer to their city by its one-time indigenous name, "Xelajú" (*Shay-la-HOO*) or, more commonly, "Xela" for short. The long version was *Xelajú Noj*, meaning "under 10 mountains." Originally part of the Mam empire, Quetzaltenango was captured in the 14th century by the Quiché people. It remained part of the Quiché kingdom until 1524, when Spanish conqueror Pedro de Alvarado captured and destroyed the city. He used the stones to build a new city called Quetzaltenango, which means "the place of many quetzals" in Mexico's Nahuatl language.

Nearly five centuries later, the new name still sticks in the collective craw of many here. Some, as a matter of pride and tradition, would never let the word "Quetzaltenango" pass their lips. Others are more pragmatic: "Xela" is just quicker to say and write.

Q25 per hour. (Instruction is in Spanish.) You can also opt for private lessons daily except Sunday for Q60 per hour—equally a bargain, we think—and delve into the fine art of salsa, merengue, cha-cha, or lambada. If you're new to Latin dancing, we recommend sticking with the relatively simpler merengue, which works well with an amazing variety of pop music back home. Call a couple of days in advance to make an appointment for private lessons and to arrange for an English-speaking instructor if you need one.

WHERE TO EAT

$ TEX-MEX ✕ **Dos Tejanos.** Tex-Mex food is here in Quetzaltenango in a big way at this restaurant inside the Pasaje Enríquez building on Parque Centro América. Look for the neon signs. Decor is that of an old Southwest cantina, with wood tables and stools in the room that also houses the bar, and chairs with backs in an amply sized adjoining room. Barbecue ribs, fajitas, and nachos make up the hearty fare. ✉ *4 Calle 12–33, Zona 1* ☎ *7765–4360* 🌐 *www.dostejanos.com* 💳 *V* ⊗ *BP.*

$ LATIN AMERICAN ✕ **El Kopetín.** Good food, attentive service, and reasonable prices make this place popular with the locals, so it can be tough to get a table later in the evening. It couldn't be described as fancy, but this restaurant's long polished bar and wood paneling raise it above the usual neighborhood dive. The menu has a number of delicious appetizers, including traditional *queso fundido* and a selection of meat and seafood dishes that are smothered in rich sauces. Saturday, the place whips up its *caldo de mariscos* (seafood stew). ✉ *14 Av. 3–51, Zona 1* ☎ *7761–8381* 💳 *AE, D, DC, MC, V.*

$$ ITALIAN ✕ **Il Cardinali.** For a home-style southern Italian atmosphere with checked tablecloths, opera music, and basketed Chianti bottles hanging from the rafters, head to Il Cardinali. The extensive, pasta-heavy menu also includes pizza and a decent wine selection. The service is friendly and quick. The front room gets chilly at night. Opt instead for

LANGUAGE SCHOOLS IN QUETZALTENANGO

Quetzaltenango has the greatest number of Spanish schools in Guatemala, and is widely known for having the country's most rigorous programs. As elsewhere, schools can line you up with homestays.

Casa Xelajú (✉ *Callejón 15, Diagonal 13-02, Zona 1* ☎ *7761-5954* 🌐 *www.casaxelaju.com*).

CBA Spanish School (✉ *12 Av. 10-27, Zona 1* ☎ *7761-8535* 🌐 *www.cbaspanishschool.com*).

Celas Maya Spanish School (✉ *6 C. 14-55, Zona 1* ☎ *7761-4342* 🌐 *www.celasmaya.edu.gt*).

Centro de Estudios Español Pop Wuj (✉ *1 Calle 17-72, Zona 1* ☎ *7761-8286* 🌐 *www.pop-wuj.org*).

Centro Ligüístico El Baul (✉ *3 Calle 17-90, Zona 5* ☎ *7765-8066* 🌐 *www.centrolinguisticoelbaul.org*).

Educación para Todos (✉ *Av. el Cenizal 0-58, Zona 5* ☎ *5935-3815* 🌐 *www.spanishschools.biz*).

El Mundo en Español (✉ *8 Av. Calle B A-61, Zona 1* ☎ *7761-3256* 🌐 *www.elmundoenespanol.org*).

El Portal Spanish School (✉ *9 Callejón A 11-49, Zona 1* ☎ *7761-5275* 🌐 *www.spanishschoolelportal.com*).

El Quetzal Spanish School (✉ *10 CAlle 10-29, Zona 1* ☎ *7765-1085* 🌐 *www.xelawho.com/elquetzal*).

Escuela de Español Juan Sisay (✉ *15 Av. 8-38, Zona 1* ☎ *7765-1318* 🌐 *www.cbaspanishschool.com*).

Eureka Spanish School (✉ *12 Av. 8-21, Zona 1* ☎ *7761-5260* 🌐 *www.spanishateureka.com*).

Inepas Spanish School (✉ *15 Av. 4-59, Zona 1* ☎ *7765-1308* 🌐 *www.inepas.org*).

Ixim No'j (✉ *1 Av. 7-34, Zona 1* ☎ *5977-1040* 🌐 *www.iximnoj.com*).

Kie Balam Spanish School (✉ *Diagonal 12 4-46, Zona 1* ☎ *7761-1636* 🌐 *www.kiebalam.com*).

La Democracia Spanish School (✉ *9 Calle 15-05, Zona 3* ☎ *7767-0013* 🌐 *www.lademocracia.net*).

Madre Tierra Spanish School (✉ *13 Av. 8-34, Zona 1* ☎ *7761-6105* 🌐 *www.madre-tierra.org*).

Miguel Ángel Asturias Spanish School (✉ *8 Calle 16-23, Zona 1* ☎ *7765-3707* 🌐 *www.spanishschool.com*).

Minerva Spanish School (✉ *24 Av. 4-39, Zona 3* ☎ *7767-4427* 🌐 *www.minervaspanishschool.com*).

Proyecto Lingüístico Quetzalteco de Español (✉ *5 Calle 2-40, Zona 1* ☎ *7765-2140* 🌐 *www.hermandad.com*).

Proyecto Lingüístico Santa María (✉ *3 Calle 10-56, Zona 1* ☎ *7765-8136* 🌐 *www.spanishgua.com*).

Sakribal Spanish School (✉ *6 Calle 7-42, Zona 1* ☎ *7763-0717* 🌐 *www.sakribal.com*).

Sol Latino Spanish School (✉ *Diagonal 12 6-58, Zona 1* ☎ *5613-7222* 🌐 *www.spanishschoolsollatino.com*).

Ulew Tinamit Spanish School (✉ *4 Calle 15-23, Zona 1* ☎ *7763-0516* 🌐 *www.spanishguatemala.org*).

Utatlán Spanish School (✉ *12 Av. 4-32, Zona 1* ☎ *7763-0446* 🌐 *www.xelapages.com/utatlan*).

Xequijel Spanish School (✉ *6 Calle 13-36, Zona 1* ☎ *7765-8309* 🌐 *www.xequijeledu.blogspot.com*).

the larger and bustling, but cozier back room. ✉ *14 Av. 3–25, Zona 1* ☎ *7761–0924* ▭ *V.*

$ THAI ✕ **Las Orquídeas.** You'll see the posters and leaflets for this small Thai restaurant—just a scant five tables and extremely informal—all over town, so by the time you get here you feel you already know the place. Look for the circular orchid-symbol sign with no name at the front door. (Orquídea means "orchid.") The English–Spanish menu is a mix-and-match affair. All the dishes, whether pad thai, coconut-milk soup, or green- or red-curry stir-fry, come with a choice of chicken, tofu, or shrimp. ✉ *4 Calle 15–45, Zona 1* ☎ *5247–5873* ⊙ *Closed Sun. and Mon.*

$ FRENCH ✕ **Royal Paris.** This bistro caters to foreign students, so the menu covers a lot of bases. Some dishes aren't the least bit Parisian, such as the succulent chicken-curry kebab. It's all prepared with flair, however. The ambience at this second-floor restaurant is definitely imported, and slightly bohemian, courtesy of the paintings of cabaret scenes. There's also a bar with an extensive wine list. **■ TIP→ Stop by on Tuesday evenings; it's movie night, with a French or Italian film (with Spanish subtitles).** ✉ *Calle 14A 3–06, Zona 1* ☎ *7761–1942* ▭ *AE, D, DC, MC, V* ⊙ *No lunch Mon.*

WHERE TO STAY

¢–$ **The Black Cat.** This slightly ramshackle hotel a few blocks off the plaza is a popular spot with travelers on a budget. Rooms on two floors of a converted residence face a small courtyard overflowing with plants. Several are arranged dorm-style with bunks, and sleep eight to 10 people. Though simple, they're clean and comfortable. There's a separate lounge where you can chat with other guests. **Pros:** good barebones budget option, central location. **Cons:** spartan rooms, some street noise. ✉ *13 Av. 3–33, Zona 1* ☎ *7761–2091* ⊕ *www.blackcathostels.net* *14 rooms, none with bath* *In-room: no a/c, no phone, no TV. In-hotel: restaurant, bar, public Internet, public Wi-Fi, no-smoking rooms* ▭ *No credit cards* *BP.*

$ **Casa Doña Mercedes.** This longtime budget standby just two blocks off the Parque Centro América has undergone a complete remodeling to upgrade its furnishings and facilities. Spacious, carpeted rooms on the upper floor contain private bathrooms; those on the first floor, all with partial brick walls, offer shared baths. All have colorful spreads and drapes. Everyone has access to shared kitchen facilities. **Pros:** friendly owner, immaculate rooms, good budget value. **Cons:** some shared baths. ✉ *6 Calle 13–42, Zona 1* ☎ *7765–4687* *8 rooms, 4 with bath* *In-room: no a/c, no phone, Wi-Fi. In-hotel: no elevator, public Internet, parking (no fee), no-smoking rooms* ▭ *V* *EP.*

$$ **Casa Mañen.** This romantic little B&B west of the central plaza blends colonial comforts with modern conveniences. The rooms—most have fireplaces—are spacious and homey, with handmade wall hangings and throw rugs and the occasional rocking chair. On the roof is a two-level terrace with a fantastic view of the city. Complimentary breakfast is served in a small dining room downstairs. The staff is incredibly friendly and will be happy to help you with travel plans. You'll get a small discount if you pay in cash. **Pros:** friendly staff, cozy surroundings. **Cons:** some street noise. ✉ *9 Av. 4–11, Zona 1* ☎ *7765–0786*

www.comeseeit.com 7 rooms, 2 suites In-room: no a/c, no phone, safe, refrigerator (some). In-hotel: restaurant, bar, no elevator, laundry service, parking (no fee), no-smoking rooms AE, D, DC, MC, V BP.

$–$$ **Hotel Modelo.** Founded in 1892, this family-run establishment is one of Guatemala's oldest, still-operating lodgings. Over the years the distinguished hotel has maintained its tradition of good service. The wood-floor rooms, furnished with antiques, surround a few small courtyards leading off the lobby. Dinner is served in a fine colonial-style restaurant. **Pros:** 19th-century ambience; attentive staff. **Cons:** some small rooms. *14 Av. A 2–31, Zona 1 7763–1376 www.hotelmodelo1892.com 19 rooms In-room: no a/c, safe (some), Wi-Fi. In-hotel: restaurant, bar, Internet terminal, parking (no fee) AE, D, DC, MC, V BP.*

4

$$ **Hotel Villa Real Plaza.** Surrounding a covered courtyard illuminated by skylights, the spacious carpeted rooms at Hotel Villa Real Plaza all have fireplaces that you'll appreciate on cool evenings. Those in a newer wing are superior to those in the dimly lit older section. The restaurant (¢–$$) has an interesting menu, whose offerings range from chicken cordon bleu to a variety of meaty stews. You'll receive a small discount if you pay with cash. **Pros:** good restaurant, business amenities. **Cons:** older rooms are dark. *4 Calle 12–22, Zona 1 7761–4045 www.hotelvillarealplazaxela.com 54 rooms In-room: no a/c, Wi-Fi. In-hotel: restaurant, room service, bar, laundry service, parking (no fee), no-smoking rooms AE, D, DC, MC, V.*

$$$ **Pensión Bonifaz.** Don't let the name fool you into thinking this is a modest establishment—Pensión Bonifaz is Quetzaltenango's most upscale hotel. Though housed in a stately old building at the central plaza's northeast corner, it has a modern interior that doesn't quite live up to its exterior. Still, it is a comfortable, well-run establishment. The nicest rooms are in the older building, where small balconies offer nice views of the plaza. A small café serves light fare for lunch, whereas the larger restaurant (¢–$$$) has a continental menu. **Pros:** good value. **Cons:** some rooms showing their age. *4 Calle 10–50, Zona 1 7761–4241 www.quetzalnet.com/bonifaz 71 rooms, 4 suites In-room: no a/c. In-hotel: restaurant, room service, bar, pool, laundry service, public Internet, public Wi-Fi, parking (no fee), no-smoking rooms AE, D, DC, MC, V EP.*

$–$$ **Villa de Don Andrés.** A turn-of-the-century building just a half-block off the Parque Centro América houses this charming budget find. Each of the five carpeted rooms is decorated with local artisan work and abuts a long, wide, bright hall that serves as a sitting room, with rocking chairs and lots of plants. All have their own baths, although Room 1's bathroom is across the hall. The one triple room at the end of the hall is huge, with one stone wall and a nonoperating fireplace that has been converted into shelving. You'll receive a small discount if you pay in cash. **Pros:** attentive owner, immaculate rooms, beautiful artisan work. **Cons:** one room has bath outside room. *13 Av. 6–16, Zona 1 7761–2014 www.villadedonandres.com 5 rooms In-room: no a/c, no phone, Wi-Fi. In-hotel: laundry service, Internet terminal, parking (no fee), no-smoking rooms AE, D, DC, MC, V BP.*

NIGHTLIFE

Guatemala's second city gets our first-place nod for a fun night out on the town. Although the center city is fine for walking in the evening, take a taxi back to your hotel if you plan to be out late.

Many places have no phone, other than a cell number belonging to someone on staff. For updates and the latest news, check the monthly, irreverent English-language publication *Xela Who,* available around town.

BARS

Casa Babylon (✉ *5 Calle 12–54, Zona 1* ☎ *7761–2320*) attracts foreign students and Guatemalans alike. They have an extensive mixed drink list. Right off the central square, **Salón Tecún** (✉ *12 Av. 4–40, Zona 1*) is a small pub inside the Pasaje Enríquez building on Parque Centro América that is popular with students.

Vegetarian restaurant **Asados Puente** (✉ *7 Calle 13–29, Zona 1* ☎ *7759–5077*) holds happy hour every night from 8 to 10 PM.

Complementing all the city's down-home offerings, classy bar **Bajo La Luna** (✉ *8 Av. 4–11, Zona 1* ☎ *7761–2242*) serves wine by the glass, pitcher, or bottle.

CAFÉS

Grab a cup of coffee or a drink on the second-floor outdoor balcony of **Balcón del Enríquez** (✉ *12 Av. 4–40, Zona 1* ☎ *7765–2296*), in the Pasaje Enríquez building on Parque Centro América. **Blue Angel Video Café** (✉ *7 Calle 15–79, Zona 1*) serves up fruit and veggie drinks while you log in via Wi-Fi on your laptop. For a taste of Xela's bohemian scene, head to the oh-so-funky **La Luna** (✉ *8 Av. 4–1, Zona 1*). Though they don't serve alcohol, the extensive hot-drink menu is enough to satisfy any espresso addict or chocophile.

DANCING

Catering to the university crowd, **El Duende** (✉ *14 Av., between 1 and 2 calles, Zona 1*) is the place to go dancing on weekends. Take your pick, depending on the night of the week, at **Kokoloko's** (✉ *15 Av. and 4 Calle, Zona 1* ☎ *5904–9028*), and dance to salsa, reggae, or world music. Happy hour is from 7 to 9 every night. Dance the night away, Latin style, at **La Parranda** (✉ *6 Calle and 14 Av., Zona 1*). Dance to a variety of music at **Pala Life Klishé** (✉ *4 Calle and 15 Av., Zona 1*) Tuesday is reggae night; Friday means disco.

LIVE MUSIC

Enjoy live music each Thursday evening at the mellow **Brooklyn Bar** (✉ *15 Av. 0–67, Zona 1*). **La Fonda del Ché** (✉ *15 Av. 7–43, Zona 1* ☎ *5569–8827*) has *trova,* a genre of protest music popular in Latin America, Tuesday through Saturday night. Nurse a glass of wine and listen to live music or a poetry reading at **El Viñedo** (✉ *15 Av. A 3–05, Zona 1*) Tuesday through Saturday. **La Mansión Marilyn** (✉ *13 Av. 5–38, Zona 1*) offers live music with a lot of Marilyn Monroe decor in the background Tuesday through Sunday.

FILMS

Enjoy a coffee, log on with your laptop, and enjoy the occasional movie night at **Cinema Coffee Shop** (✉ *12 Av. 8–21, Zona 1*). We like cozy **El Cuartito** (✉ *13 Av. 7–09, Zona 1*) for its coffee and veggie snacks. It has an outdoor patio, but the inside is a lot warmer. Tuesday's "Alternative Film Night" gets underway at 7 PM. **Cinema Paraíso** (✉ *1 Calle and 2 Av., Zona 1*) is a small café that screens artsy films. **Cubatenango** (✉ *19 Av. 2–08, Zona 1* ☎ *5508–3348*) screens Latin American films on DVD each Tuesday and Thursday at 7 PM, and serves two-for-one *Cuba Libres* (rum and cokes) each evening from 6 to 8 PM. **The Buddha** (✉ *7 Calle at 12 Av., Zona 1*) screens indie films many evenings (no fixed schedule) to the accompaniment of coffees and smoothies.

> **CHEERING ON THE GOATS**
>
> You'll have to look for it as XELAJÚ MC in the sports scores, but Quetzaltenango knows its 2007 Guatemalan National League championship soccer team as the *Superchivos* ("supergoats"), the city being the center of an important goat-raising region.

4

OUTDOOR ACTIVITIES

BICYCLING

There's great mountain biking through the hills and villages surrounding Xela. **Vrisa Bicicletas** (✉ *15 Av. 3–64, Zona 1* ☎ *7761–3237*) rents both on-road and off-road bikes by the day or week, and has maps so you can take self-guided tours of the countryside.

HIKING

Quetzaltrekkers (✉ *Casa Argentina, 12 Diagonal 8–67, Zona 1* ☎ *7761–5865* 🌐 *www.quetzaltrekkers.com*) is a nonprofit company that supports three major social-service programs by coordinating truly unforgettable hiking trips. The three-day trek to Lago Atitlán and the two-day ascent of Volcán Tajamulco both pass through spectacular countryside and several remote villages.

SHOPPING

BOOKS

Literary- and politically-minded Quetzaltenango has several fine bookstores, three with good selections in English. **El Libro Abierto** (✉ *15 Av. A 1–56, Zona 1* ☎ *7761–5195*) deals in used books, as well as postcards and organic coffee. **North & South Bookstore** (✉ *8 Calle 13–77, Zona 1* ☎ *7761–0589*) is strong in works dealing with history and politics. **Vrisa Bookstore** (✉ *15 Av. 3–64, Zona 1* ☎ *7761–3237*) has many used books in English.

MARKETS

The bustling **Mercado Minerva** (✉ *6 Calle, Zona 3*), next to the main bus terminal, is the best of the city's markets. There are plenty of interesting handicrafts to be found here. But watch your pockets—groups of skillful thieves prey on tourists coming to and from the buses.

Artesanía from most of the villages in the region can be found in the **Mercado La Democracia** (✉ *1 Calle and 15 Av., Zona 3*). Since there are relatively few shoppers, prices tend to be lower than elsewhere in the city.

Near Parque Centro América, the **Centro Comercial Municipal** (✉ *7 Calle and 11 Av., Zona 1*) has a more limited selection of souvenirs.

SPECIALTY STORES

Trama Textiles (✉ *3 Calle 10–56, Zona 1* ☎ *7765–8564* 🌐 *www.tramatextiles.org*) exhibits scarves, bags, and tablecloths woven by a local women's cooperative. **Artesanías Innova** (✉ *5 Calle 14–03, Zona 1* ☎ *7763–2189*) exhibits and sells beautiful textiles and ceramics created by nine highlands artisan cooperatives. **Creaciones Utzil** (✉ *7 Calle 29–25, Zona 3* ☎ *7763–5412*) manufactures small dolls that wear more than 100 varieties of typical Guatemalan dress. (Barbie never had a such a wardrobe.) Quetzaltenango is famous for its beautiful glass. **Vitra** (✉ *13 Av. 5–27, Zona 3* ☎ *7767–1269*) is one of the city's most noted stores. You'll find excellent hand-blown glass at affordable prices. The best-known buy-at-the-source purveyor of hand-blown glass is the artisans' cooperative **COPAVIC** (✉ *Carretera al Pacífico Km. 217.5* ☎ *7763–8028* 🌐 *www.copavic.com*). Come to watch works being created from recycled glass weekday mornings at its showroom/factory 10 km (6 mi) south of town.

Bazar de Café (✉ *13 Av. 5–38, Zona 1* ☎ *7761–4980*) sells fine roasted coffee from here in the highlands (fair-trade, of course). Purchase coffee from area cooperatives at **Café Conciencia** (✉ *12 Av. 3–35, Zona 1* ☎ *7765–8761* 🌐 *www.cafeconciencia.org*), as well as peanut butter and macadamia nuts. The **Gallo Store** (✉ *12 Av. 3–35, Zona 1*) sells T-shirts, caps, and mugs with the logo of Guatemala's best-known beer, as well as the complete line of beer itself.

AROUND QUETZALTENANGO

Quetzaltenango is hardly an urban jungle you'll need to escape, but a group of small towns clustered nearby make pleasant day or half-day trips from the city. Each carves out its identity from its church, its central plaza, and, one or two days a week, its market.

SALCAJÁ

10 km (6 mi) northeast of Quetzaltenango.

What you think is your first glimpse of Quetzaltenango is not Quetzaltenango at all, but actually the Quiché market town of Salcajá. With the growth of the metropolitan area, you'll barely know where one ends and the other begins these days, but Salcajá warrants a brief stop on your way into or out of Quetzaltenango.

Salcajá puts a different spin on Guatemalan textiles with its famous *jaspe* weavings. These are similar to the Asian *ikat* technique, and although the process is historically associated with Asia, it is assumed to have developed independently in Mesoamerica—and often likened to old-fashioned tie-dyeing. The artisan first colors strands of warp, the lengthwise yarns attached to a foot-operated treadle loom, in a resist-dyeing process, usually with hot wax that prevents exposure of some of the materials to the dye. The elaborate designs require painstaking, labor-intensive precision. You'll see the results at Salcajá's Tuesday market.

DON'T WAIT FOR THE HOLIDAYS

Have a craving for holiday eggnog? There's no need to hang on until December in this part of Guatemala. Salcajá is the center of distilling of *rompopo* (a concoction of egg yolks, honey, sugar, cinnamon, and white rum). Many households make their own in small quantities, but the town is also home to two rompopo factories. It goes down very easily… a bit too easily, in fact.

GETTING HERE AND AROUND

Salcajá sits at the turnoff to Quetzaltenango at the Cuatro Caminos crossroads on the Pan-American Highway. Chicken buses leave throughout the day from Quetzaltenango's Minerva bus terminal. The trip takes 10 minutes and costs Q3.

EXPLORING

The town's **Iglesia de San Jacinto** (✉ *Parque Central,* ☎ *No phone* 🎫 *Free* ⏲ *Daily 8–12*) dates from 1524 and is said to be the oldest surviving church in Central America. It suffered severe structural damage in a 2001 earthquake.

SAN MIGUEL TOTONICAPÁN

20 km (12 mi) northeast of Quetzaltenango, 10 km (6 mi) east of Salcajá.

This traditional highland village is famous for its wooden toys. "Toto" is full of workshops where a wide variety of handicrafts are actually produced. Come on Saturday for the market day, when you can find handloomed textiles, wax figures, furniture, painted and glazed ceramics, and a year-round assortment of handcrafted Christmas decorations.

GETTING HERE AND AROUND

Chicken buses leave throughout the day from Quetzaltenango's Minerva bus terminal. The trip takes 20 minutes and costs Q4.

ESSENTIALS

Emergencies **Police** (☎ *7766–4374*).

Medical Assistance **Farmacia Batres** (✉ *3 Calle 11–09, Zona 2, Totonicapán* ☎ *7766–3978*).

EXPLORING

Totonicapán's main church, the **Iglesia San Miguel Arcángel** (✉ *Parque Central,* ☎ *No phone* 🎫 *Free* ⏲ *Mon.–Sat. 8–11, Sun. 7–5*), dedicated to its patron, the archangel Michael, dates from 1545, although much of what you see is actually post-earthquake reconstruction done in the late 19th century.

SAN FRANCISCO EL ALTO

18 km (11 mi) northeast of Quetzaltenango, 8 km (5 mi) north of Salcajá.

What is Guatemala's largest market? Everyone guesses Chichicastenango, but it's actually the Friday affair at this highland town an easy drive from Quetzaltenango. (It's Central America's largest such doings, too.) You'll find far less of interest for visitors here than you will in Chichi, but the local color and the experience of its market, with its brilliant views and good buys on the textiles that are for sale, can't be beat. Make sure to leave time to visit the open-field animal market where everything from pigs to parrots is sold. This is pickpocket heaven, so be aware of your belongings and bring only the cash you'll need for the day.

GETTING HERE AND AROUND

Chicken buses leave throughout the day from Quetzaltenango's Minerva bus terminal. The trip takes one hour and costs Q6.

MOMOSTENANGO

30 km (18 mi) northeast of Quetzaltenango, 12 km (7 mi) north of San Francisco El Alto.

It's "Momo" in local parlance and on the front of the buses that shuttle you here from Quetzaltenango. This is one of the few places left in Guatemala where the 260-day Mayan calendar is still observed. The small town has become Guatemala's blanket central. Townspeople turn out woolen blankets (*chamarras*) by foot on treadle looms. The works were historically undyed, bearing simple designs and only the white, black, and brown colors of natural wool; however, dyeing has become a new phenomenon, with all manner of colors to choose from. Check them out, as well as high-quality woolen ponchos on Momo's Wednesday and Sunday market days.

GETTING HERE AND AROUND

Chicken buses leave throughout the day from Quetzaltenango's Minerva bus terminal. The trip takes 90 minutes and costs Q10.

SAN ANDRÉS XECUL

12 km (7 mi) northeast of Quetzaltenango, 2 km (1 mi) north of Salcajá.

A quick detour from the Pan-American Highway brings you to San Andrés Xecul, notable for its canary-yellow baroque church of the same name, which is possibly the most ornate house of worship in the country. The structure's facade contains more than 200 carved figures that echo the designs found in the huipils worn by local women. San Andrés's Thursday market begins on the plaza in front of the church and spills onto the steep streets that lead away from the town center.

GETTING HERE AND AROUND

Chicken buses leave throughout the day from Quetzaltenango's Minerva bus terminal. The trip takes 15 minutes and costs Q4.

ALMOLONGA

5 km (3 mi) south of Quetzaltenango.

In this charming village just outside of Quetzaltenango you'll find women wearing bright orange huipils and beautiful headbands. At the busy Wednesday and Saturday markets you can buy fruits cultivated at the numerous orchards in the area. A few kilometers beyond the town are several hot springs, where you can relax for a few quetzals.

LANGUAGE SCHOOL IN MOMOSTENANGO

Isolated Momostenango has almost no English speakers. Learning Spanish becomes a survival skill here. Think of that as your incentive to practice.

Patzite Spanish School (✉ *1 Calle 4–43* ☎ *7736–5149* 🌐 *www.patzite.20m.com*).

4

GETTING HERE AND AROUND

Chicken buses leave throughout the day from Quetzaltenango's Minerva bus terminal. The trip takes 10 minutes and costs Q3.

ZUNIL

9 km (5½ mi) south of Quetzaltenango, 4 km (2½ mi) south of Almolonga.

★ At the base of an extinct volcano, the radiant village of Zunil is one of the prettiest in the highlands. Mud and adobe houses are clustered around the whitewashed church that marks the center of town. On the outskirts of the village you'll find the local cemetery, which is lined with tombstones painted in soft shades of pink and blue.

Zunil is surrounded by the most fertile land in the valley, so it's no surprise most people make their living off the land. The best day to visit is Monday, when women wearing vivid purple shawls hawk fruits and vegetables grown in their own gardens.

GETTING HERE AND AROUND

Chicken buses leave throughout the day from Quetzaltenango's Minerva bus terminal. The trip takes 15 minutes and costs Q8.

EXPLORING

Zunil is a good place to pay your respects to the highland cigar-smoking deity Maximón. (Residents of Zunil call him "San Simón.") You can ask anyone in town where his likeness is—the site changes in an elaborate procession each November—as almost everyone asks a favor of him at some time or another. The idol has become a tourist attraction, and foreigners are charged a few quetzals to see him. Be sure to bring a small gift, preferably a cigar or a bit of rum. (A few extra quetzals suffice if you don't have anything.) As opposed to the practice in Santiago Atitlán, here you can place the cigar in or pour the liquid into the figure's mouth. (⇨ *See Drinking and Smoking with the Saints in Lago Atitlán section.*)

High in the hills above Zunil are the wonderful hot springs of **Fuentes Georginas.** There are four pools, two of which remain in their natural basins. Unfortunately, the spring has been losing its potency over the years, and is now only tepid. Lounging near the rocky source in the natural pool will give you the most warmth. The springs are tucked in a lush ravine in the middle of a cloud forest, so hikers should take advantage of the beautiful trails that begin here. The complex is open from 8 AM to 6 PM; admission is Q40.

WHERE TO STAY

$ **Fuentes Georginas.** Although they're a bit run-down, these nine bungalows are adequate and have fireplaces that keep you cozy at night. The best part of staying here is having round-the-clock access to the hot springs, which close to the public at 6 PM. The cabins themselves have no hot water, though. **Pros:** good budget value, rates include access to hot springs. **Cons:** spartan rooms show their age. ✉ *8 km (5 mi) from main road* ☎ *5704–2959, 7763–0596 in Quetzaltenango* 🌐 *www.lasfuentesgeorginas.com* *9 bungalows* *In-room: no a/c, no TV. In-hotel: restaurant, bar, pool, parking (no fee), no-smoking rooms* *No credit cards.*

HUEHUETENANGO

94 km (58 mi) north of Quetzaltenango.

At the foot of the Cuchumatán mountain range, Huehuetenango—it's one of those fun Guatemalan place names to say (*way-way-tay-NAHN-go*), but everybody shortens it to "Huehue"—was once part of the powerful Mam empire, which dominated most of the highland area. It wasn't until much later that the Guatemalan Quiché came into the area to stir things up, pushing the Mam up into the mountains.

Today Huehuetenango ("place of the ancestors") is a quiet town in the midst of a fertile coffee region, with few real sights of its own. It serves as a gateway to the magnificent Cuchumatán mountains and the isolated villages scattered across them.

GETTING HERE AND AROUND

Huehuetenango lies on the Pan-American Highway, 60-km (37-mi) west of the Cuatro Caminos turnoff to Quetzaltenango. The highway then continues west to the Mexican border.

Several public bus companies travel between Huehuetenango and Guatemala City. Los Halcones has departures at 7 AM and 2 PM. Rápidos Zaculeu runs buses at 6 AM and 3 PM.

ESSENTIALS

Bank **Bancared** (✉ *4 Calle 6–81, Zona 1, Huehuetenango*).

Bus Contacts **Los Halcones** (✉ *7 Av. 3–62 , Zona 1* ☎ *7764–2251*). **Rápidos Zaculeu** (✉ *3 Av. 5–25, Zona 1* ☎ *7764–1535*).

Emergencies **Police** (☎ *7764–8877*).

Medical Assistance **Farmacia Batres** (✉ *4 Calle 3–62, Zona 1, Huehuetenango* ☎ *7768–2325*). **Hospital Nacional Dr. Jorge Vides Molina** (✉ *Aldea Las Lagunas, Huehuetenango* ☎ *7764–3204*).

EXPLORING

The town surrounds its **Parque Central,** where you'll find a pretty fountain, oyster-shaped bandstand, and relief map of the region.

DON'T CALL IT A XYLOPHONE

Guatemala claims to be the birthplace of the xylophone's cousin, the marimba. The instrument was probably brought over by slaves from West Africa, but the marimba is inexorably tied to the music of this country. The marimba is congressionally declared the national musical instrument of Guatemala, and February 20 is even observed informally as the *Día Nacional de la Marimba* (National Marimba Day).

The highest-quality marimbas take about two months (and about $1,000) to build. The marimba's bars, frequently made of rosewood and tuned one octave lower than those of the xylophone, are arranged like the keys of a piano. The largest instruments span five octaves and require multiple players. Crucial to the marimba's rich, melodious sound are the resonators attached below each bar. Traditionally, gourds served that purpose, but modern instruments employ wood, or even aluminum or polyvinyl chloride tubes. A small hole is cut in each and covered with wax. (Older instruments still employ pigskin or onion skin as a covering.) Strike the bar with the mallet. The sound reverberates, giving a distinctive hum to each note.

4

The butter-yellow **Catedral de la Inmaculada Concepción** stands guard over the main square, and dates from 1874.

The ancient city of **Zaculeu,** 4 km (2 mi) from Huehuetenango, was built around AD 600 by the Mam people. The site was chosen for its strategic location, as it has natural barriers on three sides. The defenses worked all too well against the Spanish. Realizing they could not take the Zaculeu people by force, the Spaniards chose instead to starve them out. Within two months they surrendered. Today the ruins consist of a few pyramids, a ball court, and a two-room museum that gives a few insights into the world of the Mam. The site's restoration is said to be the worst in all of Guatemala, as the original archaeologists simply covered the pyramids with concrete, which was not a common building material in pre-Colombian Central America. Admission is Q25. ✉ *5 km. (3 mi) west of Huehuetenango,* ☎ *No phone* 🎫 *Q30* ⏲ *Daily 8–6.*

A short drive north of Huehuetenango, the dirt road begins to wind its way up into the mountains, where traditional villages are set between massive rocky peaks. There's a **mirador,** or scenic view, about 6 km (4 mi) from Huehuetenango.

WHERE TO EAT AND STAY

¢ LATIN AMERICAN ✕**Jardín Café.** This colorful little corner restaurant is friendly and popular among the locals. Come early for the excellent pancakes served at breakfast, or stop by for beef and chicken dishes—*pepián* (a fricassee in pumpkin and sesame sauce) or chile relleno are favorites here—at lunch or dinner. The menu includes a few Mexican favorites as well. ✉ *4 Calle and 6 Av., Zona 1* ☎ *7769–0769* 💳 *No credit cards.*

$ STEAK ✕**Las Brasas.** Grilled meats are the specialty at Huehuetenango's most elegant restaurant, although simple *típica* tablecloths are the only nod toward decor, actually making it the sole place in town with any atmosphere. The menu has a surprisingly broad range of options. There are

Restaurants
Jardín Cafe 2
Las Brasas 1
Lekaf 3

Hotels
Hotel Casa Blanca 3
Hotel Mary 1
Hotel Zaculeu 2

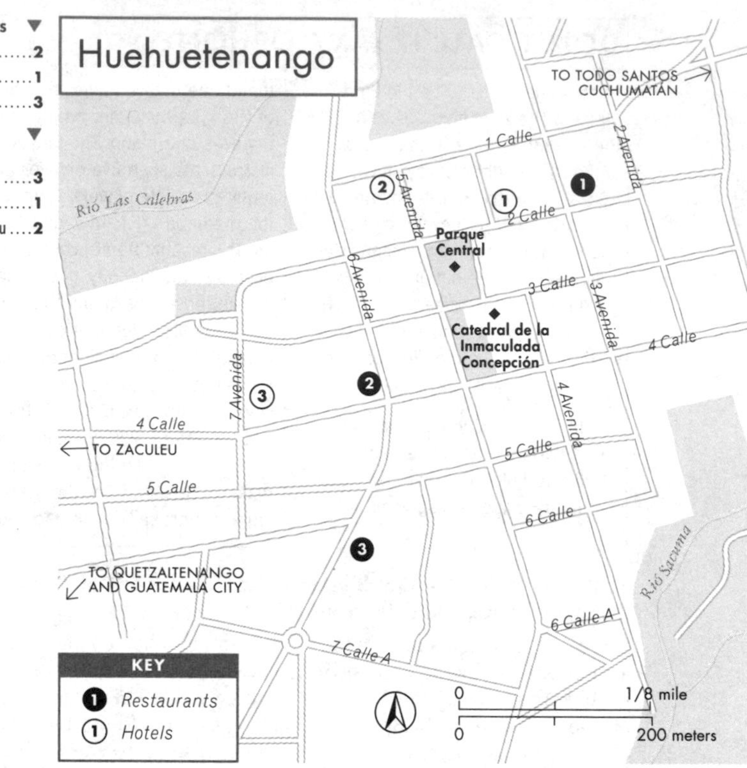

even Chinese entrées, which you won't find anywhere else in town. ✉ *4 Av. 1–55, Zona 1* ☎ *7764–2339* ▭ *V.*

$ PIZZA ✕ **Lekaf.** One of Huehue's better eateries offers everything from filet mignon to pizza, which is reputed by many locals to be the best in town. All can be washed down with a nice selection of *liquados* (fruit or yogurt smoothies). With live music on weekends, this is also a good place for after-dinner drinks. ✉ *6 Calle 6–40, Zona 1* ☎ *7764–3202* ▭ *V* ⏲ *Closed Tues.*

$ **Hotel Casa Blanca.** Who would've thought that out-of-the-way Huehuetenango would have such a top-notch hotel? Spacious rooms, excellent service, and a central location make it the town's best lodging option. Third-floor rooms have great views, especially when the bougainvillea is in full bloom. At the restaurant ($) you can choose between a table in the shady courtyard or in the cozy dining room warmed by a fireplace. **Pros:** attentive service, good restaurant, central location. **Cons:** occasional street noise. ✉ *7 Av. 3–41, Zona 1* ☎ *7769–0777* *casablanca@intellnet.com* *13 rooms* *In-room: no a/c, Wi-Fi. In-hotel: restaurant, Internet terminal, parking (no fee), no-smoking rooms* ▭ *AE, D, DC, MC, V.*

¢ **Hotel Mary.** This four-story hotel in the heart of town offers clean, if basic, accommodations. Ask to see a few rooms, as some are much better than others. **Pros:** good budget value, central location. **Cons:** spartan rooms.

⊠2 Calle 3–52, Zona 1 ☎7764–1618 28 rooms In-room: no a/c, no phone. In-hotel: restaurant, parking (no fee), no-smoking rooms ▭No credit cards.

¢ **Hotel Zaculeu.** When you pass through the front doors of this hotel north of the main square, you enter a courtyard overflowing with greenery. The older rooms, set around a portico, are brightened by locally made fabrics. They can be a bit noisy, however, especially those facing the street. The newer ones in the back are quieter, but lack character. **Pros:** good budget value. **Cons:** some rooms get street noise, some rooms have bland furnishings. *⊠5 Av. 1–14, Zona 1 ☎7764–1086 39 rooms In-room: no a/c, Wi-Fi. In-hotel: restaurant, parking (no fee), no-smoking rooms ▭V.*

LANGUAGE SCHOOL IN HUEHUETENANGO

You find all the services of a medium-size city in Huehuetenango, but very few English speakers. That means ample opportunity to practice your Spanish outside the classroom here.

Xinabajul Spanish School (*⊠4 Av. 14–44Zona 5 ☎7764–6631 www.spanishschoolinguatemala.com*).

4

SHOPPING

A few blocks to the east is the **Mercado Central,** where you can purchase local handicrafts.

TODOS SANTOS CUCHUMATÁN

40 km (24 mi) north of Huehuetenango.

Although it takes about three hours to cover the short distance from Huehuetenango to Todos Santos Cuchumatán, the bumpy ride is probably the best way to experience the tremendous height of the Cuchumatán mountain range. Whether you are driver or passenger, steel your nerves: the ride becomes anxiety-provoking at the many spots where one side of the winding dirt road drops off into a deep ravine. Despite the arduous journey, Todos Santos is one of Guatemala's most frequently visited mountain villages. Though the town was one of Guatemala's hardest hit during the civil war, with a substantial portion of the population fleeing to the safety of nearby Mexico, most residents have now returned.

GETTING HERE AND AROUND

With only extremely simple lodgings, Todos Santos realistically needs to be a day trip. If you have your own vehicle and want to brave the rough road from Huehuetenango yourself, be prepared for an exhausting drive that you'll have to make twice in one day.

The vagaries of public-bus schedules make a day trip here difficult. Soon after you arrive, you'll need to catch your return chicken bus back to Huehuetenango.

Tour operators in Quetzaltenango offer organized excursions, the easiest way to visit Todos Santos. You'll leave very early in the morning and get back in the evening, and the minivan ride will still be hair-raising, but someone else takes care of all the details for you.

EXPLORING

The town's big annual blowout revolves around the November 1 All Saints' Day holiday. (Todos Santos means "All Saints.") Many people come for the extended 10-day celebration between October 21 and November 1. The high point (or low point, depending on your perspective) of the celebration is a horse race in which the competitors ride bareback, but this is no Kentucky Derby. After each leg of the race, each rider takes a drink. His goal is not to cross a finish line, but to be the last one remaining on his horse. The booze flows copiously and, unfortunately, so does the blood from riders who tumble off their steeds (death is not uncommon). All in all, we recommend giving the race a pass.

LANGUAGE SCHOOL IN TODOS SANTOS CUCHUMATÁN

Spanish and the indigenous Mam language are your choices here. Almost no one speaks English in this remote community.

Academia Hispanomaya (✉ *Todos Santos Cuchumatán* ☎ No phone.)

Any other day of the year, Todos Santos, the spiritual heartland of the highland Mam culture, is one of those mystical, magical places in which you feel you've been transported to another world. Market days are Thursday and Saturday, with mostly produce for sale, and the attendant cacophony tossed in at no extra charge. This is one of the few remaining towns in Guatemala when men still wear traditional clothing, in this case candy-cane-stripe pants and woven shirts with long embroidered collars. The women wear stunning red, pink, and purple huipils with indigo skirts.

Las Verapaces

5

WORD OF MOUTH

"The drive to Cobán was long with some difficult mountain driving and beautiful scenery."

—vttraveler

"The highlands around Cobán are less traveled from what I understand."

—Suzie2

www.fodors.com/community

Updated by Gerard Helferich and Teresa Nicholas

Northeast of Guatemala City, the scrubby landscape gives way to forested mountains drained by wild rivers. You may feel you've stepped into northern Europe. This central section of the country is split between Baja Verapaz to the south and Alta Verapaz to the north, collectively known as Las Verapaces. Smaller Baja Verapaz is drier than Alta Verapaz, but mist-covered mountains are the norm in both. Here, the locals say, it rains 13 months out of the year. But the humidity, including a drizzly rain called *chipi-chipi,* has made this Guatemala's cardamom and coffee heartland.

Long the haunt of European budget trave lers, the area, with its dense forests, mysterious caverns, and crystalline rivers, is fast becoming Guatemala's destination for ecotourism. The largest city is workaday Cobán, whose comfortable hotels and reliable restaurants make it a good base. In addition, you'll find the rental-car outlets, bus connections, shuttle-van companies, and tour operators you'll need to discover Las Verapaces' natural wonders. The region hasn't yet seen the throngs of visitors that pass through the more touristed parts of Guatemala, so you can usually find last-minute space on organized excursions, especially if you're staying in Cobán. That said, it never hurts to make plans in advance to avoid disappointment if you have specific days in mind for rafting or caving.

If spelunking or hurtling down white-water rapids is not your idea of a vacation, you can also enjoy more tranquil activities such as bird-watching or visiting an orchid farm—or you can take a break in Cobán while you recover from your wilderness adventures. There you can tour a coffee plantation and hike a national park without even having to leave the city limits. You can visit a rustic 19th-century church or a small museum of Mayan artifacts. Or you can just relax in the main square, where you can soak up the local color and, if you're lucky, catch a parade with participants dressed in elaborate costumes, celebrating a local feast day.

ORIENTATION AND PLANNING

GETTING ORIENTED

The small city of Cobán, the administrative center of Alta Verapaz, anchors this misty highland region. The major Baja Verapaz attractions are easily accessible, lying on or near the Guatemala City highway. The sites you'll visit in Alta Verapaz orbit around Cobán, via some less-than-ideal roads.

TOP REASONS TO GO

Spot the elusive quetzal: Spend the night at the Biotopo del Quetzal, Guatemala's only preserve dedicated to protecting its national symbol, then rise at dawn to hunt for this reclusive bird.

Swim in a limpid emerald pool: Hike the lush trails at Semuc Champey, then cool off in the natural water park that has been called the most beautiful spot in Guatemala.

Go underground: Tour Las Grutas de Lanquín, or hire a guide and explore some of the region's many other limestone caves.

Scream down a white-water river: Sign onto an expedition down the Río Cahabón, whose rapids range from Class III to Class V.

Go native: Las Verapaces is the home of traditional dishes you see on menus all over Guatemala, so try the famous *kaq'ik* and other native fare in the place where they were born.

5

PLANNING

WHEN TO GO

Unlike other parts of Guatemala, Las Verapaces has rainy (May–October) and less-rainy (November–April) seasons, rather than a distinct dry time of year. **■TIP→If you're planning on doing any spelunking (opportunities abound in this region), the drier months offer a more sure-footed hike through the caves.**

Cobán's famous Rabin Ahau indigenous festival is held in late July, so make reservations far in advance if you plan to be here during that time. The same is true for Cobán's other annual celebrations: Holy Week (March or April), which features a variety of religious processions and events; the International Half Marathon (third Sunday in May), which draws runners from all over the world; the Cobán Fair (first week in August), the Guatemalan equivalent of a U.S. county fair; and the Orchid Festival (last week in November).

Las Verapaces makes a good halfway stopping point if you're traveling by road to El Petén, since the region is four to five hours in either direction from Tikal or Guatemala City. Las Verapaces also has good access to the Atlantic coast, and can easily be combined with a visit to that region.

TIMING

Most visitors don't manage to get to Las Verapaces until they already have a couple of Guatemala trips under their belts. A rushed couple of days up here lets you take in Cobán's sights and the classic day trip to Lanquín and Semuc Champey. Add another day for a visit to the Biotopo Quetzal in Baja Verapaz. The Verapaces combine well with a visit to the Petén or the Atlantic lowlands. Either can be reached from here without backtracking to Guatemala City.

GETTING HERE AND AROUND

AIR TRAVEL

There are no airports in Las Verapaces. Most people headed for this region fly into Guatemala City's Aeropuerto Internacional La Aurora.

BUS TRAVEL

Public buses based in Cobán make frequent runs to Las Verapaces' towns. Transportes Monja Blanca has regular service between Guatemala City and Cobán, passing the Biotopo del Quetzal (the driver will let you off if you ask). Relying on public transportation makes it difficult to visit some of the farther-flung attractions such as Semuc Champey or the caves at Lanquín, but there are plenty of private shuttle services and tour operators that will take you to these sites.

Bus Contact Transportes Monja Blanca (☎ *7952–1536 or 7951–1793 in Cobán or 2238–1409 in Guatemala City*).

CAR TRAVEL

Having a car is ideal for exploring Las Verapaces. Primary and secondary highways are in good shape, but beyond that, they can degenerate into dirt and gravel. Fog frequently veils rural roads at night, so try to arrive at your destination before dark. Dotting the region are numerous green DISMINUYA SU VELOCIDAD signs with a silhouette of a leaping deer, warning you to slow down for deer crossings.

HEALTH AND SAFETY

Las Verapaces doesn't offer any particular security issues, but you should exercise reasonable caution. In Cobán take the same measures you would in any city: Be aware of your surroundings, don't flash money or jewelry, keep an eye on your camera, bags, and other possessions, and avoid deserted areas. When hiking in remote zones, we recommend that you be accompanied by a guide. Finally, consult the CDC's Health Information for International Travel, and speak to your own physician about the advisability of taking anti-malaria pills.

Emergency Services Police (☎ *7952–1225 in Cobán, 7940–0050 in Salamá*).

MONEY MATTERS

Currency and traveler's checks can be exchanged in Cobán, and you can get cash at the numerous ATMs. Some banks will give you cash advances on credit cards. In smaller towns in the region you're unlikely to find ATM's, so plan accordingly.

RESTAURANTS

The region's most notable dish is *kaq'ik*, or in Spanish, *caldo de chunto,* a turkey stew. You'll find it almost everywhere, although each establishment renders the Mayan spelling a bit differently: *K* might be *C* might be *Q*. Whether urban or rural, the region is mostly the realm of small, family-run restaurants that dish up plenty of hearty food, such as venison and homemade breads.

HOTELS

Think "small" when contemplating where you'll overnight in this region, both in terms of the number of options—there aren't a lot—and the size. With few exceptions, the typical Verapaces hostelry is a small, family-run place. For that reason, reservations are a good idea any time of the year. Air-conditioning is unheard of up here, but you won't miss it.

WHAT IT COSTS IN GUATEMALAN QUETZALES

	¢	$	$$	$$$	$$$$
RESTAURANTS	under Q40	Q40–Q70	Q70–Q100	Q100–Q130	over Q130
HOTELS	under Q160	Q160–Q360	Q360–Q560	Q560–Q760	over Q760

Restaurant prices are based on the median main course price at dinner. Hotel prices are for two people in a standard double room in high season, including tax and service.

VISITOR INFORMATION AND TOURS

There are no tourist offices in Las Verapaces, but most tour operators can provide information on area attractions and arrange tours. Aventuras Turísticas, Maya'ch Expeditions, and Cobán Travels organize tours of Cobán and the region, including the Grutas de Lanquín and Semuc Champey. Proyecto Ecológico Quetzal also specializes in tours of the area, and can arrange homestays with indigenous Q'eqchí families.

Contacts Aventuras Turísticas (✉ *3 Calle 2–38 5, Zona 3, Cobán* ☎ *7951–4213* 🌐 *www.aventurasturisticas.com*). **Cobán Travels** (✉ *5 Av. 2–28, Zona 1, Cobán* ☎ *7951–7371*). **Maya'ch Expeditions** (✉ *1 Calle 14–11 5, Zona 1, Cobán*

THE HAUNTED VERAPACES

Attribute it to the mist that cloaks the region, but Las Verapaces abounds in legends of spirits, both malevolent and benign. Many a man stumbling home from the local cantina claims to have encountered the fearsome *Cadejos,* the apparition of a large, fiery-eyed dog. However, that's better than a run-in with the beautiful temptress *Simanagua,* who may lure him, sirenlike, to his demise.

The unidentified wailing that pierces the night might be the *Llorona*—the apparition of a young woman whose cries materialize at houses where someone has died. According to legend, she spends eternity searching for her lost child.

The Llorona's late-night weeping could be punctuated with the crowing of the *Saktzoxul,* the ghost-rooster. Never stop by the figlike *amate* tree at midnight. Although its sap is used as a solvent in herbal remedies, the devil is said to linger there in the wee hours.

Residents of many towns and cities in Guatemala have told these tales for generations. Is there a word of truth to any of these stories? Probably not, but don't let that spoil your fun on some dark, misty, *chipi-chipi*-shrouded night.

☎ *5658–6778* 🌐). **Proyecto Ecológico Quetzal** (✉ *2 Calle 14–36, Zona 1, Cobán* ☎ *7952–1047* 🌐 *www.ecoquetzal.org*). **Semuc Champey** (🌐 *www.semucchampey.com*).

BAJA VERAPAZ

Baja Verapaz gets fewer visitors than its better-known neighbor, Alta Verapaz. It's a primarily agricultural region where farmers cultivate sugar and vegetables, but have begun branching out into nontraditional activities such as beekeeping. The main attractions here are the moody cloud forest and Guatemala's only quetzal reserve.

BIOTOPO DEL QUETZAL

50 km (31 mi) south of Cobán; 166 km (100 mi) northeast of Guatemala City.

★ **GETTING HERE AND AROUND**

All Guatemala City–Cobán buses stop at the entrance to the reserve. Drivers know it as "el biotopo." You can also get any Cobán tour operator to organize transportation or a guided tour.

ESSENTIALS

Emergency Services **Police** (☎ *7940–0050 in Salamá*).

Medical Assistance **Farmacia Batres** (✉ *7 Av. 6–99 Zona 1, Salamá* ☎ *4219–1450*). **Hospital Nacional de Salamá** (✉ *1 Calle 1–01, Zona 4, Salamá* ☎ *7940–0125*).

EXPLORING

A 2,849-acre tract of cloud forest along the road to Cobán, the **Biotopo del Quetzal** was created to protect its resplendent namesake species, which is endangered because of the indiscriminate destruction of the country's forests.

The reserve offers the chance to see the quetzal in its natural habitat during its mating season, between April and June. Oddly enough, the best place to see the birds is not in the park itself, but in the parking lot of the Ranchito del Quetzal, 1½ km (1 mi) north. Since it is easier to spot quetzals around dawn or dusk, it's worth spending a night in the area. Even if you don't catch a glimpse of the legendary bird, there are plenty of other species to spot—you're actually far more likely to see a brilliant emerald toucan than you are a quetzal.

Expect rain here year-round, or at least the Verapaces' famed, drizzly chipi-chipi. (March and April clock in as the least-wet months.) At altitudes ranging from 1,500 to 2,300 meters (4,900 to 7500 feet), temperatures here average 16°C (60°F). The resulting luxuriant greenery of the cloud forest is gorgeous in its own right. One of the last remaining cloud forests in Guatemala, the Biotopo del Quetzal is a vital source of water for the region's rivers. Moisture that evaporates from Lago Izabal settles here as fog, which provides sustenance for the towering old-growth trees. Plants like lichens, hepaticas, bromeliads, and orchids abound.

If you're lucky, you can see howler monkeys swinging above the two well-maintained trails, the 2-km (1-mi) Los Helechos (The Ferns) and the 4-km (2½-mi) Los Musgos (The Mosses). The latter takes a short detour past a series of beautiful waterfalls. Plan on 45 minutes to an hour for the shorter trail and about double that for the longer hike. Both trails cross a river with concrete bathing pools where you can swim if you don't mind the cold. An interpretive guide is available at the stand at the trailheads. ☎ *No phone* 🎫 *Q40* ⏲ *Daily 7–4.*

WHERE TO EAT AND STAY

$ LATIN AMERICAN ✕ **Café La Granja.** Homemade everything adds a nice touch to this farmhouse-style restaurant between the Biotopo del Quetzal and Cobán. Sauces, dressings, jellies, tortillas, and cheeses are all prepared on-site. The place comes into its own with its huge farm-style breakfasts of eggs, breads, plantains, beans, and cheeses. It's a terrific place to stop if you're out early in the morning. If you go for dinner, get there early: the place closes at 7:30 PM. ✉ *Km 187, Carretera a Cobán* ☎ *7953–9003* 💳 *AE, D, DC, MC, V.*

$ 🏨 **Posada Montaña del Quetzal.** We like the one- and two-bedroom cabins in this roadside lodging near the Biotopo del Quetzal. All are set back from the road and can accommodate four to eight people. Each has a much-appreciated fireplace with ample wood supply for those chilly nights, of which there are many up here, making them much cozier than the simply furnished, stucco-wall, brick-floor rooms in the main building closer to the highway. The Posada operates its own small nature reserve; it's ideal for short hikes and is full of orchids, including the region's famed *monja blanca*. **Pros:** play area for kids; orchid garden and private nature preserve; some rooms with fireplaces. **Cons:** basic accommodations; lack of amenities and services. ✉ *Km 156, Carretera a Cobán* ☎ *5976–7680* *26 rooms, 10 cabins* *In-room: no a/c, no phone, no TV. In-hotel: restaurant, room service, pools, laundry service, Internet terminal, parking (free), some pets allowed, no-smoking rooms* *AE, D, DC, MC, V* *EP.*

> **MARIO DARY RIVERA**
>
> The Biotopo del Quetzal is officially known as the Biotopo Mario Dary Rivera in honor of the Guatemalan ecologist who fought for its creation. Dary Rivera accomplished much in his short life (1928–81). A pharmaceutical chemist by training, he undertook postgraduate studies in biology, and founded that department at Guatemala City's Universidad de San Carlos. His tireless efforts led to the creation of the country's only quetzal reserve here in Baja Verapaz in 1976.

$ ★ **Ram Tzul.** Resembling little tree-house temples, the Ram Tzul's funky cabins have rustic log-stump floors and pitched pine and cedar ceilings—and terrific views of the surrounding private nature reserve. The octagonal stained-glass windows are a little incongruous, but the bamboo furniture and studied rusticity more than make up for them. The hotel has its own trail that leads to a magnificent 60-meter (197-foot) waterfall, which is worth the visit even if you're not a guest. **Pros:** beautiful setting; incredible views from the guest rooms; private trail and waterfall. **Cons:** no pool; no Internet; lobby could use some redecorating. ✉ *Km 158, Carretera a Cobán* ☎ *2335–1805* *2335–1802* *12 rooms* *In-room: no a/c, no phone, no TV. In-hotel: restaurant, room service, bar, laundry service, parking (free)* *AE, D, DC, MC, V* *EP.*

ALTA VERAPAZ

The *alta* (high) and *baja* (low) designations to the two Verapaces are a bit of a misnomer, in that both are at relatively high elevations above the Atlantic lowlands to the east and El Petén to the north. The Alta Verapaz portion of the twin regions sits high atop limestone rock with a mostly unexplored network of caverns underneath. Using Cobán as a base, you can easily explore Alta Verapaz's two main draws, the caverns known as las Grutas de Lanquín and the hiking trails and swimming holes of Semuc Champey.

COBÁN

214 km (133 mi) northeast of Guatemala City.

Spanish King Charles V dubbed Cobán *La Ciudad Imperial* ("the Imperial City"), a designation that generates pride among residents even today. Little remains of the town's regal past, however. It has fallen victim to the wrecking ball and an out-with-the-old, in-with-new mentality of successive city governments. This mostly indigenous city of 70,000 bustles with prosperity, thanks to its position as a hub of the

CLOSE UP

The National Bird

Perhaps no bird is tied to the culture and symbolism of a country the way the resplendent quetzal is to Guatemala. As the national emblem, it appears on the country's coat of arms and flag, and it even gives its name to the currency. The elusive quetzal has been revered since the days of the ancient Maya, who called it the winged serpent. Though the Maya often captured quetzals to remove their tail feathers, killing one was a capital offense.

Tradition holds that the quetzal was the spiritual guide of Maya warrior Tecún Umán, Guatemala's national hero. When Tecún Umán was mortally wounded in battle with Spanish explorers, the story says his quetzal alighted on his chest, staining itself with its dying master's blood, forever giving the male bird its distinctive scarlet breast. Legend also says that its sadness over Tecún Umán's death silenced the quetzal's once beautiful song. The quetzal has long symbolized freedom; it is said the bird cannot survive in captivity, a fact that has been proven false by the quetzals that live and breed in Mexico City's zoo.

Central American cloud forests remain the natural habitat of the resplendent quetzal (*Pharomachrus mocinno*), one of six quetzal species, and misty Las Verapaces offers Guatemala's most likely place to spot one. Although the female quetzal is attractive, the male is spectacular, with its distinctive crimson belly, blue-green back, and long tail. (Think "robin" for the body size, but the tail more than doubles that length.) Its conspicuous appearance notwithstanding, the quetzal can be difficult to spot in the lush foliage of the cloud forest. April through June, mating season, is your best bet, when males and females take turns incubating their eggs.

lucrative coffee and cardamom industries, and to its role as the center of a growing tourism region.

The longtime residents of Cobán are the Q'eqchí Maya. Though they are seldom featured in the tourism brochures, many women still wear traditional clothing. *Cortes* (woven skirts), each made of 8 meters (27 feet) of fabric, are gathered and usually worn to just below the knees. They are traditionally paired with embroidered *huipiles* fashioned from a rectangular piece of fabric with a hole cut out for the neck and the sides sewn up, but today many women wear lacy, machine-made blouses instead.

GETTING HERE AND AROUND

Transportes Monja Blanca runs comfortable buses between Guatemala City and Cobán. Buses depart every hour or so from 4 to 4 at both ends of the route, and the trip takes five hours. As of this writing, a new bus terminal is being constructed outside of Cobán, near Viveros Verapaz; when it's completed, all buses will arrive and depart from there.

If you're driving from Guatemala City, take the Carretera Atlántica to El Rancho, where you'll take Route 17 north to reach Cobán. Gas stations line the route.

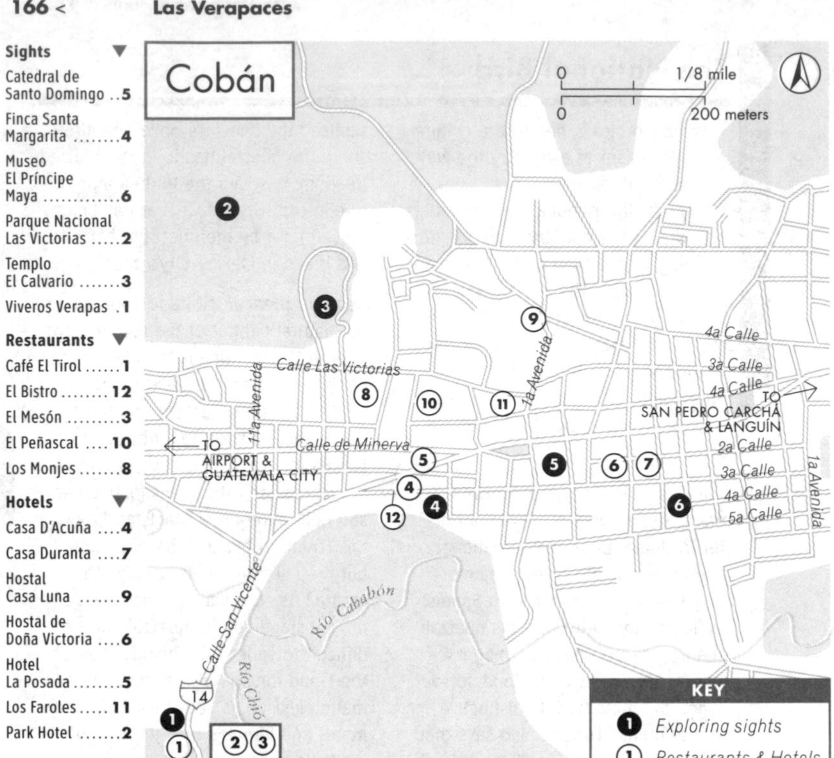

Several agencies in Cobán rent cars for about Q400 a day, which is a great deal if you want to spend some time exploring the area on your own. Companies with good reputations include Inque and Tabarini. Reserve ahead of time, especially on the weekends.

Cobán is divided into 10 *zonas,* but your visit will likely be confined to the four central sectors. Numbered *avenidas* (avenues) run north–south, *calles* (streets) run east–west, and the same grid of addresses appears in each zone. 1 Calle, the main east–west downtown street, serves as the boundary between Zonas 1 and 2 west of the cathedral, and between Zonas 3 and 4 east of the cathedral.

SAFETY AND PRECAUTIONS

Cobán is not particularly dangerous, but you should exercise the usual precautions you would in any city. In particular, avoid hiking alone in the Nacional Parque Las Victorias, where robberies have been reported.

ESSENTIALS

Bank **Banco Reformador** (✉ *1 Av. 2–66, Zona 1, Cobán* ☎ *7952–1011*).

Bus Contacts **Transportes Monja Blanca** (✉ *8 Av. 15–16, Zona 1, Guatemala City* ☎ *2238–1409* ✉ *2 Calle 3–77, Zona 4, Cobán* ☎ *7952–1536 or 7951–1793*).

Emergency Services **Police** (☎ *7952–1225*).

A BIT OF HISTORY

In the history of a country with a frequently violent past, one man stands out for his devotion to peace. Dominican priest Bartolomé de Las Casas (1484–1566) crusaded tirelessly in opposition to the atrocities committed by Spanish colonists against indigenous peoples and advocated for an end to their use as slaves. Though more frequently associated with neighboring Mexico—in his honor, his name was appended to that of southern Mexico's indigenous city par excellence, San Cristóbal de las Casas—the priest's ideals were tested strongly here in Las Verapaces. As the home of the Rabinal Maya, one of the most feared indigenous groups in Mesoamerica, the region was the site of fierce fighting in the early 1500s. Spanish colonists were unable to overcome the Rabinal with brute force, but their atrocities against the original inhabitants of the land continued.

Las Casas struck an unusual bargain with his compatriots: if the military stayed away, he would deliver the land without spilling a single drop of blood. Spain reluctantly agreed, and Las Casas began translating hymns and scripture into local languages. The Rabinal chief, realizing the Spanish weren't going to go away, agreed to be baptized. His people followed suit, and the "conquest" of the region meant that the area was soon dotted with orderly Spanish-style villages. It became known as Las Verapaces, "The Lands of True Peace."

Historians debate Las Casas's legacy. He initially advocated replacing indigenous labor with African slaves, a position he later recanted when he saw the harsh treatment the Africans received at the hands of the Spanish. And the measures Las Casas proposed for bringing peace did dilute the strength and dominance of indigenous culture. However, during Guatemala's darkest years in the 1980s, those who yearned for true peace frequently invoked the memory of the iconic Dominican priest.

5

Medical Assistance Farmacia Zuiva (✉ *1 Av. 2–78, Zona 2, Cobán* ☎ *7952-9750*). **Hospital Regional de Cobán** (✉ *8 Calle 1–24, Zona 11, Cobán* ☎ *7952–2050*).

Rental Cars Inque (✉ *3 Av. 1–18, Zona 4, Cobán* ☎ *7952–1994*). **Tabarini** (✉ *8 Av. 2–27, Zona 2, Cobán* ☎ *7952–1504* 🌐 *www.tabarini.com*).

TOP ATTRACTIONS

❹ **Finca Santa Margarita.** For a nation so involved with the coffee industry, Guatemala offers few opportunities for visitors to watch its principal export being produced. The Finca, three blocks west of Cobán's Parque Central, is a pleasant exception. Here you can take a 45-minute tour of an operating coffee farm and witness the process of planting, growing, harvesting, and processing coffee beans. Owned by the Dieseldorff family, which has lived in Cobán for more than a century, the wooden buildings have a distinct Old World feel. ✉ *3 Calle 4–12, Zona 2* ☎ *7951–3067* 🎫 *Q30* 🕒 *Weekdays 8:30–11 and 2–4, Sat. 8:30–11.*

2 **Parque Nacional Las Victorias.** Near Templo El Calvario, the park sits on what used to be a privately owned plantation. Today it is filled with lush vegetation and winding paths that have great views of the town. There are also picnic facilities and a play area for kids. Robberies have occurred here; we advise against making the visit without a guide. Aventuras Turísticas leads daily tours to the park. ✉ *11 Av. and 3 CalleZona 1* ☎ *7951–3090* *Q6* *Daily 8–5*

3 **Templo El Calvario.** A short walk from the modern markets of central Cobán sits the city's best known sight, which offers one of the best views in the area.

Tradition holds that an indigenous hunter happened upon a pair of sleeping jaguars here, but decided not to kill them. He later returned to the location to find an image of Jesus, which town elders took as a sign that a church should be built at the site. The present El Calvario is not that original church; the structure you see dates from 1810, and sits at the top of a cobblestone path with 130 steps, each representing a bead of the rosary. A series of small shrines, each sheltering a cross darkened with ash, lines the path up to the church. The lowest shrine is traditionally devoted to prayers of any type. The middle stop is for requests related to affairs of the heart. The highest shrine, near the church entrance, is the place to pray for good health. If you light a votive candle, pay attention to the way the flame burns: local belief says an upright, vertical flame is a sure sign your prayer will be answered; any flickering of smoke or tilting of the flame portends a less certain response. ✉ *3 Calle and 7 Av., Zona 1* ☎ *No phone* *Free* *Daily 5:30–6.*

WORTH NOTING

5 **Catedral de Santo Domingo.** The whitewashed church bordering the main square is worth peeking into, although it is quite understated. To the right of the cathedral is the convent. Built in the late 1500s, it is one of Cobán's oldest surviving buildings, and now serves as the diocesan offices. In front, an odd, modern orange-and-yellow bandstand mars the central park and blocks your ability to get a good photo of the cathedral. Residents have dubbed it "the tortilla press," and most would be just as happy to see it torn down. ✉ *1 Av. and 1 Calle, Zona 3* ☎ *7951–3396.*

La Islas. This very pleasant balneario, or "resort," is located in the town of San Pedro Carchá, 6 km (4 mi) east of Cobán. On a clear-running river, Las Islas ("the islands") tempts bathers with a variety of natural and man-made falls and pools, as well as a water slide. The grounds are spacious and well maintained, with picnic tables, changing rooms, and a restaurant that opens on weekends. On Sundays there's also a small handicrafts market with half a dozen vendors. ✉ *San Pedro Carchá* ☎ *No phone Q10 Daily 7–4.*

OFF THE BEATEN PATH

While you're in the area, you may want to stop by **San Pedro Carchá**, a modern market town serving local farmers. Although San Pedro doesn't offer much in the way of conventional tourist sights, it does present a good opportunity to see how average Guatemalans live. There's a large daily market (✉ *9 Av. 9–08*) that spills out into the surrounding streets, offering everything from fresh produce to fabrics, poultry to household items. Set on the Plaza Principal is the Parroco de San Pedro, a white church with a pretty ochre-and-rose interior.

6 **Museo Príncipe Maya.** A 10-minute walk from the plaza, this museum has a private collection of ancient Mayan artifacts recovered from El Petén, Alta Verapaz, and Quiché. Though the exhibit is relatively small, the variety of pieces is impressive. Known for its miniature Olmec quartz figurines, the museum also has fearsome masks, giant sacrificial pots, a reconstructed tomb, jade jewelry, and weapons. ✉ *6 Av. 4–26, Zona 3* ☎ *7952–2809* 🎫 *Q20* ⏲ *Mon.–Sat. 9–6.*

GOOD HABITS

Guatemala's national flower, the *monja blanca* (*white nun*), grows in abundance here. Legend holds that a colonial-era nobleman asked a young woman of meager means to marry him. She happily accepted, but her family saw the marriage as their ticket to riches and placed incessant demands on their new son-in-law. She died of despair over her family's behavior and turned into a delicate white orchid with petals resembling a nun's habit.

5

1 **Viveros Verapaz.** Run by the friendly Millie Mittelstaedt de Hernández, this magnificent orchid farm is a good place for an afternoon jaunt. The farm grows 400 different species native to Guatemala, and Mittelstaedt clearly enjoys sharing her passion with visitors, pointing out breathtaking blossoms and describing the painstaking process of coaxing the temperamental ornamentals to bloom. The orchids flower in late November through February; Cobán's International Orchid Festival is held annually the last week of November. ✉ *Carretera Antigua, 2 km (1 mi) south of Cobán* ☎ *5700–7722* 🎫 *Q10* ⏲ *Mon.–Sat. 7–4.*

WHERE TO EAT

$ CAFE ✕ **Café El Tirol.** The owner of this popular café grew up on a coffee plantation near Cobán. Duly qualified, she serves the largest selection of caffeinated beverages in this coffee-growing region. Hot coffee, cold coffee, coffee with liquor, coffee with chocolate, and a wide assortment of teas make up most of the menu. She also whips up some of the best breakfasts in town. The café is on the grounds of the Viveros Verapaz. ✉ *Carretera Antigua, 2 km (1 mi) south of Cobán* ☎ *5700–7722* 💳 *No credit cards* ⏲ *Closed Sun.*

$ ECLECTIC Fodor's Choice ★ **El Bistro.** This is a "must stop" when you're in Cobán. Have a seat in one of the intimate dining rooms or out in the garden and enjoy delicious international dishes. Though the menu includes nicely prepared pastas and pizzas, the grilled meats, accompanied by grilled vegetables and a variety of homemade salsas, are especially succulent. All the vegetables, and even the lamb and pork, are grown organically on El Bistro's own farm outside of town. The coffee stands out even in a city known for the brew, and the breakfasts here are legendary. The homemade desserts are the best in the city; a brownie or a slice of carrot cake makes a great midday snack. The restaurant's gift shop also offers the highest-quality handicrafts in Cobán. ✉ *4 Calle 3–11, Zona 2* ☎ *7951–0482* 💳 *AE, DC, MC, V.*

CLOSE UP

The German Connection

The economic prosperity of Las Verapaces traces back to the wave of German immigrants who settled here in the 1870s. Invited by President Justo Rufino Barrios to inhabit and work the land, they turned the region into a center for coffee and cardamom production.

Subsequent generations of Germans never saw much need to assimilate, and kept their language, German citizenship, and ties to their homeland. That never bothered anyone until the 1930s, when a few swastika flags began fluttering over Cobán. When Guatemala declared war on Hitler in 1941, the Germans were given a choice: renounce their German citizenship or be expelled. Many chose to leave. Others stayed, became Guatemalan citizens, and continued working in the industries they had established. You can see evidence of their presence in the German surnames up here—you're as likely to meet a Schmidt as you are to encounter a Rodríguez—but there's no need to dust off your high-school German. They all speak Spanish these days.

$ LATIN AMERICAN **El Mesón.** The lime meringue pie alone is worth a trip to this charming log cabin–turned restaurant just south of Cobán, but you'll likely want to precede dessert with a full Verapaces-style meal. The ubiquitous regional turkey stew kaq'ik is on the menu, of course, but you can also try roast lamb, beef, or rosemary chicken. ✉ *Km 207.7, Carretera a Cobán* ☎ *7951–0141* ▭ *AE, D, DC, MC, V.*

$ LATIN AMERICAN **El Peñascal.** This large restaurant is popular with a local crowd, and at lunchtime you're likely to find a soccer match playing on the projection TV. The decor is simple, with tile floors, tall ceilings, and guitars hanging from the walls. The menu is extensive and includes pastas, grilled meats, seafood, sandwiches, and burgers, but the specialties here are traditional dishes such as *kaq'ik* (preceded by a bowl of hot chocolate), *suban-ick* (chicken and pork in a delicious tomato sauce), *jocón* (chicken in a mild green sauce), and *sopa de tortuga* (turtle soup). Save room for the homemade pies. ✉ *5 Av. 2–61, Zona 1* ☎ *7951–2102* ▭ *AE, D, DC, MC, V.*

¢ ECLECTIC **Los Monjes.** This modern, family-style restaurant is a good place to stop for lunch or a snack after touring the nearby Parque Nacional or El Calvario. Located on the second floor of a small shopping center, overlooking the street, it offers a wide variety of grilled meats and seafood, as well as lighter fare such as burgers, sandwiches, pizzas, pasta, and salads. ✉ *7 Av. 1–17, Zona 1* ☎ *7951–0219* ▭ *V.*

WHERE TO STAY

¢ **Casa D'Acuna.** The owners of El Bistro also run a small, clean, and exceptionally inexpensive hostel next door. Lining a long first-floor corridor, the rooms have either double or bunk beds; all have shared baths. **Pros:** central location; orchid-filled courtyard; friendly staff. **Cons:** basic accommodations. ✉ *4 CAlle 3–11, Zona 2* ☎ *7951–0482* 📠 *7951–0449* *7 rooms* *In-room: no a/c, no phone, no TV. In-*

hotel: restaurant, Internet terminal, parking (free), no-smoking rooms ▭ *AE DC, MC, V* 🍴 *EP.*

$$ **Casa Duranta.** This hotel in a century-old house offers great in-town value and gives old Cobán standby La Posada some competition. The building is constructed, colonial-style, around a lovely garden. Rooms contain two queen-size beds, tile floors, huge bathrooms, and lots of wrought iron. Enjoy the evenings on the chairs outside your room on the wide veranda lining the perimeter of the garden. Top it all off with a knowledgeable owner, and you have one of our favorite lodgings in the area. The restaurant serves local cuisine and is open daily except Monday. **Pros:** beautiful garden, pleasant veranda. **Cons:** some distance from city center, street noise in front rooms. ✉ *3 Calle 4–46, Zona 3* ☎ *7951–4188* 🌐 *www.casaduranta.com* *10 rooms* *In-room: no a/c, no phone, Wi-Fi. In-hotel: restaurant, laundry service, Internet terminal, Wi-Fi, parking (free), no-smoking rooms* ▭ *AE, D, DC, MC, V* 🍴 *EP.*

Fodor's Choice ★

¢ **Hostal Casa Luna.** If your tastes run toward the simple, then this modestly furnished backpackers' hostel near the center of Cobán makes for a good budget find. Three of the six rooms are for one or two people; the other three have bunk beds and can sleep up to four; bathrooms are shared. Plenty of hammocks are hanging out in the garden and are nice to come back to at the end of a long day. The proprietors also run Cobán Travels tour company. **Pros:** budget price; good location; friendly atmosphere. **Cons:** spartan accommodations; lack of privacy; maintenance not the best. ✉ *5 Av. 2–28, Zona 1* ☎ *7951–3528* *6 rooms* *In-room: no a/c, no phone, safe (some), no TV (some). In hotel: laundry service, Internet terminal, W-Fi, parking (paid), some pets allowed, no-smoking rooms* ▭ *AE, D, DC, MC, V* 🍴 *EP.*

$ **Hostal de Doña Victoria.** The rustic Doña Victoria was built as a convent more than 400 years ago. It's filled with charming antiques; rocking chairs and overstuffed couches line the wide stone porch encircling the patio, which is also graced with an old stone well. Rooms are spacious and have beds piled high with blankets for the cold Cobán nights. **Pros:** charming atmosphere; central location; good value. **Cons:** may be a little too rustic for some tastes. ✉ *3 Calle 2–38, Zona 3* ☎ *7951–4213* *11 rooms* *In-room: no a/c, no phone. In-hotel: restaurant, laundry service, Internet terminal, parking (free), some pets allowed, no-smoking rooms* ▭ *V* 🍴 *EP.*

$$ **Hotel La Posada.** True charm pervades La Posada, a lovely colonial home overlooking Cobán's central plaza, which the current owner's grandmother opened as a hotel in 1939. Rooms have wooden floors and exposed beams and are furnished with antiques. Some have special touches like wardrobes and writing desks, and three have fireplaces. Painted blue chairs and cloth hammocks fill the porch overlooking the pretty garden. In the reception area is a Ping-Pong table, which is popular with families. Request a room away from the street if you're bothered by traffic noise. A cozy restaurant with a fireplace serves international as well as Guatemalan favorites. **Pros:** charming atmosphere, central location, good restaurant. **Cons:** street noise. ✉ *1 Calle 4–12, Zona 2* ☎ *7952–1495* 🌐 *www.laposadacoban.com* *16 rooms* *In-room:*

Fodor's Choice ★

5

no a/c, no phone, no TV (some), Wi-Fi. In-hotel: 2 restaurants, room service, laundry service, Internet terminal, Wi-Fi, parking (free), no-smoking rooms ▭ *AE, D, DC, MC, V* 🍽 *EP.*

THERE SHE IS . . .

The Rabin Ahau, Cobán's biggest festival of the year, takes place the last week in July. Gathering indigenous groups from around the country, the event is a great way for visitors to see a variety of authentic native costumes, as well as experience traditional music and dance. The culmination is a Guatemalan-style beauty contest on Saturday night to crown the festival queen, the *Reina Rabin*.

$ **Los Faroles.** This centrally located hotel is popular with Guatemalan business travelers, who appreciate its unusual combination of convenience and tranquillity, thanks to its position on a quiet street one (uphill) block away from the main square. The spotless rooms are simply furnished, with one double bed. Next door is a small coffee roasting plant (owned by the same family), which fills the air with a delightful scent. **Pros:** central location, quiet street, good value. **Cons:** basic accommodations, down steep hill from main square. ✉ *2 C. 3–61, Zona 1* ☎ *7951–1140 and 4136–3490* *21 rooms, 1 suite* *In-room: no a/c, no phone, Wi-Fi. In-hotel: restaurant, room service, Wi-Fi, parking (free), no-smoking rooms* ▭ *V* 🍽 *EP.*

$$ **Park Hotel.** You start seeing the signs advertising this hotel on the Atlantic Highway as you leave Guatemala City, and long before you get here you've memorized the name and location. The place, a few kilometers south of Cobán, is huge, and in that regard very *un*-Verapaces-like, humming with all the activity—gym, shops, playground, meeting rooms—of a hotel that bills itself as a "resort and conference center." Rooms are scattered around the lush grounds; some have fireplaces. The hotel has a lot of amenities and is a good value. **Pros:** park-like setting; many amenities; great for kids. **Cons:** large-hotel feel; outside of town. ✉ *Km 196.5 Carretera a Cobán, Santa Cruz de Verapaz* ☎ *7952–0807* *128 rooms, 8 suites* *In-room: no a/c, no phone (some). In hotel: 2 restaurants, room service, bar, tennis court, gym, laundry service, Wi-Fi, parking (free)* ▭ *AE, D, DC, MC, V* 🍽 *EP.*

SHOPPING

El Bistro (✉ *4 Calle 3–11, Zona 2* ☎ *7951–0482*), Cobán's best restaurant, also has the city's best selection of high-quality handicrafts, specializing in textiles from the highlands. **Finca Santa Margarita** (✉ *3 Calle 4–12, Zona 2* ☎ *7951–3067*), the working coffee plantation near the center of Cobán, has excellent, very reasonably priced coffee for the caffeine addicts on your shopping list. **Monja Blanca** (✉ *4 Calle 3–12, Zona 2* ☎ *7952–1250*) is a small jewelry shop specializing in silver. **Mercado de Artesanias** (✉ *2 Av. between 2 and 3 calles, directly behind the city government building, Zona 1* ☎ *No phone*)offers souvenirs but not much in the way of high-quality handicrafts.

OUTDOOR ACTIVITIES

CAVING The Cuevas de Rey Marco, near the village of San Juan Chamelco, are relatively untouched caves. Tours take you into the caves only a few hundred yards, but for experienced spelunkers the potential for further

CLOSE UP

The Magic Bean

When locusts destroyed Guatemala's blue-indigo and red-cochineal harvests in the early 19th century, ending its lucrative role in the dye industry, no one imagined that a tentative replacement crop called coffee would one day drive the country's economy. The country has all the factors necessary—moderately high altitude, mineral-rich volcanic soil, adequate rainfall, and distinct rainy and dry seasons—to be a major player in the coffee world.

The Asociación Nacional del Café, the Guatemalan Coffee Association, recognizes and certifies eight regional coffees. Tasters wax poetic about **Antigua** in particular, using terms such as "spicy," "smoky," "flowery," and "chocolaty" to describe the highly nuanced flavors of Guatemala's arguably most famous coffee. Like Antigua, the nearby **Fraijanes** and **Acatenango**—the association added the latter as a designated region in 2007—are cultivated in soil enriched by volcanic ash, and are protected from the climatic vagaries of ocean air, giving these three coffees their well-known bright acidity. Volcanic soil is also the key to the flavor of **Atitlán** and **San Marcos,** but their wetter climates, particularly in San Marcos's case, make for softer, fuller-bodied coffees. Guatemala's three nonvolcanic regions—rainy **Cobán,** moderately wet **Oriente,** and dry, remote **Huehuetenango**—also give rise to full-bodied brews.

Guatemala has become the darling of fair-trade advocates: much of the industry here remains the province of small producers, especially around Lake Atitlán. The isolation of regions such as Huehuetenango necessitates close-by milling and drying of beans by local cooperatives, thereby keeping much of the labor in the community and creating a sustainable product. Some 95% of Guatemalan coffee is shade-grown, a green, migratory bird–friendly method of cultivating the product, requiring lower use of pesticides and fertilizers and resulting in less soil erosion. However, production costs for many small operations have begun to exceed prices fetched on the world market—shade-grown means smaller yields, for example—forcing an increasing number of individual farmers off their land and into the cities. Still, coffee has helped transform historically poorer areas of the country, such as the Oriente, near the Honduran border. Producers look to fair-trade certification as a way to produce a better product and reap a higher resulting price. The Germany-based Fairtrade Labelling firm presently certifies several producers here with its fair-trade imprimatur.

The rub for the coffee-loving visitor is that it's difficult to find a decent cup of the stuff here. True to the realities of economics in the developing world, the quality product goes for export, leaving a lower-grade bean behind for the local market. Nor does it help that Guatemalans heavily lace their coffee with sugar. Your best bet is an upscale hotel or restaurant, one in tune with international tastes and that will have export-quality coffee on hand. Souvenir shops also have good product for you to take home.

exploring is limitless, as the caverns stretch for many miles beneath the mountains of the Sierra Yalijux. Getting inside is difficult; expect to crawl through the entrance and cross a waist-high river.

SOCCER Cobán's more-than-respectable soccer team, Cobán Imperial, plays regularly in the hilltop **Estadio Verapaz,** five blocks northwest of the bus station. Sit in the bleachers or on the grassy hillside. Look for the sandwich board in the main square for information about upcoming matches. Tickets are Q30.

LANGUAGE SCHOOLS

Centro de Idiomas Oxford (✉ *4 Av. 2–16, Zona 3, Cobán* ☎ *7951–2836* 🌐 *www.olcenglish.com*).

Escuela de Español Muq'bil'Be (✉ *6 Av. 5–39, Zona 3* ☎ *7951–2459* 🌐 *www.spanishschoolscoban.com*).

LANQUÍN

63 km (39 mi) east of Cobán.

This pretty village, founded in the 16th century, is on the doorstep of some impressive natural wonders, namely the caverns of Lanquín and the limpid pools of Semuc Champey. There's not much to see in town, other than the small, 400-year-old church, but it's the place to stay if you want to arrive at the nearby sites early in the morning.

GETTING HERE AND AROUND

Lanquín is about five hours from Guatemala City (take the Carretera Atlántica to El Rancho, where you'll take Route 17 north, then switch to a mountainous dirt road). It's about an hour and a half from Cobán, where you can rent a car, take a public bus or a collective van, or sign on to an organized tour to get to the caves.

EXPLORING

Portions of the **Grutas de Lanquín,** a system of caves cut through by underground rivers, are easy to explore. The first 30 minutes of the hour-long hike consist of a trail with iron railings to help you keep your footing among the huge stalagmites. Things get hairier toward the end, and you'll want an experienced guide who knows exactly how to help you navigate the path. Visit toward sunset and you'll see thousands of bats leave their dwellings and head for the starry night sky. Entering the caves is worth it, despite the garish labels painted on the rock formations. You could probably figure out yourself what the formations are, but signs point them out to you anyway: *sapo* (toad), *oveja* (sheep), *tigre* (tiger), or *señora* (woman). **■TIP→ You'll get wet and dirty, so wear old clothes. The interiors of the caverns are illuminated, but you'll appreciate a small flashlight.** ☎ *No phone* *Q30; Q10 parking* ⏲ *Daily 8–5.*

WHERE TO STAY

$ **Hotel El Recreo Lanquín Champey.** This large wooden hotel at the mouth of the Grutas is a good choice for budget travelers. There are sparsely furnished single and double rooms as well as several stone-and-concrete cabañas out back. Some rooms share a bathroom. There's also space for camping. The restaurant serves decent Guatemalan fare. **Pros:** close to Grutas de Lanquín and Semuc Champey; extensive grounds. **Cons:** access only via mountainous dirt road; swimming pools not well maintained. ✉ *Km 272, near Grutas de Lanquín* ☎📠 *7983–0057 or 5155–8279* *38 rooms, 4* cabañas *In-room: no a/c, no TV, no phone. In-hotel: restaurant, bar, 2 pools, laundry service, Internet terminal, Wi-Fi, some pets allowed, parking (free)* ▭ *V* 🍽 *EP.*

DID YOU KNOW?

A *National Geographic* team was able to map the entire underground system in 1993, when, in an exceptionally parched year, the water sank to record low levels.

OUTDOOR ACTIVITIES

WHITE-WATER RAFTING

Rafting expeditions on the Río Cahabón, a challenging river near Lanquín, usually last from one to five days. The easiest sectors log in at Class III, but can go up to Class V. Guatemala City–based **Maya Expeditions** (✉ *15 Calle A 14–07, Zona 10, Guatemala City* ☎ *2363–4955* 🌐 *www.mayaexpeditions.com*) arranges trips down the raging river. Local Cobán outfitter **Aventuras Turísticas** (✉ *3 Calle 2–385, Zona 3, Cobán* ☎ *7951–4213* 🌐 *www.aventurasturisticas.com*) arranges single- or multi-day expeditions on the Cahabón.

SEMUC CHAMPEY

10 km (6 mi) south of Lanquín.

GETTING HERE AND AROUND

Fodor's Choice ★

Semuc Champey is close to Lanquín, but it's along a gravel road, and depending on the time of year, you may need a four-wheel-drive vehicle. Every tour operator in Cobán offers all-day excursions to the park, and two companies in Cobán run collective vans. **Transportes Martínez** (☎ *5877–7305*) has vans leaving Cobán every hour on the hour from 5 AM to 5 PM, returning to Cobán every hour on the hour from 3 AM to 3 PM; the fare for the 2-hour ride is Q20 each way. **Astralan** (☎ *7951–1662*) leaves Cobán every hour on the hour from 5:30 AM to 5 PM and returns to Cobán every hour on the hour from 5 AM to 4:30 PM; the fare is Q25 to Lanquín and Q40 to Semuc Champey. As of this writing, a new bus terminal is being built on the edge of Cobán, and when it is completed all collective vans will leave from there.

EXPLORING

Often praised as the most beautiful spot in Guatemala, **Semuc Champey** lives up to that lofty billing. The site appears to be a series of emerald pools surrounded by dense forest and limestone canyon. On further investigation you'll notice that the pools actually form the top of a natural arch through which the raging Río Cahabón flows. Local legend has it that various explorers have tried to enter the underground passage by lowering themselves over the lip of the arch; many turned back right away, while some were swallowed up, their bodies never recovered.

You'll find a series of trails of various lengths here. Bring practical shoes. We recommend starting in the morning with the hour-long Mirador trail which takes you high above the site to give you a feel for the lay of the land (and the water). After that tiring trek, you'll appreciate the shorter, 20-minute Champey trail which leads you to the whirlpools for a refreshing swim. (There are no lifeguards here; swim at your own risk.) The half-hour Cahabón trail takes you back to the park entrance past the point where the river emerges from the cave. If possible, try to avoid holidays, when crowds of visitors dilute the natural experience of the park. ✉ *10 km (6 mi) south of Lanquín* ☎ *No phone* 🎫 *Q50; Q10 parking* ⏲ *Daily 8–6.*

The Atlantic Lowlands

6

WORD OF MOUTH

"The highlight of the region (in my opinion) is the trip up and down the Rio Dulce."

—hopefulist

"I spent a week in Copán studying Spanish last fall, and definitely found a lot to do in the area. Every afternoon was full! I found Copán a pleasant place to spend a whole week."

—mmb23

www.fodors.com/community

By Jeffrey Van Fleet

Guatemala's short Caribbean shoreline doesn't generate the same buzz as those of neighboring Belize and Mexico. The coast—Guatemalans all call it the Atlántico, even though it's the Caribbean you're seeing—stretches a scant 123 km (74 mi). But whatever you call it, there's plenty to keep you occupied in the lowlands on this side of the country.

Tourist brochures tout this coast as "The Other Guatemala" because predominantly indigenous and Spanish cultures of the highlands give way to an Afro-Caribbean tradition that listens to the rhythms of far-off Jamaica rather than taking its cue from Guatemala City.

Although the indigenous culture here isn't as striking as that in the highlands, traces of the Mayan empire, such as the impressive ruined cities of Quiriguá and, just across the border in Honduras, Copán, mark the movement of this ancient people through the lowlands, and you'll run across many inland people who speak only their native Q'eqchí. Living in remote mountain villages, they sometimes must walk a full day or more to get to the market towns. The coastal towns of Livingston and Puerto Barrios are home to the Garífuna, an Afro-Caribbean people who speak a Creole language all their own. In this region largely untouched by tourism is the stunning Lago Izabal, one of Guatemala's great, don't-miss excursions.

Although this region borders the Caribbean, you shouldn't expect *that* Caribbean, the one of white-sand beaches and azure-blue seas. St. Barts it is not, but a visit here makes a pleasant contrast to the rest of Guatemala. After a stay in the chilly highlands, this region of banana plantations, tropical ports, and slowly moving ceiling fans will seem downright languid and sultry. You'll enjoy your trip here much more if you adapt to the local rhythm of life. Wake at sunrise and take care of most of your activities in the morning. With a good book in hand, find a hammock in which to relax during the steamy midday hours. Hit the street again in the late afternoon and evening, when the temperatures are a bit cooler.

ORIENTATION AND PLANNING

GETTING ORIENTED

Think of this region's highlights as being laid out in a large oval loop oriented northeast and southwest. At the northeastern end on Guatemala's short Caribbean coast lie Puerto Barrios, the region's largest city, and its more fun, more interesting sibling, Livingston, which can be reached only by boat across the Bahía Amatique (Amatique Bay). The Río Dulce flows from Livingston southwest to Lago Izabal, Guatemala's largest lake. River and lake meet at the town also usually referred to as Río Dulce, the southwest curve of the loop. From there a short drive brings

TOP REASONS TO GO

Cruise through a canyon: A boat trip up or down the canyoned Río Dulce is Guatemala's signature eco-excursion.

Groove to the punta: Toto, I don't think we're in the highlands anymore. The region's most popular music has its roots in far-away Africa.

Ponder the intricacies of the Maya: Quiriguá, in Guatemala, and Copán, just over the Honduran border, are two of the Mayan world's best preserved ruins complexes. The minutiae of their stelae are still intact to this day.

Soak those aching muscles: The hot springs at various points along the Río Dulce make perfect places for a dip, and all the boat excursions make a stop.

Take a walk on the wild side: Some of the country's best birding and wildlife observation strings along the Río Dulce and Lago Izabal.

you back to the Carretera Atlántica (Atlantic Highway), either southwest to Guatemala City, or northeast back to the coast. Off the route back to Puerto Barrios lie the Mayan ruins of Quiriguá and the more famous Mayan city of Copán, just across the border in Honduras.

Lago Izabal. A seamless lake/river waterway connects inland Fronteras to the town of Río Dulce and the Caribbean coast. The river portion, also called Río Dulce, is one of the country's great tropical excursions.

Along the Atlantic Coast. "Sultry and steaming" describes the weather, music, and cuisine along Guatemala's short Caribbean coast. Lively port towns give you a cultural mix entirely different than what you've seen on the Antigua-Atitlán-Chichi circuit.

Copán (Honduras). One of Mesoamerica's most famous complexes of Mayan ruins sits just across the Guatemalan–Honduran border. It would be a shame to come this far and not take it in.

PLANNING

WHEN TO GO

This side of the country has less distinct rainy and dry seasons; rains are more evenly spaced throughout the year. Ironically, June and July, when the rainy season is getting underway in the rest of the country, are the driest months in the Caribbean region. The best time to visit is November–December, when temperatures are most tolerable. It's best to avoid the region during March and April, when the heat is dizzying and farmers burning their fields in preparation for annual planting leave the skies thick with view-obliterating smoke.

TIMING

Few Guatemala first-timers venture to this part of the country, but you can do justice to the Atlantic lowlands' highlights in four or five days. A trip on Río Dulce (the river) and Lago Izabal with a chance to explore its endpoints, Río Dulce (the town) and Livingston, warrants a couple of days. Although many visitors do Copán as a one-day, cross-border jaunt, a two- or three-day visit is more relaxed. This region fits in nicely with a visit to Las Verapaces or El Petén. Either can be reached easily without heading back to Guatemala City.

GETTING HERE AND AROUND

The Carretera Atlántica (Highway CA–9) forms the northeast–southwest transportation backbone of the region, starting out at Guatemala City and leading to the coast at Puerto Barrios. Perpendicular to this, Highway CA–13 intersects at La Ruidosa, leading northwest to the town of Río Dulce, and beyond to the Petén. Get much farther off this beaten path and you have the option of traveling by water (in some cases you must). Río Dulce (the river) connects Río Dulce (the town) with Livingston on the coast. Livingston can also be reached via boat across Amatique Bay from Puerto Barrios.

AIR TRAVEL

There are presently no flights to the Atlantic lowlands. You'll arrive at La Aurora International Airport in Guatemala City and make your way overland to this region.

BOAT TRAVEL

Ferries make the 90-minute trip between Puerto Barrios and Livingston twice daily. Smaller *lanchas* that leave on an as-needed basis do the same run in about 30 minutes. Drivers belong to a Livingston-based cooperative called Asotransali. There is also boat service for the two-hour trip from Livingston to Río Dulce for approximately Q100. Requena's Charter Service travels the route between Punta Gorda, Belize, and Puerto Barrios and Livingston. Travel time is 90 minutes to Livingston, and another 90 minutes to Puerto Barrios. Tickets cost $18, payable in U.S. currency.

Boat Contacts Asotransali (✉ *Municipal docks, Livingston* ☎ *7947–0870*). **Requena's Charter Service** (☎ *501/722–2070 in Punta Gorda, Belize* 🌐 *www.belizenet.com/requena*).

BUS TRAVEL

The highly regarded Litegua is the public-transportation workhorse of the region, with frequent, comfortable buses connecting the capital with Puerto Barrios and Río Dulce.

Bus Contact Litegua (*Calle Principal, Fronteras [Río Dulce]* ☎ *7930–5251*).

CAR TRAVEL

From Guatemala City most people drive to the Atlantic lowlands via the Carretera Atlántica. The journey to Río Dulce or Puerto Barrios takes about five hours. The stumbling block is always the amount of traffic heading out of the capital. Descending the curving roads through the mountains you can feel the temperature and humidity rising.

There is no place to rent a car in this region. Take care of those needs back in Guatemala City.

HEALTH AND SAFETY

The heat and sun in the Atlantic lowlands can be intense. Be prepared with a good sun hat and lightweight clothing that covers your arms and legs. Shorts don't protect legs from the sun, tall grass, insects, and dust. Also pack plenty of sunscreen and insect repellent.

Robberies have been known to occur in Puerto Barrios and Livingston and at the marina in Río Dulce, so be on your guard. Use the same precautions you would anywhere else—don't wear flashy jewelry and watches, keep your camera in a secure bag, and don't handle money in public. Remain alert for pickpockets, especially in crowded markets. Only hike in the countryside with a reputable guide. Women should never hike alone. As is the case with many other excursions in Guatemala, a visit to the Siete Altares park near Livingston should only be undertaken with an organized group.

Emergency Services Police (☎ *7943–2074 in Esquipulas, 7948–7643 in Puerto Barrios, 7948–3244 in Santo Tomás de Castilla, 7930–5166 in Río Dulce*).

MONEY MATTERS

If you need to exchange cash in the Atlantic lowlands, Banrural has the most branches in the region.

Contacts Banrural (✉ *9 Calle and 1 Av, Puerto Barrios* ☎ *7948–2490* ✉ *Calle Principal, Fronteras [Río Dulce]* ☎ *7930–5159* ✉ *Calle Principal, Livingston* ☎ *7947–0974* ✉ *5 Av. 2-65, El Estor* ☎ *7949–7507*).

6

WHAT IT COSTS IN GUATEMALAN QUETZALES

	¢	$	$$	$$$	$$$$
Restaurants	under Q40	Q40–Q70	Q70–Q100	Q100–Q130	over Q130
Hotels	under Q160	Q160–Q360	Q360–Q560	Q560–Q760	over Q760

Restaurant prices based on the median main course price at dinner. Hotel prices are for two people in a standard double room in high season, including tax and service.

RESTAURANTS

A warm climate means restaurants here are bright, airy alfresco or semi-open places. The outdoor seating is a refreshing change from the chill if you've been in the highlands. As for the food, think one word: coconut, or *coco* in Spanish. It pervades everything here. You might order *leche de coco* (coconut milk), or *pan de coco* (coconut bread). *Sere* is a hearty fish stew cooked in coconut milk. *Rice and beans*—the name is always in English—is the Caribbean adaptation on the beans and rice you've been eating elsewhere in Guatemala. This variation is steeped in (what else?) coconut milk. Another key ingredient here is cassava, locally known as *yuca,* which is used in a labor-intensive bread. This region is also where you'll find some of Guatemala's best seafood.

HOTELS

The Atlantic lowlands mix medium-size resort complexes—they may bill themselves as having a beach, but you'll more likely spend time in the hotel pool—and small, family-run lodgings. All do a brisk business

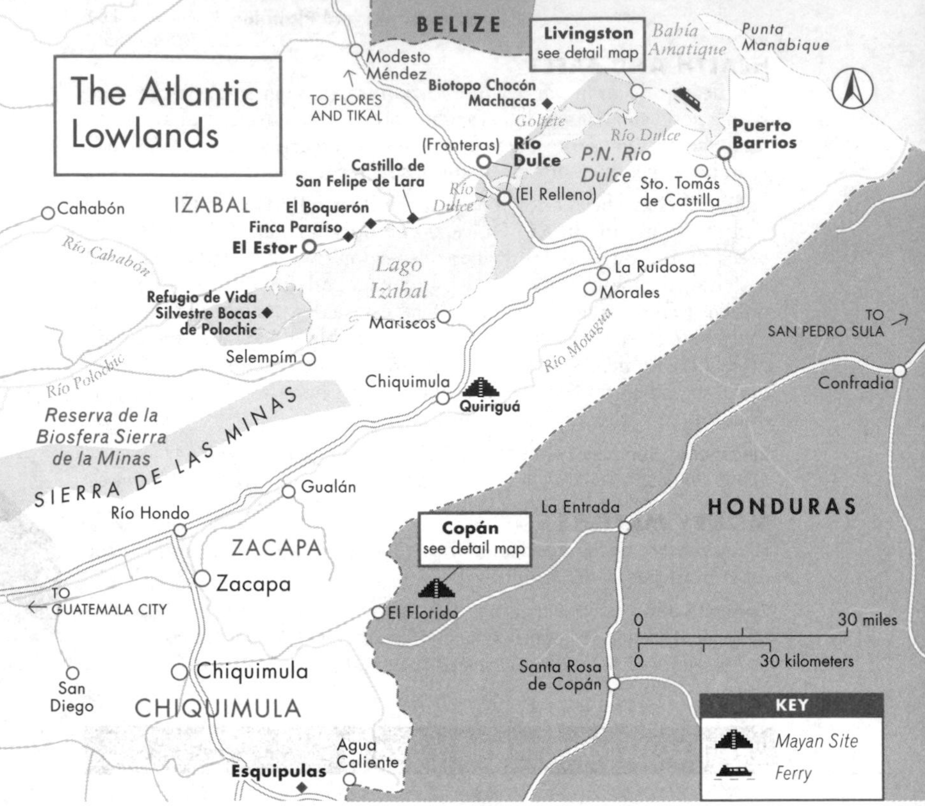

on weekends, when Guatemalans head out from the city; make reservations if you plan to be here then. Other than Christmas and Easter weeks, rates remain constant year-round.

VISITOR INFORMATION AND TOURS

Other than the information booth staffed by INGUAT, the national tourist office, at the cruise terminal at Santo Tomás de Castilla, and only accessible to boat passengers, there are no official visitor-information offices in the area. Heading to a tour operator or hotel will certainly get you on the right path.

LAGO IZABAL

Mention "Guatemala" and "lake" in the same sentence, and you'll likely think of the highlands' Lago Atitlán, but the famed Izabal deserves as much attention. The country's largest lake sits in the midst of a tropical-forested region alive with wildlife, and is connected to the Atlantic coast by the Río Dulce. Before railroads, and then highways, took over the transportation heavy lifting in this region, the lake was part of one of Guatemala's major cargo routes . . . and a favorite haunt of pirates.

RÍO DULCE

280 km (148 mi) northeast of Guatemala City, 30 km (19 mi) northwest of La Ruidosa.

Fodor's Choice ★ The term "Río Dulce" denotes two geographic entities. First and foremost, it designates the beautiful waterway connecting the coastal town of Livingston with Lake Izabal, and is one of Guatemala's signature sights. It also refers to a town of that name, although that isn't actually its name at all. (Highway signs do direct you to RÍO DULCE, however.) The municipal entity that everyone calls "Río Dulce" consists of two towns on opposite shores of the river—Fronteras on the north and El Relleno on the south—connected by the country's longest bridge at 850 meters (2,790 feet). At first glance, the town has little to keep you here, although unexpectedly good restaurants and hotels nearby are easily reached by road or water. The *lancheros* (captains) who congregate on the river will take you anywhere in the immediate area for under Q50.

GETTING HERE AND AROUND

Río Dulce is a major transportation hub: drive south and you'll hit the road connecting Guatemala City with the Caribbean coast; head north and you'll eventually reach El Petén.

6

Litegua offers direct bus service to Río Dulce from Guatemala City several times daily, leaving the capital throughout the day and night. Tickets cost Q50. Linea Dorada runs between Guatemala City and Flores in El Petén, passing through Río Dulce, the route's halfway-ish point. Buses leave the capital daily at 10. The trip to Río Dulce takes about five hours, getting you in around 3 AM. Tickets cost Q48.

A few tour operators have offices in Río Dulce. Gray Line Guatemala runs shuttles to and from Guatemala City and Antigua from here. Otitours, which is based here, also runs shuttles to the capital, Antigua, Tikal, and Copán, Honduras.

ESSENTIALS

Bus Contacts Linea Dorada (✉ *16 Calle 10–03, Zona 1, Guatemala City* ☎ *2290–7990*). **Litegua** (✉ *Calle Principal, Fronteras [Río Dulce]* ☎ *7930–5251* 🌐 *www.litegua.com*).

Emergencies Police (☎ *7930–5166 in Río Dulce*).

Tours Gray Line Guatemala (✉ *16 Calle and 7 Av., Puerto Barrios* ☎ *7948–1254* ✉ *Calle Principal, Fronteras [Río Dulce]* ☎ *7930–5196* 🌐 *www.graylineguatemala.com*). **Otitours** (✉ *Parque Las Brisas, Fronteras, Río Dulce* ☎ *7930–7674*).

EXPLORING

Once an important Mayan trade route, the Río Dulce later became the route over which the conquistadors sent the gold and silver they plundered back to Spain. All this wealth attracted Dutch and English pirates, who attacked both the ships and the warehouses on shore. In hopes of curtailing these buccaneers, colonists built a series of fortresses on the river's northern banks. In 1955 the Guatemalan government reconstructed the ruined fortress of **Castillo de San Felipe de Lara** (✉ *Southwest of Fronteras* ☎ *No phone* 💵 *Q25* ⏲ *Daily 8–5*). Spanish colonists constructed the fortress in 1595 to guard the inland waterway from pirate incursions. It was used as a prison between 1655 and 1660. You can reach it by the road leading west from Río Dulce or by a short boat ride. A 1999 earthquake in this region destroyed the river pier, as well as damaging portions of the fort. If you wish to visit, rather than simply see the structure from the water, you'll need to approach the park overland rather than upriver.

The northern banks of the Golfete, an expansive body of water between Lago Izabal and Río Dulce, are covered by the 17,790-acre **Biotopo Chocón Machacas.** Among the stretches of virgin rain forest and the extensive mangrove swamp here are gentle manatees—shy marine mammals also known as sea cows because of their enormous size. Manatees are as elusive as quetzals, so as you boat through the reserve you're more likely to see other animals such as sea otters. Some of the creeks go through thick forests where giant mahogany, ceiba, and mangrove trees hang over the water to form tunnels so thick they block out the sun. A tiny island surrounded by the park's dozens of creeks and lagoons has a well-maintained 1-km (.5-mi) nature trail that is easily walked by visitors with stiff boating legs. The trail has such interesting examples of old-growth trees as the San Juan, a tall, straight tree with yellow blossoms, and such exotic plants as orchids and bromeliads.

The only way to get to the reserve is on a 45-minute boat trip from Río Dulce or Livingston. Most launches up and down the river will stop at the park entrance if requested, but they rarely enter the park. Most major hotels on the Río Dulce rent boats with guides for individual or group tours. ✉ *Northeast of Fronteras* ☎ *No phone.*

WHERE TO EAT AND STAY

$ AMERICAN ✕ **Bruno's.** Although lodging is an option here, Bruno's is best known as a popular hangout for the yachting crowd. Most of the regular patrons arrive by boat. You'll feel at home here in the lively American-style restaurant featuring a great international menu. Expats enjoy sandwiches, burgers, and other light fare as they watch football on the big-screen TV. ✉ *Under bridge, on north side* ☎ *5692–7292* ▭ *AE, D, DC, MC, V.*

$$$ Fodor's Choice ★ **Catamaran Island Hotel.** On the north bank of the Río Dulce, this lovely resort takes advantage of its location with a restaurant built right over the water. The specialties are grilled steaks and fresh fish, including the delicious robalo plucked from the river. A string of spacious bungalows is cooled by river breezes, the nicest feature of which are the porches, perfect for watching boats. The staff can arrange boat trips along the river and to Livingston. Although the Banana Palms *below* is bigger and grander, we prefer Catamaran Island's more traditional resort-like experience. **Pros:** resort feel without being overrun with guests; many activities. **Cons:** many activities, so not good if you're looking for seclusion. ✉ *5 km (3 mi) east of Fronteras* ☎ *7930–5494, 2367–1545 in Guatemala City* 🌐 *www.catamaranisland.com* *35 rooms* *In-room: no phone, no TV, Wi-Fi. In-hotel: restaurant, room service, bar, tennis court, pool, Internet terminal, no-smoking rooms* ▭ *AE, D, DC, MC, V* *BP.*

$ **Hacienda Tijax.** There is only very basic accommodation here, but people come for the eco-activities, not the rooms. Built out over the water, this jungle lodge—the name is pronounced *Tee-HAHSH*—offers a number of types of accommodations, from cozy birdhouse-shaped

THE BANANA TRILOGY

Although Rigoberta Menchú gets most of the attention as Guatemala's Nobel Prize laureate, the country has another in novelist, diplomat, and journalist Miguel Ángel Asturias (1899–1974), who won the 1967 Nobel Prize for literature. Asturias spent his life and career alternately in Guatemala and abroad, living in forced or self-imposed exile during the tenures of the country's many right-wing military governments. He did a stint in Paris as a reporter for several Latin American newspapers during the 1920s, those "Lost Generation" years of Ernest Hemingway and Gertrude Stein.

Asturias never lived in the Atlantic lowlands, but he is inexorably tied to the region, having immortalized the hot and humid eastern coast in his 1950's *Viento Fuerte* (Strong Wind, or in some translations The Cyclone), 1954's *El Papa Verde* (The Green Pope), and 1960's *Los Ojos de los Enterrados* (The Interred). Known collectively as "The Banana Trilogy," these books chronicle the pain inflicted on the country by the United Fruit Company.

cabanas to large two-story bungalows with kitchens and dining rooms. A series of swinging bridges over a mangrove swamp lets you stroll to the adjacent nature reserve. Also nearby is a plantation where you can learn how rubber is extracted from trees. The lodge is also known for its restaurant, which serves a variety of Italian dishes, including homemade pesto. There are also plenty of vegetarian dishes. **Pros:** many activities; ecologically minded staff. **Cons:** rustic rooms. ✉ *Northeast of Fronteras* ☎ *7930–5505* 🌐 *www.tijax.com* *27 cabins, 20 with bath* *In-room: no a/c, no phone, kitchen (some), no TV, Wi-Fi. In-hotel: restaurant, bar, pool, water sports, no elevator, no-smoking rooms* *AE, D, DC, MC, V.*

$$$$ **Hotel Banana Palms.** Río Dulce's largest resort is also one of its more luxurious properties. Guests flock for the weekend from Guatemala City, leaving the hotel relatively quiet during the week. It's set amid lovely forested grounds near the San Felipe fortress. Rooms are all suites, with small kitchens, living rooms, and bedrooms containing one or two queen-size beds. Second-floor suites have private decks with individual hot tubs. The Banana Palms is a good option for families, since it has a separate children's pool, and games such as foosball, Ping-Pong, and billiards. **Pros:** many activities, always something going on. **Cons:** difficult to procure space on weekends; many activities, so not good if you're looking for seclusion. ✉ *300 meters east of Castillo San Felipe* ☎ *7930–5022, 2334–2598 in Guatemala City* 🌐 *www.bananapalms.com.gt* *33 rooms* *In-room: kitchen, refrigerator. In-hotel: restaurant, bar, pool, gym, beachfront, no elevator, laundry service, Internet terminal, parking (no fee), no-smoking rooms* *AE, D, DC, MC, V.*

¢ **Posada del Río.** An in-town lodging on the Fronteras side of the bridge offers very simple rooms with a bed, television, chair, and little else. It's a good value if you don't need many amenities. Reception is on the first floor; all rooms are on the second, as well as a small communal balcony. The hotel is undergoing expansion at this writing, with the addition of rooms expected to be complete in late 2010. **Pros:** good rock-bottom budget value; friendly owners. **Cons:** spartan rooms; construction noise can be disruptive during the day. ✉ *Under bridge, Fronteras* ☎ *7930–5167* *16 rooms* *In-room: no a/c, no phone. In-hotel: no elevator, parking (no fee), no-smoking rooms* *No credit cards* *EP.*

NIGHTLIFE

Head to **Hotel Backpackers** (✉ *Under bridge, El Relleno* ☎ *7930–5480*) for a beer at the waterfront bar. It's a fun place to while away the evening, and it's a bar with a conscience, to boot. All the proceeds go to benefit **Casa Guatemala Orphanage** (🌐 *www.casa-guatemala.org*), so drink up.

OUTDOOR ACTIVITIES

The natural crown jewel of this region is Río Dulce, which winds its way between Lake Izabal and the coast through a 13,000-hectare (32,000-acre) national park. Excursions approach the park by land, but we recommend making the two- to three-hour trip up or down the river to immerse yourself in the experience and have fun feeling a bit like Indiana Jones. The *colectivos* (public boats) leave from the dock near the Río Bravo Restaurant when they have at least eight passengers (the *lancheros* will keep you waiting all afternoon if the boat is not full). The rate is usually about Q100 per person. Private boats can also be hired, but they cost around Q750, depending on how well you negotiate the price, really only useful if you have your own group. All public launches stop at Bird Island, a roosting place for several hundred cormorants, and Flower Lagoon, a small inlet covered in bobbing water lilies and magnolias. There's also a stop at a hot springs that tumbles into a shallow river. Definitely bring your bathing suit. Mornings are cooler, and the water is calmer. Afternoons give way to heat and choppier rides.

EL ESTOR

40 km (24 mi) southwest of Fronteras.

Although the vast majority of this little town's population is Q'eqchí, there's also a decidedly Caribbean influence. Locals describe El Estor as *tranquilo,* which means easygoing or laid-back, and this becomes evident as you stroll around the brick streets. There's a waterfront walk where you can look for birds along the shores of Lago Izabal; El Estor is on a migratory path, so hundreds of species can be spotted here. The town, which grew up around the nickel mine to the west, seems to have drifted to sleep after the facility was shut down. Plans to reopen the mine by Canadian mining firms have generated much animosity among people in the area, some of whom have been evicted from their land. Anti-Canadian sentiment lurks under the surface here. Many travelers from Canada stay low-key about their nationality when visiting El Estor.

The drive here from Río Dulce takes you past expansive banana plantations as well as cattle ranches. Look for the massive ceiba trees along the road. They are sacred to the Maya—the only reason they were left standing when the rest of the forest was cleared. Also try to spot

THE BANANA REPUBLIC

From the docks in Puerto Barrios gigantic freight-liners leave daily with enormous crates of bananas stacked like children's blocks. Groups of farm workers can be spotted along the roadside, each carrying nothing more than a small knit bag. Men from one village often seek work as a group to increase their chances of being hired. Although the minimum wage is about $3.50 a day, some will work for half that amount. They usually return home on Sunday, the one day of the week they don't live on the farms.

Most of what is written about the banana industry in Guatemala focuses on the bad old days of the legendary United Fruit Company. The term "banana republic" was coined to describe neighboring Honduras, but it could just as easily have described Guatemala during the first half of the 20th century. The company got its start here in 1901, when financier and United head Minor Keith won the right to transport mail between Guatemala and the United States. That expanded into telegraph services and the construction of the Atlantic railroad between Guatemala City and Puerto Barrios, all in addition to their traditional activities of growing and processing fruit. United Fruit and its rival Standard Fruit gradually became dominant political and economic forces in the country, pulling strings and dictating policy.

Thankfully, those days are gone. United Fruit ceased operations under that name in 1970, and, through a series of mergers and acquisitions, became Chiquita Brands International in 1984. Standard Fruit became Dole about the same time. Bananas are still big business here—Guatemala's $270 million industry accounts for 5.8% of the world's banana supply—and Dole and Chiquita remain owners of huge plantations in the lowlands. But neither company exercises the control over Guatemalan affairs they once wielded.

6

strangler figs, which wrap themselves around the trunks of palms. Eventually they overcome the palms, which die from lack of sunlight.

GETTING HERE AND AROUND

Only the first 15 km (9 mi) of the road from Río Dulce to El Estor are paved. After that, expect gravel. Very basic public buses run by Fuente del Norte connect the towns hourly throughout the day.

Bus Contact Fuente del Norte (*El Estor* ☎ *7930–5251* 🌐 *www.autobusesfuentedelnorte.com*).

EXPLORING

Fodor'sChoice ★ Perhaps the most beautiful of Guatemala's natural wonders, **El Boquerón** is a narrow limestone canyon whose 180-meter (590-foot) walls are covered in foliage heavy with hanging moss. Hummingbirds dance around lavish blooms, blue morpho butterflies flutter between branches, and kingfishers dive at minnows. Sometimes howler monkeys visit the trees nearby—listen for their thunderous cries in the late afternoon. All along the canyon you can climb rocks and explore caves filled with clinging bats. Close to the entrance is a turnoff past a giant ceiba tree that leads to several thatch huts along the river; the proprietors, Antonio and Miguel, provide roughly fashioned *kayukos* (canoes) that you can rent for a ride through the canyon. The water is clean and cool, and great for swimming except after a heavy rain, when all the local rivers turn a muddy brown. ✉ *3 km (2 mi) east of El Estor.*

Known for its steaming waterfall, think of **Finca El Paraíso** as a natural spa for the tired traveler. (The entire complex is technically a mixed-use farm, with livestock and crops.) Don't be dissuaded from a trip here even if the weather is hot and humid, as the falls descend into an icy cold river. A trail from the front gate leads to a short yet somewhat bumpy climb to the falls—be careful, as the rocks can be slippery. Around the falls are small indentations in the rock that serve as natural saunas. You can also hike upstream to the narrow cave at the source of the river. The rock formations here are otherworldly. About 2 km (1 mi) downstream from the hot springs is a simple restaurant that serves hearty meals. From here you can also rent horses and ride to the springs. ✉ *16 km (10 mi) east of El Estor* ☎ *7949–7122 or 7949–7131* *Q10.*

Declared a protected area in 1997, **Refugio de Vida Silvestre Bocas del Polochic** is home to more than 250 species of birds, including blue herons, kingfishers, and snowy egrets. If you're lucky, you'll spot the blue-throated motmot. On the western end of Lago Izabal, the country's largest wetland encompasses more than 51,000 acres. The Fundación Defensores de la Naturaleza (Defenders of Nature Foundation) manages the private reserve. From the office in El Estor you can arrange a guided boat trip to the reserve and a visit to the Q'eqchí village of Selempín, with meals prepared by local women. The foundation also runs a remote ecolodge at the base of the Sierra de las Minas. The thatch-roof lodge has rooms with bunk beds and a full kitchen. **■ TIP→ A midnight thunderstorm is magical, but regardless of the weather you'll hear the roar of howler monkeys well into the evening.** ✉ *Defensores de la Naturaleza, 10 km (6 mi) south of El Estor* ☎ *7949–7427* 🌐 *www.defensores.org.gt.*

WHERE TO EAT AND STAY

$ LATIN AMERICAN ✕ **Restaurante Chaabil.** The name means "beautiful" in the language of the Q'eqchí, and that's an apt description for the best eatery in El Estor. Built over the water, the palm-thatched building is the perfect place for a breakfast with a view of the majestic Sierra de las Minas or for a dinner accompanied by a spectacular sunset over Lago Izabal. You may even get a chance to snap a photo of a fisherman delivering the catch of the day. Call ahead of time to enjoy a bowl of seafood *tapado,* a hearty stew prepared with coconut milk and plantains, or stop by anytime for lake perch or river robalo. For dessert, try a pineapple smoothie. ✉ *West of main square* ☎ *7949–7272* ▭ *No credit cards.*

$ **Hotel Marisabela.** This hotel has clean, simply furnished rooms, the best four of which overlook the lake. A third-floor balcony with wooden lounge chairs is the best place in town for an afternoon siesta. Although the restaurant (¢–$) always looks closed, it's open for business. Just call out "*¡Buenas tardes!*" until one of the workers appears. The Italian dishes are authentic and filling. **Pros:** good budget value; tasty restaurant; some rooms with lake views. **Cons:** spartan rooms; not all rooms have lake views. ✉ *8 Av. and 1 Calle* ☎ *7949–7206* *12 rooms* *In-*

room: no phone, no TV. In-hotel: restaurant, no elevator, parking (no fee), no-smoking rooms ▭ *No credit cards.*

¢–$ **Hotel Vista al Lago.** This hotel was once the general store that gave El Estor its name. Now run by the loquacious Oscar Paz, it has clean, cozy rooms. The wide wooden balcony is a great place to observe the town's waterfront. Before checking in, make sure the town hall next door has no plans for a dance; otherwise the thumping music will keep you awake until 4 AM. **Pros:** good budget value; friendly staff; owner is a wealth of information about the area. **Cons:** some street and music noise some evenings. ✉ *Next to town hall, 6 Av. 1–13* ☎ *7949–7205* ✉ *vistalago@intelnett.com* *21 rooms* *In-room: no a/c (some), no TV. In-hotel: no elevator, parking (no fee), no-smoking rooms* ▭ *AE, D, DC, MC, V.*

SHOPPING

You can watch how the beautiful weavings of Guatemala are made at the **Q'cqchí Women's Weaving Workshop** (✉ *North of main square* ☎ *No phone* ⏲ *Mon.–Sat. 8–noon and 3–5*). Every year small numbers of women come from their villages to live at the workshop, where they spend a year learning the age-old crafts of loom and belt weaving. Every woman who successfully completes the course is given a loom to take back to her village, and is encouraged to teach other women how to weave.

6

QUIRIGUÁ

186 km (115 mi) northeast of Guatemala City, 96 km (60 mi) southwest of Puerto Barrios.

GETTING HERE AND AROUND

Public transportation to Quiriguá is convoluted. Driving yourself is realistically the best way to arrive here. To get here, take the turnoff at Km 203 of the Atlantic Highway, near Chiquimula.

EXPLORING

Fodor's Choice ★ Unlike the hazy remnants of chiseled images you see at most other archaeological sites in Central America, **Quiriguá** has some that are seemingly untouched by winds and rain. They emerge from the rock faces in breathtaking detail. Quiriguá, a Mayan city that dates from the Classic period, is famous for the amazingly well-preserved stelae, or carved pillars, which are the largest yet discovered, and dwarf those of Copán, Honduras, some 50 km (30 mi) south. Construction began on the Guatemalan lowlands' most important Mayan ruins about AD 500. Its hieroglyphics tell its story: Quiriguá served at the time as a satellite state under the control of Copán. By the height of its power in the 7th century, Quiriguá had overpowered Copán, but just as quickly fell back into submissive status.

The stelae depict Quiriguá's ruling dynasty, especially the powerful Cauac Chan (Jade Sky), whose visage appears on nine of the structures circling the Great Plaza. Stela E, the largest of these, towers 10 meters (33 feet) high and weighs 65 tons. Several monuments, covered with interesting zoomorphic figures, still stand. The most interesting of these

THE BLACK CHRIST

Quick! Name Guatemala's most-visited destination. Antigua? Chichicastenango? Tikal? Even if it's not on your itinerary, an estimated one million Guatemalans and their fellow Central Americans flock to the southeastern city of Esquipulas, 222 km (133 mi) east of Guatemala City, each year to visit the whitewashed Basílica de Esquipulas (✉ *Parque Central, Esquipulas* 🎫 *Free* ⏲ *Daily 6 AM–8 PM*).

Guatemala's most famous church houses the figure of the *Cristo Negro* (Black Christ), an object of veneration for the faithful throughout Central America. Italian immigrant Quirio Cataño carved the dark-wood figure in 1585, and several miracles have been attributed to it. Eighteenth-century Archbishop Pedro Pablo de Figueroa of Guatemala claimed to have been cured himself of illness by the Cristo Negro; he ordered a fine church constructed to house the figure. The end result was the baroque, four-towered church, completed in 1758, that sits on Esquipulas's central park. Pope John XXIII elevated the church to basilica status in 1961.

The line of pilgrims forms at the east side of the basilica, and snakes slowly to the image housed in a glass case behind the main altar. Many drop to their knees as they approach the case. Notes of thanks and tiny medallions depicting various body parts cured festoon the area around the image. The line out of the basilica moves even more slowly. Tradition says that the faithful should not turn their backs on the Black Christ, and many exit the church walking backwards.

depicts Cauac Chan's conquest of Copán and the subsequent beheading of its then-ruler, 18 Rabbit. The remains of an acropolis and other structures have been partially restored.

In ancient times Quiriguá was an important Mayan trading center that stood on the banks of the Río Motagua (the river has since changed its course). The ruins are surrounded by a stand of rain forest—an untouched wilderness in the heart of banana country. Quiriguá still lives in the shadow of its better-known neighbor across the border, and of Tikal in the Petén in northern Guatemala, but it is one of Guatemala's most accessible Mayan sites. A small museum on-site gives insight into the history of Cauac Chan and his contemporaries. ☎ *No phone* 🎫 *Q60* ⏲ *Daily 7:30–5.*

ALONG THE ATLANTIC COAST

If you've made it this far, you've arrived at Guatemala's Caribbean coast. The sultry air, the swaying coconut palms, and the banana freighters that ply the Bahía de Amatique are a world away from the highlands that everyone comes to see. The Afro-Caribbean ethnic makeup is distinctive too, as is the language you'll hear, but won't quite be able to identify. (It's Garífuna, a Creole-based tongue.) To borrow the adjective from the tourist brochures, this is Guatemala at its most "different."

OFF TO NEW YORK?

American diplomat and explorer John Lloyd Stephens (1805–52) visited Quiriguá in 1841, and hatched an ambitious plan to dismantle the site's structures, float them down the Motagua River, and ship them to New York for permanent exhibition. Stephens had visited Copán two years earlier and purchased that site for a mere $50, with plans to remove its structures in the same manner. He argued that a museum could better protect the stelae from the ravages of rain and sun. Fortunately for history, the asking price for Quiriguá was far more than Stephens was willing to pay.

Despite the questionable scheme, historians today consider Stephens one of the great Mayanists of the 19th century. His *Incidents of Travel in Central America, Chiapas and Yucatán* and his extensive mapping of regional ruins are regarded as important period contributions to this field of knowledge.

LIVINGSTON

37 km (23 mi) northeast of Río Dulce.

Visitors always compare Livingston with Puerto Barrios across the bay, and the former wins hands down, for its sultry, seductive Caribbean flavor. Wooden houses, many on stilts, congregate in this old fishing town, once an important railroad hub, but today inaccessible by land from the outside world. Although it sits on the mainland, Livingston might as well be a Caribbean island—the culture seems closer to that of Jamaica than to the rest of Guatemala. Livingston proudly wears its Garífuna heritage on its sleeve. The culture is unique to Central America's eastern coast, and descends from the intermarriage of African slaves with Caribbean indigenous peoples.

Although it is not, Livingston might also just as well be an island. No roads connect the town with the rest of Guatemala, boats providing the only access. Livingston's single paved road is the only evidence left of its heyday as a major port for coffee and other crops during the late 19th century. Livingston's population now makes its living mostly from fishing. By day the soft lick of waves on the shore measures out the slow pace that makes this laid-back community so attractive. At night roving bands of musicians take to the streets.

Anyone expecting white-sand beaches and azure waters is bound to be disappointed. The narrow beach that stretches north from the river mouth is not especially attractive. It is, however, a great place to explore, as it is home to several bars and a little shop where Pablo Marino sells handmade drums, shakers, and wood carvings. Afternoon breezes off the ocean make resting on the beach a good place to pass the torrid afternoons. Once you arrive here, shed your worries and settle under a coconut palm.

CLOSE UP

Dance the Punta

You won't quite be able to put your finger on what it is: It's not reggae. It's not salsa. It's not hip-hop. But the punta resembles all three, and you'll hear the music everywhere along the Caribbean coast, here and in neighboring Belize and Honduras.

Scholars surmise that the name *punta* is actually a corruption of the word *bunda*, meaning "buttocks" in the Mandé language of West Africa, from where the music was imported. The name fits: dancers remain nearly stationary from the waist up, but engage in intense hip gyrations, right to left in a circular motion, while dancing on the balls of their feet. Historically, drums, rattles, and turtle shells provided the percussion-only accompaniment; these days, synthesizers and guitars have taken over that role, creating an all-the-rage style of music known as punta rock. Garífuna lyrics were the one-time norm; English and Spanish have become more common, helping to propel the punta beyond this region to prominence in World Music playlists.

GETTING HERE AND AROUND

The only way to get to or from the town is by boat. Daily ferry service leaves Puerto Barrios at 10:30 AM and 5 PM and Livingston at 5 AM and 2 PM. The trip takes about 90 minutes. Launches that connect the two cities take about 30 minutes, but they don't depart until they are full. This can really dent your plans, especially if you are leaving late in the day. (You usually don't need to wait more than 45 minutes.) The ride across Amatique Bay can get choppy by afternoon. Opt for a morning crossing if your schedule permits. There is boat service from Puerto Barrios to Honduras (Q200) and Livingston (Q180). There is also boat service from Livingston to Río Dulce for approximately Q100.

Asotransali is an association that represents 50 private boat captains in Livingston and can help you arrange à la carte tours on the Río Dulce or to Siete Altares. Look for their sign at the public dock. Happy Fish Travel, affiliated with the restaurant of the same name in Livingston, arranges area tours. Negotiate the price with the captain for a private Río Dulce tour, but expect to pay around Q1,000 for a full-fledged tour.

■ TIP→ Livingston's streets have official names. However, other than the main street, called Calle Principal, no one uses them or even seems to know them.

SAFETY AND PRECAUTIONS

There have been numerous robberies of tourists on the way to Siete Altares, so be sure to go with a guide and an organized group. Never walk in the countryside around Livingston alone or, especially, after dark.

ESSENTIALS

Tours Asotransali (✉ *Municipal docks, Livingston* ☎ *7947–0870*). **Happy Fish Travel** (✉ *Calle Principal, Livingston* ☎ *7947–0661*).

Restaurants ▼
Happy Fish 2
Restaurante Bahía Azul 1
Tilingo Lindo 3

Hotels ▼
Casa Rosada 1
Finca Tatín 4
Hotel Garifuna 2
Hotel Villa Caribe 3

Livingston

← TO SIETE ALTARES
Calle Principal
Calle Principal
Bahía de Amatique
Municipal Dock
TO RÍO DULCE, PUERTO BARRIOS, PUNTA GORDA (BELIZE)

KEY
Restaurants
Hotels

WHERE TO EAT

$ CARIBBEAN **✕ Happy Fish.** The thatch roof and painfully slow-turning ceiling fans are right out of *Night of the Iguana* or any other tropical movie of your choice. The seafood is phenomenal here at one of the town's most popular restaurants, which draws locals and tourists in equal numbers. We like the seafood *tapado,* a sweet fish stew. You can check your e-mail at the Internet terminal while you're waiting. ✉ *Calle Principal* ☎ *7947–0661* ▭ *MC, V.*

$ CARIBBEAN **✕ Restaurante Bahía Azul.** The walls are literally covered with travel information at Bahía Azul, the most popular tourist restaurant in town. If you're thinking about a trip, you can probably arrange it here. At the curve on the main street, its porch is a great place to watch people stroll past. The large menu includes everything from sandwiches to lobster. Most nights include live drumming by a local band. ✉ *Calle Principal* ☎ *7947–0151* ▭ *AE, D, DC, MC, V* ⊙ *BP.*

$ MIDDLE EASTERN **✕ Tilingo Lindo.** For the best curry this side of the Darién Gap head to this small bistro, which sits near the beach. The menu features such international favorites as Israeli *shockshuka* (an egg soup), chow mein, and chicken à l'orange. Meals all come with tasty salads and garlic bread. The intimate, rustic feel will keep you content while you wait for your meal, which takes a while to arrive. ✉ *North end of Calle Principal at the beach* ☎ *No phone* ▭ *No credit cards.*

CLOSE UP

The Garífuna

Guatemala's Atlantic coast presents a different ethnic makeup than the rest of the country. It has a substantial percentage of mixed indigenous and African descent known as the Garífuna. They speak one of Guatemala's 23 constitutionally recognized non-Spanish (and one of two non-Mayan-based) languages.

The Garífuna word for Garífuna is "Garinagu," but British-colonial powers called them the "Black Caribs," a term which sounds decidedly politically incorrect today. In the eyes of the British, "black" distinguished them from the "good" (from a British perspective) "Yellow Caribs," indigenous Arawak peoples in the British West Indies that had not intermarried with African slaves. Following a 1797 revolt on the Caribbean island of St. Vincent, British authorities exiled the Garífuna to the island of Roatán, off the coast of Honduras, then under British control. From there they dispersed to the mainland, settling Central America's Caribbean coast from Belize through northern Nicaragua.

Some 17,000 of their descendants live today in Guatemala. Music, dance traditions, and the Garífuna language remain here on the coast, even if old-timers lament the creeping outside influences, namely Spanish, rap, and reggae. Migration from Central America (largely in the 1980s) means that today the United States contains the world's largest Garífuna population.

WHERE TO STAY

$ Fodor's Choice ★ **Casa Rosada.** This string of waterfront bungalows can best be described as Guatemala's most luxurious way of roughing it. Each is furnished with bright highland furniture and a pair of beds draped with mosquito nets. Don't be scared off by the shared baths; they're clean and comfortable, and the showers have hot water. The main building houses a restaurant serving excellent meals on a pretty patio overlooking the water. The dinner menu changes daily, but always includes lobster and other favorites. Dinner, at 7 sharp, is by candlelight. **Pros:** friendly staff; rustic luxury. **Cons:** shared baths; basic rooms. ✉ *Near public dock* ☎ *7947–0303* 🌐 *www.hotelcasarosada.com* *10 bungalows, none with bath* *In-room: no a/c, no phone, no TV. In-hotel: restaurant, no elevator, laundry service, no-smoking rooms* *No credit cards* *EP.*

¢ **Finca Tatín.** A rustic bed-and-breakfast run by a friendly Argentine family, Finca Tatín is far off the beaten path, 20 minutes by boat from Livingston. The inn, which doubles as a Spanish school, rents canoes, which are a great way to see the river without the roar of a motor. A generator supplies the electricity here from 6 to 11 PM; the rest of the day, solar panels take their turn. **Pros:** ecologically minded staff; solar electricity part of day; friendly owners. **Cons:** rustic rooms. ✉ *8 km (5 mi) south of Livingston* ☎ *5902–0831* 🌐 *www.fincatatin.centroamerica.com* *5 bungalows, 4 rooms without bath* *In-room: no a/c, no phone, no TV. In-hotel: restaurant, no-smoking rooms* *No credit cards.*

¢ **Hotel Garífuna.** Run by a cordial Livingston family, Hotel Garífuna puts you in the heart of a lively neighborhood. The rooms in this two-story building open onto a porch overlooking the street or a tree-filled backyard. Expect very basic accommodation here, but the friendly owners make up for the fact that you have just a bed or two, a table, and a fan. **Pros:** friendly owners. **Cons:** some street noise. ✉ *Off the main street* ☎ *7947–0183* 🖷 *7947–0184* *8 rooms* *In-room: no a/c, no TV. In-hotel: no elevator, laundry service, Internet terminal, no-smoking rooms* 💳 *No credit cards.*

TIP

Be aware that young men wait on Livingston's town dock to "escort" you to your hotel. They may even tell you your chosen lodging is "full" or "closed," and recommend an alternative, from which they get a commission. Don't buy it. "Tipping" them to leave you alone is your prerogative.

$$$$ Fodor's Choice ★ **Hotel Villa Caribe.** Livingston's finest hotel, the Villa Caribe has some great views of the Caribbean from its hilltop perch. The extensive grounds overflow with foliage. Spacious rooms, in a thatch-roof building, all have private balconies and ocean views. Palm trees surround the large pool, where you can relax in one of the lounge chairs or order a drink at the bar. The restaurant serves seafood dishes, such as coconut shrimp and robalo, but is almost always empty. The staff can arrange trips up the Río Dulce and to spots around the Bahía de Amatique. **Pros:** attentive staff, stylish luxury. **Cons:** restaurant dead most of the time. ✉ *On the main street* ☎ *7947–0072, 2334–1818 in Guatemala City* 🌐 *www.villasdeguatemala.com* *40 rooms, 2 suites* *In-room: no phone, refrigerator. In-hotel: 2 restaurants, room service, bar, pool, beachfront, no elevator, laundry service, Internet terminal, no-smoking rooms* 💳 *AE, D, DC, MC, V.*

NIGHTLIFE

Nightlife in Livingston has always been synonymous with one word: Ubafu. Everyone, resident and visitor alike, stops by this popular bar on the Calle Principal to enjoy the distinctive punta music. Your other option is to stop by various hotels and restaurants—namely the Villa Caribe and Bahía Azul—which also present shows of Garífuna music many evenings. These places are lively and enjoyable, but fall a bit into the watered down for tourists category.

BARS The **Ubafu,** a Rasta-inspired shack (note the Bob Marley posters) on the main street, is Livingston's most famous and enduring bar, and the best place to see punta rock music as the locals enjoy it.

OUTDOOR ACTIVITIES

A short hike or boat ride (5 km [3 mi]) north of Livingston takes you to a gorgeous little jungle river called Siete Altares, a series of deep pools that are ideal for swimming. The name translates as "Seven Altars," the altars of which are seven lovely waterfalls. Arrange for a guided tour with the friendly folks at **Bahía Azul** (☎ *7947–0151*) or **Happy Fish** (☎ *7947–0303*). A walking tour costs about Q120, and usually takes in a stroll through Livingston; a bag lunch is included. Other tours replace the hike with a boat ride and cost about double. The one-way walk takes about 90 minutes, but is a fantastic way to experience nature here.

6

PUERTO BARRIOS

295 km (183 mi) from Guatemala City. Puerto Barrios is 2 hours by ferry from Livingston.

The friendly but down-at-the-heels port city of Puerto Barrios preserves the atmosphere of an old banana town. Its wide streets, mostly detached buildings—many are old stilt houses built in the traditional Caribbean style—and heavy tropical air give it a small-town feel, belying its population of 40,000. Nearby Santo Tomás de Castilla has now replaced it as the country's largest port, but the city still serves as the region's administrative, economic, and transportation center.

"Barrios," as everyone calls it, was once a thriving port for the United Fruit Company, thanks to the formerly operating railroad that connected it with Guatemala City. The commercial boom, however, has long since subsided; its port still functions, but most operations have been transferred to Santo Tomás. Officially, there's little to keep you here—the thriving market, while interesting, is geared to the workaday needs of the populace rather than any must-have souvenirs—but because transportation schedules don't always mesh well in this region, you may find yourself here for a night. With a couple of nice, but not-*too*-flashy resorts nearby, staying here is not a hardship.

GETTING HERE AND AROUND

Litegua operates comfortable buses from Guatemala City to Puerto Barrios. Trips to the capital from Puerto Barrios also leave approximately hourly during the day, and slightly less frequently in the evening. Be sure to ask for the comfortable *clase* service on the company's double-decker buses, which run three times daily.

Gray Line Guatemala runs shuttles to Guatemala City and Antigua from Puerto Barrios. Transportes El Chato can set you up with transport and tours from here to nearby Belize.

ESSENTIALS

Bus Contact Litegua (✉ *6 Av. 9–10, Puerto Barrios* ☎ *7948–1172* 🌐 *www.litegua.com*).

Emergencies Police (☎ *7948–7643 in Puerto Barrios, 7948–3244 in Santo Tomás de Castilla*).

Medical Assistance Hospital Nacional (✉ *Colonia San Manuel, Puerto Barrios* ☎ *7948–3073*).

Tours Gray Line Guatemala (✉ *16 Calle and 7 Av., Puerto Barrios* ☎ *7948–1254* 🌐 *www.graylineguatemala.com*). **Transportes El Chato** (✉ *1 Av. and 10 Calle, Puerto Barrios* ☎ *7948–5525*).

WHERE TO EAT AND STAY

$ CARIBBEAN ✕ **Restaurante Safari.** A longtime favorite in Puerto Barrios, this grass-roof restaurant is one of the few right on the water. On a hot afternoon or steamy night the ocean breezes are a tremendous relief. Seafood is the specialty here, especially the *tapado*, a hearty fish-coconut soup. ✉ *End of 5 Av. at water* ☎ *7948–0563* ▭ *AE, D, DC, MC, V.*

$$$$ **Amatique Bay Resort & Marina.** Sprawling resorts like this waterfront complex are the newest trend in Guatemala. The beautiful natural surroundings are somewhat diminished by all the effort to make things luxurious. The impressive pool, complete with a replica of a Spanish galleon that shoots water from its cannons, has slides for children and an island bar for adults. Few of the sunny suites have views of the ocean, but they are equipped with everything you would find in a well-furnished apartment, including washers and dryers. **Pros:** many activities, always something going on; fun for kids. **Cons:** large numbers of day visitors from cruise ships; luxury can seem overdone here. ✉ *Finca Pichilango, north of Puerto Barrios* ☎ *7948–1800, 2421–3333 in Guatemala City* 🌐 *www.amatiquebay.net* *61 rooms* *In-room: kitchen, Wi-Fi. In-hotel: 2 restaurants, room service, 3 bars, pools, bicycles, no elevator, laundry service, Internet terminal, no-smoking rooms* *AE, D, DC, MC, V* *AI.*

$$$$ **Green Bay Hotel.** Set amid a tropical garden, this string of thatch bungalows faces the expansive waters of the Bahía de Amatique. The grounds are adjacent to a forest-draped hill with a small waterfall. You can relax by the pool or on the private beach, or arrange a cruise on the bay and up the Río Dulce. Boats pick up guests at the dock in Puerto Barrios; phone ahead to let them know you're coming. **Pros:** many activities, always something going on. **Cons:** many activities, so not good if you're looking for seclusion. ✉ *Cayos del Diablo, 8 km (5 mi) west of Puerto Barrios* ☎ *7948–2361, 2337–2500 Ext. 8 in Guatemala City* 🌐 *www.greenbay.com.gt* *49 rooms* *In-room: Wi-Fi. In-hotel: restaurant, room service, 2 bars, 2 pools, beachfront, airport shuttle, no-smoking rooms* *AE, D, DC, MC, V* *AI.*

6

COPÁN (HONDURAS)

Explorer Christopher Columbus landed on the northern coast of Honduras in 1502, claiming the region for Spain. He was far from the first person to set foot here, however. This land had already seen great civilizations rise and fall. Nowhere is this more evident than in Copán, one of the most breathtaking archaeological sites in Central America. What makes Copán so fascinating to archaeologists is not just its astounding size, but its small details. Here they have uncovered carvings that tell the history of this great city, as well as that of others in the region. If you want to understand the ancient civilizations of Quiriguá in Guatemala or Teotihuacán in Mexico, first come to Copán.

For 2,000 years the Maya resided in what is now western Honduras, creating the distinctive art and architecture that can still be seen at the ancient city of Copán. The Lenca, who are believed to have lived alongside the Maya, had an equally vibrant, although less well-known, culture. Dominating the region after the fall of the Maya, the Lanca had no intention of being subjugated when the Spanish arrived in the 16th century. Chief Lempira brought tribes together to battle the conquistadors; his murder at the hands of the Spanish at a "peace conference" provided Honduras with its first national hero. The country's currency is named for the great warrior.

CRUISE DAY AT SANTO TOMÁS

Take one sleepy town. Turn it into Guatemala's largest commercial port. Make it the headquarters of the country's navy. Then build a cruise-ship terminal. The result is a small boom, the likes of which the village of Santo Tomás de Castilla never thought possible.

During the October to May cruise season, boats from Holland America, Norwegian, P&O, and Regent Seven Seas dock at the port's modern, spacious Terminal de Cruceros (cruise terminal) on a few Western Caribbean and Panama Canal itineraries. The facility offers money exchange—you can get by with U.S. dollars if you go on an organized shore excursion—post office, telephones, Internet computers, a lively crafts market, and an office of INGUAT, the national tourist office. Most passengers opt for an organized shore excursion.

Few visitors spend much time in Santo Tomás itself. In the mid-19th century Belgian immigrants settled the town, but scant evidence of their presence remains save for the preponderance of French and Flemish names in the local cemetery.

For urban life, Guatemala–Caribbean style, Puerto Barrios beckons, a quick taxi ride away. Livingston is a 30-minute water-taxi jaunt across the bay. Many passengers go for resort-chic and spend their shore time at the nearby Amatique Bay Resort, swimming, watersliding, kayaking, horseback riding, or bicycling. Boat rides from Livingston up the Río Dulce are also popular.

The ruins at Quiriguá are the most accessible Mayan complex in this part of the country, but operators can also fly you from Puerto Barrios's airstrip to Copán, across the border in Honduras, and all the way up to Tikal, for about $500.

COPÁN RUINAS

13 km (8 mi) east of Guatemalan border at El Florido, 168 km (104 mi) southwest of San Pedro Sula, Honduras.

With a squat colonial church watching over its eastern edge, the central square of Copán Ruinas calls to mind an era long past. You may think you've gone back in time, as horse-drawn wagons are not an uncommon sight on the surrounding cobblestone streets.

GETTING HERE AND AROUND

Many Guatemala-based travelers do cross-border jaunts as long organized day trips out of Guatemala City or Antigua. Guatemala's border post is El Florido, a town with no real lodging or dining options, other than a few food stands. Guatemala and Honduras belong to a joint immigration and customs union (along with El Salvador and Nicaragua), making border formalities between the two countries easy. Simply show your passport. Any days spent in Honduras count toward your maximum 90 days permitted to spend in Guatemala. The border is open 24 hours.

CLOSE UP

Copán History

The first king during the Classic Period, Yax Kuk Mo (or "Blue-Green Quetzal Macaw"), came to power around AD 435. Very little is known about him or his successors until the rise of the 12th king, Smoke Jaguar (628–695). Under his rule Copán grew to be one of the largest cities in the region. His successor, King 18 Rabbit (695–738), continued the quest for complete control of the region. The city's political structure was shaken, however, when he was captured by the soldiers of Quiriguá, a city in what is today part of Guatemala. He was brought to that city and beheaded.

During his short reign, Smoke Monkey (738–749) was increasingly challenged by powerful noble families. Smoke Monkey's son, Smoke Shell (749–763), tried to justify his power by playing up the historical importance of great warrior kings. He ordered the construction of the elaborate Hieroglyphic Stairway, the longest Classic Mayan inscription yet to be discovered, which emphasized the supremacy in battle of Copán's rulers. The 16th king, Dawning Sun (763–820), continued to glorify warfare in his architecture, but it was too late. By this time, Copán and its political authority were in decline.

Crossing the border with a rental vehicle complicates matters slightly. You'll need documented permission from your Guatemalan rental company to take the vehicle out of the country.

EXPLORING

Although most visitors come here to see the astounding Mayan ruins east of town, you can also learn a bit about that culture at the **Museo Copán Ruinas.** Though most of this charming little museum's descriptions are in Spanish, the ancient tools and artworks speak for themselves. The exhibit on *el brujo* ("the witch") is especially striking, displaying the skeleton and religious artifacts of a Mayan shaman. ✉ *West side of Parque Central* ☎ *No phone* 🎫 *L60* ⏲ *Daily 9–5.*

A cadre of colorful parrots greets you at the gate to **Copán,** one of the most breathtaking archaeological sites in Central America. Down a tree-lined path you'll find a series of beautifully reconstructed temples. The intricate carvings on the stone structures, especially along the Hieroglyphic Stairway, are remarkably well preserved. Here you can marvel at the artistry of a city that many have called the "Athens of Central America."

The area open to the public covers only a small part of the city's ceremonial center. Copán once extended for nearly 2 km (1¼ mi) along the river, making it as large as many Mayan archaeological sites in Guatemala. It's also just as old—more than 3,000 years ago there was an Olmec settlement on this site. Because new structures were usually built on top of existing ones, the

A QUESTION OF NAMES

The archaeological site is Copán. The nearby town is Copán Ruinas. You'd think it would be the other way around.

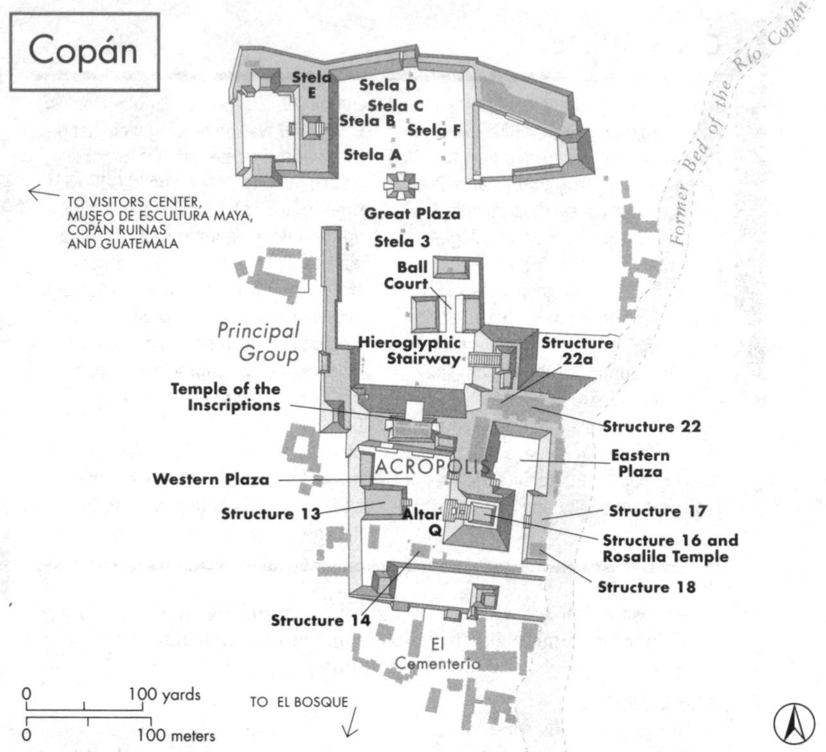

great temples that are visible today were built during the reigns of the city's last few rulers.

As you stroll past cieba trees on your way to the archaeological site, you'll find the **Great Plaza** to your left. The stelae standing about the plaza were monuments erected to glorify rulers. Some stelae on the periphery are dedicated to Smoke Jaguar, but the most impressive, located in the middle of the plaza, depict 18 Rabbit. Besides stroking the egos of the kings, these monuments had religious significance. Vaults for ritual offerings have been found beneath most of them.

The city's most important **ball court** lies south of the Great Plaza. One of the largest of its kind in Central America, it was used for more than simple entertainment. Players had to keep a hard rubber ball from touching the ground, perhaps symbolizing the sun's battle to stay aloft. Stylized carvings of macaw heads that line either side of the court may have been used as markers for keeping score—and the score was worth keeping, since the losers were probably put to death.

Near the ball court is one of the highlights of Copán, the **Hieroglyphic Stairway.** This amazing structure, covered with a canopy to protect it from the weather, contains the world's largest collection of hieroglyphs. The 63 steps immortalize the battles won by Copán's kings, especially those of the much revered King Smoke Jaguar. Once placed chronologically, the history can no longer be read because an earthquake knocked many steps free, and archaeologists replaced them in a random order. All may not be lost: experts have located an early photograph of the stairway that helps unlock the proper sequence.

The **Western Court** is thought to have represented the underworld. The structures, with doors that lead to blank walls, appear symbolic. On the east side of the plaza is a reproduction of Altar Q, a key to understanding the history of Copán. The squat platform shows a long line of Copán's rulers passing power down to their heirs. It ends with the last great king, Dawning Sun, facing the first king, Yax Kuk Mo.

LANGUAGE SCHOOLS IN COPÁN RUINAS

Guatemala isn't the only place in Central America to study Spanish. Copán Ruinas is a pleasant little place to learn the language, with many activities to keep you busy in your spare time.

Guacamaya Spanish School (✉ *100 meters north of Parque Central* ☎ *504/651–4360* 🌐 *www.guacamaya.com*).

Ixbalanque Spanish School (✉ *350 meters west of Parque Central* ☎ *504/651–4432* 🌐 *www.ixbalanque.com*).

6

The **Acropolis** was partly washed away by the Río Copán, which has since been routed away from the ruins. Dawning Sun was credited with the construction of many of the buildings surrounding this grand plaza. Below the Acropolis are tunnels that lead to some fascinating discoveries. Underneath Structure 16 are the near-perfect remains of an older building, called the **Rosalila Temple.** This structure, dating from 571, was subsequently buried below taller structures. Uncovered in 1989, the Rosalila was notable in part because of the paint remains on its surface—rose and lilac—for which it was named. Another tunnel called **Los Jaguares** takes you past tombs, a system of aqueducts, and even an ancient bathroom.

Two other parts of Copán that served as residential and administrative areas are open to the public, and they offer a glimpse into the daily lives of ordinary people. **El Bosque** (literally, "the Forest") lies in the woods off the trail to the west of the Principal Group. **Las Sepulturas** ("the graves"), which lies 2 km (1 mi) down the main road, is a revealing look into Mayan society. Excavations have shown that the Maya had a highly stratified social system in which the elite owned houses with many rooms.

East of the main entrance to Copán, the marvelous **Museo de Escultura Maya** provides a close-up look at the best of Mayan artistry. All the sculptures and replicas are accompanied by informative signs in English as well as Spanish. Here you'll find a full-scale replica of the Rosalila Temple, if you don't want to brave the tunnels (or the extra admission price) to see the original thing. The structure, in eye-popping shades of red and green, offers an educated guess at what the ceremonial and political structures of Copán must have looked like at the time they were in use.

The entrance fee covers admission to the ruins, as well as to nearby sites like El Bosque and Las Sepulturas. Admission to the tunnels to Rosalila and Los Jaguares is extra (L300), as is admission to the Museo de Escultura Maya (L150). It's a good idea to hire a guide, as they are very knowledgeable about the site, and there is minimal signage inside the complex to illustrate just what you are seeing. English-speaking ones charge about L500 for a two-hour tour for a group of up to 10 people. A small cafeteria and gift shop are near the entrance. ✉ *1 km (½ mi) east of Copán Ruinas* ☎ *No phone* 🎟 *L300* ⏲ *Daily 8–4.*

WHAT IT COSTS IN HONDURAS (LEMPIRAS)				
	$	$$	$$$	$$$$
Restaurants	under L75	L75–L150	L150–L225	over L225
Hotels	under L750	L750–L1,500	L1,500–L2,250	over L2,250

Restaurant prices are per person, for a main course at dinner. Hotel prices are for two people in a standard double room in high season, including Honduras's 16% tax.

WHERE TO EAT

$–$$ LATIN ✕ **Carnitas Nía Lola.** Housed in a charming wooden building, this long-time favorite has sweeping views of the valley from its second-story dining room. Wonderful smells emanate from the meats on the grill, which is crowned with a stone skull reminiscent of those at the nearby ruins. One of the favorite dishes here is the *carne encebollado,* sizzling beef topped with onions and accompanied by a mound of french fries. ✉ *2 blocks south of the Parque Central* ☎ *No phone* ▭ *AE, MC, V.*

$ LATIN ✕ **Llama del Bosque.** Named for a colorful flower, this cheerful little place is tucked away on a side street. It feels much larger than it really is because of the sloped wooden ceiling that soars above the dining room. This is the place to come for barbecued meats—try the *pinchos,* which are chunks of beef brought to your table on long skewers. You're guaranteed not to go home hungry. ✉ *1½ blocks west of Parque Central* ☎ *504/651–4431* ▭ *AE, MC, V.*

WHERE TO STAY

Most hotels in Copán Ruinas can put together multi-day Web-only packages that include accommodation and guided tours of the ruins.

$ ★ **Hacienda San Lucas.** In a century-old hacienda, this country inn is one of the most charming lodgings in the area. Flavia Cueva's tender care shows in all the details, from the carefully crafted wooden furniture in the simple but elegant rooms to the hammocks swinging from the porch outside. The restaurant serves steaming tamales, tasty adobo sauce, and aromatic coffee. Take a walk to Los Sapos, a Mayan archaeological site where huge stones were carved into the shape of frogs, or go horseback riding through the cool Copán Valley. **Pros:** attentive owner; good value. **Cons:** removed from town center. ✉ *1½ km (1 mi) south of Copán* ☎ *504/651–4495* 🌐 *www.haciendasanlucas.com* *8 rooms* *In-room: no a/c. In-hotel: restaurant* ▭ *No credit cards.*

$ **Hotel Marina Copán.** Facing Parque Central, this colonial-era building has been lovingly converted into the town's prettiest hotel. The second-story restaurant overlooks the sparkling pool, shaded by clusters of banana trees. Brilliant bougainvillea lines the paths to the rooms, which are filled with hand-hewn wood furniture and cooled by lazily turning ceiling fans. At the bar you can listen to mariachi music on Friday and Saturday night. **Pros:** central location; great guides. **Cons:** occasional street noise. ✉ *Northwest corner of Parque Central* ☎ *504/651–4070, 877/893–9131 in North America* 🌐 *www.hotelmarinacopan.com* *44 rooms, 5 suites* *In-hotel: 2 restaurants, room service, bar, pool, gym, spa, laundry service, parking (no fee)* 💳 *AE, MC, V.*

$$$ **Hotel Posada Real de Copán.** The closest lodging to the archaeological site, this Spanish-style hotel is in the hills just outside of town. The open-air lobby, filled with tropical flowers, adds to the ambience. Inside the tile-roof buildings are generously proportioned rooms with views of the lush gardens. After a day exploring the dusty ruins, swim a few laps in the palm-shaded pool or relax in the nearby hot tub. **Pros:** closest hotel to ruins; luxurious rooms. **Cons:** far from town center. ✉ *2 km (1 mi) east of Copán Ruinas* ☎ *504/651–4480* 🌐 *www.posadarealdecopan.com* *80 rooms* *In-room: Wi-Fi. In-hotel: restaurant, room service, bar, pool, no elevator, parking (no fee)* 💳 *AE, MC, V.*

$$ **Plaza Copán.** Watch horses clip-clop around the cobbled streets of Copán Ruinas from your terrace at this hotel on Parque Central. Ask for one of the rooms on the top floor, which have views of the town's red-tile roofs. Relax with a drink by the little pool in the central courtyard, which is shaded by tall palm trees. The restaurant, set behind a lovely colonnade, appropriately called Los Arcos, serves traditional fare. **Pros:** centrally located, good views. **Cons:** occasional street noise. ✉ *Southeast corner of Parque Central* ☎ *504/651–4508* 🌐 *www.plazacopanhotel.com* *20 rooms* *In-room: refrigerator, Wi-Fi. In-hotel: restaurant, bar, pool, no elevator* 💳 *AE, MC, V.*

The Pacific Lowlands

WORD OF MOUTH

"It's a shame: Guatemalans all know their Pacific coast, but we foreigners have barely discovered it yet. It's a quick, easy jaunt to get here from the center of the country. I especially like Monterrico, this cool, kind of funky little beach town. Maybe it will all stay a secret just a little while longer."

—Jeffrey Van Fleet

www.fodors.com/community

By Jeffrey Van Fleet

Even old Guatemala hands scratch their heads when someone mentions its little-known Pacific coast. The country's 266-km (160-mi) Pacific shoreline could lay the groundwork for a string of beach resorts like those in neighboring Mexico, but a rugged coast, dark-sand beaches, and water too rough for swimming conspire to make things otherwise. Except for the beach town of Monterrico, a fun-in-the-sun vacation culture has barely developed here, and even there, no one would mistake the locale for Acapulco.

This is Guatemala's breadbasket, and agriculture—primarily cattle raising and sugar and cotton production—has brought a level of prosperity to the Pacific Lowlands little seen elsewhere in the country. The region is also the country's hot new real-estate market. Condominiums and vacation homes are springing up, not just on the coast, but inland, too. With Guatemala City hemmed in by mountains north and west, south provides the path of least resistance for metro-area growth to spill.

For such a little-known region, the Pacific lowlands offer a surprising variety of activities. The beach is your obvious choice, with Monterrico your best bet—some would say your only true choice—in that regard. Monterrico and the coast east to the Salvadoran border host sea-turtle conservation projects. Nearby Puerto San José is developing as the center of Guatemala's sportfishing industry. If you arrive in Guatemala on a Pacific cruise, your first encounter with the country will be the next-door port of Puerto Quetzal. From there, all manner of shore excursions, in this region and elsewhere in Guatemala, are yours for the choosing. The area around Santa Lucía Cotzumalguapa and Retalhuleu has some of Guatemala's best white-water rafting. Takalik Abaj and El Baúl, two of the country's lesser-known indigenous ruins, are here, too. The proximity of Mexico to this region means that both Mayan sites show considerable influence from peoples farther north. Retalhuleu is also Guatemala's amusement-park center, and makes for a pleasing stop if you're traveling with the kids.

Best of all, it's a cinch to get to this part of the country. You can be here in an hour or so on decent roads from Guatemala City, Antigua, Lake Atitlán, or Quetzaltenango. If you seek a respite from the chill of the highlands, here is Guatemala's most accessible warm-weather destination. Paradoxically, travelers most familiar with this region are those with little interest in Guatemala at all. For drivers traveling to and through Central America, this region's Highway CA–2 zips between Mexico and El Salvador and makes for a faster, straighter, flatter route through the country than the parallel Pan-American Highway (CA–1) through the mountainous highlands to the north. But if you have the time, consider slowing down and spending some here.

TOP REASONS TO GO

Zoning out at the beach: Guatemala's sights assault your senses. A break at the beach town of Monterrico might be the relaxing antidote the doctor ordered.

Pondering the mystery of the sea turtles: The odds seem against Guatemala's three turtle species surviving at all, but carry on they do along this coast.

Reeling in the big one: Or brag about the one that got away. Guatemala's sportfishing industry centers on Puerto San José.

Careening down the rapids: The Pacific lowlands are home to four white-water rivers ideal for beginner or intermediate rafters.

Building up your repertoire of Mayan ruins: You've done the big ruins. Two lesser-known sites, both with considerable Mexican influence, let you delve further into Mayan history.

ORIENTATION AND PLANNING

GETTING ORIENTED

Guatemala's mountainous highlands front the Pacific lowlands on the north, with the landscape tumbling down to the ocean in less than two hours. The small cities of Retalhuleu and Santa Lucía Cotzumalguapa anchor the western part of this region. The old port city of Puerto San José and the lively beach town of Monterrico sit on the far eastern end of the coast, not far from the border with El Salvador. In the middle of the lowlands sits the not-so-interesting city of Escuintla, the region's economic hub, a place you may pass through but likely not stay in.

Retalhuleu. Guatemalans best know the western gateway to the Pacific lowlands for its two large amusement parks just outside of town.

Takalik Abaj. Olmec met Maya at this lesser-known but well-preserved Preclassic site of granite stelae and pyramids near Retalhuleu.

Santa Lucía Cotzumalguapa. The country's sugar capital and white-water center is also home to the ruins of El Baúl, a Mayan site showing considerable influence from the Pipil people of Mexico.

Escuintla. An outdoor safari zoo east of town just might transport you in your mind to far-off East Africa.

Puerto San José. The oldest port city in Guatemala, and the center of its fishing industry, will be your first glimpse of the country if you arrive on a Pacific cruise.

Monterrico. Guatemala's only real beach town, slightly ramshackle Monterrico is the perfect kick-off-your-shoes destination, still little known and on the cusp of its own Jimmy Buffet era.

PLANNING

WHEN TO GO

The year here divides into rainy (May–October) and dry (November–May) seasons. Unlike those in most of the rest of Guatemala, hotels here do observe high and low seasons corresponding to the weather, and set rates accordingly. Beach lodgings also raise rates on weekends. Even though comparatively few travelers come here, the Pacific lowlands fit nicely into a visit to points just north. A good highway connects the eastern coast at Puerto Quetzal with Guatemala City and Antigua, putting you here in about 90 minutes, and Retalhuleu is a one-hour drive south (and downhill all the way) from Quetzaltenango in the highlands.

TIMING

In spite of its ease of access, few international travelers know this region at all. Two or three days can easily be tacked onto a visit to the capital, Antigua, Lake Atitlán, or Quetzatenango.

GETTING HERE AND AROUND

AIR TRAVEL

The Pacific lowlands have no airport, but the capital's Aeropuerto Internacional La Aurora on the south side of Guatemala City puts you within an hour or two of most places in this region.

BOAT TRAVEL

There is no boat travel through the rough waters along this stretch of coast. Your only experience on boats will be the ride on the *lanchón* ferries that transport you and your vehicle across the Canal de Chiquimulilla that separates Monterrico from the mainland, and that only if you travel via Avellanas, which very few visitors do these days.

BUS TRAVEL

Virtually every tour operator in Guatemala City, Antigua, and Panajachel can set you up with a minivan shuttle to the beach. Most travel via Antigua. Large Greyhound-style public buses (*pullmans*) ply the region, too, although many routes require you to change in the hub city of Escuintla.

CAR TRAVEL

Although this region fronts the ocean, you'll find few ways to travel along the coast other than the 40 km (24 mi) road that hugs the Pacific between Puerto San José and Monterrico. Highway CA–2, 45 km (27 mi) inland parallel to the ocean, forms the east–west transportation backbone of this region, connecting Mexico and El Salvador. The four-lane Highway CA–9—it's the country's best—begins in Guatemala City and runs south to the coast at Puerto Quetzal. You'll pay a Q12 toll at Km 51 north of the hub city of Escuintla. Highway CA–2 intersects at Escuintla, heading west to Santa Lucía Cotzumalguapa and Retalhuleu. Continuing on CA–9, a large highway interchange sits at the coast. Follow signs to PUERTO SAN JOSÉ for points west, and to IZTAPA for Monterrico and the eastern Pacific coast. At Iztapa itself, a Q20 toll bridge crosses to an island for the last 25 km (15 mi) to Monterrico. Watch out for the iguanas that dart across the two-lane road.

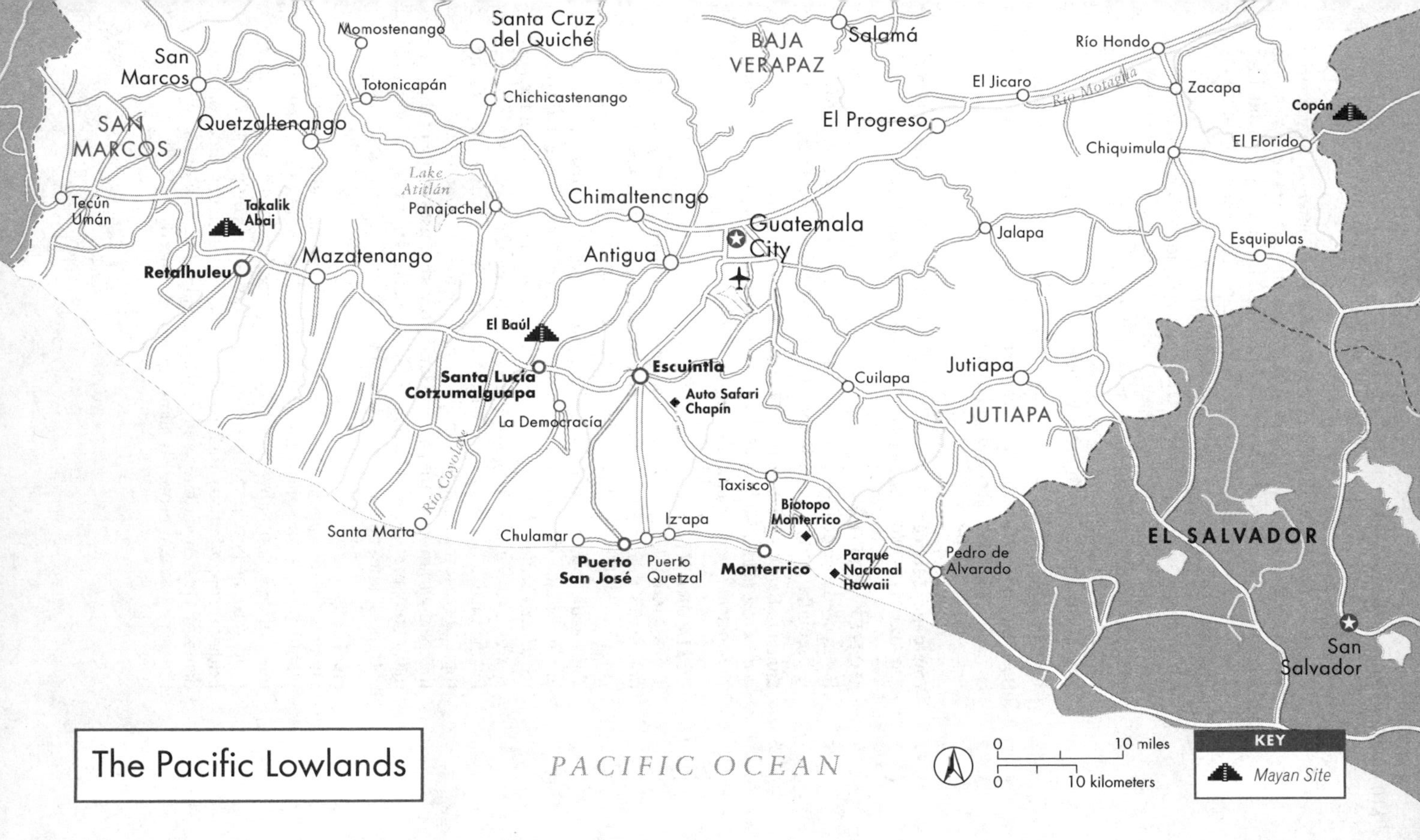
The Pacific Lowlands
Momostenango
Santa Cruz del Quiché
San Marcos
Totonicapán
Chichicastenango
BAJA VERAPAZ
Salamá
Río Hondo
El Jicaro
Río Motagua
Zacapa
Copán
El Progreso
SAN MARCOS
Quetzaltenango
Chiquimula
El Florido
Lake Atitlán
Tecún Umán
Takalik Abaj
Panajachel
Chimaltenango
Guatemala City
Jalapa
Esquipulas
Retalhuleu
Mazatenango
Antigua
El Baúl
Santa Lucía Cotzumalguapa
Escuintla
Auto Safari Chapín
Cuilapa
Jutiapa
JUTIAPA
La Democracía
Río Coyolate
Taxisco
Biotopo Monterrico
Santa Marta
Chulamar
Iztapa
Puerto San José
Puerto Quetzal
Monterrico
Parque Nacional Hawaii
Pedro de Alvarado
EL SALVADOR
San Salvador
PACIFIC OCEAN
0
10 miles
0
10 kilometers
KEY
Mayan Site

HEALTH AND SAFETY

The heat and sun in the Pacific lowlands can be intense. Be prepared with a good sun hat and lightweight clothing that covers your arms and legs. Shorts don't protect legs from the sun, tall grass, insects, and dust. Also pack plenty of sunscreen and insect repellent. The mosquitoes are voracious at the beach. Replenish regularly with lots of fluids.

This is a mostly safe region of the country, and with standard travel precautions—no flashy jewelry, keep valuables well hidden—you should be fine. Strong undercurrents mean swimming poses a risk along the entire coast. Exercise extreme caution, and never swim alone, good advice anywhere, but imperative here.

Both Escuintla and Retalhuleu are home to large public hospitals.

Hospitals Hospital Nacional (✉ *Carretera a Taxisco, Km 59.5, Escuintla* ☎ *7889–5146*). **Hospital Nacional** (✉ *Blvd. Centenario and 3 Av., Zona 2, Retalhuleu* ☎ *7771–0116*).

Emergency Services Police (☎ *7888–1120 in Escuintla, 7881–1333 in Puerto San José, 7771–0002 in Retalhuleu, 7882–5032 in Sant Lucía Cotzumalguapa*).

MONEY MATTERS

If you need to exchange money in the Pacific Lowlands, the place to do it is Escuintla, Monterrico, Retalhuleu, or Santa Lucía Cotzumalguapa.

Contacts Banco Agromercantil (✉ *7 Calle 3–07, Zona 1, Escuintla* ✉ *5 Av. and 5 Calle, Retalhuleu* ✉ *3 Av. 6–78, , Santa Lucía Cotzumalguapa*). **BanRural** (✉ *Carretera a Hawaii and Calle Principal, Monterrico*).

RESTAURANTS

Think "lodging"—yours or another—when considering your dining options in this region. Hotels tend to have the best restaurants, and you're welcome whether or not you're staying there.

The Pacific lowlands bring together a number of dishes from elsewhere in Guatemala, with a few specialties of its own. No surprise that you'll see a hearty *caldo de mariscos* (seafood stew) on most restaurant menus, as well as *sopa de tortuga* (turtle soup). Given the fragile state of the Pacific turtle population, we suggest avoiding that second one. On the topic of what to avoid, you might also be on the lookout for *chanfaina*, the local variation on the Spanish lamb stew that uses many of the animal's body parts. In this region of Guatemala it's more likely prepared with beef, but still with everything tossed in.

HOTELS

Lodgings in this region go for the resort look and feel, although no one would ever mistake them for a Club Med. They tend to be small, but most offer a pool, always appreciated in the lowland heat. If you're headed to the beach, make advance reservations if you plan to be here Friday through Sunday nights—the weekend is getaway time for residents of Guatemala City and nearby El Salvador. Any other night of the week you can probably show up unannounced.

WHAT IT COSTS IN GUATEMALAN QUETZALES					
	¢	$	$$	$$$	$$$$
RESTAURANTS	under Q40	Q40–Q70	Q70–Q100	Q100–Q130	over Q130
HOTELS	under Q160	Q160–Q360	Q360–Q560	Q560–Q760	over Q760

Restaurant prices are based on the median main course price at dinner. Hotel prices are for two people in a standard double room in high season, including tax and service.

VISITOR INFORMATION

There are no official visitor-information offices in the area, but heading to a tour operator or hotel will certainly put you on the right path.

RETALHULEU

62 km (74 mi) south of Quetzaltenango, 192 km (115 mi) southwest of Guatemala City.

Guatemala has some pretty complex place names, but no one even bothers trying to pronounce this one. It's *ray-tahl-hoo-LAY-oo* if you care to venture a try—that means "sign of hollows in the earth"—but everyone just goes with "Reu" (*RAY-oo*) for short. This friendly, one-time cacao town has become Guatemala's very own Orlando, with two huge amusement parks just outside town. Water sports beckon between here and the coast, and on the way east to neighboring Santa Lucía Cotzumalguapa. The nearby indigenous ruins of Takalik Abaj are just a short trip west toward the Mexican border.

7

GETTING HERE AND AROUND

Autobuses Fuente del Norte operates comfortable hourly buses between its own terminal in Retalhuleu and the capital. The trip takes three hours, and tickets cost Q45.

ESSENTIALS

Bus Contact Autobuses Fuente del Norte (✉ *7 Av. and 10 Calle, Retalhuleu* ☎ *5540–9989 in Retalhuleu, 2471–0952 in Guatemala City*).

WHERE TO STAY

$$ **Hotel Posada de Don José.** Retalhuleu's prestige address is this medium-size, colonial-style hotel a couple of blocks from the Central Park. It is frequented by business travelers during the week and vacationing families on the weekend. The large rooms are arranged on two floors around the pool area, and contain dark-wood furnishings and two beds each. Ask for a room that doesn't overlook the busy 5 Calle. ■ **TIP→ The poolside restaurant is the best in town. Pros:** good value; friendly staff. **Cons:** some street noise in rooms facing front; some noise from interior pool during day. ✉ *5 Calle 3–67, Zona 1* ☎ *7771–0180* 🌐 *www.hotelposadadedonjose.com* *21 rooms* *In-room: Wi-Fi. In-hotel: restaurant, room service, bar, pool, no elevator, laundry service, public Internet, parking (no fee), no-smoking rooms* 💳 *AE, D, DC, MC, V.*

THEME-PARK CENTRAL

Retalhuleu is home to two well-designed, Disney-like theme parks operated by IRTRA, a Guatemalan labor organization. Both sit just north of town on the highway to Quetzaltenango. Wet and wild, **Xocomil** is a water park of which there are many in this part of the country. The Mayan-themed structures tend a bit toward the cheesy side, but it's a well-integrated design that encompasses waterslides, wave pools, and more tranquil children's pools in the park. (✉ *Km 180.5, Carretera a Quetzaltenango* ☎ *7722–9400, 2423–9000 in Guatemala City* 🌐 *www.irtra.org.gt* ⏲ *Tues.–Sun. 9–5* 🎟 *Q75; Q50, kids 5–12, under 5 free*).

We'll call the adjoining **Xetulul** a bit more "Epcot Center-y." It expands on Xocomil's Mayan theme, but incorporates pavilions devoted to colonial Guatemala, as well as Spain, Italy, and France into its complex, with several fun amusement rides to boot. (✉ *Km 180.5, Carretera a Quetzaltenango* ☎ *7722–9450, 2423–9000 in Guatemala City* 🌐 *www.irtra.org.gt* ⏲ *Thurs.–Sun. 10–6* 🎟 *Q200; Q100, kids 5–12, under 5 free*).

TAKALIK ABAJ

11 km (6½ mi) northwest of Retalhuleu.

GETTING HERE AND AROUND

Your own car is easiest for reaching Takalik Abaj. The turnoff to the ruins is at Km 190.5 east of Retalhuleu on Highway CA–2. The site lies 5 km (3 mi) north of the highway, the pavement ending the last two kilometers.

EXPLORING

Olmec meets Mayan at **Takalik Abaj,** a little-known complex of ruins tucked away in the southwestern corner of the country. Historically, this lowland location gave far better access to central and southern Mexico than did sites elsewhere in Guatemala, and the Olmec influence was stronger here than other places around the country. Inhabitants of Takalik Abaj also formed strong commercial ties with Kaminaljuyú, on the site of present-day Guatemala City.

The name means "standing stones" in Quiché, a moniker given to the site by those who uncovered it in the 1880s. (No one is certain what its original inhabitants called the place, as is the case with the majority of Guatemala's indigenous ruins.) What is known is that the site dates from the Preclassic period, and was inhabited from the 8th century BC to AD 9th century, peaking about AD 200. The standing-stone name is apt: Takalik Abaj is home to almost 300 well-preserved stelae, made of granite, unlike the limestone used at ruins in northern Guatemala's Petén region. Several small pyramids round out the offerings on the site.

Guides staff the booth at the site entrance, and can provide you with a tour. These folks don't see a lot of visitors, so a Q15 tip is always appreciated. Alternatively, the nearby Takalik Maya Lodge can set you up with a tour. ✉ *11 km (6½ mi) northwest of Retalhuleu* ☎ *No phone* ⏲ *Daily 10–6* 🎟 *Q25.*

WHERE TO STAY

$$$$ **Takalik Maya Lodge.** You negotiate a rough road to get here—it's a few kilometers north of the entrance to its namesake ruins—but a stay on this working coffee, rubber, and macadamia plantation is worth the trip. The colonial-style rooms are in the plantation house, and, except for having to share bathrooms, are quite nice. Two large, newer, separate bungalows are designed to be their own mini-Mayan palaces. The lodge has a lot of mix-and-match packages that contain lodging only, all meals, or several tours, among them horse and bicycle rides, as well as tours of the nearby ruins. **Pros:** comfortable rooms, many activities. **Cons:** rough road to get here. ✉ *Turn at Km 190.5 on Pacific Hwy.* ☎ *5651–1097, 2369–7206 in Guatemala City* 🌐 *www.takalik.com* *7 rooms, none with bath, 2 bungalows* *In-room: no a/c, no phone, no TV. In-hotel: restaurant, bar, pool, parking (no fee), no-smoking rooms* *AE, D, DC, MC, V* *FAP.*

SANTA LUCÍA COTZUMALGUAPA

104 km (63 mi) east of Retalhuleu, 88 km (53 mi) southwest of Guatemala City.

Tidy, prosperous Santa Lucía Cotzumalguapa is the town that sugar built. The small city is worth a stop to visit a couple of lesser-known indigenous ruins. Several nearby rivers also put Santa Lucía in the midst of one of the country's best white-water regions. However, you'll have to hook up with a trip in Guatemala City, as none depart from here.

7

GETTING HERE AND AROUND

Santa Lucía Cotzumalguapa is tricky to reach by public transportation since almost all long-distance buses take the CA–2 bypass and don't go into town at all. Your best bet if you have no wheels is to transfer buses at Escuintla for nearly hourly service direct into Santa Lucía Cotzumalguapa.

EXPLORING

In the midst of working fields of sugarcane north of town, **Finca El Baúl** clumps together a collection of stelae from the Preclassic to Late Classic periods (AD 250–900). The site shows influences of the indigenous Pipil people, who spoke the Nahuatl language of central Mexico, as well as the Maya. Though billed as an outdoor museum, you'll find little explanation of what you're seeing at El Baúl. Most visitors come here, rather, to observe the occasional Mayan rituals that still take place on the site. There's no fixed schedule, but if you do stumble upon an observance, be unobtrusive. A few visitors wandering aimlessly through the fields have been robbed. We recommend a taxi to get here and back. Most drivers know the place and are happy to serve as your guide and protector. ✉ *4 km [2½ mi] north of Santa Lucía Contzumalguapa* ☎ *5312–1073* *Daily 7–4* *Q10.*

For a far better grounding in the Mayan history of the region than you can get at El Baúl, head to the Finca Las Ilusiones, also a one-time sugarcane plantation. The site is officially known as the **Museo de Cultura Cotzumalguapa,** and takes in a collection of stelae and stones

SUGAR IS ENERGY

Guatemala's $500 million sugar industry centers around Santa Lucía Cotzumalguapa. The annual *zafra*, or cutting of cane, lasts from November to May, roughly corresponding to the dry season. The 2008 to 2009 season generated 47.8 million *quintales* of sugarcane (one quintal = 46 kg = 100 lb., the traditional unit used to measure output in the industry.) Guatemala's 15 *ingenios* (sugar producers) go through various stages in the process of converting cane to refined sugar, and the heat and moisture generated produce about 750 gigawatt-hours of electricity—enough excess energy to supply their own needs as well as 10% of the country's power. That packet of sugar you put in your Guatemalan coffee, another of the country's signature agricultural products, just might have generated the electricity needed to brew your morning cup.

gathered from nearby archaeological sites. Most of these come from Bilbao, on the northern edge of Santa Lucía, which housed a collection of carved stones. The 80-ton, so-called Monument 21 remains at the Bilbao site, and has been copied in fiberglass for display at this museum. The remainder of the Bilbao stones here are authentic. ✉ *Km 87.5, Carretera al Pacífico, on eastern edge of Santa Lucía Contzumalguapa* ☎ *No phone* ⏲ *Daily 7–noon and 2–4* 💵 *Q10.*

OUTDOOR ACTIVITIES

June through October is the season for daylong rafting excursions to the beginners' Río Coyolate (Class II–III), the slightly more difficult Río Nahualate (Class III), and the Río Naranjo (Class III–IV) for experienced rafters only. All are within striking distance of Santa Lucía Cotzumalguapa and Retalhuleu, but all excursions leave from Guatemala City. Also departing from the capital are one-day excursions on the Río Los Esclavos (Class III–IV) near Escuintla.

Maya Expeditions (✉ *15 Calle A 14–07,* ☎ *2363–4955* 🌐 *www.maya-expeditions.com*) offers trips that range from easy to challenging.

ESCUINTLA

37 km (22 mi) east of Santa Lucía Cotzumalguapa, 57 km (35 mi) south of Guatemala City.

"Ghastly" and "exhaust-ridden" are two of the terms travelers use to describe the region's largest city. If you're negotiating the Pacific lowlands by public transportation, you'll likely pass through this hub as a transfer point. There's little to keep you here, save for one unusual attraction east of town.

GETTING HERE AND AROUND

The four-lane Highway CA–9, the country's best, heads due south from Guatemala City to Escuintla, where it intersects with Highway CA–2 at large interchange just outside of town.

Transportes Esmeralda operates service between Guatemala's main bus terminal in Zona 4 and Escuintla every half-hour throughout the day. Travel time is just under one hour.

ESSENTIALS

Bus Contact Transportes Esmeralda (✉ *Terminal de Buses, Zona 4, Guatemala City* ☎ *2232–3643 in Guatemala City*).

EXPLORING

It's not exactly a game park in Kenya, but **Auto Safari Chapín** creates a Guatemalan version of the experience. This large outdoor zoo gives you a drive-through safari encounter. Among the 100 species of animals here, the facility is especially strong in it population of giraffes, zebras, hippos, and rhinos. ✉ *Km. 87.5, Carretera a Taxisco 2363–1105* 🌐 *www.autosafarichapin.com* ⏲ *Tues.–Sun. 9:30–5* 🎫 *Q60; Q50, kids under 10.*

PUERTO SAN JOSÉ

42 km (25 mi) south of Escuintla, 99 km (59 mi) south of Guatemala City.

7

Guatemala's oldest port dates from 1853, its construction spurred by the then-nascent coffee trade. Its importance has been eclipsed since the 1980s by the more modern Puerto Quetzal, next door to the east. Puerto San José serves as the westernmost mainland point on the Canal de Chiquimulilla, a waterway separating a sliver of land from the rest of Guatemala. Puerto San José is the center of the Pacific coast's just-beginning-to-burgeon sportfishing trade. It has also been a traditional beach-vacation destination for residents of Guatemala City, but is being supplanted by nearby Monterrico.

GETTING HERE AND AROUND

Transportes Esmeralda operates service between Guatemala's main bus terminal in Zona 4 and Puerto San José every half-hour throughout the day. Travel time is about two hours.

The four-lane Highway CA–9 leads due south from Guatemala City via Escuintla and ends at the ocean. Take the PUERTO SAN JOSÉ exit at the large interchange on the coast.

ESSENTIALS

Bus Contact Transportes Esmeralda (✉ *Terminal de Buses, Guatemala City* ☎ *2232–3643 in Guatemala City*).

WHERE TO STAY

$$$ 🏨 **Hotel Martita.** At first blush, you wouldn't choose a hotel near the center of a port town, but this hotel in the center of Puerto San José does things up big and draws a ton of weekend vacationers from Guatemala City. The place is thoroughly sparkling and modern, with air-conditioned comfort, a great pool, with one for the kids on the side, and a yummy restaurant. If you find yourself needing to stop in Puerto San José—we admit that's far from a likely possibility—this is a good bet. **Pros:** attentive service, great pools. **Cons:** center of town, difficult to find space on weekends. ✉ *Av. del Comercio* ☎ *7881–1337, 2474–1383 in Guatemala City* 📠 *7881–1337,*

2474–1337 in Guatemala City ⇨ *38 rooms, 13 villas* ♿ *In-hotel: restaurant, room service, bar, pool, laundry service, public Internet, parking (no fee)* ▭ *AE, D, DC, MC, V* 🍽 *BP.*

THE LADINOS

In Guatemala's historically stratified society, a vaguely defined group called the *Ladinos* occupies the middle rungs of the socioeconomic ladder. The word generally describes anyone with mixed European-indigenous blood, and the Pacific lowlands and Guatemala City are the most Ladino-populated areas of the country. The term has become a largely self-defined one. People entirely of Mayan ancestry, but who live in an urban area, speak Spanish at home, and wear Western clothing, may choose to identify themselves as "Ladino," even if technically they are not.

OUTDOOR ACTIVITIES

Guatemala's southern coast is one of the best bill-fishing spots in the world, especially during fall and spring. Several world records have been recorded here. The targets are sailfish that can reach up to 150 pounds, but enormous yellow tuna and blue marlin are often caught in the outer waters. November through April is prime season here, but anglers say you're likely to reel something in all year long. (Peak season for yellow-fin tuna and dorado are the North American summer months.) **Sailfish Bay Lodge** (☎ *2426–3909 in Guatemala City, 800/638–7405 in U.S.* ⊕ *www.sailfishbaylodge.com*) is one of the best companies in the area, offering a variety of excursions from Iztapa, near Puerto San José. Only multiday packages are offered, beginning at $2,084 per person, double occupancy in the lodge's two-story bungalows, including meals, airport transfers, chartered boats, and last-night accommodation in Guatemala City.

MONTERRICO

35 km (21 mi) east of Puerto San José, 134 km (80 mi) south of Guatemala City.

Look up "laid-back beach town" in the dictionary, and you just might find a picture of Monterrico, the only town in the country with such a vibe. Don't expect Puerto Vallarta, but Monterrico is a wonderful little place with a growing selection of lodgings, and even the upscale hotels aren't too pricey. Weekends are usually full here—you can be here from Guatemala City in just over two hours, and a huge number of the capital's residents do exactly that—but come during the week and you'll likely have the place to yourself.

Drawbacks include black volcanic sand that is very hot on bare feet at midday (wear sandals), and a wicked undertow that can pull you out to sea before you realize what is happening. (Lifeguards watch over a small section of beach on weekends only. Exercise extreme caution, and never swim alone, good advice anywhere, but especially here.)

CRUISE DAY AT PUERTO QUETZAL

The port of Puerto Quetzal has nudged out next-door Puerto San José as the Pacific coast's largest container port. Its newest incarnation is that of a port of call for ships of five cruise lines during the October–May season. Puerto Quetzal offers a distinct advantage that its competing Atlantic port at Santo Tomás de Castilla does not: the proximity here to the central and western highlands means that Antigua, Lake Atitlán, and Chichicastenango all appear on the list of shore excursions offered—that last one is an option on Thursday and Sunday market days only—all too far to reach from the Caribbean as a day trip. Cunard, Holland America, Norwegian, Regent Seven Seas, P&O, and Royal Caribbean call at Puerto Quetzal on select Panama Canal—and South America—cruise itineraries.

GETTING HERE AND AROUND

Don't forget that Monterrico is on an island, separated from the mainland by the Canal of Chiquimulilla. Just east of Puerto San José is the small town of Iztapa, also on the mainland side of the canal. A Q20 toll bridge crosses to the island and the 35 km (21 mi) road to Monterrico. An alternate, less convenient route takes you via Escuintla, then southeast to the town of Taxisco. From there, head south to the tiny hamlet of Avellanas, where you board a ferry—the flat-bed boats are called *lanchónes,* and most are big enough for only one or two vehicles at a time—to make the 25-minute trip down the canal. The ferry cost is Q85 per vehicle and Q50 per passenger.

Public bus connections to Monterrico are complicated. You need to transfer in Escuintla, then take a smaller bus to the administrative capital of Taxisco, and then board a final bus to Monterrico, when you negotiate the ferry at Avellanas. For that reason, we recommend minivan shuttle transport if you lack your own wheels. Any company in Guatemala City, Antigua, or Panajachel can fix you up.

EXPLORING

The only named street—and the only paved street, for that matter—is Calle Principal, which ends at the beach. Lodgings are scattered a block inland from the beach along dirt streets leading east and west.

The **Biotopo Monterrico,** officially, the Monterrico Natural Reserve for Multiple Uses, encompasses 6,916 acres along Guatemala's Pacific coast and includes everything from mangrove swamps to dense tropical forests. This is a haven for ornithologists, as the reserve is home to more than 100 species of migratory and indigenous birds. Marine turtles swim ashore from July to January, and you can often see them digging nests for their eggs at night. We recommend an organized tour of the reserve. Although the visitor center sits in town a couple of blocks east of Calle Principal, visiting on your own is logistically difficult. **Naturaltours** (✉ *East of Calle Principal* ☎ *5958–9491*) leads boat tours—in Spanish only—of the canal, mangroves, and lagoons. Rise and shine, for they begin at 5 AM, an hour necessary to take advantage of the best wildlife-viewing opportunities. ✉ *Southeast of Monterrico* ☎ *No phone* 🎫 *Free.*

7

WHERE TO EAT AND STAY

$ SEAFOOD ✕ **La Taberna del Pelícano.** The thatch-roof place a couple of blocks east of Calle Principal with two resident pelicans on the premises—hence the name—is our favorite stand-alone restaurant in Monterrico. You'll appreciate when the server lights a mosquito coil under your wooden table, and you'll dine on a yummy selection of pastas and seafood, all to the accompaniment of soft music. Peruse the book-exchange shelf while you wait. ✉ *Beach road east of Monterrico* ☎ *5584–2400* ▭ *No credit cards* ⊙ *Closed Mon. and Tues.*

$$$ **Atelie del Mar.** A wonderfully friendly Finnish–Guatemalan couple operates this bright, cheery hotel on the beach road west of town. The Guatemalan half of the pair brings her artist's talents—ask for a tour of her on-premises studio—to the rooms, which are decorated in bright tropical colors, with one or two beds per room, two chairs, small armoire, and a stone-basin sink and shower in the bathroom. A small staff whips up great food and serves it out in the thatch-roof rancho next to the pool. **Pros:** friendly owners; art studio on site; Wi-Fi (a rarity in Monterrico). **Cons:** hotel at end of dirt road, dark walk at night. ✉ *Beach road west of Monterrico* ☎ *5752–5528* 🌐 *www.hotelateliedelmar.com* *16 rooms* *In-room: no a/c (some), no phone, no TV, Wi-Fi. In-hotel: restaurant, bar, pool, no elevator, Internet terminal, parking (no fee), no-smoking rooms* ▭ *AE, D, DC, MC, V.*

$$$ **Dos Mundos Pacific Resort.** Set a bit outside the center of town, Monterrico's most sumptuous lodging comes courtesy of the folks who brought you Panajachel's Hotel Dos Mundos. It's another winner, even if such luxury seems a bit out of place in this funky beach town. Bungalows are arranged around the beachfront grounds, and contain tile floors, carved-wood furniture, and individual porches. The combination of ceiling fans and air-conditioning keeps things delightfully cool, as do a dip in the pool or a refreshing drink at the large rancho-style restaurant and bar. **Pros:** resort amenities; Wi-Fi; a/c. **Cons:** several blocks from center of town; lacks Monterrico beach vibe. ✉ *La Curvina, beach road east of Monterrico* ☎ *7848–1407* 🌐 *www.dosmundospacific.com* *14 rooms* *In-room: no phone, no TV, Wi-Fi. In-hotel: restaurant, room service, bar, pools, parking (no fee), no-smoking rooms* ▭ *AE, D, DC, MC, V* *BP.*

$$$ **Hotel Hawaian Paradise.** The second word in this lodging's name is missing an I, but this newest of the area's lodgings isn't missing any comfort. Just outside the tiny hamlet of Hawaii, 8 km (5 mi) east of Monterrico, the place is hopping for such a remote locale. (The paved roads ends just outside Monterrico, meaning you negotiate the last few kilometers on a dirt road. Rooms and apartments are bright and modern, and all have terrific ocean views. The hotel offers a 20-percent discount on its normal rates Monday–Thursday nights. **Pros:** resort amenities; lots of activity; a/c. **Cons:** several kilometers from town, rough road to get here. ✉ *Km. 33, Carretera a Hawaii* ☎ *5361–3011, 2338–2869 in Guatemala City* 🌐 *www.hawaianparadise.com* *7 rooms, 4 apartments* *In-room: DVDs, no phone, safe. In-hotel: restaurant, bar, pool, no elevator, Internet terminal, no-smoking rooms* ▭ *AE, D, DC, MC, V.*

GUATEMALAN SEA TURTLES

This far eastern stretch of Guatemala's Pacific coast is home to three species of marine turtle: the green, the leatherback, and, most prominently, the olive ridley turtle. For thousands of years, all three have engaged in an elaborate nesting ritual here, usually July to January, with peak nesting season taking place in August and September.

Every two to four years, female turtles come ashore, nesting 2 to 5 times in a 12-day period. Each turtle digs a pit with her flippers and scoops out a chamber for depositing about 100 eggs. She fills and conceals the chamber before heading back out to sea. After a 60-day incubation period, the hatchlings emerge. In the ultimate team effort, they scurry up the sides of the chamber, kicking sand down to the bottom, and gradually raising the level of the base of the pit, from which they escape and make a mad dash to the sea. Biologists believe that the nesting site's sand leaves an imprint on the hatchlings—though it's not known exactly how—that draws the females back as adults to the same stretch of beach to continue the millennia-old ritual.

Unfortunately, turtle eggs are prized by poachers. (Walk into a bar and you'll probably see them on the appetizer menu. Local lore holds they are aphrodisiacs.) Guatemalan authorities have struck a pragmatic bargain: egg harvesting can continue, as long as the harvesters donate 20% of their eggs to local hatcheries. Two organizations based here lead those conservation efforts, incubating donated eggs and, when the hatchlings emerge, returning them to the sea. Even with such conservation efforts, many of the hatchlings will not make it to adulthood. Many fall victim to sharks, boat rudders, and fishing nets. The fact that the turtle population survives at all is a remarkable feat of nature.

CECON (*The Center for Conservation Studies* ✉ *2 blocks east of Calle Principal, Monterrico* ☎ *5847–7777, 2331–0914 in Guatemala City* 🌐 *www.usac.edu.gt/cecon.php* 🎫 *Q8* ⏲ *Daily 7–5*), based at Guatemala City's Universidad de San Carlos, operates the Biotopo Monterrico and an interesting in-town visitor center that documents the life cycle of the turtles, as well as iguanas and caimans. It also manages Monterrico's most popular event, and one of Guatemala's most fun: the weekly turtle release during the July to January nesting season. Each Saturday at 5:30 PM the week's hatchlings return to the sea in a well-attended event. For a Q10 ticket you can sponsor a turtle, and release it at the starting line, and watch it scurry across the sand and make it to the finish line. The tide is the goal, of course—whoever said turtles are slow never witnessed this race. Win or lose, your Q10 goes to a good cause.

The Petén-based **ARCAS** (✉ *Parque Nacional Hawaii, 8 km [5 mi] east of Monterrico* ☎ *5849–8988, 2478–4096 in Guatemala City* 🌐 *www.arcasguatemala.com*), whose name is the Spanish acronym for "Association for Rescue and Conservation of Wildlife," maintains an operation in Hawaii National Park, east of Monterrico near the Salvadoran border. ARCAS is always looking for volunteers, both experts and lay people, with a passion for conservation.

LANGUAGE SCHOOL IN MONTERRICO

Monterrico offers Guatemala's one opportunity for studying Spanish in a beachside locale.

Proyecto Lingüístico Monterrico (✉ *Calle Principal* ☎ *5619–8200* 🌐 *www.monterrico-guatemala.com/spanish-school.htm*).

$$ **Hotel Pez de Oro.** The hotel whose name translates as "fish of gold" is best known for its Italian restaurant. Stop by for dinner even if you aren't staying here. Thatch-roof, tile-floor bungalows are scattered around the grounds, each with carved-wood furniture and ceiling fans that keep each unit surprisingly cool. **Pros:** good budget value; friendly owners; yummy Italian restaurant. **Cons:** spartan rooms. ✉ *Beach road east of Monterrico next to Tortugario* ☎ *2368–3684 in Guatemala City* 🌐 *www.pezdeoro.com* *18 cabins* *In-room: no a/c, no phone, no TV. In-hotel: restaurant, bar, pool, beachfront, parking (no fee), no-smoking rooms* *V* *EP.*

$–$$ **Johnny's Place.** Traditionally Monterrico's most happening place gives you several lodging options that will work out, no matter what your budget. They range from multi-person dorm rooms to fully equipped bungalows—they're made of concrete and are still a bit on the basic side, but comfortable, nonetheless. If you're feeling flush with your quetzals, and are here with a small group, opt for the two-story, stone-and-brick deluxe bungalow, the only unit here with air-conditioning, hot water, and television. ■ **TIP→ Even if you don't stay here, stop by for a meal—** everybody in town usually does at some point during their stay. **Pros:** cool beach vibe; good restaurant. **Cons:** rooms are spartan. ✉ *Beach road east of CAlle Principal* ☎ *5812–0409* 🌐 *www.johnnysplacehotel.com* *5 rooms, 6 bungalows* *In-room: no a/c (some), no phone, no TV (some). In-hotel: restaurant, bar, pool, beachfront, no elevator, parking (no fee), no-smoking rooms* *V* *EP.*

$$$ **Utz Tzaba Beach Hotel.** This is a realistic option only if you have a car, but the Utz Tzaba is a good small-resort choice. (The name means "beautiful coast.") Rooms make a semicircle around the lush green grounds fronting the beach, and have high ceilings and tile floors. Bungalows sleep up to seven people, and come with one or two bedrooms and fully equipped kitchenettes. (The bungalow rate does not include breakfast for that reason, but rooms do.) A separate kids' pool and playground make this a good option if you're traveling with the family. Internet access is difficult in this part of the country, but these folks offer Wi-Fi. **Pros:** good value; resort amenities. **Cons:** several kilometers from town, need car to stay here. ✉ *Km 21.8, Carretera a Monterrico* ☎ *7848–1479* 🌐 *www.utz-tzaba.com* *10 rooms, 4 bungalows* *In-room: refrigerator (some), kitchen (some). In-hotel: restaurant, bar, pool, Internet terminal, public Wi-Fi, parking (no fee), no-smoking rooms* *AE, D, DC, MC, V* *BP, EP.*

El Petén

8

WORD OF MOUTH

"Temple IV is the tallest building at Tikal, about 230 feet high, rising above the forest canopy. There was a flock of toucans walking around in a tree just below us. You can see the other temples rising up out of the forest and green parrots chasing each other and when the sun starts going down, the colors of the temples change."

—stotz

www.fodors.com/community

Updated by Lan Sluder

The jungles of El Petén were once the heartland of the Mayan civilization. The sprawling empire—including parts of present-day Mexico, Belize, Honduras, and El Salvador—was once made up of a network of cities that held hundreds of thousands of people, but a millennium ago this fascinating civilization went into a mysterious decline and soon virtually disappeared. The temples that dominated the horizon were swallowed up by the jungle.

Today ancient ruins seem to just crop up from El Petén's landscape. In comparison with the rest of Guatemala, which has 15 million people in an area the size of Tennessee, El Petén is relatively sparsely populated, although this is changing. Fifty years ago El Petén had fewer than 20,000 residents. Due to massive immigration from other areas of Guatemala, El Petén now has more than half a million people (almost twice the population of the entire country of Belize). Still, nature reigns supreme, with vines and other plants quickly covering everything that stands still a little too long. Whatever your primary interest—archaeology, history, birding, biking—you'll find plenty to do and see in this remote region.

Four-wheel-drive vehicles are required to get to many of the archaeological sites (but not to Tikal), while others, such as those in the Mirador Basin, are reachable only by boat or on foot. The difficulty doesn't just enhance the adventure, it gives you time to take in the exotic scenery and rare tropical flora and fauna that are with you all the way. Most major roads in the Petén are now beautifully paved, and the towns of Flores and Santa Elena bustle with activity.

The Petén may be vast and remote, but the traveler's focus takes in a far more limited area. Ruins dot the entire region, but excavation has begun on only a few of them. In the center of the region on Lago Petén Itzá sits Flores, its administrative center, and its twin town of Santa Elena, the site of the regional airport. Northeast lie the famed ruins of Tikal.

HISTORY

At its peak, the Mayan civilization developed one of the earliest forms of writing, the very first mathematical system to use zero, complex astronomical calculations, advanced agricultural systems, and an inscrutable belief system. It was during this zenith that spectacular cities such as Tikal were built. By the time the Europeans arrived, the Mayan civilization had already mysteriously collapsed.

Until the 1960s the Petén region was a desolate place. This all changed when the Guatemalan government began offering small tracts of land in El Petén for US$25 to anyone willing to settle it. The landless moved in droves, and today the population is more than 500,000—a 25-fold increase in around 50 years.

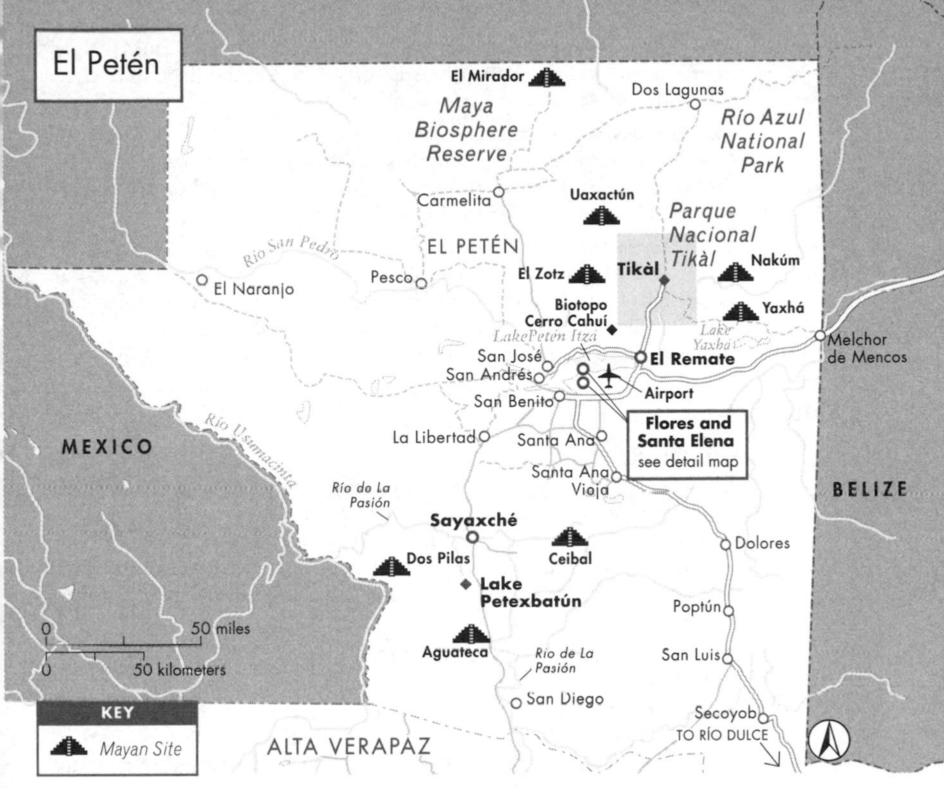

Unemployment in El Petén is high, and tourism—mostly associated with Tikal and other Mayan sites—is the main industry. Many make ends meet through subsistence farming, logging, hunting for *xate* (palm leaves used in the floral industry) in the wild, and marijuana cultivation. Exploration for oil is underway in a few areas as well.

ORIENTATION AND PLANNING

GETTING ORIENTED

The Petén is rugged country, where major roads are few and far between and highways are all but nonexistent. But because there are only two airports—one in Guatemala City, the other in Flores—you're forced to do most of your travel by land. Many of the roads in El Petén are still unpaved, the exceptions being the road from Santa Elena–Flores to Tikal, the road from Río Dulce in the south to Santa Elena–Flores, and a few others.

Proximity to Las Verapaces and the Atlantic lowlands—it's four to five hours from either region—make the Petén a reasonable overland combination with either, and air links to Guatemala City simplify travel here from almost any other region of the country.

Tikal. Arguably the most impressive of all Mayan sites, and rivaling even Machu Picchu in Peru and Angkor Wat in Cambodia in its ancient splendor, Tikal is a must-see.

Tikal Environs. Set at the end of causeway in Lake Petén, the town of Flores is a charming and walkable small town, with almost a Mediterranean air. The village of El Remate, closer to Tikal and on the lake, is another pleasant base for exploring the region.

Other Mayan Sites in El Petén. The complexes of Yaxhá, Nakúm, Uaxactún, and El Zotz are scattered around Tikal. They're all close, but poor roads limit the number of visitors, especially during the rainy season. Farther removed, southwest of Flores, off the road to Cobá in Las Verapaces, are the town of Sayaxché and its nearby Ceibal ruins.

PLANNING

WHEN TO GO

It's very warm here year-round. The rainy season is May to November. Occasional showers are a possibility the rest of the year, but shouldn't interfere with your plans. March and April are the hottest months, with December and January a few degrees cooler than the rest of the year. July and August see an influx of visitors during prime North American and European vacation time.

GETTING HERE AND AROUND

AIR TRAVEL

Aeropuerto Internacional Santa Elena (FRS), or the Mundo Maya International Airport, often just referred to as the Flores airport, is less than ½ mi (1 km) outside town. Taxis and shuttles meet every plane and charge about 20 quetzales per person to take you into Flores. The airport has service to and from Belize City, Guatemala City, and Cancún.

TACA and TAG operate flights between Guatemala City and Santa Elena-Flores that take less than an hour and cost from around US$110 each way or US$190 round-trip.

Contacts TACA (☎ *7926–1238, 2470–8222 in Guatemala City* 🌐 *www.taca.com*). **TAG** (☎ *2360–3038* 🌐 *www.tag.com.gt*).

BUS TRAVEL

Linea Dorada and Autobuses del Norte (ADN) offer direct bus service between Guatemala City and Santa Elena and Flores. The 9-hour trip on air-conditioned buses with comfortable reclining seats, TVs, and bathrooms costs around Q180 one-way (US$23) or Q350 (US$45) round-trip. Call at least one day ahead for reservations. Inexpensive local service is available, but those buses stop in every village along the way, which adds hours to the trip.

In Santa Elena the San Juan Hotel serves as the local bus terminal. Here you can catch a bus operated by San Juan Travel that makes the 1 1/2 hour, 42-mi (70-km) trip on a good paved road to Tikal at 6, 8, 9, and 10 am and return trips at 2, 4, 5 and 6 pm. Service may be reduced during slow periods. They cost around Q30 one way or Q60 round-trip per person. Local buses serving other destinations like Sayaxché depart from the market in Santa Elena. They are inexpensive but very slow.

The 42-mi (70-km) paved route between Flores–Santa Elena and Tikal is served by scheduled minibus shuttles, operated by San Juan Travel and other companies. They cost around Q30 one-way or Q60 round-trip per person. The trip takes about 1½ hours.

Contacts Autobuses del Norte (✉ E Bus Terminal, 4a Calle, Santa Elena ☎ 7924-8131). **Linea Dorada** (✉ *Calle 4a, Santa Elena* ☎ *7926–0528* ✉ *Calle de la Playa, Flores* ☎ *2232–9658*). **San Juan Travel** (✉ *2 Calle, Santa Elena* ☎ *7926–0042*).

CAR TRAVEL

Main roads in El Petén, such as between Flores/Santa Elena and Tikal, are paved and in very good shape. Secondary roads, however, often are in poor repair and not very well marked. Some roads are impassable during the rainy season, so check with the tourist office before heading out on seldom traveled roads, such as those to the more remote ruins surrounding Tikal.

If you're not booked on a tour, the best way to get around El Petén is by renting a four-wheel-drive vehicle. The major rental agencies, including Budget and Hertz, have offices at Aeropuerto Internacional Santa Elena. Koka, a local company, also rents vehicles from an office in the airport, as does Tabarini, which usually has a good selection. Prices start at around US$30 a day, or US$50 a day for an SUV. You need a valid driver's license from your own country to drive in Guatemala.

Local Agencies Budget (✉ *Aeropuerto Internacional Santa Elena* ☎ *7950–0741*). **Hertz** (✉ *Aeropuerto Internacional Santa Elena* ☎ *7950–0204*). **Koka** (✉ *Aeropuerto Internacional Santa Elena* ☎ *7926–1233*). **Tabarini** (✉ *Aeropuerto Internacional Santa Elena* ☎ *7926–0253 or 7926–0277*).

TAXI TRAVEL

Taxis from the Santa Elena–Flores airport to Tikal are around US$30. A taxi from the Santa Elena airport into Flores is Q20 (about US$2.50) per person.

EMERGENCIES

El Petén's only hospital is in San Benito, a suburb of Santa Elena. Medical facilities in El Petén are not as modern as in the rest of the country. If you're really sick, consider getting on the next plane to Guatemala City. Centro Médico Maya in Santa Elena has physicians on staff, though little or no English is spoken.

Contact Emergency Services Police (☎ *7926–1365*). **Centro Médico Maya** (✉ *4 Av., Santa Elena* ☎ *7926–0180*). **Hospital Nacional** (✉ *San Benito* ☎ *7926–1333*).

Pharmacy Farmacia Nueva (✉ *Av. Santa Ana, Flores* ☎ *7926–1387*).

MONEY MATTERS

There are several banks in Santa Elena, but few anywhere else in the region. Those on Calle 4, the main street, have ATMs that work with foreign ATM cards with MasterCard or Visa logos on the PLUS or CIRRUS systems. Several gas stations between Santa Elena and Ixlú also have bank ATMs. Flores has one bank, but it does not have an ATM. Many ATMs only take four-digit pin numbers.

Banks Banrural (✉ *4 Calle at 3 Av., Santa Elena* ☎ *7926–1002*). **Banco Industrial** (✉ *4 Calle, Santa Elena* ☎ *7926–0281*).

SAFETY

Most crimes directed at tourists in El Petén have been pickpocketings, muggings, and thefts from cars. However, there have been a number of incidents over the years involving armed groups stopping buses, vans, and private cars at Tikal park.

In town, don't wear flashy jewelry and watches, keep your camera in a secure bag, and don't handle money in public. Hire taxis only from official stands at the airport, outside hotels, and at major intersections. If you can avoid it, don't drive after sunset. One common ploy used by highway robbers is to construct a roadblock, such as logs strewn across the road, and then hide nearby. When unsuspecting motorists get out of their cars to remove the obstruction, they are waylaid. ⚠ **If you come upon a deserted roadblock, don't stop; turn around.**

The increase in adoption of Guatemalan children has caused some people—particularly rural villagers—to fear that children will be abducted by foreigners. Limit your interaction with children you do not know, and be discreet when taking photographs.

ABOUT THE RESTAURANTS

In El Petén you have a couple of choices for dining: *comedores,* which are small eateries along the lines of a U.S. café or diner, with simple and inexpensive local food; and restaurants, that, in general, are a little nicer and serve a wider selection of food, often with an international or American flavor. Restaurants are mostly in Flores and other towns. Elsewhere you'll probably eat in hotel or lodge dining rooms.

Some restaurants serve wild game, or *comida silvestre.* Although often delicious, the game has usually been taken illegally. You might see *venado* (venison), *coche del monte* (mountain cow or peccary), and *tepezcuintle* (paca, a large rodent) on the menu.

ABOUT THE HOTELS

El Petén now has a wide range of lodging options, from suites at luxurious lakeside resorts to stark rooms in budget hotels. Flores has many lodging choices, though most are mediocre at best, and the number of hotels there keeps prices competitive. The hotels in the much larger Santa Elena, the gateway to the island town of Flores, are generally larger and more upscale than the places in Flores, but with less atmosphere. El Remate, about 22 mi (35 km) from Flores on the road to Tikal, is a pleasant alternative, with several excellent small, mostly inexpensive hotels. At Tikal itself are three lodges that have the great advantage of being right at the park. On the north side of Lago de Petén Itzá are several hotels, including a couple of the most upscale in the region: Francis Ford Coppola's La Lancha and the largest resort hotel in the area, Hotel Camino Real Tikal.

WHAT IT COSTS IN GUATEMALAN QUETZALES					
	¢	$	$$	$$$	$$$$
Restaurants	under Q40	Q40–Q70	Q70–Q100	Q100–Q130	over Q130
Hotels	under Q160	Q160–Q360	Q360–Q560	Q560–Q760	over Q760

Restaurant prices are per person for a main course at dinner. Hotel prices are for two people in a standard double room, including tax (up to 22%) and service.

Many hotels in El Petén have high and low seasons. They charge higher rates during the dry season, December through April, especially at the peak times of Christmas and Easter, and sometimes also during the July to August vacation season. Advance reservations are a good idea during these periods, especially at Tikal park lodges.

TOURS

Flores-based Martsam Travel, run by Lileana and Benedicto Grijalva, offers many different types of tours in the area. Tikal Travel in Melchor de Mencos at the Belize–Guatemala border has well-priced tours of Tikal and other Mayan sites in El Petén. Tip tour guides about 10% of the tour price.

Contacts Martsam Travel (✉ *Calle Centroamérica and Av. 30 de Junio, Flores* ☎ *7926–0346* ☎📠 *7926–3225*). **Tikal Travel at Río Mopan Lodge** (✉ *Melchor de Mencos* ☎ *7926–5196* 🌐 *www.tikaltravel.com*).

VISITOR INFORMATION

ARCAS, which returns illegally captured animals to the wild, is a great resource on the flora and fauna of El Petén. The staff at INGUAT, Guatemala's tourism promotion agency, is courteous, professional, and knowledgeable. INGUAT has two offices in El Petén, one in Flores at the central plaza and one at Aeropuerto Internacional Santa Elena. CINCAP (Centro de Información sobre de Naturaleza, Cultura y Artesanías), on the central plaza in Flores, also has tourism information and historical exhibits on the Petén.

Contacts ARCAS (✉ *Barrio La Ermita, 6 mi [10 km] east of Santa Elena in San Benito* ☎ *5208–0968* 🌐 *www.arcasguatemala.com*). **CINCAP** (✉ *Parque Central, Flores* ☎ *7926–0718*). **INGUAT** (✉ *On Parque Central, Flores* ☎ *7926–0669* ✉ *Aeropuerto Internacional Santa Elena* ☎ *7926–0533 at airport*).

TIKAL

Fodor's Choice ★

22 mi (35 km) north of El Remate, 42 mi (68 km) northeast of Flores.

GETTING HERE AND AROUND

A paved, well-patrolled 42-mi (70-km) highway connects Flores-Santa Elena and Tikal, passing through the town of El Remate at about its halfway point.

TIMING

You can visit Tikal on a day trip and get a good sense of its grandeur. Depending on your schedule, you may choose to spend the night either at Tikal park so you can see the ruins in the morning (a must for

TOP REASONS TO GO

TIKAL
Tikal is usually ranked as the most impressive of all Mayan sites. You'll never forget the jungle setting, rich with wildlife and birds.

OTHER MAYAN RUINS
Tikal is the best known, but hardly the only important Mayan site in El Petén. El Mirador was a giant city-state, perhaps larger than Tikal, and in the Mirador Basin are the remains of at least four other centers, including Nakbé, El Tintal, Xulnal, and Wakná.

FLORES AND PETÉN ITZÁ
The island town of Flores has a charming European feel, with red-roof houses and cobblestone streets.

SHOPPING FOR HANDICRAFTS
The indigenous population creates countless kinds of handicrafts. There's an open-air market in Santa Elena, and Flores has a number of little shops. The village of El Remate is known for its unique wood carvings, and the border town of Melchor also has shops catering to tourists.

birders), or in Flores, El Remate, or elsewhere along the shores of Lake Petén Itzá. You can easily spend two days, or longer, exploring the ruins. You may want to hire a guide for your first day, then wander about on your own on the second. If you have additional time, consider an extension in El Petén. The town of Flores, with its lakeside bistros and cobblestone streets, merits at least a half-day stroll.

SAFETY AND PRECAUTIONS

Taxis and tourist buses seem to be magnets for bandits in El Petén. The bandits take passengers' valuables; occasionally passengers have been assaulted. Keep in mind that some 300,000 international visitors come to Tikal every year, and the vast majority of them have no problems with crime.

Tikal is one of the most popular tourist attractions in Central America—and with good reason. Smack in the middle of the 222-square-mi (575-square-km) Parque Nacional Tikal, the towering temples are ringed on all sides by miles of virgin forest. The area around the ruins is great for checking out creatures that spend their entire lives hundreds of feet above the forest floor in the dense canopy of trees. Colorful birds like yellow toucans and scarlet macaws are common sights.

Although the region was home to Mayan communities as early as 600 BC, Tikal itself wasn't established until sometime around 200 BC. One of the first structures to be built here was a version of the North Acropolis. Others were added at a dizzying pace for the next three centuries. By AD 100 impressive structures like the Great Plaza had already been built. But even though it was a powerful city in its own right, Tikal was still ruled by the northern city of El Mirador. It wasn't until the arrival of a powerful dynasty around AD 300 that Tikal arrogated itself to full power. King Great Jaguar Paw sired a lineage that would build Tikal into a city rivaling any of its time. It's estimated that by AD 500 the city covered more than 18 square mi (47 square km) and had a population of close to 100,000.

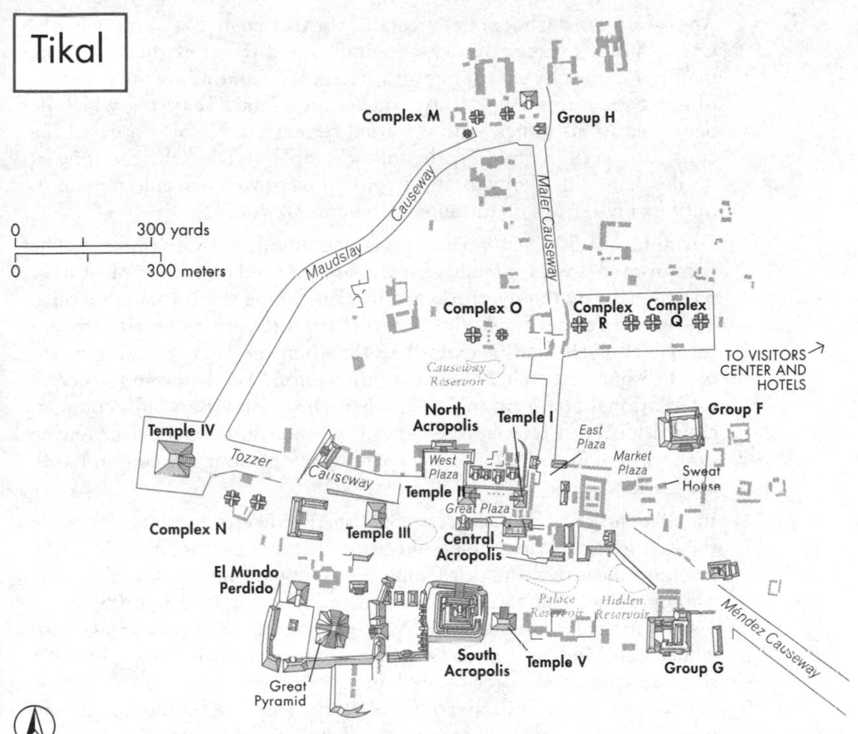

The great temples that still tower above the jungle were at that time covered with stucco and painted with bright reds and greens, and the priests used them for elaborate ceremonies meant to please the gods and assure prosperity for the city. What makes these structures even more impressive is that the Maya had no metal tools to aid in construction, had no beasts of burden to carry heavy loads, and never used wheels for anything except children's toys. Of course, as a hierarchical culture they had a slave class, and the land was rich in obsidian, a volcanic glass that could be fashioned into razor-sharp tools.

By the 6th century Tikal governed a large part of the Mayan world, thanks to a leader called Caan Chac (Stormy Sky), who took the throne around AD 426. Under Caan Chac, Tikal became an aggressive military and commercial center that dominated the surrounding communities with a power never before seen in Mesoamerica. The swamps protected the city from attack and allowed troops to spot any approaching enemy. Intensive agriculture in the *bajos* (lowlands) provided food for the huge population. A valuable obsidian trade sprang up, aided by the city's strategic position near two rivers.

Tikal thrived for more than a millennium, forming strong ties with two powerful centers: Kaminal Juyu, in the Guatemalan highlands, and Teotihuacán, in Mexico City. The city entered a golden age when

Ah-Cacao (Lord Chocolate) ascended the throne in AD 682. It was Ah-Cacao and his successors who commissioned the construction of the majority of the city's most important temples. Continuing the tradition of great structures, Ah-Cacao's son commissioned Temple I, which he dedicated to his father, who is buried beneath it. He also ordered the construction of Temple IV, the tallest temple at Tikal. By the time of his death in 768 Tikal was at the peak of its power. It would remain so until its mysterious abandonment around AD 900.

For almost 1,000 years Tikal remained engulfed by the jungle. The conquistadors who came here searching for gold and silver must have passed right by the overgrown ruins, mistaking them for rocky hills. The native Peténeros certainly knew of the ancient city's existence, but no one else ventured near until 1848, when the Guatemalan government dispatched archaeologists to the region. Tikal started to receive international attention in 1877, when Dr. Gustav Bernoulli commissioned locals to remove the carved wooden lintels from across the doorways of Temples I and IV. These were sent to a museum in Basel, Switzerland.

In 1881 and 1882 English archaeologist Alfred Percival Maudslay made the first map showing the architectural features of this vast city. As he began to unearth the major temples, he recorded his work in dramatic photographs—you can see copies in the museum at Tikal. His work was continued by Teobert Maler, who came in 1895 and 1904. Both Maler and Maudslay have causeways named in their honor. In 1951 the Guatemalan air force cleared an airstrip near the ruins to improve access for large-scale archaeological work. Today, after more than 150 years of digging, researchers say that Tikal includes some 3,000 buildings. Countless more are still covered by the jungle. ✉ *Parque Nacional Tikal* ☎ *No phone* 🌐 *www.tikalpark.com* 🎟 *Q150 (increased from Q50 in 2007)* ⏲ *Daily 6–6.*

EXPLORING

WITH A GUIDE Guides can be booked at the guide-booking desk near the visitor center. They make the visit more interesting, though don't believe everything they tell you, as some guides have their own pet theories on the decline of the Maya or other subjects that they love to expound to tourists. Near the parking lot at Tikal is an information kiosk where you can hire guides. Rates are highly negotiable, but expect to pay about US$60 for a tour for up to four or five people. In a large group you may pay as little as US$8–US$10 per person. If you're staying more than one day, hire a guide for the first day, and then wander on your own after that.

ON YOUR OWN Wear comfortable shoes and bring water—you'll be walking about 6 mi (10 km) if you intend to see the whole site. As you enter Tikal, keep to the middle trail. You'll soon arrive at the ancient city's center, filled with awe-inspiring temples and intricate acropolises. The pyramid that you approach from behind is **Temple I,** known as the Temple of the Great Jaguar because of the feline represented on one of its carved lintels. It's in what is referred to as the **Great Plaza,** one of the most beautiful and

EXPLORING TIPS

Visitors are not allowed inside the ruins after opening hours, which are 6 AM to 6 PM.

We do hear tales of tourists sneaking in or slipping guards bribes to pass, but we advise against that. The trails are not lit and climbing the pyramids is risky in the dark. There's also a slight menace of robbery.

If you stay at one of the three lodgings on the grounds, you get a jump-start on the day-tour visitors and have the advantage of being here late in the afternoon, after everyone else has left.

If you purchase your entrance ticket after 3 PM, you can use the same ticket for your next day's entry.

dramatic in Tikal. The Great Plaza was built around AD 700 by Ah-Cacao, one of the wealthiest rulers of his time. His tomb, comparable in magnitude to that of Pa Cal at the ruins of Palenque in southern Mexico, was discovered beneath the Temple of the Great Jaguar in the 1960s. The theory is that his queen is buried beneath **Temple II,** called the Temple of the Masks for the decorations on its facade. It's a twin of the Temple of the Great Jaguar. In fact, construction of matching pyramids distinguishes Tikal from other Mayan sites.

The **North Acropolis,** to the west of Ah-Cacao's temple, is a mind-boggling conglomeration of temples built over layers and layers of previous construction. Excavations have revealed that the base of this structure is more than 2,000 years old. Be sure to see the stone mask of the rain god at Temple 33. The **Central Acropolis,** south of the Great Plaza, is an immense series of structures assumed to have served as administrative centers.

If you climb to the top of one of the pyramids, you'll see the gray roof combs of others rising above the rain forest's canopy but still trapped within it. **Temple V,** to the south, underwent a $3 million restoration project and is now open to the public. **Temple IV,** to the west, is the tallest-known structure built by the Maya. Although the climb to the top is difficult, the view is unforgettable.

To the southwest of the plaza lie the **South Acropolis,** which hasn't been reconstructed, and a 105-foot-high pyramid, similar in construction to those at Teotihuacán. A few jungle trails, including the marked Interpretative Benil-ha Trail, offer a chance to see spider monkeys and other wildlife. Outside the park, a somewhat overgrown trail halfway down the old airplane runway on the left leads to the remnants of old rubber-tappers' camps, and is a good spot for bird-watching.

At park headquarters are two small archaeological museums that display Mayan artifacts. They are a good resource for information on the enigmatic rise and fall of the Maya people, though little information is in English.

Museo Lítico or Stelae Museum has stelae found at Tikal and interesting photos from early archaeological excavations. ✉ *Near visitor center* 🎫 *Q10 ($1.20)* ⏲ *Daily 9–5.*

Museo Tikal, also known as the Tikal Sylvannus G. Morley Museum, has a replica of Ha Sawa Chaan K'awil's burial chamber and some ceramics and bones from the actual tomb (the jade, however, is a replica). ✉ *Near visitor center* 🎫 *Free with ticket from Museo Lítico* ⏲ *Daily 9–5.*

WATCH FOR THE ANIMALS!

Obey Tikal's 45 kph (27 mph) speed limit; it's designed to give you time to stop for animals that cross the road within the confines of the park. Be particularly careful of the raccoon-like coatimundi that locals call a *pizote*, which scurries with abandon across the road. At the park entrance a guard gives you a time-stamped ticket to be collected by another guard when you arrive at the visitor center. If you cover the 9-mi (15-km) distance in less than 20 minutes, you'll be deemed to have been speeding and possibly fined.

WHERE TO STAY

There are three hotels on the park grounds: Tikal Inn, Jungle Lodge, and Jaguar Inn. At all of these you pay for the park location rather than good amenities and great service. Electric power is from generators, which usually run from around 5 or 6 AM to 10 or 11 PM, although batteries may provide limited lighting throughout the night. None of the hotels at the park has air-conditioning. Since the hotels here have a captive audience, service is not always as friendly or helpful as it could be, and reservations are sometimes "lost," even if you have confirming e-mail. Camping is also available, at the park campsite (US$4–US$7) or at the Jaguar Inn. Several *comedores* are at the entrance to the park, Comedor Tikal and Imperio Maya currently being the best, and you can also get snacks and drinks in the parking lot and at the hotels. All of the hotels have room-only rates, but if you are booking through a travel agent you may be required to take a package that includes meals and a Tikal tour.

$$ **Jaguar Inn.** Although this small hotel won't win any travel awards and has the feel of a backpacker's place, it's considerably less expensive than the other two hotels in the park and has a good restaurant. The small rooms have tile floors and wooden furnishings, with Guatemalan fabrics. You can also camp here for Q40 (US$5) per person, including rental of a hammock and mosquito net. **Pros:** cheapest lodging at the park, camping available. **Cons:** basic rooms somewhat jammed together, no pool. ✉ *Parque Nacional Tikal* ☎ *7783–3647 (front desk) or 7926–0002* (reservations) 🌐 *www.jaguartikal.com* *13 rooms in cabins, 1 dorm, camping area* *In-room: no phone, no TV. In-hotel: restaurant, Wi-Fi hot spot* 💳 *DC, MC, V.*

$$$$ **Jungle Lodge.** Built 50 years ago to house archaeologists working at Tikal, this hotel has cute duplexes with porches but not much privacy. The bungalows are spacious, with double beds and tile floors. There are whirling ceiling fans, but the generator is shut off from 11 PM to 5 AM, so you may be hot at night. Two new suites have king beds and whirlpool baths. If your budget allows, choose one of the bungalows or suites. The restaurant ($$) was rebuilt in late 2006, and serves unremarkable

food, though in a pleasant dining room. **Pros:** best of the three lodges in the park, clean and adequate accommodations. **Cons:** you are paying for location, food is mediocre. ✉ *Parque Nacional Tikal* ☎ *7861–0447* 🌐 *www.junglelodgetikal.com* *12 rooms with shared baths, 34 bungalows, 2 suites* *In-room: no phone, no TV. In-hotel: restaurant, bar, pool, laundry service, Internet terminal* ▭ *MC, V* 🍽 *BP.*

$$$$ **Tikal Inn.** This cluster of comfortable bungalows, set farthest from the park entrance, wraps around a well-manicured garden and a pool. It's set apart from the other lodgings, affording a bit of privacy. The rooms have a modern feel, yet they have thatch roofs and stucco walls decorated with traditional fabrics. Avoid the rooms near the parking lot, as guests who want to watch the sunrise over the park gather there and can be noisy. A restaurant ($$) has a menu that changes daily. **Pros:** good location in the park, has a swimming pool. **Cons:** poor service at times, rooms are hot, limited hot water and electricity. ✉ *Parque Nacional Tikal* ☎ *7926–1917* ☎ *7926–0065* 🌐 *www.tikalinn.com* *18 rooms, 18 bungalows* *In-room: no phone, no TV. In-hotel: restaurant, bar, pool, laundry service, Internet terminal* ▭ *AE, DC, MC, V.*

TIKAL ENVIRONS

Flores, a charming small town in Lake Petén connected to the mainland by a causeway, is the main point of interest for most visitors. Stay in a small inn or hotel, eat at lakeside bistros, and explore the cobblestone streets on foot. Santa Elena, at the entrance to Flores, is a bustling commercial center but is far less frequented by tourists. El Remate, a village on the shore of the lake, has a number of small, mostly budget, hotels, and is a handy jumping-off point for Tikal if you don't stay in the park.

8

FLORES

★ *133 mi (206 km) north of Río Dulce, 38 mi (61 km) northeast of Sayaxché.*

The red-roof town of Flores, on an island surrounded by the waters of Lago Petén Itzá, is on the site of the ancient city of Tatyasal. This was the region's last unconquered outpost of Mayan civilization, until finally falling to the Spanish in 1697. The conquerors destroyed the city's huge pyramids.

Today the provincial capital is a pleasant place to explore, with its narrow streets lined with thick-walled buildings painted pink, blue, and purple. Flowering plants droop over balconies, giving the town a tropical flavor. There's a central square presided over by a colonial church.

Sadly, most of the hotels in Flores are also pedestrian, rarely rising above mediocrity. Flores is crying out for a truly special small inn, one that's as charming as the town itself.

Connected to the mainland by a bridge and causeway—don't be put off by the Burger King at the entrance to the causeway—Flores serves as a base for travelers to El Petén. It's also the center of many nongovernmental organizations working for the preservation of the Mayan Biosphere, an endangered area covering nearly all of northern Petén. Flores is also one of the last remaining vestiges of the Itzá, the people who built Mexico's monumental Chichén Itzá.

In the 1800s, before it was a departure point for travelers headed for the ruins, Flores was called Devil's Island because of the prison on top of the hill (a church stands there now). Since 1994 the building has been home to the **Centro de Información sobre la Naturaleza, Cultura, y Artesanía de Petén** (✉ *North side of Parque Central* ☎ *7926–0718* ⏲ *Weekdays 8–5*). This center has a small museum with photographs of the region and information about local resources, such as allspice, chicle (a chewing-gum base made from tree sap), and *xate* (a shade palm used in floral decorations). A gift shop sells wood carvings, woven baskets, cornhusk dolls, and even locally made peanut butter.

GETTING HERE AND AROUND

From the airport in Santa Elena, Flores is a short Q20 per-person taxi ride. Minibuses (Q25 per person) will bring you from Tikal park. Flores itself is best seen on foot or in tuk-tuks (small motorcycle rickshaw taxis). Note, however, that a massive street resurfacing project in 2009–10 has ripped up many of the cobblestone streets in town, making walking temporarily less pleasurable.

TIMING

You can easily experience the highlights of Flores in a day or less, but it's a pleasant place to relax for longer. If visiting Tikal park from Flores, you'll require an additional one to two days.

SAFETY AND PRECAUTIONS

Flores generally is a safe small town, but avoid flashing wads of money or jewelry, and don't wander alone on isolated streets after dark.

WHERE TO EAT

¢–$ LATIN AMERICAN

✗ **Café Arqueológico Yaxha.** This restaurant combines a cultural and educational experience with good food. German architect Dieter Richter, who has worked on projects at Yaxha and Naranjo, started this café. You can browse a collection of books, photos, maps, and other information about the Mayan world while you enjoy a hamburguesa (Q35) or a Mayan dish such as *Pollo Xni Pec* (chicken in a chili sauce served with rice and yucca, Q48). You can also book tours to Yaxha and elsewhere. ✉ *Av. 15 de Septiembre* ☎ *5830–2060* 💳 *MC, V.*

¢–$$$ STEAKHOUSE

✗ **Capitán Tortuga.** The large, cartoonlike Capitán Tortuga sign may fool you into thinking this restaurant is just for kids, but the excellent grilled steak and seafood options make this one of Flores's best restaurants. The *pinchos* (grilled kebabs) are cooked on an open barbecue, sending enticing aromas throughout the restaurant. There's a nice patio out back, which offers tremendous sunset views of the lake. ✉ *Calle 30 de Junio and Callejón San Pedrito* ☎ *7926–0247* 💳 *MC, V.*

¢–$ CAFÉ

✗ **Cools Beans/El Café Chilero.** Sit in a leafy garden and sip a latte or lemonade at this cool coffeehouse. Breakfast is around Q15, and light meals are served the rest of the day. ✉ *Calle 15 de Septiembre near causeway* ☎ *5571–9240* 💳 *MC, V* ⏲ *Closed Tues.*

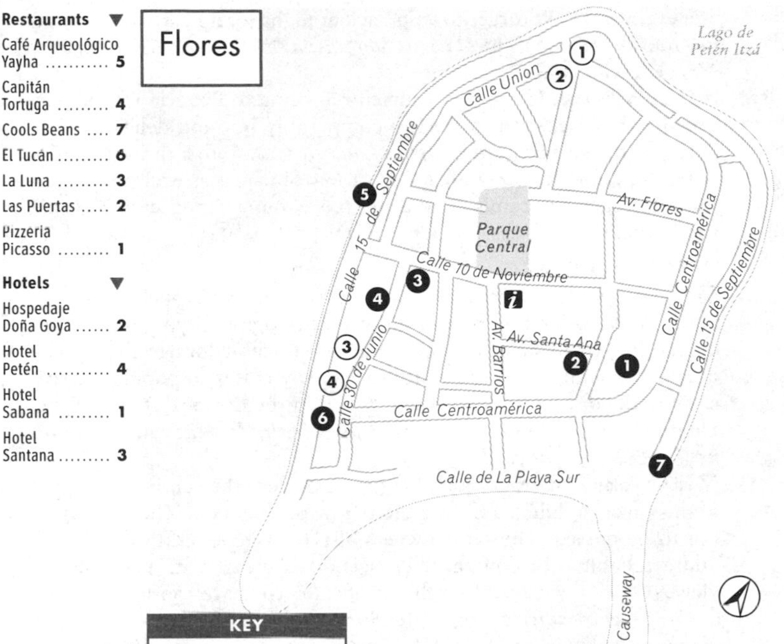

¢–$$ MEXICAN ✕ **El Tucán.** Toucans and parrots, part of the menagerie belonging to the owner, share the breezy terrace with diners. The small dining room, decorated with highland weavings, also has good views of one of Flores's cobblestone streets. The menu includes a variety of traditional meals, though Mexican cuisine is the specialty here. The bread is baked on the premises. ✉ *Calles 15 de Septiembre and Centroamérica* ☎ *7867–5137* ▭ *AE, D, DC, MC, V* ⏲ *Closed Sun.*

$–$$$ CONTINENTAL ★ ✕ **La Luna.** With its homemade paper lamp shades illuminating lovely blue walls, La Luna inspires romance on any moonlit night. But you can just as easily fall in love with what we think is the most creative restaurant in town when you stop in for a delicious lunch. Choose from inventive dishes, including wonderful vegetarian options like the stuffed squash in white sauce. Many people drop by for a drink at the bar. ✉ *Calle 30 de Junio* ☎ *7926–3346* ▭ *AE, DC, MC, V* ⏲ *Closed Sun.*

¢–$ LATIN AMERICAN ✕ **Las Puertas.** On a quiet side street, Las Puertas was named for its six screened doors. It's a favorite hangout for locals and travelers alike. The friendly couple who run the place take great pride in serving only the freshest foods. Notable are the delicious sandwiches made with homemade bread and mozzarella cheese and the giant goblets of incredible iced coffee. In the afternoon you can relax with a fruit drink as you play one of the many board games. Films are shown in the afternoon and evening. Don't forget to stop back at night for a hearty dinner and live music. ✉ *Calle Central at Av. Santa Ana* ☎ *7926–1061* ▭ *AE, DC, MC, V* ⊙ *Closed Sun.*

¢–$ PIZZA ✕ **Pizzeria Picasso.** If you find yourself returning to Pizzeria Picasso, it's because the brick-oven pizza is incomparably hot and delicious. The decor, featuring a print of Picasso's *Guernica,* is another draw. If you're not in the mood for pizza, there is a variety of pastas as well. Save room for cheesecake or tiramisu and a cup of steaming cappuccino. ✉ *Calle Centroamérica* ☎ *7926–0673* ▭ *AE, DC, MC, V* ⊙ *Closed Mon.*

WHERE TO STAY

¢ **Hospedaje Doña Goya.** A rooftop terrace with hammocks swinging in the breeze is the best part of this budget lodging. If you prefer, grab a good book and sink into one of the comfortable lounge chairs. The hotel is clean and well run, which explains why it is so popular. Arrive early in the day to secure a room. A bed in the dorm is Q25. ✉ *Calle Union* ☎ *7926–3538* *6 rooms, 3 with bath, dormitory* *In-room: no TV* ▭ *No credit cards.*

$$ **Hotel Petén.** An arabesque plunge pool graces the central courtyard of this lovely lodging. Taking a dip to escape the midday heat is a treat not to be missed. The same owners also operate several other hotels and a reliable tour company. **Pros:** modern hotel with great sunset views of the lake. **Cons:** four flights of stairs to get to top-floor rooms. ✉ *Calle Centroamerica, off Calle 30 de Junio* ☎ *7926–0692* *21 rooms* *In-hotel: restaurant, bar, pool, laundry service, Internet terminal* ▭ *AE, DC, MC, V* *BP.*

$–$$ **Hotel Sabana.** This small hotel, with four floors in one section and five in another, offers simple rooms that open onto a terrace overlooking the pool. A sundeck has nice views of the lake. This is a reliable choice in a less expensive hotel if you want a pool and need some creature comforts such as air-conditioning and a TV. **Pros:** dependable choice with some amenities. **Cons:** a lot of stairs to climb. ✉ *Calle Union and Av. Libertad* ☎ *7926–1248* *www.hotelsabana.com* *28 rooms* *In-hotel: restaurant, bar, pool, laundry service* ▭ *AE, DC, MC, V.*

$–$$ ★ **Hotel Santana.** Sitting right on the water, this bright pink hotel is one of the best lodging choices on the island. All the rooms open up onto wide balconies with wicker chairs where you can enjoy the view. Rooms at the back have lake views. The sunny central courtyard surrounds a pleasant pool. **Pros:** a top choice in Flores, lovely views of the lake. **Cons:** mishmash of building styles and materials, but it seems to work. ✉ *Calle 30 de Junio, Playa Poniente* ☎ *7926–0662* *www.santanapeten.com* *35 rooms* *In-room: safe. In-hotel: restaurant, pool, laundry service, Internet terminal* ▭ *AE, DC, MC, V.*

NIGHTLIFE

Discoteca Raices (✉ *Av. Periférico* ☎ *5521–1843*) is the island's only true disco. The bar at the **Mayan Princess** (✉ *Av. La Reforma and Av. 14 de Noviembre* ☎ *No phone*) shows nightly movies on a big-screen TV.

Las Puertas (✉ *Calle Central at Av. Santa Ana* ☎ *7926–1061*) has live music every night. The artsy **La Luna** (✉ *Calle 30 de Junio* ☎ *7926–3346*) has a pleasant atmosphere.

SPORTS AND THE OUTDOORS

BOATING

Boat trips on Lake Petén Itzá can be arranged through most hotels in Flores or by haggling with boat owners who congregate behind the Hotel Santana. Tours often include a stop at Paraíso Escondido, a small mainland park northwest of Flores.

SANTA ELENA

¼ mi (½ km) south of Flores.

Although it lacks the charms of neighboring Flores, gritty Santa Elena is pretty much unavoidable. Most services that you'll need for your trip to El Petén are usually offered here. There are also more upscale hotels here than in Flores.

GETTING HERE AND AROUND

Tuk-tuks—the motorized three-wheeled taxi rickshaws manufactured in Asia—ply the streets of Flores and Santa Elena. Five minutes and Q5 will get you between the two.

TIMING

Santa Elena is a place to sleep in a decent hotel, get money from an ATM, and buy picnic supplies. There's little to see in Santa Elena itself. At most, you'll use it as a base for exploring other parts of El Petén, so how long you stay here depends on your exploration plans.

SAFETY AND PRECAUTIONS

Some gas stations in Santa Elena have armed guards 24 hours a day, so that should tell you something. The better hotels are quite safe, however, and most visitors never experience any crime.

8

WHERE TO STAY

$$ **Hotel del Patio-Tikàl.** Built in traditional Spanish style, this modern hotel is easily recognizable by its stone walls and barrel-tile roof. Rooms, some of which are in need of refurbishing, face a small patio with a trickling fountain. Ask for a room on the first floor, as these have much larger windows. The patio restaurant sits under big arches leading to a grassy courtyard, making it a much more pleasant place to relax than the musty bar. ✉ *Corner of Calle 2 and Av. 8* ☎ *7926–1229* 🌐 *www.caminoreal.com.gt* *21 rooms* *In-room: safe. In-hotel: restaurant, room service, bar, pool, gym, laundry service, Internet terminal* ▭ *AE, D, DC, MC, V* *BP.*

$$ **Hotel La Casona del Lago.** The style looks a tad out of place here (think Caribbean pastels), but no matter. Santa Elena's newest, spiffiest hotel sits on the lakeshore and has splendid views of Flores across the water, especially from the top-floor restaurant and bar. Rooms are bright and spacious, with large windows, tile floors, two double beds each, and a desk, and are arranged around three sides of the pool. This place also tosses in amenities such as Wi-Fi, rarely seen in this part of the country. ✉ *1 Calle* ☎ *7952–8700, 2336–2841 in Guatemala City* *33 rooms* *In-hotel: restaurant, bar, pool, laundry service, Internet terminal, Wi-Fi hot spot, laundry service* ▭ *AE, D, DC, MC, V.*

$$$$ **Petén Espléndido.** You're not on Flores, but the views of that pretty island from your private balcony are the next best thing. The pool, surrounded by palm trees, is a great place to spend an afternoon sunbathing. Sit at one of the shaded tables on the terrace or in the pretty dining room and enjoy the *especial del día* (daily special). The hotel is popular among business travelers, who appreciate the fully equipped convention center. Families enjoy the paddleboats on the lake. **Pros:** the top full-service hotel in Santa Elena, only elevator in the Petén, nice views of Flores. **Cons:** a bit formal, smallish rooms. ✉ *At foot of bridge leading to Flores* ☎ *7926–0880* 🌐 *www.petenesplendido.com* *62 rooms* *In-room: safe. In-hotel: restaurant, room service, bar, pool, Internet terminal, laundry service* 💳 *AE, DC, MC, V.*

$$$$ ★ **Villa Maya.** You could lie in bed and count the birds flying by your window at these modern villas at Lake Petenchel, east of Santa Elena. Some 50 species have been spotted in the area. If you're more interested in wildlife, ask an attendant where to find the troop of spider monkeys that roams the grounds and the adjacent rain forest. All 56 rooms, in two-level bungalows spread out around the grounds, are tastefully decorated with colorful weavings and mahogany accents, and have terrific views. Vans shuttle you to and from Tikal. **Pros:** beautiful lake views, quiet and peaceful setting. **Cons:** not convenient to a selection of restaurants and shopping. ✉ *5 mi (8 km) east of Santa Elena* ☎ *5415–1592, 2334–8136 in Guatemala City* 🌐 *www.villasdeguatemala.com* *56 rooms* *In-room: no phone, no TV. In-hotel: restaurant, room service, bar, pools, bicycles, laundry service, Internet terminal, laundry service* 💳 *AE, DC, MC, V.*

SPORTS AND THE OUTDOORS

There are several caves in the hills behind Santa Elena with interesting stalactite and stalagmite formations and subterranean rivers. The easiest to visit is Aktun Kan, just south of town.

Ixpanpajul Parque Natural (✉ *Ruta a Santa Elena, Km 468* ☎ *2336–0576* 🌐 *www.ixpanpajul.com*) is a private nature reserve sitting on a large stand of primary rain forest. Hiking the suspended bridges of the skyway will give you a bird's-eye view of the indigenous flora and fauna that make the rain forest the most biodiverse ecosystem on the planet. The park also offers myriad adventure opportunities, from nighttime ATV tours to horseback rides to mountain-bike excursions. The Tarzán Canopy Tour (zip line) costs Q125. There is camping (from Q30 per person), and rental cabañas are available. The entrance to the reserve is 6 mi (10 km) south of Santa Elena.

EL REMATE

18½ mi (30 km) northeast of Flores.

A mellow little town on the eastern shore of Lago Petén Itzá, El Remate is known mostly for its wood carvings, made by families that have dedicated themselves to this craft for generations. Just west of El Remate is the Biotopo Cerro Cahuí, and you can rent a canoe or kayak (around Q10 or US$1.20 an hour) at El Remate to explore the lake. Because it's less than one hour from both Tikal and Yaxhá, El Remate makes a good base for exploring the area.

With more than 1,500 acres of rain forest, **Biotopo Cerro Cahuí** (✉ *West of El Remate* ☎ *No phone* 🎫 *Q20*) is one of the most accessible wildlife reserves in El Petén. It protects a portion of a mountain that extends to the eastern edge of Lago Petén Itzá, so there are plenty of opportunities for hiking. Two well-maintained trails put you in proximity of birds like ocellated turkeys, toucans, and parrots. As for mammals, look up to spot the long-armed spider monkeys or down to see squat rodents called *tepezcuintles.* Tzu'unte, a 4-mi (6-km) trail, leads to two lookouts with views of nearby lakes. The upper lookout, Mirador Moreletii, is known by locals as Crocodile Hill, because from the other side of the lake it looks like the eye of a half-submerged crocodile. Los Ujuxtes, a 3-mi (5-km) trail, offers a panoramic view of three lakes. Both hikes begin at a ranger station, where English-speaking guides are sporadically available. Some robberies and attacks on tourists have taken place in the reserve, so ask locally about safety conditions before you explore on your own.

GETTING HERE AND AROUND

El Remate is about a half-hour from Flores by car.

TIMING

Most visitors use El Remate as a base for visits to Tikal and other nearby Mayan sites, so the length of stay depends on how much time you want to spend seeing ruins.

WHERE TO EAT AND STAY

¢–$ LATIN AMERICAN ✕ **La Estancia Cafetería.** Owner Victor Morales's specialty is an exquisite whitefish served with vegetables sautéed in butter on a wooden platter. Every once in a while he cooks up some fresh venison. Even though the driveway is usually filled with cars, this eatery is easy to miss—look for the Orange Crush sign. ✉ *1¼ mi (2 km) south of El Remate* ☎ *No phone* 💳 *No credit cards.*

$–$$ **La Casa de Don David.** Owners Don David Kuhn and his wife, Doña Rosa, have lived in the area for almost 30 years, and are a great source of travel tips. The hotel's Web site also has a wealth of information on the area. Rooms are simple and clean, with private baths, and some have air-conditioning. La Casa is known for its second-story restaurant, which has good home cooking. One meal is included in the room rate—you can choose to have breakfast or dinner here. The hotel offers good, well-priced tours to Tikal, Yaxha, El Mirador, and other sites. **Pros:** knowledgeable host, attractive grounds, good restaurant. **Cons:** not a lot of frills. ✉ *On road to Biotopo Cerro Cahuí* ☎ *5306–2190 or 7928–8469* 🌐 *www.lacasadedondavid.com* *15 rooms* *In-room: no TV. In-hotel: restaurant, laundry service, Internet terminal* 💳 *MC, V* *BP.*

$$–$$$ **La Mansión del Pájaro Serpiente.** Perched high on the hillside, La Mansión del Pájaro Serpiente has some of the prettiest accommodations in El Petén. You have a choice of rooms in either standard or deluxe bungalows. Canopy beds grace the larger bedrooms, which are furnished in dark tropical woods and have big windows that let in lots

of light. You can throw open the windows to catch the lake breezes, so sleeping is comfortable. Up a nearby hill is a swimming pool, and farther up you'll find a covered terrace with several hammocks. The grounds are lovingly maintained, and there are even resident peafowl. The open-air restaurant serves local and international dishes. **Pros:** pretty little cabins set on a hillside, lake views (though it's not directly on the lake), lovely grounds, swimming pool. **Cons:** not for visitors who can't walk up and down steep hills. ✉ *On main hwy. south of El Remate* ☎ *7926–4246* ✉ *tikalnancy@hotmail.com* *10 rooms* *In-room: no phone, no TV. In-hotel: restaurant, bar, pool, laundry service* *No credit cards.*

SPORTS AND THE OUTDOORS

The fun folks at **Tikal Canopy Tour** (✉ *Near entrance gate to Tikal park, about 40 minutes by car from Flores* ☎ *5819–7766* 🌐 *www.canopytikal.com*) have expeditions that take you to the true heart of the rain forest—not on ground level, but more than 100 feet up in the air. In the canopy you'll see monkeys and maybe even a sloth. The tour, which costs US$30 per person, ends with an exhilarating 300-foot-long ride down a zip line.

SHOPPING

Although most souvenirs here are similar to those found elsewhere in Guatemala, the beautiful wood carvings are unique to El Petén. More than 70 families in this small town dedicate themselves to this craft. Their wares are on display on the side of the highway right before the turnoff for the Camino Real and La Lancha hotels on the road to Tikal, and also in small shops in El Remate.

NORTH SHORE, LAKE PETÉN ITZÁ

8 mi (13 km) west of El Remate.

The small villages of San Pedro, San José, and San Andrés, on the northwest shore of Lake Petén Itzá, have beautiful views of the sparkling lake. Several upscale lodges and hotels have opened here, and the area is accessible via bus or car on an improved (but bumpy) dirt road from El Remate or Santa Elena, or in the clockwise direction from San Benito.

WHERE TO STAY

$$$$ ★ **Camino Real Tikal.** To experience the natural beauty of the jungles surrounding Lago Petén Itzá without sacrificing creature comforts, many people head to Camino Real Tikal. It's possible to spend several days at the hotel without exhausting the possibilities—kayaking on the lake, hiking in a private reserve, swimming in the pool, lounging in the lakeside hammocks, and experiencing a traditional Mayan sauna. A dozen three-story thatch-roof villas set high on the hillside hold the rooms, all of which have porches with views of the sparkling lake. **Pros:** most upscale large hotel in El Petén, beautiful setting. **Cons:** somewhat remote, rooms a bit dated. ✉ *Lote 77, Parcelamiento Tayasal, 3 mi (5 km) west of El Remate, San José* ☎ *7926–0204* 🌐 *www.caminoreal.com.gt* *72 rooms* *In-room: safe, refrigerator. In-hotel: 2 restau-*

rants, room service, bars, pool, gym, water sports, bicycles, Internet terminal, laundry service ▭ *AE, DC, MC, V* 🍽 *BP.*

$$$$ Fodor's Choice ★ **La Lancha.** Francis Ford Coppola's latest lodging venture isn't quite as luxe as his two properties in Belize, though it is the only one with air-conditioning, but everything is done in exquisite taste. Guatemalan and Balinese textiles and handmade furniture make rooms cozy. All the casitas glimpse Lake Petén Itzá, though the pricier, larger lake-view units have the stunning, splurge-worthy views. The lake-view units, however, are many steps farther down the hillside. The restaurant serves delicious Guatemalan food, and the lake views from your table are incredible. A new gift shop above the restaurant sells crafts at reasonable prices. **Pros:** lovely lake views, good restaurant, all done in good taste. **Cons:** expensive (for Guatemala), somewhat remote, lots of steep steps, you can hear your neighbors in the duplex units. ✉ *8 mi (13 km) west of El Remate, San José* ☎ *7928–8331, 800/746–3743 in U.S.* 🌐 *www.blancaneauxlodge.com* *10 casitas* *In-room: no phone, no TV. In-hotel: restaurant, room service, bar, pool, bicycles, Wi-Fi hot spot, laundry service* ▭ *AE, MC, V* 🍽 *CP.*

$$$$ Fodor's Choice ★ **Ni'tun Ecolodge.** After hiking through the jungle, you'll love returning to this charming cluster of cabins owned by a former coffee farmer. The point is to disturb the environment as little as possible, so the buildings are constructed of stone and wood left behind by farmers clearing land for fields. The common areas, including a massive kitchen downstairs and an airy bar and reading room upstairs, are delightful. Ni'tun also runs Monkey Eco Tours, so you can choose from itineraries ranging from one-day trips to nearby villages to a seven-day journey to El Mirador. It's easiest to get here by boat (a 20-minute trip) from Flores. **Pros:** small, very personal lodge experience, excellent food, engaging owner. **Cons:** somewhat off the beaten path. ✉ *1 mi (2 km) west of San Andrés, northwest of Flores* ☎ *5201–0759* 🌐 *www.nitun.com* *4 cabins* *In-room: no TV. In-hotel: restaurant, bar, Internet terminal* ▭ *AE, DC, MC, V* ⊗ *Closed late May–early June* 🍽 *BP.*

8

OTHER MAYAN SITES IN EL PETÉN

Although Tikal is the most famous, El Petén has hundreds of archaeological sites, ranging from modest burial chambers to sprawling cities. The vast majority have not been explored, let alone restored. Within a few miles of Tikal are several easy-to-reach sites. Because they're in isolated areas, it's a good idea to go with a guide.

EXPLORING

Nakúm lies deep within the forest, connected to Tikal via jungle trails that are sometimes used for horseback expeditions. You cannot visit during the rainy season, as you'll sink into mud up to your ankles. Two building complexes and some stelae are visible. ✉ *16 mi (26 km) east of Tikal.*

The 4,000-year-old city of **Uaxactún** (pronounced Wah-shank-TOON) was once a rival to Tikal's supremacy in the region. It was conquered by Tikal in the 4th century and lived in the shadow of that great city for centuries. Inscriptions show that Uaxactún existed longer than any other Mayan city, which may account for the wide variety of structures. Here you'll find a Mayan observatory.

Uaxactún is surrounded by thick rain forest, so the trip can be arduous, but as it's difficult to get here, you most likely won't have to fight the crowds as you do at neighboring Tikal, leaving you free to enjoy the quiet and mystical air of the ruins. The rock-and-dirt road is passable during the drier seasons and nearly impossible at other times without a four-wheel-drive vehicle. You'll need to secure a permit to visit Uaxactún. The administration building in Tikal is on the road between the Jaguar Inn and the Jungle Lodge. Obtaining a permit is sometimes easier said than done, but with a little persistence and perhaps a small *mordida* (bribe), you should be able to get past the guards into the administration area where they grant the free permits. Sometimes police will ask to accompany you on the trip, which is helpful for two reasons: it prevents potential robberies, and, most important, will give you an extra person to push if your vehicle gets stuck. The police may ask you for some money; a Q20 tip goes a long way toward making your trip smooth. ✉ *16 mi (24 km) north of Tikal.*

Overlooking a beautiful lake of the same name, the ruins of **Yaxhá** are divided into two sections of rectangular structures that form plazas and streets. The city was probably inhabited between the Preclassic and Classic periods. The ruins are being restored by a German organization. Lake Yaxhá, surrounded by virgin rain forest, is a good bird-watching spot. During the rainy season only a four-wheel-drive vehicle—or setting out on horseback, motorcycle, or on foot—will get you to Yaxhá; the rest of the year the road is passable. ✉ *30 mi (48 km) south of Flores, 19 mi (30 km) east of Tikal.*

A popular ecotourism destination, **El Zotz** consists of the remnants of a Mayan city. On a clear day you can see the tallest of the ruins at Tikal from these unexcavated ruins. The odd name, which means "the bat" in Q'eqchí, refers to a cave from which thousands of bats make a nightly exodus. Troops of hyperactive spider monkeys seem to have claimed this place for themselves, swinging through the treetops and scrambling after each other like children playing a game of tag. Unlike those in Tikal, however, these long-limbed creatures are not used to people and will shake branches and throw twigs and fruit to try to scare you away. Mosquitoes are fierce especially in rainy season; bring your strongest repellent. ✉ *15 mi (24 km) west of Tikal.*

El Mirador, once equal in size and splendor to Tikal, may eventually equal Tikal as a must-see Mayan ruin. It's just now being explored, but elaborate plans are being laid to establish a huge park four times the size of Tikal. The Mirador Basin contains the El Mirador site itself, four other known Mayan cities that probably were as large as Tikal (Nakbé, El Tintal, Xulnal, and Wakná), and many smaller but important sites—perhaps as many as 80 to 100 cities. The Mirador Basin is home to an incredible diversity of plant and animal life, including 200 species of birds, 40 kinds of animals (including several endangered ones, such as jaguars), 300 kinds of trees, and 2,000 different species of flora. It has been nominated as a UNESCO World Heritage Site. Currently, fewer than 2,500 visitors get to El Mirador annually, as it's a difficult trek requiring five or six days of hiking (round-trip). The jumping-off point for the trek is Carmelita Village, about 50 mi (84 km) north of Flores. There are no hotels in the Mirador Basin, and no roads except for dirt paths. Local tour companies can arrange treks. ✉ *40 mi (66 km) northwest of Tikal.*

Mayan Sites

9

WORD OF MOUTH

"Tikal is amazing. The tour buses are gone by late afternoon and we saw less than a dozen tourists the entire time we were there. You can see the other temples rising up out of the forest and green parrots chasing each other and when the sun starts going down, the colors of the temples change. A few more people joined us. Here we sit, maybe 8 people, from different countries, taking each other's pictures, high above the jungle canopy and watching the sun set on buildings that were an integral part of the lives of a people whose civilization disappeared over a thousand years ago."

—stotz

www.fodors.com/community

Updated by Jeffrey Van Fleet

Visiting Guatemala without touring any Mayan sites is like going to Greece and not seeing the Acropolis and the Parthenon. For at least five millennia, the Maya left their imprint on Mesoamerica, and today some of the Mayan world's most awe-inspiring ruins are yours to explore. Even the most accessible sites aren't overrun with hordes of travelers—at some you may be the only visitor, other than perhaps a troop of howler monkeys or a flock of parrots.

A MAYAN PRIMER

CHRONOLOGY

The **Preclassic** (circa 3000 BC to AD 250) period was influenced by the Olmec, a civilization centered on the Gulf Coast of present-day Mexico. During this period cities began to take root, especially in the Guatemala and neighboring Belize lowlands. It's at this time that Takalik Abaj in the Pacific lowlands and Naranjo in the Petén were first settled.

By the **Late Preclassic** (circa 300 BC to AD 250) period, the Maya had developed an advanced mathematical system, an impressively precise calendar, and one of the world's five original writing systems.

During the **Classic** (circa 250 BC to AD 900) period, Mayan artistic, intellectual, and architectural achievements excelled. Vast city-states were connected by a large number of paved roadways, some of which still exist today. The great cities of Tikal and Quiriguá, along with Copán, just across the border in Honduras, were just a few of the powerful centers that controlled the Classic Mayan world.

The single largest unsolved mystery about the Maya is their rapid decline during the **Terminal Classic** (AD 800 to 900) period and the centuries following. Scholars have postulated that climate change, pandemic disease, drought, stresses in the social structure, overpopulation, deforestation, and changes in the trade routes could have been responsible. Nevertheless, smaller communities at Ceibal, Nakúm, and El Baúl were thriving during this period.

The Maya of the **Postclassic** (AD 900 to early 1500s) period were heavily affected by growing powers in central Mexico. Architecture, ceramics, and carvings from this period show considerable outside influence. Although still dramatic, Postclassic cities such as Chichén Itzá and Uxmal pale in comparison to their Classic predecessors. The period in what is now Guatemala was marked by a slow migration to the highlands. By the time of the Spanish conquest in the 16th century, the Maya were scattered, feuding, and easy to conquer.

KEY DATES

Note: Most of the dates are approximate, and some are disputed.

BC

3114 Date of the creation of the world, or 0.0.0.0.0 according to the Long Count calendar
3000 Early Olmec and Mayan civilizations thought to have begun
900 Olmec writing system developed
800 Tikal established
700 First written Mayan language
500 First Mayan calendars carved in stone
200 First monumental buildings erected at Tikal and El Mirador

AD

159 Copán established
400–600 Tikal becomes leading city-state, with population of perhaps 200,000
426 Accession of Caan Chac begins Tikal's period of military dominance
628 Accession of Smoke Jaguar begins Copán's golden age
682 Accession of Ah-Cacao begins Tikal's golden age
695 Accession of 18 Rabbit begins four decades of Copán's regional military dominance
738 Quiriguá defeats Copán
899 Tikal abandoned
900 Classic period of Mayan history ends
900–1500 Maya civilization in decline, many cities abandoned
984 Copán abandoned
1517 Spanish arrive in Yucatán peninsula, Mexico, and begin conquest of Maya
1517–1625 Diseases introduced from Europe cause death of majority of Maya
1523–1527 Spanish conqueror Pedro de Alvarado subjugates most Mayan communities in the Guatemalan highlands
1695 Tikal ruins rediscovered by Spanish
1724 Spanish abolish *encomienda* system of forced Mayan labor
1834 Copán ruins rediscovered
1841 Quiriguá ruins rediscovered
1881 Early archaeological work begins at Tikal, by Alfred Maudslay
1927–1929 Aviator Charles Lindbergh's flights instrumental in mapping El Petén and pinpointing location of ruins
1956 William Coe and others begin excavations at Tikal
1960–1996 Guatemala's 36-year civil war causes massive displacement of Mayan communities in the highlands and Verapaces
1980s War's "scorched earth" campaign targets certain Mayan communities for destruction
1989 Rediscovery of Copán's Rosalila Temple
1992 Rigoberta Menchú, a Maya woman, wins Nobel Peace Prize
1996 Signing of peace accords ends war, eliminates army's role in domestic security, and gives co-official status to 21 Mayan languages
2006 Mel Gibson's *Apocalypto,* set in a crumbling Mayan civilization, and with actors speaking Yucatec Maya, was filmed in Veracruz
2012 The end of the world, 13.0.0.0.0 in the Long Count calendar

HISTORY IN BRIEF

Theories abound about the origin of the name *Guatemala*, but the prevailing consensus is that the word means "land of the trees" in one of the original Proto-Mayan languages. The name is apt. Guatemala's forested lowlands provided a fertile home for the region's Maya for centuries. On the topic of names, the original names of most of Guatemala's Mayan sites have been lost to history. Archaeologists in the 19th and 20th centuries routinely gave their rediscoveries new monikers. Uaxactún in El Petén is perhaps the most extreme case: its pronunciation (*wah-shak-TOON*) is thought to be a play on the name of Washington, D.C., the home of the Carnegie Institution, which funded the original expedition there. Call it inertia, but the new names have stuck.

Anthropologists believe that humans from Asia crossed a land bridge, in what is now the Bering Strait in Alaska, into North America more than 25,000 years ago. Gradually these Paleoindians, or "Old Indians," whose ancestors probably were Mongoloid peoples, made their way down the continent, establishing Native American or First Nation settlements in what is now the United States and Canada. Groups of them are thought to have reached Mesoamerica, which includes much of central Mexico, Guatemala, Belize, Honduras, and El Salvador, around 20,000 to 22,000 years ago.

These early peoples were hunter-gatherers. The Olmec civilization, considered the mother culture of later Mesoamerican civilizations including that of the Maya, arose in central and southern Mexico 3,000 to 4,000 years ago. The Olmecs developed the first writing system in the New World, dating from at least 900 BC. They also had sophisticated mathematics and created complex calendars. The Olmecs built irrigation systems to water their crops.

As long ago as around 3000 BC—the exact date is in question and has changed as archaeologists have made new discoveries—the Maya began to settle in small villages in the region. They developed an agriculture based on the cultivation of maize (corn), squash, and other fruits and vegetables. What would become the great city-states of the region, including Tikal in El Petén, were first settled around 900 to 700 BC.

Two or three centuries before the time of Christ, several Mayan villages grew into sizeable cities. The Maya began to construct large-scale stone buildings at Tikal and elsewhere. Eventually, Tikal, Copán, in Honduras, and other urban centers each would have thousands of structures—palaces, temples, residences, monuments, ball courts, even prisons. Although the Maya never had the wheel, and thus no carts or wagons, they built paved streets and causeways, and they developed crop-irrigation systems.

At its height, in what is known as the Classic period (250 BC to AD 900), the Mayan civilization consisted of about 50 cities, much like ancient Greek city-states. Each had a population of 5,000 to 100,000 or more. Tikal, the premier city in the region, may have had 200,000 residents in and around the city during its heyday. The peak population of the Mayan civilization possibly reached 2 million or more.

Mayan culture put a heavy emphasis on religion, which was based on a pantheon of nature gods, including those of the sun, moon, and rain. The Mayan view of life was cyclical, and Mayan religion strove to accommodate human life to the cycles of the universe.

Contrary to what scholars long believed, however, Mayan society had many aspects beyond religion. Politics, the arts, business, and trade were all important and dynamic aspects of Mayan life. Dynastic leaders waged brutal wars on rival city-states. Under its ruler Lord Smoke Ahau, Caracol, the largest city-state in Belize, conquered Tikal in AD 562, and less than a hundred years later, conquered another large city, Naranjo (also in El Petén).

The Maya developed sophisticated mathematics. They understood the concept of zero and used a base-20-numbering system. Astronomy was the basis of a complex Mayan calendar system involving an accurately determined solar year (18 months of 20 days, plus a 5-day period), a sacred year of 260 days (13 cycles of 20 days), and a variety of longer cycles culminating in the Long Count, based on a zero date in 3114 BC, or 0.0.0.0.0—the date that the Maya believed was the beginning of the current cycle of the world.

The Mayan writing system is considered the most advanced of any developed in Mesoamerica. The Maya used more than 800 "glyphs," small pictures or signs, paired in columns that read from left to right and top to bottom. The glyphs represent syllables and, in some cases, entire words, that can be combined to form any word or concept. There is no Mayan alphabet. Mayan glyphs can represent either sounds or ideas, or both, making them difficult to accurately interpret. The unit of the writing system is the cartouche, a series of 3 to 50 glyphs, the equivalent of a word or sentence in a modern language.

As in most societies, it's likely that the large majority of the Maya spent much of their time simply trying to eke out a living. In each urban area the common people lived in simple thatch dwellings, similar to those seen in the region today. They practiced a slash-and-burn agriculture. Farmers cleared their small plots by burning the bush, then planting maize, squash, sunflowers, and other crops in the rich ash. After two or three years, when the soil was depleted, the plot was left fallow for several years before it could be planted again.

Beginning around AD 800, parts of the Mayan civilization began to decline. In most areas the decline didn't happen suddenly, but over decades and even centuries, and it took place at different times. For example, the cities in the northern lowlands of Mexico's Yucatán, such as Chichén Itzá, flourished for several more centuries after Tikal and Copán were abandoned.

Scholars still debate the reasons for the decline. Climatic change, lengthy droughts, overpopulation, depletion of arable land, social revolutions by the common people against the elites, epidemics, and the impact of extended periods of warfare all have been put forth as reasons. It may well have been a combination of factors, or there may have been different causes in different regions.

Whatever the reasons, the Mayan civilization never regained its Classic-period glory. By the time the Spanish arrived in the early 1500s, only a few of the Mayan cities, mainly in the highlands of Guatemala, were still thriving. Most of the great cities and trading centers, including Tikal and Copán, had long been abandoned.

Seeking gold and other plunder, the Spanish began their conquest of the Maya in the 1520s. Some Mayan states offered fierce resistance, and the last Mayan kingdom, in Mexico, was not vanquished until almost 1700. There was one enemy against which the Maya were defenseless: European disease. Smallpox, chicken pox, measles, flu, and other infectious diseases swept through the Mayan settlements. Scientists believe that within a century, nearly 90% of the Maya had been wiped out by "imported" diseases. Mayan resistance to European control continued from time to time. In 1847 indigenous Maya in the Yucatán rose up against Europeans in the bloody Caste Wars, which lasted until 1904.

Much of the Mayan civilization was buried under the tropical jungles for centuries, and Westerners knew little about it. In the process of trying to convert the Maya to Christianity in the 16th century, the Spanish burned most of the codices, Mayan "books" made of deer hide or bleached fig-tree paper. Only in the last few decades have scholars made progress in deciphering Mayan glyphic writing.

In 1839 two British adventurers, John Lloyd Stephens and Frederick Catherwood, visited Central America and explored a number of the Mayan sites. Their books, especially *Incidents of Travel in Central America, Chiapas, and Yucatán,* with text by Stephens and illustrations by Catherwood, brought the attention of the world to the Mayan past.

In the late 1800s the first systematic archaeological excavations of Tikal were begun. Alfred Maudslay, an Englishman, conducted excavations at Tikal in 1881–82, and Harvard's Peabody Museum did fieldwork there between 1895 and 1904. Sylvanus Morley, a well-known Mayan expert, conducted work at Tikal at times between 1914 and 1928. In 1956 the University of Pennsylvania began the first large-scale excavation project at Tikal. Since then, many university and museum teams have conducted extensive fieldwork. The 1989 excavation of Copán's previously unknown and well-preserved Rosalila Temple stunned the archaeological world and offered new insights into Mayan architecture and decor.

Guatemala's 1960–96 civil war, the longest in Latin American history, caught Maya descendents in the crossfire between government and insurgents. The war reached its most brutal phase during the 1982–83 military dictatorship of General Efraín Ríos Montt, whose forces targeted several Mayan communities for extinction. By war's end, more than 200,000 people had died. To its great credit, Guatemala has made tremendous strides toward reconciliation in the 1½ decades since a peace treaty was signed, yet suspicions linger among indigenous generations who remember the worst of the war.

The end of the world, or at least its current cycle, will take place on December 21, 2012, according to the Long Count calendar of the ancient Maya.

DOS AND DON'TS FOR VISITING RUINS

Don't ever take any artifact from a Mayan site, not even a tiny pottery shard. The theft of Mayan antiquities is a serious crime. Luggage is often searched at the international airport, and if any Mayan artifacts are found you could be in hot water.

Do climb the temples and enjoy the views from the top. At most sites you're free to climb the ruins. The views from El Castillo at Xunantunich, from structures at Cerros of Chetumal Bay, and from Lubaantun to the sea, are among the most memorable. Be warned, though: most of the steps are very steep.

Do descend into Xilbalba. The Maya called the underworld Xilbalba. You can experience it by visiting one of the caves once used by the Maya. Though not Mayan ruins, per se, the elaborate system of caverns around Cobán, under Alta Verapaz, was thought by many to be the entrance to Xilbalba, and you can still stumble upon ceremonial rituals taking place in the caves of Lanquín.

Do look for wildlife at the ruins and en route. Guatemala preserves many of its Mayan ruins in national parks, which are home to many birds and wild creatures. On the drive through Tikal National Park, for example, you'll pass through broadleaf jungle, and you may see brocket deer, howler monkeys, oscellated turkey, and coatimundi.

ARCHITECTURE

One look at the monumental architecture of the Maya, and you might feel transported to another world. The breathtaking structures are even more impressive when you consider that they were built 1,000 to 2,000 years ago or more, without iron tools, wheels, or pulleys. The following is a brief explanation of the architecture you see at a Mayan ruin.

INFLUENCES

Mayan architecture, even the great temples, may echo the design of the typical thatch hut ordinary Maya used for thousands of years. The rectangular huts had short walls made of a limestone mud and were topped by a steeply tilted two-sided thatch roof. Caves—ever-important Mayan ceremonial sites—were also influential. Many aboveground Mayan temples and other monumental structures have cave-like chambers, and the layout of Mayan cities probably reflected the Mayan cosmology, in which caves played a critical role.

BUILDING MATERIALS

With few exceptions, the large buildings in Mayan cities were constructed mostly from limestone, which was widely available in this region. Quarries were often established close to a building site so that workers didn't have to haul stone long distances. The Maya used limestone for mortar, stucco, and plaster. Limestone was crushed and burned in wood-fired kilns to make lime. A cement-like mortar was made by combining one part lime with one part of a white soil called *sahcab,* and then adding water.

The Maya also used wood, which was plentiful in Mesoamerica. In fact, some of the early temples were probably constructed of wood poles and thatch, much like the small houses of the Maya; unfortunately, these buildings are now lost.

TOOLS

The Maya were behind the curve with their tool technology. They didn't have iron tools, pulleys to move heavy weights, or wheels to build carts. They didn't have horses or other large animals to help them move materials. Instead, they used large numbers of laborers to tote and haul stones, mortar, and other building materials.

Obsidian, jade, flint, and other hard rocks were used to make axes, knives, and saws. The Maya had masons' kits to cut and finish limestone, and they had the equivalent of a plumb bob and other tools to align and level stones. The Maya were skilled stoneworkers, although the degree of finish varied from city to city.

CITY LAYOUT

In most Mayan cities large plazas were surrounded by temples and large pyramids, probably used for religious ceremonies and other important public events. Paved causeways connected the plazas. Away from the city center were sprawls of "suburbs"—smaller stone buildings and traditional thatch huts. Most cities had ball courts, and although the exact rules are unclear, players used a ball of natural rubber (rubber was discovered by the Olmecs) and scored points by getting the ball through a hoop or goalpost. "Sudden death" had a special meaning—the leader of the losing team was sometimes killed by decapitation.

Adventure and Learning Vacations

WORD OF MOUTH

"We have always enjoyed school and home visits. Even when we couldn't communicate with our hosts very much, we've always felt that this was a worthwhile experience. The people have always been friendly and we enjoyed seeing their homes and spending time with them. Many people feel that this is one of the highlights of the trip."

—PIPERPAT

"Travel agencies all over Antigua sell trips ($6–$8) to Pacaya Volcano that leave at about 6 AM and return around 1 PM. The 1 hour and 15 minute drive could be in a van, a minibus, or a schoolbus. Buy the walking stick for Q5—it's the best 75 cents you'll ever spend."

—Happy LC

Updated by Jeffrey Van Fleet

Tour operators, both in Guatemala and outside the country, can help you arrange an adventure or learning vacation. You can experience Mayan culture in the jungle-covered ruins at Tikal or at Copán, just across the border in Honduras. Antigua and Quetzaltenango are known for language study and for getting you started on volunteer-vacation opportunities, but Spanish courses are yours for the having at many locales around Guatemala. There are also volcanoes to explore, adventure sports to try, and wildlife to view. Many companies organize trips that will take you to neighboring countries, too.

PLANNING YOUR ADVENTURE

CHOOSING A TRIP

With dozens of choices for special-interest trips to Guatemala, there are a number of factors to keep in mind when deciding which company and package will be right for you.

How strenuous do you want your trip to be? Adventure vacations are commonly split into "soft" and "hard" adventures. Hard adventures, such as strenuous treks (often at high altitudes) or Class IV or V rafting, generally require excellent physical conditioning and previous experience. Most hiking, biking, canoeing/kayaking, and similar soft adventures can be enjoyed by persons of all ages who are in good health and accustomed to a reasonable amount of exercise. A little honesty goes a long way—recognize your own level of physical fitness and discuss it with the tour operator before signing on. Once you start out, there's no turning back.

How far off the beaten path do you want to go? Depending on your tour operator and itinerary, you'll often have a choice between relatively easy travel and comfortable accommodations or more strenuous daily activities accompanied by overnights spent in basic lodgings or at campsites. Ask yourself if it's the *reality* or the *image* of roughing it that appeals to you. Be honest, and go with a company that can provide what you're looking for.

Is sensitivity to the environment important to you? If so, determine whether it is equally important to your operator. Does the company protect the fragile environments you'll be visiting? Are some of the company's profits designated for conservation efforts or put back into the communities visited? Does it encourage indigenous people to dress up (or dress down) so that your group can get great photos, or does it respect their cultures as they are? Many of the companies included in this chapter are actively involved in environmental conservation and projects with indigenous communities. Their business's future depends on keeping this fragile ecological and cultural mix alive.

What sort of group is best for you? At its best, group travel offers curious, like-minded people companions with which to share the day's experiences. Do you enjoy mixing with people from other backgrounds, or would you prefer to travel with people from one similar to your own? Inquire about group size; many companies have a maximum of 10 to 16 members, but 30 or more is not unknown. The larger the group, the more time spent (or wasted) at rest stops, meals, and hotel arrivals and departures.

If groups aren't your thing, most companies will customize a trip for you. In fact, this has become a major part of many tour operators' business. Your itinerary can be as flexible or as rigid as you choose. Such travel offers all the conveniences of a package tour, but the "group" is composed of only you and your travel companions. Responding to a renewed interest in multigenerational travel, many tour operators also offer family trips, with itineraries carefully crafted to appeal both to children and adults.

How much extra pre-trip help do you want? Gorgeous photos and well-written tour descriptions go a long way toward selling a company's trips. Once you've chosen your trip, though, there's a lot of room for your operator to help you out, or leave you out in the cold. For example, does the operator provide useful information about health (suggested or required inoculations, tips for dealing with high altitudes)? A list of frequently asked questions and their answers? Recommended readings? Equipment needed for sports trips? Visa requirements? A list of client referrals? All of these things can make or break a trip, and you should know before you choose an operator whether or not you want their help getting answers to all these questions.

Are there hidden costs? Make sure you know what is and is not included in basic trip costs when comparing companies. International airfare is usually extra. Sometimes domestic flights are, too. Is trip insurance required, and if so, is it included? Are airport transfers included? Visa fees? Departure taxes? Gratuities? (Rarely, to those last three.) Although some travelers prefer the option of an excursion or free time, many, especially those visiting a destination for the first time, want to see as much as possible. Paying extra for a number of excursions can significantly increase the total cost of the trip. Many factors affect the price, and the trip that looks cheapest in the brochure could well turn out to be the most expensive. Don't assume that roughing it will save you money, as prices rise when limited access and a lack of essential supplies on-site require costly special arrangements.

MONEY MATTERS

Tours in Guatemala can be found at all price points, but local operators are usually the best deal. Excursions that use as many local people and resources as possible are generally cheaper, and also give the greatest monetary benefit to the local economy. These types of tours are not always listed in guidebooks or on the Internet, so often they have to be found in person when you're on the ground or by word of mouth. Safety and date specificity can fluctuate. Guides don't always speak English, and are not always certified. Amenities such as lodging and transportation may be very basic in this category. Some agencies pay attention to the environment; others do not. You really have to do your research on every operator, no matter the cost, to be sure you get what you need. When you find the right match, the payoff in terms of price and quality of experience will be worth the pre-trip research time you invested.

On the other end of the spectrum, the large (often international) tour agencies are generally the most expensive; however, they provide the greatest range of itinerary choices and highest quality of services. They use the best transportation, like private planes, buses, and boats, which rarely break down. First-rate equipment and safe, reliable guides are the norm. Dates and times are set in stone, so you can plan your trip down to the time you step in and out of the airport. Guides are usually English-speaking, certified, and well paid. When food and lodging are provided they are generally of high quality. If you are a traveler who likes to have every creature comfort provided for, look for tour operators more toward this end of the spectrum.

WHAT TYPE OF TRIP?

Adventure Tours. Adrenaline-pumping sports thrills for the active traveler.

Beaches and Relaxation. Find a place to hang your hammock after a volcanic-mud bath.

Ecotourism. Spot a resplendent quetzal while staying at a thatched jungle lodge in pristine cloud forests.

Cultural Tourism. Living and learning the local culture.

Language Schools. Learn Spanish while staying with a local family.

Mayan Ruins. Trek to pyramids hidden by lush jungle and surrounded by the roar of howler monkeys.

Volunteer Vacations. Get your hands dirty saving the rain forest, protecting sea turtle breeding grounds, or helping those less fortunate.

LODGING

Overnight stays can cost as much or as little as you want them to. To its great credit, Guatemala offers ample accommodation in every price range—no one has been priced out of the market here—and even the high end of the spectrum isn't too outrageously priced. Independent travelers tend to favor budget hotels and hostels costing little more than a few dollars a night, whereas luxurious five-star hotels geared to package tourists are becoming common. Your preference will help determine what type of tour operator is best for you.

Most multiday tours include lodging, often at a discounted rate, and they generally have options that accommodate most budgets through a number of hotels. On the other hand, many hotels have their own tour agency or will sell tours at a discounted rate to particular agencies. You can book through either one—it just depends on the specific tours and hotels that interest you. In many instances you don't have to book accommodation through your tour agency; however, you will often save money if you are combining services such as transportation, food, tours, and guides. If you are interested in specific hotels, such as beach resorts or ecolodges, in many cases your best tour options will be directly through these establishments. Considering the small size of Guatemala, many of its sights can be seen on a one-day tour, which allows you to leave your luggage at the hotel for less hassle.

EQUIPMENT

Good gear is essential. Sturdy shoes, a small flashlight or headlamp, rain gear, mosquito protection, and medicine are all things you should bring with you no matter what kind of tour you're taking. For more technical sports, your choice of tour operator will determine whether you bring your own gear, buy new gear, or rent what they already have. The decision will probably be yours in most cases. Tour operators can generally provide equipment, but the quality of this equipment varies a great deal. If you're going to use equipment that will be provided, ask your operator for a written statement of the gear to be used.

When you arrive, check that your expectations have been met, and complain if they haven't. Many companies do use top-of-the-line equipment; however, the occasional company will cut corners. Prices on equipment purchased in Guatemala tend to be significantly higher (roughly 20% to 40%) than in North America or Europe. If you prefer or require a specific brand of equipment, bringing your own is a good idea. Airlines accommodate most types of equipment and will likely have packing suggestions if you call ahead. For instance, most bicycle shops can take apart and box up your bike for plane transport. Airlines charge additional fees for surpassing size and weight limits. Shipping equipment to Guatemala tends to be expensive, and if you're not using an agency such as FedEx or DHL (actually, even if you are!), expect the unexpected.

ADVENTURE AND LEARNING VACATIONS

ADVENTURE TOURS

If you're looking for a heart-thumping adrenaline rush, Guatemala has a lot to offer. From hiking active volcanoes to rafting raging Class IV rapids, the country has an abundance of adventure tours. Wherever you go, you're not very far from a zip line through the cloud forest or sportfishing for a 900-pound black marlin.

Season: Year-round
Locations: Antigua, Lake Atitlán, Río Dulce, Livingston
Cost: From $395 for four days from Guatemala City
Tour Operators: Guatemala Ventures, Old Town Outfitters

If lava is what you seek, Old Town Outfitters will take you climbing to the best of Guatemala's 33 volcanoes on their seven-day tour. The highly active Pacaya and the dormant Agua volcanoes near Antigua are the first ascents, and the multiple-night climbs of Acatenango

CLOSE UP

Tour Operators

Abercrombie & Kent (☎ *630/725-3400 or 800/554-7016* 🌐 *www.abercrombiekent.com.*)

Adventure Life (☎ *800/344-6118* 🌐 *www.adventure-life.com.*)

AdventureSmith Explorations (☎ *800/728—2875 or 530/583-1775* 🌐 *www.adventuresmithexplorations.com.*)

Elderhostel (☎ *800/454-5768* 🌐 *www.elderhostel.org.*)

G.A.P. Adventures (☎ *416/260-0999 or 800/465-5600* 🌐 *www.gapadventures.com.*)

Garifuna Tours (☎ *504/448-1069* 🌐 *www.garifunatours.com.*)

GATE Travel (☎ 608/791-5283 🌐 *www.gate-travel.com.*)

Geographic Expeditions (☎ *415/922-0448 or 800/777-8183* 🌐 *www.geoex.com.*)

Global Crossroad (☎ *972/252-4191* 🌐 *www.globalcrossroad.com.*)

Grayline Tours (☎ *303/394-6920* 🌐 *www.grayline.com.*)

Guatemala Ventures (☎ *7832-3383* 🌐 *www.guatemalaventures.com.*)

Journey Latin America (☎ *020/8747-8315* 🌐 *www.journeylatinamerica.co.uk.*)

Maya Tour (☎ *954/889-6292* 🌐 *www.mayatour.com.*)

Old Town Outfitters (☎ *502/5399-0440* 🌐 *www.adventureguatemala.com.*)

Overseas Adventure Travel (☎ *800/221-0814* 🌐 *www.oattravel.com.*)

Pop-Wuj (☎ *7761-8286* 🌐 *www.pop-wuj.org.*)

Tucan Travel (☎ *020/8896-1600* 🌐 *www.tucantravel.com.*)

Wildland Adventures (☎ *800/345-4453 or 206/365-0686* 🌐 *www.wildland.com.*)

and Fuego volcanoes make up the latter part of the trip. The climb to the top of Central America's highest peak, Tajamulco Volcano (4218 meters/13,840 feet), is an optional three-day addition. For something a bit cooler, try their four-day kayak trip down the Río Dulce, which ends on the Caribbean, at Guatemala's preeminent Garífuna village. If you're interested in high-adrenaline sports, try Guatemala Ventures' Pacific coast to Atlantic coast tour, which combines hiking, biking, and rafting on an eight-day journey across Guatemala's most stunning landscapes. Exact destinations are tailored to meet your skill level.

ECOTOURISM

Ecotourism, a style of touring natural habitats to see flora and fauna while minimizing one's ecological impact, really began in the jungles of Costa Rica. It quickly spread across Central America and around the world. Guatemala offers plenty of nature- and wildlife-related activities.

Season: Year-round

Locations: Flores, Petexbatún Lake, Aguateca, Yaxhá, Tikal, Ixpanpajul Natural Park
Cost: From $1,280 for eight days from Guatemala City
Tour Operators: Adventure Life, Guatemala Ventures, Old Town Outfitters

The volcanic slopes, cloud forests, and lowland jungle regions of Guatemala are home to many rare bird species such as quetzals, the mountain trogon, blue-throated green motmot, hairy woodpecker, hummingbirds, toucans, and macaws. Nineteen ecosystems in total can be found here, and they are home to not just birds, but more than 250 species of mammals and 200 species of reptiles and amphibians. Many are found only in isolated pockets around the country. Adventure Life explores the Petén jungle region heavily, via trekking and kayaking excursions, bringing you to Flores, Petexbatún Lake, the Aguateca, Yaxhá, and Tikal ruins, as well as Ixpanpajul Natural Park. Guatemala Ventures has one-day tours to many of the parks and other locations throughout the country. Old Town Outfitters offers hiking, biking, and kayaking trips to a number of these regions.

CULTURAL TOURISM

From ancient civilizations and indigenous groups to small pueblos rebounding from decades of civil war, there's no shortage of interest in Guatemala's diverse people. Here are some of the many tour companies that can take you to encounter groups that rarely meet the outside world and have remained unchanged for centuries. Always do your research before taking tours like this—it's important that your operator conduct business with the local people in an ethical, respectful way.

Season: March, April, and July
Locations: Guatemala City, Quiché, San Lucas Tolimán, Lake Atitlán, Antigua
Cost: From $1,175 for 10 days from Guatemala City
Tour Operators: GATE Travel

The Maya are the living soul of Guatemala, but many difficulties surround their adaptation to the modern world. GATE's program helps you understand Mayan roots and spirituality, as well as the history and politics of Guatemala. Human-rights issues, poverty, community leadership, and migration are touched upon. GATE can also tailor programs for U.S.-based educational and religious groups.

LANGUAGE SCHOOLS

You can study a day of Spanish with room and board in Guatemala for about the same price as a martini in a London club, which is why the activity has caught on. Prices are much lower than in universities, and many of the courses are accredited. We list a selection of programs in each chapter.

Season: Year-round
Locations: Antigua, Quetzaltenango
Cost: From $595 for one week from Guatemala City
Tour Operators: G.A.P. Adventures, Pop-Wuj, Tucan Travel

Guatemala is one of Latin America's language hot spots, where thousands of foreigners of all ages can be found practicing Spanish in the country at any given time. G.A.P.'s 14-day Guatemala Spanish Adventure teaches you Spanish as you visit locations such as Antigua, Lake Atitlán, Tikal, and Poptún, using hands-on learning as you bargain at the Chichicastenango market or chat up locals at a Salsa bar. Tucan Travel's eight-day Spanish program is more typical of Guatemalan schools. Like many others, it's based in Antigua, where you will have 20 hours of classes per week, area tours, and local homestays. Volunteer community work projects are a must for all Pop-Wuj Spanish studies in Quetzaltenango. The projects are divided between community/social and medical/health care and will differ based on the type of language skills you want to acquire.

MAYAN RUINS

Centered in northeastern Guatemala, the Mayan civilization once stretched from Mexico to as far south as Costa Rica. Ruins of their magnificent stelae, temples, and ball courts are scattered throughout the region, Tikal and Copán, just across the border in Honduras, being the most prominent; but many other smaller complexes leave visitors just as breathless.

GUATEMALA

Season: Year-round

Locations: Flores, Tikal, Río Dulce, Antigua, Panajachel, Lake Atitlán, Chichicastenango, Totonicapán

Cost: From $1,895 for 14 days from Guatemala City

Tour Operators: Abercrombie & Kent, Adventure Life, AdventureSmith Explorations, Elderhostel, G.A.P. Adventures, Geographic Expeditions, Journey Latin America, Maya Tour, Overseas Adventure Travel, Tucan Travel, Wildland Adventures

A wide range of tour companies operate in the region, and infinite combinations of ruins and other sightseeing tours are possible. Abercrombie & Kent offers a five-day Guatemala Extension as an add-on to tours of other countries in the region, focusing on Tikal, Antigua, and Lake Atitlán. Elderhostel's two-week The Maya and More tour takes in Tikal and Copán, as well as similar sites in neighboring Belize. G.A.P. Adventures' Mayan Explorer program, among many others, gives you 14 days visiting the Mayan ruins on Mexico's Yucatán peninsula, such as Chichén Itzá and Palenque, moving all the way south to Guatemala and Tikal. Journeys Latin America's Hidden Maya brings you to the best ruins and sites in northeast Guatemala, plus Copán in Honduras, with a few days exploring the reef at Caye Caulker in Belize. AdventureSmith Explorations offers a five-day excursion between Tikal and Palenque stopping at lesser known ruins such as Yaxchilan and Bonampak along the way. Wildland Adventures extends the previous trip seven more days to add travels to Lake Atitlán and Copán, Honduras.

With Adventure Life's Mundo Maya you visit Tikal and Lake Atitlán like many other trips, but also the isolated and off-the-beaten-track highland town of Totonicapán. While there, you'll visit local artisans'

CLOSE UP

Getting the Most from Your Spanish Study

Some 100 language schools in Quetzaltenango, another 80 in Antigua, and many more scattered around the country make Guatemala one of the world's premier destinations for learning Spanish. With so many options to choose from, how do you select a program? We've culled suggestions from students and instructors, both inside and outside Guatemala:

1. Use the Internet, but recognize its limitations. These institutions are businesses, and put their best feet forward in their promotional materials. Don't decide based solely on a flashy Web site.

2. Check online evaluations of programs. We like the Web site *www.123teachme.com* for student evaluations of about 80 Guatemala Spanish schools.

3. Choose location carefully. Guatemala offers you Spanish study in big city or small town. If you want to be where the action is, then Antigua or Quetzaltenango are for you, but their huge student population is precisely what turns some off. You'll be more isolated in another locale, but survival may be precisely the motivation you need to get out there and learn the language.

4. Don't ignore schools' other offerings. Some schools can teach you to cook, dance, or even basics in a Mayan language. Many organize travel outings with other students. Some are affiliated with volunteer programs.

5. Arrive in Guatemala in advance. If your schedule permits, arrive at your desired destination a couple of days early and visit a few schools. We understand the reassurance of arranging everything in advance, but courses normally start each week, giving you flexibility to make last-minute decisions.

6. Verify what is and is not included in the price. The quoted fee may be for tuition only, or may include books and course materials or room and board with a local family. Some schools also levy an inscription fee to cover costs of processing your registration.

7. Be wary of long-term discounts. Most schools discount tuition if you sign up for a month or two at a time, but if you discover early on that the program isn't for you, refunds are difficult to impossible to obtain. Don't lock yourself into anything long-term unless you are certain you'll stick with it.

8. Consider a homestay. Living with a host family increases your out-of-class practice with the language, and most schools can set you up with one. Ask to meet two or three families to find the right fit.

9. Practicar. Hablar. You study Spanish in Guatemala to immerse yourself in the language. If you spend all your time outside of class at Reilly's bar in Antigua—we like Reilly's, honest, but it's expat central—your progress will be minimal. Get out there and talk to Guatemalans.

10. Be realistic in your expectations. You won't come away from a typical two-week beginner's course reading the original text of *Don Quixote*. It will be survival Spanish on which you can build.

workshops and indigenous markets. Geographic Expeditions combines Tikal, Antigua, Lake Atitlán, and Copán with luxury resorts, including film director Francis Ford Coppola's La Lancha lodge. Maya Tour's excursions of varying lengths take you on the standard Tikal–Quiriguá–Copán route, and combine these sites with Mayan complexes in neighboring countries. Overseas Adventure Travel combines visits to Guatemala's and Honduras's Mayan ruins with sights in neighboring Central American countries. Tucan Travel offers a variety of mix-and-match excursions taking in Mayan ruins in Guatemala and neighboring countries.

HONDURAS

Season: Year-round
Locations: Copán
Cost: From $455 for three days from Guatemala City
Tour Operators: Garifuna Tours, Grayline Tours, Journey Latin America

Only one ruin complex in Honduras approaches the scale of Guatemalan sites: Copán. Discovered in 1839 and still hidden by dense vegetation, the site is still being researched. Journey Latin America can combine almost any of their tours with a three-day, standard trip to Copán from Guatemala City, which gives you approximately two full days at the ruins. (Many Guatemalan tour operators do a rushed one-day trip to Copán from Antigua or the capital. You'll spend most of your time traveling to and from.) Grayline Tours has an eight-day guided excursion with several days exploring the ruins at Copán followed by Roatán, the largest of Honduras's Bay Islands, for the remainder of your trip. Garífuna Tours includes Copán on their 11-day trip that also covers bird-watching in two Honduran national parks and relaxation at Roatán.

VOLUNTEER VACATIONS

Whether you help protect endangered sea turtles or help a struggling community build houses and schools, volunteering can be one of the most rewarding travel experiences you could ever have—plus there are plenty of opportunities to practice your Spanish and see some sights along the way.

Season: Year-round
Locations: Antigua, Lake Atitilán, Tikal, Flores
Cost: From $1,450 for four weeks from Guatemala City
Tour Operators: Global Crossroad

Global Crossroad's various volunteer programs deal with women's empowerment, children's daycare, and English instruction. The programs start at one month in length, and the initial weeks include Spanish-language study.

UNDERSTANDING GUATEMALA

VOCABULARY

	ENGLISH	SPANISH	PRONUNCIATION
BASICS			
	Yes/no	Sí/no	see/no
	OK	De acuerdo	de a-**kwer**-doe
	Please	Por favor	pore fah-**vore**
	May I?	¿Me permite?	may pair-**mee**-tay
	Thank you (very much)	(Muchas) gracias	(**moo**-chas)**grah**-see-as
	You're welcome	De nada	day **nah**-da
	Excuse me	Con permiso	con pair-**mee**-so
	Pardon me	¿Perdón?	pair-**dohn**
	Could you tell me?	¿Podría decirme?	po-dree-ah deh-**seer**-meh
	I'm sorry	Disculpe	Dee-**skool**-peh
	Good morning!	¡Buenos días!	**bway**-nohs **dee**-ahs
	Good afternoon!	¡Buenas tardes!	**bway**-nahs **tar**-dess
	Good evening!	¡Buenas noches!	**bway**-nahs **no**-chess
	Goodbye!	¡Adiós!/¡Hasta luego!	ah-dee-**ohss/ah**-stah-**lwe**-go
	Mr./Mrs.	Señor/Señora	sen-**yor**/sen-**yohr**-ah
	Miss	Señorita	sen-yo-**ree**-tah
	Pleased to meet you	Mucho gusto	**moo**-cho **goose**-toe
	How are you?	¿Cómo está usted?	**ko**-mo es-**tah** oo-sted
	Very well, thank you	Muy bien, gracias.	**moo**-ee bee-**en**, **grah**-see-as
	And you?	¿Y usted?	ee oos-**ted**
DAYS OF THE WEEK			
	Sunday	domingo	doe-**meen**-goh
	Monday	lunes	**loo**-ness
	Tuesday	martes	**mahr**-tess
	Wednesday	miércoles	me-**air**-koh-less
	Thursday	jueves	hoo-**ev**-ess
	Friday	viernes	vee-**air**-ness

ENGLISH	SPANISH	PRONUNCIATION
Saturday	sábado	**sah**-bah-doh

MONTHS

January	enero	eh-**neh**-roh
February	febrero	feh-**breh**-roh
March	marzo	**mahr**-soh
April	abril	ah-**breel**
May	mayo	**my**-oh
June	junio	**hoo**-nee-oh
July	julio	**hoo**-lee-yoh
August	agosto	ah-**ghost**-toh
September	septiembre	sep-tee-**em**-breh
October	octubre	oak-**too**-breh
November	noviembre	no-vee-**em**-breh
December	diciembre	dee-see-**em**-breh

USEFUL PHRASES

Do you speak English?	¿Habla usted inglés?	**ah**-blah oos-**ted** in-**glehs**
I don't speak Spanish	No hablo español	no **ah**-bloh es-pahn-**yol**
I don't understand (you)	No entiendo	no en-tee-**en**-doh
I understand (you)	Entiendo	en-tee-**en**-doh
I don't know	No sé	no seh
I am American	Soy americano	soy ah-meh-ree- **kah**-no
What's your name?	¿Cómo se llama usted?	**koh**-mo she **yah**-mah oos ted
My name is . . .	Me llamo . . .	may yah-moh
What time is it?	¿Qué hora es?	keh o-rah es
My name is . . .	Me llamo . . .	may **yah**-moh
What time is it?	¿Qué hora es?	keh **o**-rah es
It is one, two, three . . . o'clock.	Es la una. . . . Son las dos, tres	es la **oo**-nah/sohn lahs dohs, tress

ENGLISH	SPANISH	PRONUNCIATION
How?	¿Cómo?	**koh**-mo
When?	¿Cuándo?	**kwahn**-doh
This/Next week	Esta semana/ la semana que	**es**-teh seh-**mah**-nah/lah seh-**mah**-entra nah keh **en**-trah
This/Next month	Este mes/el próximo mes	**es**-teh mehs/el **proke**-see-mo mehs
This/Next year	Este año/el año que viene	**es**-teh **ahn**-yo/el **ahn**-yo keh vee-**yen**-ay
Yesterday/today/ tomorrow	Ayer/hoy/mañana	ah-**yehr**/oy/mahn-**yah**-nah
This morning/ afternoon	Esta mañana/tarde	**es**-tah mahn-**yah**- nah/ **tar**-deh
Tonight	Esta noche	**es**-tah **no**-cheh
What?	¿Qué?	keh
What is it?	¿Qué es esto?	keh es **es**-toh
Why?	¿Por qué?	pore **keh**
Who?	¿Quién?	kee-**yen**
Where is . . . ?	¿Dónde está . . . ?	**dohn**-deh es-**tah**
the bus stop?	la parada del autobus?	la pah-**rah**-dah del oh-toh-**boos**
the post office?	la oficina de correos?	la oh-fee-**see**- nah deh koh-**reh**-os
the museum?	el museo?	el moo-**seh**-oh
the hospital?	el hospital?	el ohss-pee-**tal**
the bathroom?	el baño?	el **bahn**-yoh
Here/there	Aquí/allá	ah-**key**/ah-**yah**
Open/closed	Abierto/cerrado	ah-bee-**er**-toh/ ser-ah-doh
Left/right	Izquierda/derecha	iss-key-**er**-dah/ dare-**eh**-chah
Straight ahead	Derecho	dare-**eh**-choh
Is it near/far?	¿Está cerca/lejos?	es-**tah** **sehr**-kah/
I'd like . . .	Quisiera . . .	kee-see-ehr-ah

ENGLISH	SPANISH	PRONUNCIATION
a room	un cuarto/una habitación	oon **kwahr**-toh/ leh-hoss **oo**-nah ah-bee-tah-see-**on**
the key	la llave	lah **yah**-veh
a newspaper	un periódico	oon pehr-ee-**oh**- dee-koh
a stamp	la estampilla	lah es-stahm- **pee**-yah
I'd like to buy . . .	Quisiera comprar . . .	kee-see-**ehr**-ah kohm-**prahr**
a dictionary	un diccionario	oon deek-see-oh- **nah**-ree-oh
soap	jabón	hah-**bohn**
suntan lotion	Loción bronceadora	loh-see-**ohn** brohn- seh-ah-**do**-rah
a map	un mapa	oon **mah**-pah
a magazine	una revista	**oon**-ah reh-**veess**-tah
a postcard	una tarjeta postal	**oon**-ah tar-**het**-ah post-**ahl**
How much is it?	¿Cuánto cuesta?	**kwahn**-toh **kwes**-tah
Telephone	Teléfono	tel-**ef**-oh-no
Help!	¡Auxilio! ¡Ayuda! ¡Socorro!	owk-**see**-lee-oh/ ah-**yoo**-dah/ soh-**kohr**-roh
Fire!	¡Incendio!	en-**sen**-dee-oo
Caution!/Look out!	¡Cuidado!	kwee-**dah**-doh

SALUD (HEALTH)

I am ill	Estoy enfermo(a)	es-**toy** en-**fehr**-
Please call a doctor	Por favor llame a un médico	pohr fah-**vor ya**-meh ah oon med-ee-koh
acetaminophen	acetaminofen	a-say-ta-**mee**-no-fen
ambulance	ambulancia	ahm-boo-**lahn**-see-a
antibiotic	antibiótico	ahn-tee-bee-**oh**-tee-co
aspirin	aspirina	ah-spi-**ree**-na
capsule	cápsula	**cahp**-soo-la
clinic	clínica	**clee**-nee-ca

ENGLISH	SPANISH	PRONUNCIATION
cold	resfriado	rays-free-**ah**-do
cough	tos	toess
diarrhea	diarrea	dee-ah-**ray**-a
fever	fiebre	fee-**ay**-bray
flu	Gripe	**gree**-pay
headache	dolor de cabeza	doh-**lor** day cah- **bay**-sa
hospital	hospital	oh-spee-**tahl**
medication	medicamento	meh-dee-cah-**men**-to
pain	dolor	doh-**lor**
pharmacy	farmacia	fahr-**mah**-see-a
physician	médico	**meh**-dee-co
prescription	receta	ray-**say**-ta
stomach ache	dolor de estómago	doh-**lor** day eh-**sto**-mah-go

MENU GUIDE

Rice, beans, and tortillas are the heart of Guatemala's comida típica (typical food). It's possible to order everything from sushi to crepes in Guatemala City and Antigua, but most Guatemalans have a simple diet built around rice, beans, and the myriad fruits and vegetables that flourish here. Guatemalan food isn't spicy, certainly not like that of neighboring Mexico, but the Highlands' ubiquitous pepián can pack a kick. But many dishes are seasoned with the same five ingredients—onion, salt, garlic, cilantro, and red bell pepper.

SPANISH	ENGLISH
GENERAL DINING	
Almuerzo	Lunch
Bocas	Appetizers or snacks (literally "mouthfuls") served with drinks in the tradition of Spanish tapas.
Cena	Dinner
Comedor	An inexpensive café; a plato de día is always found at a comedor
Desayuno	Breakfast
Plato del día	Heaping plate of rice, beans, fried plantains, cabbage salad, tomatoes, macarrones (noodles), and fish, chicken, or meat—or any variation thereof
ESPECIALIDADES (SPECIALTIES)	
Arroz con frijoles	Rice sautéed with black beans
Arroz con mariscos	Fried rice with fish, shrimp, octopus, and clams, or whatever's fresh that day
Arroz con pollo	Chicken with rice
Caldo de chunto	Turkey stew
Caldo de mariscos	Seafood stew
Camarones	Shrimp
Ceviche	Chilled, raw seafood marinated in lime juice, served with chopped onion and garlic
Chicharrones	Fried pork rinds
Chilaquiles	Meat-stuffed tortillas
Chile relleno	Stuffed bell pepper

SPANISH	ENGLISH
Chorreados	Corn pancakes, served with natilla (sour cream)
Corvina	Sea bass
Empanadas	Savory or sweet pastry turnover filled with fruit or meat and vegetables
Empanaditas	Small empanadas
Escabeche	Pickled relish, usually served with fish
Fiambre	Salad with cold cuts and vegetables, frequently served on All Saints' Day
Kaq'ik	Turkey stew, interchangeable with caldo de chunto
Langosta	Lobster
Langostino	Prawns
Palmitos	Hearts of palm, served in salads or as a side dish
Pepián	Chicken fricassee in pumpkin and sesame sauce
Pescado ahumado	Smoked marlin
Picadillo	Chayote squash, potatoes, carrots, or other vegetables chopped into small cubes and combined with onions, garlic, and ground beef
Pozol	Corn soup
Rice and beans	A Caribbean dish cooked in coconut milk, not to be confused with arroz con frijoles
Salsa caribeño	A combination of tomatoes, onions, and spices that accompanies most fish dishes on the Caribbean coast
Sere	Fish stew cooked in coconut milk

POSTRES (DESSERTS) & DULCES (SWEETS)

Cajeta de coco	Fudge made with coconut and orange peel
Cajeta	Molasses-flavored fudge

SPANISH	ENGLISH
Dulce de leche	Thick syrup of boiled milk and sugar
Flan	Caramel-topped egg custard
Mazamorra	Cornstarch pudding
Pan de maiz	Sweet corn bread
Torta chilena	Flaky, multilayered cake with dulce de leche filling
Tres leches cake	"Three milks" cake, made with condensed and evaporated milk and cream
Frutas (Fruits)	
Aguacate	Avocado
Anón	Sugar apple; sweet white flesh; resembles an artichoke with a thick rind
Banano	Banana
Bilimbi	Looks like a miniature cucumber crossed with a star fruit; ground into a savory relish
Carambola	Star fruit
Cas	A smaller guava
Coco	Coconut
Fresa	Strawberry
Granadilla	Passion fruit
Guanábana	Soursop; large, spiky yellow fruit with white flesh and a musky taste
Guayaba	Guava
Mango	Many varieties, from sour green to succulently sweet Oro (golden); March is the height of mango season
Manzana de agua	Water apple, shaped like a pear; juicy but not very sweet
Marañon	Cashew fruit; used in juices
Melocotón	Peach
Melón	Cantaloupe

SPANISH	ENGLISH
Mora	Raspberry
Naranja	Orange
Palmito	Heart of palm
Papaya	One of the most popular and ubiquitous fruits
Pera	Pear
Piña	Pineapple
Plátano	Plaintain
Sandía	Watermelon
Bebidas (Beverages)	
Agua pura	Purified water
Café con leche	Coffee with hot milk
Café negro	Black coffee
Cerveza	Beer
Fresco natural	Fresh-squeezed juice
Horchata	Cinnamon-flavored rice drink
Leche de coco	Coconut milk
Licuado	Fruit shake made with milk (con leche) or water (con agua)
Refrescos	Tropical fruit smoothie with ice and sugar
Ron	Rum

Travel Smart

WORD OF MOUTH

"There are basic guidelines that you need to follow, such as knowing where you are at all times, being very aware of your surroundings, keeping your belongings close to your body, taking cabs at night (even in the smaller towns), and having some knowledge of Spanish was really helpful as well. Guatemala is still very much a third world country. As long as you are aware of the risks associated with traveling to such an environment, and you keep your travel wits about you, you should be okay."

—carlyshells

www.fodors.com/community

GETTING HERE & AROUND

Roughly the same size as Tennessee, Guatemala occupies the full breadth of Central America and has both Pacific and Caribbean coastlines. The main bulk of the country is the mountainous southern half, which contains 21 of Guatemala's 22 departments. Guatemala City, the country's capital, is in the south. It's the biggest urban area in Central America, and opinions of both visitors and locals are divided on whether *la ciudad* (the city), as it's often called, is a chaotic nightmare or a taste of the real Guatemala. Although most international flights land here, many visitors go straight to nearby Antigua (only 45 km [28 mi] away) or Lake Atitlán (60 km away) rather than staying in the capital.

TRAVEL TIMES FROM GUATEMALA CITY

To	By Air	By Bus
Antigua	n/a	1 hour
Panajachel	n/a	3 hours
Quetzaltenango	n/a	3½ hours
Flores	1 hour	7 to 9 hours
Lago Izabal	n/a	4 hours
Puerto Barrios	n/a	6 hours
Monterrico	n/a	2½ hours
Cobán	n/a	4 hours

AIR TRAVEL

Guatemala City is the country's main hub: from Dallas or Houston the flying time is 2 hours; from Miami, 2½ hours; from Los Angeles, 7 hours; from New York, Chicago, or Toronto via Miami or Mexico City, about 7 hours.

Airlines and Airports Airline and Airport Links.com (🌐 *www.airlineandairportlinks.com*) has links to many of the world's airlines and airports.

Airline Security Issues Transportation Security Administration (🌐 *www.tsa.gov*) has answers for almost every question that might come up.

AIRPORTS

Nearly all international flights arrive at the gleaming Aeropuerto Internacional La Aurora (GUA) in Guatemala City, the country's main air hub. It sits inside the city proper, not far from the lodgings in the New City.

The arrivals hall has a temperamental ATM that is occasionally out of money or out of order. You can buy quetzals at an exchange office, open until about 9 PM, when the airport begins to shut down operations for the night, but passengers with a valid ticket can stay there overnight to wait for early flights.

The road between the airport and Guatemala City is sometimes targeted by thieves and carjackers, especially at night. Try to choose a flight that arrives in daylight hours. If you do travel into Guatemala City after dark, ask your hotel if they have a transfer service. Otherwise arrange a private shuttle or take a registered taxi or the shuttle bus, never the public bus.

⚠ **Rush-hour traffic on the road between Antigua and Guatemala City can double the time of the normal 1-hour trip. Always leave plenty of time to arrive.**

Tikal is served by the smaller Aeropuerto Internacional Mundo Maya (FRS), just outside Flores. More commonly known as Aeropuerto Santa Elena, it's mainly used for internal flights from Guatemala City, although it receives daily TACA flights from Cancún, Mexico, and some flights from Belize.

There are several other small airports in Guatemala—Puerto Barrios, for example—but these are usually served by private jets or charter aircraft, rather than scheduled flights.

In Guatemala there's a $30 departure tax on all international flights, but it's usually included in your ticket price. Check with your airline. All the same, you have to pay a so-called airport security fee of Q20 in cash at the airport. For local flights, departure tax is Q5.

Airport Information Aeropuerto Internacional La Aurora (✉ *Guatemala City* ☎ *2331-8192*). **Aeropuerto Internacional Mundo Maya** (✉ *Santa Elena* ☎ *7926-0113*).

GROUND TRANSPORTATION

La Aurora airport is about 6½ km (4 mi) from Guatemala City and 24 km (15 mi) from Antigua. The easiest and safest way to reach both cities from the airport is by registered taxi or private shuttle. Taxis to Guatemala City cost about $15 and take between 15 and 30 minutes; the trip to Antigua can take anything between 1 and 2 hours, depending on traffic, and costs about $25. Only take a numbered cab from the official booth, never one touting for service.

Shuttles are private minibus services. You can either book a shuttle in advance for yourself or you can share one with other passengers going in the same direction. Shuttles to Antigua leave regularly and cost $35 for a private service, or $12 to $15 per person on a shared service. STA is one of the best-known local shuttle services.

Public buses connect the airport to Guatemala City, but have a bad reputation for safety. Avoid them.

The 2-km (1-mi) taxi ride between Aeropuerto Mundo Maya and Flores costs around $3.

Contacts Servicios Turísticos Atitlán (☎ *7762-2246* 🌐 *www.visit-antigua.com/vans.htm*).

FLIGHTS

TO AND FROM GUATEMALA

All scheduled international flights into Guatemala land at Guatemala City, with the exception of flights to Flores from Belize City and Cancún.

WORD OF MOUTH

After your trip, be sure to rate the places you visited and share your experiences and travel tips with us and other Fodorites in "Member Reviews and Ratings" and "Travel Talk Forums" on www.fodors.com.

Central American airline TACA flies direct from Los Angeles and Miami, as well as from El Salvador, Honduras, Nicaragua, and Costa Rica. TACA flights are usually punctual and include a meal service, though missing luggage is a sometimes-reported problem. The airline codeshares with itineraries of United Airlines.

There are daily flights from Dallas and Miami on American and from Houston on Continental. Delta flies from Atlanta. Mexicana flies from Mexico City, and Iberia has flights from Madrid. Panamanian airline COPA links Guatemala with Panama City and U.S. connections.

Some of the best deals around are with Spirit Airlines, a low-cost airline that flies three times weekly from Fort Lauderdale to Guatemala. US Airways, which flies daily from Charlotte, North Carolina, also has good prices.

Belizean airline Tropic Air has two daily flights from Flores to Belize City. TACA flies from Cancún.

Airline Contacts AmericanAirlines (☎ *800/433-7300, 2422-0000 in Guatemala*). **Continental Airlines** (☎ *800/231-0856, 2385-9610 in Guatemala*). **COPA** (☎ *800/359-2672, 2361-1577 in Guatemala*). **Delta Airlines** (☎ *800/241-4141, 2263-0600 in Guatemala*). **Iberia** (☎ *800/772-4642, 2332-0911 in Guatemala*). **Mexicana** (☎ *800/531-7921, 2333-6001 in Guatemala*). **Spirit Airlines** (☎ *800/772-7117, 2385-8743 in Guatemala*). **TACA** (☎ *800/400-8222, 2470-8222 in Guatemala*). **Tropic Air** (☎ *800/422-3435, 7926-0348 in Guatemala*). **USAirways** (☎ *800/622-1015, 2470-0880 in Guatemala*).

WITHIN GUATEMALA

TACA has both morning and afternoon departures between Guatemala City and Flores. You can buy flights online before your trip, but booking through a Guatemalan travel agent can sometimes reduce the cost. Standard return fares usually cost around $200. TAG operates the same route once a day for a similar fare.

Airline Contacts TACA (☎ *800/400–8222 in U.S., 2470–8222 in Guatemala*). **TAG** (☎ *2360–3038*).

BOAT TRAVEL

There's a daily water-taxi service at 9 AM from Punta Gorda, Belize, to Puerto Barrios, Guatemala. The trip takes about 1½ hours and returns at 2 PM; tickets cost $18 each way. A similar service operates between Livingston and Punta Gorda on Tuesday and Friday; it's a 50-minute trip. Requena's Charter Service is a reputable Belize-based outfit. Other operators have booths on the waterfronts of all three towns: you turn up and buy a ticket on the spot.

Note that life jackets are typically not provided on boats and that the seas can be rough. Postpone your trip if the weather looks bad, and don't be shy about waiting for another boat if the one offered looks unseaworthy or overcrowded.

Contact Requena's Charter Service (☎ *501/722–2070 in Punta Gorda, Belize* 🌐 *www.belizenet.com/requena*).

BUS TRAVEL

ARRIVING AND DEPARTING

Many travelers arrive in and depart from Guatemala by bus. The services listed here are all so-called "first-class" buses, which means little more than that there is a toilet on-board and air-conditioning. Departures are usually punctual. Several second-class buses operate international routes, but have neither Web sites, reliable enquiry numbers nor, at this writing, fixed terminals, due to the Guatemala City transport authority's chaotic attempt at terminal reorganization.

Popular with budget travelers, Ticabus is an international bus company connecting all of Central America. It has direct daily services from Guatemala City to Tapachula in Mexico ($17; five hours) and El Salvador ($17; five hours). Connecting services go to Nicaragua, Honduras, Costa Rica, and Panama, but usually involve one or two overnight stops. Hedman Alas is a Honduran company that connects Guatemala City and Antigua with Copán Ruinas, San Pedro Sula, and Tegucigalpa in Honduras ($68). Línea Dorada runs services from Guatemala City to Tapachula, Mexico; and from Flores to Belize City and Chetumal, Mexico. It offers connecting services to other Mexican cities.

Contacts Hedman Alas (☎ *2362–5072* 🌐 *www.hedmanalas.com*). **Línea Dorada** (☎ *2232–5506* 🌐 *www.tikalmayanworld.com*). **Ticabus** (☎ *2459–2848* 🌐 *www.ticabus.com*).

GETTING AROUND GUATEMALA

Guatemalan buses come in three very different subspecies. Locals still favor the recycled Bluebird school buses known as *camionetas*; but the newer, pricier *pullmans*—once Greyhound coaches—are gaining popularity, especially for longer trips. Quicker and more comfortable are private minibus shuttle services: you can hire one for yourself or buy a seat on services with scheduled departures.

Dressed up in the gaudiest paint jobs around and blaring merengue, camionetas whiz along at breakneck speeds. They often start out from terminals near a market, but will screech to a halt whenever a potential passenger appears on the roadside. People pile in like hens in a coop, giving rise to the tourist nickname "chicken buses." Camionetas can get you just about anywhere cheaply and quickly, making them great for short trips. Tightly squeezed seating, short routes, and their drivers' disregard for basic road rules means they probably aren't a good idea on longer journeys. Their schedules are also loose, sometimes delaying departures until buses fill up. Be aware that on some routes the last bus of the day isn't always a sure thing, so always ask before waiting around.

Drivers and their assistants, called *cobradors* or *ayudantes,* are often a bit gruff, but really know their stuff: they can tell you whether you're on the right bus and remind you when and where to get off. Within cities, you pay the cobrador as you board (Q2 to Q4 is the norm); on intercity buses a fare collector passes through the bus periodically to take your fare, showing an amazing ability to keep track of riders who haven't paid. Large bags are typically stowed on top—this may make you nervous, but thefts aren't common. Except for occasional pickpocketings, incidents involving foreign travelers on public buses are rare.

Several companies operate long-distance pullmans, the self-styled first-class service, between Guatemala's main cities. On a few routes there are *de lujo* (deluxe) express buses with air-conditioning and other comforts, which cost a few dollars more. Take the pictures shown at bus terminals and on Web sites with a pinch of salt, and keep your comfort expectations low even on deluxe routes: maintenance standards fluctuate wildly and you never really know what you're getting until you board the bus. You can buy tickets in advance at bus terminals, but it's usually unnecessary for routes within Guatemala: arrive at bus terminals about a half-hour before your departure.

From Guatemala City ADN (Autobuses del Norte) has services to Flores and Río Dulce. Litegua operates many daily regular and first-class services between Guatemala City and Puerto Barrios. Línea Dorada offers direct bus service between Guatemala City and Flores. Servicios Turísticos Atitlán, known as STA, is one of the best-known shuttle companies.

Bus Information ADN (☎ *2251–0610* 🌐 *www.adnautobusesdelnorte.com*). **Litegua** (☎ *2220–8840* 🌐 *www.litegua.com*). **Línea Dorada** (☎ *2232–5506* 🌐 *www.tikalmayanworld.com*). **Servicios Turísticos Atitlán** (☎ *7762–2246* 🌐 *www.visit-antigua.com/vans.htm*).

CAR TRAVEL

Although it's easy to get around Guatemala without a car, it's much easier to visit small villages and explore the countryside if you have one. Taking to Guatemala's roads requires some courage, however. Local drivers pay scant attention to speed limits or traffic rules. Outside the big cities potholed road surfaces are common, and mountain roads are often bordered by sheer drops. If you are not used to driving very defensively, taking buses or private shuttles may be a better idea. Always allow extra travel time for unpredictable events, making sure to bring along snacks and drinks.

It's possible to enter Guatemala by land from Mexico, Belize, El Salvador, and Honduras. The Pan-American Highway, which passes through most major cities, connects the country with Mexico at La Mesilla and with El Salvador at San Cristóbal. It's also possible to travel to El Salvador via the coastal highway, crossing at Pedro de Alvarado or Valle Nuevo. Pacific routes to Mexico pass through Tecún Umán and El Carmen–Talismán.

To reach Belize, take the highway east from Flores, passing El Cruce before reaching the border town of Melchor de Mencos. There are also two routes into Honduras, through El Florido or Cinchado.

Travelers often get harassed or swindled at border towns. There is no entry fee, although you may be asked for a bribe. Rental agencies sometimes allow you to cross the border with their car, but you usually have to pay a fee to do so.

You can drive in Guatemala with a valid U.S. license for up to 30 days. Get an international driver's license if you plan to drive longer. Most roads leading to larger towns and cities are paved; those leading to small towns and villages are generally dirt roads. *Doble-tracción,* or four-wheel drive, is a necessity in many remote areas, especially at the height of the rainy season. Gas stations can also be scarce, so be sure to fill up before heading into rural areas. Consider bringing some extra fuel along with you. Don't count on finding repair shops outside the major towns.

Many locals ignore traffic laws, so you should be on your guard. *Alto* means "stop" and *Frene con motor* ("use engine to break" or downshift) means that a steep descent lies ahead. Travel only by day, especially if you are driving alone. Keep your eyes peeled for children or animals on the road. If you arrive at a roadblock such as a downed tree, do not attempt to remove the roadblock, simply turn around. Highway robbers often deliberately fell trees to ensnare drivers.

GASOLINE

There are plenty of gas stations in and near big cities in Guatemala. On long trips, fill your tank whenever you can, even if you've still got gas left, as the next station could be a long way away. An attendant always pumps the gas and doesn't expect a tip, though a small one is always appreciated. Plan to use cash, as credit cards are rarely accepted.

Most rental cars require premium unleaded gas, called *súper,* which costs about Q22 per *galón.* A growing number of *autoservicio* (self-service) pumps knock a quetzal off the gallon price.

PARKING

On-street parking generally isn't a good idea in Guatemala, as car theft is very common. Instead, park in a guarded parking lot. Many hotels have their own guarded parking lots.

RENTAL CARS

For safaris into the mountains, or for exploring smaller roads in areas like Petén, a *doble tracción* or *cuatro por cuatro* (four-wheel-drive vehicle) stands you in good stead. If money isn't an object, consider renting one no matter where you go: unpaved roads, mud slides in rainy season, and a general off-the-beaten-path landscape are status quo here. Note that most Belize agencies do not permit you to take their vehicles over the border into Guatemala or Mexico, and vice versa.

Compact cars like a Kia Picanto or VW Fox start at around $40 a day; for $50 to $60 you can rent a Mitsubishi Lancer, a VW Golf, or a Polo. Four-wheel-drive pickups start at $70 a day, though for a full cabin you pay up to $120. International agencies sometimes have cheaper per-day rates, but locals undercut them on longer rentals. Stick shifts are the norm in Guatemala, so check with the rental agency if you only drive automatics.

Contacts Ahorrent (☎ *2383–2802*). **Tabarini** (☎ *2331–2643*).

Major Agencies Alamo (☎ *800/522–9696, 2362–2701 in Guatemala*). **Avis** (☎ *800/331–1084, 2331–2750 in Guatemala*). **Budget** (☎ *800/472–3325, 2332–7744 in Guatemala*). **Hertz** (☎ *800/654–3001, 2470–3800 in Guatemala*). **National Car Rental** (☎ *800/227–7368, 2362–2701 in Guatemala*).

ROAD CONDITIONS

Immense improvements have been made to Guatemala's ravaged roads, and the primary highway network is in great shape. Potholed and unpaved surfaces are common when you get off main roads. Mountain roads are peppered with hairpin bends, and often don't have guardrails; conditions are particularly tough in the rainy season. Always pick a four-wheel-drive vehicle for travel off the beaten path.

Ongoing roadworks and the sheer volume of traffic can double journey times between major cities. Don't count on going any faster than 50 MPH on paved roads; 15 to 20 MPH is more normal on dirt roads.

Guatemalan road signage is far from perfect. There are usually signs pointing to large towns, but routes to smaller towns may not be clearly marked. Look for intersections where people seem to be waiting for a bus—that's a good sign that there's an important turnoff nearby. Markers on major highways designate distances in kilometers from Guatemala City, which, itself, is usually denoted on signs as GUATEMALA.

FROM	TO	DISTANCE
Guatemala City	Antigua	24 km (15 mi)
Antigua	Panajachel	60 km (37 mi)
Antigua	Quetzaltenango	215 km (134 mi)
Guatemala City	Cobán	212 km (132 mi)
Cobán	Flores	190 km (118 mi)
Flores	Tikal	60 km (37 mi)
Flores	Puerto Barrios	284 km (176 mi)
Guatemala City	Puerto Barrios	296 km (184 mi)
Guatemala City	Monterricot	134 km (80 mi)

ROADSIDE EMERGENCIES

Guatemala has no private roadside assistance clubs—ask rental agencies carefully about what you should do if you break down. You can also call the police or Provial, the state roadside assistance team, but expect both to take a long time to arrive. Operators on both lines usually speak only Spanish.

Emergency Services Guatemalan National Police (☎ *110*). **Provial** (☎ *1520*).

RULES OF THE ROAD

Drivers in Guatemala stick to the right. Seat belts are required, and the law is enforced. Using a cellular phone while you are driving is not permitted. There are few speed-limit signs, and police sometimes ignore speeders, though enforcement of all traffic laws is becoming more routine. As you approach small towns, watch out for *túmulos,* the local name for speed bumps.

Guatemala's highways are an adventure, especially when they run along the edges of cliffs soaring high above a valley. Trucks and buses drive unbelievably fast along these routes; if you don't feel comfortable keeping up the pace, pull over periodically to let them pass. The narrow roads mean you can be stuck motionless on the road for an hour while a construction crew stands around a hole in the ground. If you observe the rules you follow at home, you should be fine. Just don't expect everyone else to follow them.

CRUISE TRAVEL

Guatemala isn't a major cruise destination, but some ships on Panama Canal and South America cruises call at Puerto Quetzal, on the Pacific coast. A few Western Caribbean itineraries stop at Santo Tomás de Castilla, on the Caribbean coast.

Cruise Lines Holland America Line (☎ *206/281-3535 or 877/932-4259*). **Norwegian Cruise Line** (☎ *305/436-4000 or 800/327-7030*). **Princess Cruises** (☎ *661/753-0000 or 800/774-6237*). **Regent Seven Seas Cruises** (☎ *877/505-5370*).**Royal Caribbean International** (☎ *866/562-7625*).

SHUTTLE TRAVEL

Shuttles in Guatemala are private minivans that can seat eight to 15 passengers. You can either hire one for yourself or pay for a seat on a shared service. They're faster and more comfortable than public buses and maintain a fairly reliable schedule. We highly recommend them as a way to travel between popular destinations. Advance reservations are usually required.

Shuttles can be arranged at the airport, at travel agencies, and through most hotels and hostels. Popular routes, like those between Guatemala City, Antigua, Chichicastenango, Panajachel, and Quetzaltenango run three to five times daily; other routes may have less frequent departures.

A private shuttle between Antigua and Guatemala City airport costs $35 to $40;

a seat on the same shuttle is $12. Atitrans, Gray Line, and Servicios Turísticos Atitlán are three reputable companies that operate shuttles throughout the country.

Guatemala Companies Atitrans (☎ *7832-3371*). **Gray Line Guatemala** (☎ *2383-8600*). **Servicios Turísticos Atitlán** (☎ *5583-8328* 🌐 *www.visit-antigua.com/vans.htm*).

TAXI TRAVEL

Most Guatemalan cities are small enough to walk around, but taxis can be a good idea late at night or for longer trips. Meters are the norm in Guatemala City; everywhere else you need to agree upon your fare in advance. Wherever possible, get your hotel or restaurant to call you a cab, otherwise try to pick vehicles with a clearly painted number on the side, which means they're registered. Taxis in many communities are covered, three-wheeled Bajaj vehicles manufactured in India. Locals refer to them as *tuk-tuks*. You can often hire a taxi for a day or half-day trip, and many willingly shuttle you between Guatemala City and Antigua for $35. Taxi drivers aren't generally willing to change large bills, so carry enough for your trip and a small tip.

ESSENTIALS

ACCOMMODATIONS

Guatemala has lodging options for every budget, be it backpackers' digs, reliable international hotels, far-flung ecolodges, classy colonial inns, or rustic retreats with local flair.

By law, all lodgings are no-smoking. This includes your room, all common areas, and all outdoor areas on the property.

TIP→ Assume that hotels operate on the European Plan (EP, no meals) unless we specify that they use the Breakfast Plan (BP, with full breakfast), Continental Plan (CP, continental breakfast), Full American Plan (FAP, all meals), or Modified American Plan (MAP, breakfast and dinner), or are all-inclusive (AI, all meals and most activities).

APARTMENT AND HOUSE RENTALS

Short-term furnished rentals aren't common in Guatemala, and colonial-style villas in Antigua and occasionally Atitlán make up the bulk of the options. The biggest selection is at Ah! Guatemala, whereas Great Rentals has more unusual properties. Sublet.com and Vacation Rentals By Owner deal with more modest, run-of-the-mill apartments, often as cheap as $300 a week.

Contacts **Ah! Guatemala** (*www.ahguatemala.com/travel_and_tourism*). **Great Rentals** (☎ *512/493–0368* *www.greatrentals.com*). **Sublet.com** (*www.sublet.com*). **Villas International** (☎ *415/499–9490 or 800/221–2260* *www.villasintl.com*). **Vacation Rentals By Owner** (*www.vrbo.com*).

Exchange Clubs **Home For Exchange** (*www.homeforexchange.com*).

BED AND BREAKFASTS

The Guatemalan definition of B&B might not coincide with yours. The term is frequently extended to luxury hotels that happen to include breakfast in their price; indeed, these make up most of the pickings at Bed & Breakfast.com and Bed & Breakfast Inns Online. The lists at Ah! Guatemala and A Thousand Inns include many homier midrange establishments. For cheap, family-run places, try Traveller's Point.

Reservation Services **A Thousand Inns** (*www.1000inns.com*). **Ah! Guatemala** (*www.ahguatemala.com/travel_and_tourism/bed_and_breakfast*). **Bed & Breakfast.com** (☎ *512/322–2710 or 800/462–2632* *www.bedandbreakfast.com*). **Bed & Breakfast Inns Online** (☎ *615/868–1946 or 800/215–7365* *www.bbonline.com*). **Traveller's Point** (*www.travellerspoint.com*).

HOSTELS

Guatemala has no HI-affiliates, but Traveller's Point and Hostel World have ample listings and booking services. Consider sorting out your first few nights in advance, then get recommendations from fellow travelers for your next port of call.

Information **Hostels.com** (*www.hostels.com*). **Hostel World.com** (*www.hostelworld.com*). **Travellers' Point** (*www.travellerspoint.com*).

ECOLODGES

The International Ecotourism Society has online resources to help you pick someplace really green. The Rainforest Alliance gives you tips online for being a greener tourist and rates Guatemalan lodgings on their sustainability practices. Responsible Travel is an online travel agency for ethical holidays.

Information **International Ecotourism Society** (*www.ecotourism.org*). **Rainforest Alliance** (*www.ra.org*). **Responsible Travel** (*www.responsibletravel.com*).

COMMUNICATIONS

INTERNET

Internet access is widely available to travelers in Guatemala. Many high-end hotels offer some kind of in-room access for laptop users (often Wi-Fi), but note that you are sometimes charged extra for using this. Many hostels and language schools are also well connected, and usually charge reasonable rates.

All big cities have a choice of cybercafés, and even remote locations usually have at least one. Rates range between Q5 to Q12 an hour. Many have Internet-phone services.

Contacts Cybercafes (www.cybercafes.com) lists over 4,000 Internet cafés worldwide.

PHONES

The good news is that you can now make a direct-dial telephone call from virtually any point on earth. The bad news? You can't always do so cheaply. Calling from a hotel is almost always the most expensive option; hotels usually add huge surcharges to all calls, particularly international ones. In some countries you can phone from call centers or even the post office. Calling cards usually keep costs to a minimum, but only if you purchase them locally. And then there are mobile phones (⇨ *below*), which are sometimes more prevalent—particularly in the developing world—than landlines; as expensive as mobile phone calls can be, they are still usually a much cheaper option than calling from your hotel.

The country code for Guatemala is 502. To call Guatemala from the United States, dial the international access code (011) followed by the country code (502), and the eight-digit phone number, in that order. Guatemala does not use area codes.

CALLING WITHIN GUATEMALA

Guatemala's phone system is usually reliable. You can make local and long-distance calls from your hotel—usually with a surcharge—and from any public phone box or call center (known as *locutorios*). All Guatemalan phone numbers have eight digits.

Local calls in Guatemala are cheap. Most pay phones operate with phone cards, so it's worth buying one if you plan to make many local calls. You can buy a phone card in most grocery stores, or at Telgua offices. **■TIP→ Do not use the black, red, or blue wall-mounted phones with signs that read FREE COLLECT CALL. They charge a whopping $10-per minute to the number being called and have a 5-minute minimum.**

Useful Numbers Local Directory Assistance (in Spanish) (☎ *124*). **Operator Assistance (in Spanish)** (☎ *121*).

CALLING OUTSIDE GUATEMALA

To make international calls from Guatemala, dial 00, then the country code, area code, and number. Many public call centers (*locutorios*) use Internet telephone and so have very cheap rates, but communication quality can vary. Midrange and budget hotels sometimes have similarly competitive services. You can also make international calls from pay phones using a prepaid calling card. You can make collect calls to North America through the international operator.

The country code for the United States is 1.

You can use AT&T, Sprint, and MCI services from Guatemalan phones, though some pay phones require you to put coins in to make the call. Using a prepaid calling card is generally cheaper.

Useful Numbers International Operator (for collect calls) (☎ *147–120*).

Access Codes AT&T (☎ *From Guatemala City 138–126, from the rest of Guatemala 9999–190*). **MCI** (☎ *9999–189*). **Sprint** (☎ *9999–195*).

CALLING CARDS

Guatemala's public pay phones use prepaid calling cards, which you can purchase at small markets, pharmacies, and Telgua offices. Ask for a *tarjeta telefónica*. They come in denominations of Q20, Q30, and Q50; calls within Guatemala cost 50 centavos per minute.

MOBILE PHONES

Mobile phones are immensely popular in Guatemala—landlines are hard to get and expensive to maintain, so locals rely heavily on their cells for basic communication needs. Guatemalan mobile phones use the GSM network. If you have an unlocked

LOCAL DO'S AND TABOOS

CUSTOMS OF THE COUNTRY

■ Guatemala has a large indigenous population that maintains many Mayan traditions and religious rites. Be judicious when taking photographs at such events, and if in doubt, ask for permission. There are few taboos to worry about when interacting with Ladinos (non-indigenous Guatemalans).

■ Ask when someone or something is due to arrive and you're likely to get "*ahorita*" (now-ish) as a reply. Guatemalan timing is rather more flexible than North American, and you should be prepared to be patient. Buses and airplanes are usually fairly punctual, however. In Guatemala it is acceptable to make a quick hiss or whistle to get someone's attention—you may find that you even take up the habit yourself, particularly with waiters. You also may hear men catcall women in this way, which, unfortunately, is not considered terribly rude either.

GREETINGS

■ Guatemalans use formal salutations (*buenos días, buenas tardes,* and *buenas noches*) to greet strangers, business associates, and people with whom they don't have a close relationship. The formal "you" form, *usted,* is also common in such situations. Women often greet each other with a kiss on the cheek. Among men a handshake is the norm, sometimes accompanied by a friendly backslap.

SIGHTSEEING

■ In Guatemala's major cities you can dress pretty much as you would at home. In smaller villages, however, people are more conservative, so ditch the microminis and short shorts in favor of less revealing clothing.

■ With the exception of luxury buses and shuttles, the seats on Guatemalan buses are expected to fit three abreast. Always make room for others on buses. It's perfectly fine to step into the aisle to let someone take a middle or window seat.

OUT ON THE TOWN

■ Although drinking alcohol—especially beer—is very normal for Guatemalan men, Guatemalan women tend not to drink very much, if at all. Smoking is prohibited in all public venues, including bars and restaurants.

■ Public displays of affection are fine between heterosexual couples in big cities, but expect conservative—or even aggressive—reactions to same-sex couples.

■ If you are invited to someone's house for a meal, take along a small gift for the hostess.

LANGUAGE

■ Spanish is spoken by the majority of Guatemalans, many of whom might speak a Mayan language as their first language. Wherever tourist traffic is heavy, English speakers are plentiful. Spanish is the only way to communicate off the beaten path. Language schools are a huge business in Guatemala, and many offer quick "crash" courses which can help start you off on the right linguistic foot. Be aware that many Guatemalans will answer "yes" even if they don't understand your question, so as not to appear unkind or unhelpful. To minimize such confusion, try posing questions as "Where is so-and-so?" rather than "Is so-and-so this way?"

■ A phrase book and language-tape set can help get you started.

■ *Fodor's Spanish for Travelers* (available at bookstores everywhere) is excellent.

triband phone, and intend to call local numbers, it makes sense to buy a prepaid Guatemalan SIM card on arrival—rates will be much better than using your U.S. network.

There are three main mobile companies in Guatemala. Movistar, owned by Telefónica, has the cheapest rates: Q0.50 to Q1 per minute for local calls and Q1 to the U.S. Claro, owned by Telgua, is more expensive (Q1 for local calls and Q4 for U.S. calls) but has better coverage. Tigo is a happy medium. Prepaid SIM cards from all three companies cost between Q150 and Q200; prepaid phone packages start at around Q225 to Q500. You can then top up your credit with cards sold at most small grocery stores. Occasionally there are so-called half-price-minute sales, where you are credited twice the face value of your top-up card. Shops and stands from all three companies abound in the big cities, with more opening all the time.

■ TIP→ Many language schools rent mobile phones to their students, or have special deals for buying one.

Contacts Claro (🌐 *www.claro.com.gt*). **Mobal** (☎ *888/888–9162* 🌐 *www.mobalrental.com*) rents mobiles and sells GSM phones (starting at $99) that will operate in 140 countries. Per-call rates vary throughout the world. **Movistar** (🌐 *www.movistar.com.gt*). **Planet Fone** (☎ *888/988–4777* 🌐 *www.planetfone.com*) rents cell phones, but the per-minute rates are expensive. **Tigo** (🌐 *www.tigo.com.gt*).

CUSTOMS AND DUTIES

You're always allowed to bring goods of a certain value back home without having to pay any duty or import tax. But there's a limit on the amount of tobacco and liquor you can bring back duty-free, and some countries have separate limits for perfumes; for exact figures, check with your customs department. The values of so-called "duty-free" goods are included in these amounts. When you shop abroad, save all your receipts, as customs inspectors may ask to see them as well as the items you purchased. If the total value of your goods is more than the duty-free limit, you'll have to pay a tax (most often a flat percentage) on the value of everything beyond that limit.

WORD OF MOUTH

Was the service stellar or not up to snuff? Did the food give you shivers of delight or leave you cold? Did the prices and portions make you happy or sad? Rate restaurants and write your own reviews in "Member Reviews and Ratings" or start a discussion about your favorite places in "Travel Talk Forums" on www.fodors.com. Your comments might even appear in our books. Yes, you, too, can be a correspondent!

Visitors may enter Guatemala duty-free with a camera, up to six rolls of film, any clothes and articles needed while traveling, 500 grams of tobacco, 3 liters of alcoholic beverages, 2 bottles of perfume, and 2 kg of candy. Unless you bring in a lot of merchandise, customs officers probably won't even check your luggage, although a laptop may attract some attention.

It's illegal to export most Mayan artifacts. If you plan on buying such goods, do so only at reputable stores, and keep the receipt. You may not take fruits or vegetables out of Guatemala.

U.S. Information U.S. Customs and Border Protection (🌐 *www.cbp.gov*).

EATING OUT

When it comes to food, Guatemala seems eclipsed by its neighbor, Mexico. It's an unfair oversight, though: there are plenty of delicious dishes unique to the country. As most top-end restaurants specialize in European or American fare, you'll have to look to cheaper places (including markets and street vendors) for truly Guatemalan flavors. See our Flavors of Guatemala feature at the front of the book to learn more about regional specialties.

Guatemalans don't eat huge quantities of meat, but a little shredded chicken, ground beef, chorizo, or ham seems to make its way into just about every dish, so vegetarian options can be limited. In big cities Chinese and Italian restaurants abound, and are a good way for veggie lovers to stop feeling "beaned out." All the same, *ensalada de aguacate* (avocado salad), *pan de banana* (banana bread), and flan (a crème caramel dessert) never get dull.

Only the most expensive restaurants in Guatemala accept credit cards. The restaurants that we list (all of which are indicated by a ✕ symbol) are the cream of the crop in each price category. By law, all dining establishments are no-smoking, including any restaurant outdoor seating areas.

MEALS AND MEALTIMES

Lunch (*comida* or *almuerzo*) is the main meal and runs from noon to 2 or 3. Many restaurants do set-price meals of two or three courses at lunchtime. For Guatemalans, dinner is less important and often is just a light snack not long after sundown. Restaurants in major tourist areas offer more substantial fare and stay open later, but most places are all but deserted by 9.

Unless otherwise noted, the restaurants listed in this guide are open daily for lunch and dinner.

PAYING

In restaurants with waiter service, you pay the check (*la cuenta*) at the end of the meal. At street-food stands and in markets, you pay upfront. Credit cards are accepted in more expensive restaurants, but it's always a good idea to check before you order, especially as some establishments only accept one kind of credit card.

For guidelines on tipping see Tipping, below.

WINES, BEER, AND SPIRITS

Alcohol is available in just about every restaurant in Guatemala, though cheaper places have more limited choices. Beer is the local alcoholic drink of choice. Lager is the most popular style, usually served ice-cold. Good local brands include Gallo, Dorada, Brahva, and Cabro. Gallo also brews a dark beer called Moza.

Guatemala has no real wine market to speak of, but restaurants catering to tourists often have imported bottles from Chile and Argentina, and, less often, the United States. Imported liquor is easy to find in supermarkets; *ron* (rum) and *aguardiente* ("firewater" distilled from sugarcane) are favorite local tipples.

The official drinking age in Guatemala is 18, but this is rarely enforced.

ELECTRICITY

You won't need a converter or adapter, as the electrical current in Guatemala is 110 volts, the same as in the United States. Outlets in both countries take U.S.–style plugs. **TIP→ Power surges are fairly common, so consider carrying a surge stabilizer if you travel with expensive electrical items, such as a laptop.** In a few remote areas lodges and hotels may generate their own electricity. After the generators are turned off at night, light comes only from kerosene lanterns or your flashlight.

EMERGENCIES

In a medical or dental emergency, ask your hotel staff for information on and directions to the nearest private hospital or clinic. Taxi drivers should also know how to find one, and taking a taxi is often quicker than an ambulance. If you do need an ambulance, it's best to call for one from the hospital you want to go to; alternatively, you can call the Cruz Roja (Red Cross). Many private medical insurers provide online lists of hospitals and clinics in different towns. It's a good idea to print out a copy of these before you travel.

For theft, wallet loss, small road accidents, and minor emergencies, contact the nearest police station. Expect all dealings with the police to be a lengthy, bureaucratic business—it's probably only worth bothering if you need the report for insurance claims.

The government tourist office, INGUAT, operates an Asistur service, available toll-free 24 hours a day from any telephone in the country. Its English-speaking operators can put you in touch with the proper authority during emergencies.

Guatemala City uses three-digit phone numbers for calling police, fire, and ambulance. The rest of the country uses standard eight-digit numbers. We list them in each chapter.

Pack a basic first-aid kit, especially if you're venturing into more remote areas. If you'll be carrying any medication, bring your doctor's contact information and prescription authorizations. Getting your prescription filled in Guatemala might be problematic, so bring enough medication for your entire trip—and extras in case of travel delays.

Foreign Embassies United States (✉ *Av. La Reforma 7–01, Zona 10, Guatemala City* ☎ *2326–4000, 2331–2354 for after-hours emergency assistance* 🌐 *guatemala.usembassy.gov*).

General Emergency Contacts Asistur (☎ *1500*).

HEALTH

Guatemala's public hospitals are chronically underfunded, under-equipped, and understaffed. Although they will tend to you in an emergency, wherever possible, seek private medical care. Most big cities have at least a couple of private clinics or hospitals; there's usually at least one English-speaker on the staff. Treatment at such clinics can be very expensive, so medical insurance is a necessity.

SHOTS AND MEDICATIONS

Malaria is prevalent in areas below 1,500 meters (4,900 feet)—both Antigua and Lake Atitlán are too high to be at risk. Another mosquito-borne disease, dengue, is also a threat, particularly on the Pacific coast. The best way to prevent both is to avoid being bitten: cover up your arms and legs and use ample repellent, preferably one containing DEET. The CDC recommends chloroquine as a preventative antimalarial for adults and infants in Guatemala. To be effective, the weekly doses must start a week before you travel and continue four weeks after your return. There is no preventative medication for dengue.

SPECIFIC ISSUES IN GUATEMALA

In Guatemala it's best to drink only bottled water, called *agua purificada* or *agua mineral* in Spanish. It is available even at the smallest stores and is much cheaper than in North America.

The major health risk in Guatemala is traveler's diarrhea, so skip uncooked foods and unpasteurized milk and milk products. Ask for your drinks *sin hielo,* meaning "without ice." In Guatemala most top-of-the-line hotels have ice that's perfectly safe. Pepto-Bismol or Imodium (known generically as loperamide) can be purchased over the counter in Guatemala, but bring along your own stash in case you aren't near a pharmacy. Drink plenty of purified water or tea—chamomile is a good folk remedy. Pharmacies also sell sachets of rehydration salts (*suero oral*), or you can make your own: ½-teaspoon salt (*sal*) and 4-tablespoons sugar (*azúcar*) dissolved in a quart of water.

HOURS OF OPERATION

Most banks are open 9 to 4, but some stay open until 7 PM and many keep Saturday hours until noon. Many museums are closed Monday. Most have normal business hours, but some close for a couple of hours at midday. Tikal opens daily 8 to 6. Shops are generally open 10 to 7, many closing for a 1 to 3 lunch break. Small grocery stores known as *tiendas* usually keep longer hours than these.

HOLIDAYS

Año Nuevo (**New Year's Day**), January 1; *Semana Santa* (**Holy Thursday through Easter**), April 1–4, 2010, April 21–24,

2011, and April 5–8, 2012; *Día del Trabajador* (**Labor Day**), May 1; *Día del Ejército* (**Army Day**), June 30; *Nuestra Señora de la Asunción* (**Feast of the Assumption**), August 15 (Guatemala City only); *Día de la Independencia* (**Independence Day**), September 15; *Día de la Revolución* (**Revolution Day**), October 20; *Todos los Santos* (**All Saints' Day**), November 1; *Navidad* (**Christmas**), December 25. At this writing, Guatemala's congress is debating a bill that would move some secular holidays to the nearest Monday. Each town and region also has its own *fiesta* (festival), where carnival-like celebrations can last a whole week.

MAIL

Most Guatemalan towns have a post office, although your best bet is to send mail from a large city. Service at El Correo, the Guatemalan mail system, is improving, thanks to consultation and assistance from Canada Post. Most post offices open from 8:30 to 5:30. Airmail letters to North America cost Q6.50 and take a week or two to arrive. High-end hotels can usually send your mail for you, too.

Your hotel may be willing to receive mail for you. American Express also offers free mail collection at its main city offices for its cardholders.

Contacts El Correo (☎ *2413–0202* 🌐 *www.elcorreo.com.gt*).

SHIPPING PACKAGES

Expect packages you send through the Guatemalan mail system to take a very long time to arrive. They usually get there in the end, but it's worth paying extra for recorded delivery (*correo registrado*). Many stores can ship your purchases for you, for a cost. Valuable items are best sent with private express services. Couriers operating in Guatemala include DHL, UPS, and FedEx. Delivery within two to three business days for a 1-kg. (2.2-lb) package starts at about Q500.

Express Services DHL Worldwide Express (☎ *2379–1111*). **FedEx** (☎ *2411–2100*). **UPS** (☎ *2421–6000*).

MONEY

Guatemala can be remarkably cheap, especially when you're traveling in the villages of the highlands. Mid-range hotels and restaurants where locals eat are an excellent value. Rooms at first-class hotels and meals at the best restaurants, however, approach those in developed countries. Trips into remote parts of the jungle and specialty travel like river rafting and deep-sea fishing are also relatively expensive.

You can plan your trip around ATMs—cash is king for day-to-day dealings—and credit cards (for bigger spending). U.S. dollars can be changed at any bank and are accepted as payment at many businesses catering to tourists—large bills may provet difficult to change; leave all other currencies at home. Traveler's checks are useful only as a reserve. They can be exchanged for local currency at some banks, but few businesses accept them as payment.

Prices throughout this guide are given for adults. Substantially reduced fees are almost always available for children, students, and senior citizens.

TIP→ It is nearly impossible to find Guatemala's currency, the quetzal, outside the country, and if you can, it will be at a very unfavorable exchange rate. Wait until you arrive to change money.

ITEM	AVERAGE COST
Cup of Coffee	Q4–Q8
Glass of Beer	Q8
Sandwich	Q10
Museum Admission	Free–Q25
Set-price lunch	Q15–Q25

ATMS AND BANKS

ATMs—known locally as *cajeros automáticos*—are easy to find in Guatemalan cities. Screens on most offer you a choice of Spanish or English, and a growing number offer the indigenous Quiché language, too. Cards on the Cirrus and Plus networks can be used in ATMs bearing these signs: CREDOMATIC, BANCARED, BI, and 5B. Major banks in Guatemala include BAM, BanRural, and Bantrab. In some smaller cities finding an ATM is trickier. Technically, you should be able to go into the bank to withdraw money through a teller using your ATM card, but it's easier just to take ample cash supplies with you. **■ TIP→ ATMs often empty out before holiday weekends, so withdraw your cash beforehand.** Be sure your pin number only has four digits, as most Guatemalan ATMs don't accept longer ones. Make withdrawals from ATMs in daylight, never at night. Where possible, choose ATMs inside banks rather than freestanding ones.

CREDIT CARDS

Throughout this guide, the following abbreviations are used: **AE,** American Express; **D,** Discover; **DC,** Diners Club; **MC,** MasterCard; and **V,** Visa.

Visa is the most widely accepted credit card in Guatemala, followed by MasterCard and American Express. Diners Club and Discover might not even be recognized. If possible, bring more than one credit card, as some establishments accept only one type. You can usually pay by credit card in top-end restaurants, hotels, and stores; the latter sometimes charge a small surcharge for using credit cards. Many transportation and tour companies also take plastic.

It's a good idea to inform your credit-card company before you travel, especially if you're going abroad and don't travel internationally very often. Otherwise, the credit-card company might put a hold on your card owing to unusual activity—not a good thing halfway through your trip. Record all your credit-card numbers—as well as the phone numbers to call if your cards are lost or stolen—in a safe place, so you're prepared should something go wrong. Both MasterCard and Visa have general numbers you can call (collect if you're abroad) if your card is lost, but you're better off calling the number of your issuing bank, since MasterCard and Visa usually just transfer you to your bank; your bank's number is usually printed on your card.

■ TIP→ Before you charge something, ask the merchant whether or not he or she plans to do a dynamic currency conversion (DCC). In such a transaction the credit-card *processor* (shop, restaurant, or hotel, not Visa or MasterCard) converts the currency and charges you in dollars. In most cases you'll pay the merchant a 3% fee for this service in addition to any credit-card company and issuing-bank foreign-transaction surcharges.

Dynamic currency conversion programs are becoming increasingly widespread. Merchants who participate in them are supposed to ask whether you want to be charged in dollars or the local currency, but they don't always do so. And even if they do offer you a choice, they may well avoid mentioning the additional surcharges. The good news is that you *do* have a choice. And if this practice really gets your goat, you can avoid it entirely thanks to American Express; with its cards, DCC simply isn't an option.

Reporting Lost Cards American Express (☎ *800/528–4800 in the U.S. or 336/393–1111 collect from abroad*). **Diners Club** (☎ *800/234–6377 in the U.S. or 303/799–1504* *collect from abroad or 2338–6801 in Guatemala).* **Discover** (☎ *800/347–2683 in the U.S. or 303/902–3100 collect from abroad).* **MasterCard** (☎ *800/627–8372 in the U.S. or 636/722–7111 collect from abroad or 1–800/999–1480 in Guatemala).* **Visa** (☎ *800/847–2911 in the U.S. or 410/581–9994 collect from abroad or 1–800/999–0115 in Guatemala).*

CURRENCY AND EXCHANGE

Guatemala's currency is the quetzal, named after the national bird, and is equal to 100 centavos. Single quetzals come as both coins and bills. There are also 1-, 5-, 10-, 25-, and 50-centavo coins. Bills come in denominations of ½ (brown), 1 (green), 5 (purple), 10 (red), 20 (blue), 50 (orange), and 100 (tan). (The ½-quetzal bill is rarely seen these days.) The central bank has announced plans to introduce bills of 200 (aqua), 500 (gray), and 1,000 (ocher) quetzals sometime during 2010. At this writing, the exchange rate is 8.3 quetzals to the U.S. dollar.

U.S. dollars are widely accepted in Guatemalan shops and restaurants that cater to tourists, though the conversion rate will not be quite as good as at banks. Street-side money changers abound, but you'll be safer from scams if you change your money at a bank, even though the rates aren't quite as good. You can exchange money easily at the airport and at border crossings.

WORST-CASE SCENARIO

All your money and credit cards have just been stolen. In these days of real-time transactions, this isn't a predicament that should destroy your vacation. First, report the theft of the credit cards. Then get any traveler's checks you were carrying replaced. This can usually be done almost immediately, provided that you kept a record of the serial numbers separate from the checks themselves. If you bank at a large international bank like Citibank or HSBC, go to the closest branch; if you know your account number, you may be able to get a new ATM card. **Western Union** (☎ *800/325–6000* 🌐 *www.westernunion.com*) sends money almost anywhere, and has many authorized agents in Guatemala. Have someone back home order a transfer online, over the phone, or at one of the company's offices, which is the cheapest option. The U.S. State Department's **Overseas Citizens Services** (🌐 *www.travel.state.gov/travel* ☎ *202/501–4444*) can wire money to any U.S. consulate or embassy abroad for a fee of $30. Just have someone back home wire money or send a money order or cashier's check to the state department, which will then disburse the funds as soon as the next working day after it receives them.

PACKING

Whatever you do, pack light—casual, comfortable, hand-washable clothing. T-shirts and shorts are acceptable near the beach, while more conservative attire is appropriate in smaller towns. If you're heading to Antigua, the Verapaces, or the highlands, especially during the winter months, bring a sweater or jacket, as nights and early mornings can be chilly. Sturdy sneakers or hiking shoes or boots with rubber soles are essential. A pair of sandals (preferably ones that can be worn in the water) are indispensable, too. Jewelry—even the fake stuff—only attracts the wrong sort of attention. Scarves or beads are safer accessories.

"Insect repellent, sunscreen, sunglasses" is your packing mantra, and an umbrella or stashable raincoat are handy, too. Long-sleeve shirts and long pants will also protect your skin from the relentless sun and ferocious mosquitoes. Tissues and anti-bacterial hand wipes make trips to public toilets more pleasant. A handbag-sized flashlight is also very useful: blackouts and streets without proper lighting are commonplace. In the jungle, a camping mosquito net is invaluable when staying at places with no screens on the windows (or no windows at all). Snorkelers should try to bring their own equipment if there's room in the suitcase.

PASSPORTS AND VISAS

To enter Guatemala all U.S. citizens, regardless of age, need a passport valid for at least six months beyond their arrival. You are automatically granted a 90-day tourist visa at immigration. You may be asked to show a return or onward transportation ticket. Guatemala participates in a joint-immigration agreement with El Salvador, Honduras, and Nicaragua. Any side trips to those neighboring countries count toward your 90 days, too. If you plan to stay longer, you either need to leave that four-country region for 72 hours, or renew your visa at the office of the Departamento de Extranjería, a division of Guatemalan immigration, in the capital. This takes five days, and you'll need to leave your passport there. You can take that step once.

Info Departamento de Extranjería (✉ *7 Av. 1–17, Guatemala City* ☎ *2361–8476* 🌐 *www.migracion.gob.gt*).

U.S. Passport Information U.S. Department of State (☎ *877/487–2778* 🌐 *travel.state.gov/passport*).

GUATEMALA REQUIREMENTS	
Passport	Must be valid for 6 months after date of arrival.
Visa	Issued automatically to Americans on arrival.
Vaccinations and Medication	No vaccinations required; antimalarial medication advised for areas below 1,500 meters (4,900 feet).
Driving	U.S. driver's license accepted; CDW is compulsory on car rentals and will be included in the quoted price.
Departure Tax	US$30, usually included in ticket price, and Q20, payable in cash at the airport.

RESTROOMS

Guatemalan restrooms—look for the SANITARIOS sign—use Western-style toilets; cleanliness standards are often low, especially in public facilities such as bus and gas stations. Despite this, you often have to pay a small fee (a quetzal or two) to use these toilets. **■TIP→ Toilet paper is a rarity, so carry tissues with you.** Antibacterial hand wipes are also useful. Guatemalan plumbing generally can't handle toilet paper; throw it in the basket by the toilet instead.

SAFETY

Guatemala has a bad reputation for safety, and it's true that pickpocketings, muggings, and car thefts are common. However, most Central Americans are extremely honest and trustworthy. It's not uncommon for a vendor to chase you down if you accidentally leave without your change. Taking a few simple precautions when traveling in Guatemala is usually enough to avoid being a target.

Attitude is essential: strive to look aware and purposeful at all times. Look at maps before you go outside, not on a street corner. Hire taxis only from official stands at the airport, and ask hotels or restaurants to order you a cab. If you do hail one on the street, do so only at major intersections.

Don't wear anything that looks—or is—valuable. Even small items attract attention (your wedding ring, for example) and are best left behind. Limit your accessories to cheap beads and the like. Whipping out a flashy camera on a busy city street isn't a good idea either. Keep a very firm hold of handbags when out and about, and keep them on your lap in restaurants, not dangling off your chair.

Take special care when driving. If you can avoid it, don't drive after sunset. A common ploy used by highway robbers is to construct a roadblock, such as logs strewn across the road, and then hide nearby.

When unsuspecting motorists get out of their cars to remove the obstruction, they are waylaid. If you come upon a deserted roadblock, don't stop; turn around. In cities, always park in car parks, never on the street; and remove the front of the stereo, if possible.

Many popular destinations have a special tourist police service, known as the *Policía Turística* or just "Politur," a joint venture of INGUAT and the National Police. (Their presence is most evident in Antigua and at Tikal.) Aimed at reducing crimes against tourists, they're more like a private security service than a police force. As well as keeping a lookout at street corners, they'll accompany you on hikes and walks in places where safety is an issue.

Guatemalans don't have much faith in their regular police force: many officers are involved in highway-robbery and protection rackets. At best the police are well-meaning but under-equipped, so don't count on them to come to your rescue in a difficult situation.

The lonely slopes of the volcanoes near Antigua and Lake Atitlán have been frequented by muggers, so go with a group of people, a reputable guide, or a member of the Tourist Police, and carry only minimal valuables.

The increase in adoption of Guatemalan children has provoked the fear by many here, particularly rural villagers, that children will be abducted by foreigners. **Limit your interaction with children you do not know, and never take photos of children without asking permission of their parents first.**

The most important advice we can give you is that, in the unlikely event of being mugged or robbed, do not put up a struggle. Nearly all physical attacks on tourists are the direct result of their resisting would-be pickpockets or muggers. Comply with demands, hand over your stuff, and try to get the situation over with as quickly as possible—then let your travel insurance take care of it.

Nature can be menacing, too. A strong undertow lurks in the waters off the Pacific coast, making swimming there risky. Beaches have few, if any, lifeguards.

GOVERNMENT ADVISORIES

Violent crime is a serious issue in Guatemala and tourists have been victims.

Guatemala has four active volcanoes and earthquakes are a constant possibility. You can check the tectonic situation before your trip at **The U.S. Government Federal Management Agency (FEMA)** (🌐 *www.fema.gov*). June through November is hurricane season: both the Caribbean and Pacific coasts are often affected. During this time heavy rain frequently causes landslides, blocking roads and occasionally causing more serious destruction.

General Information and Warnings
U.S. Department of State (🌐 *www.travel.state.gov*).

PICKPOCKETS

Pickpockets are the most common threat in Guatemala. They typically work in pairs or in threes: one will distract you while another slips a hand into your pocket or backpack during the commotion. Distractions could include someone bumping into you, spilling something on you, or asking you for the time. Crowded markets or street corners are hot spots for this, especially if your hands are full with your luggage or purchases. Remember that children and old women are just as likely to be pickpockets as men; many are so skillful you won't realize you've been robbed until later.

Keep your money in a pocket rather than a wallet, which is easier to steal. If you carry a purse, choose one with a zipper and a thick strap that you can drape across your body; adjust the length so that the purse sits in front of you at or above hip level. On buses and in crowded areas, hold purses or handbags close to your body; thieves use knives to slice the bottom of a bag and catch the contents as they fall out.

Try to keep your cash and credit cards in different places, so that if one gets stolen you can fall back on the other. Avoid carrying large sums of money around, but always keep enough to have something to hand over if you do get mugged. Another good idea is to keep a dummy wallet (an old one containing an expired credit card and a small amount of cash) in your pocket, with your real cash in an inside or vest pocket: if your "wallet" gets stolen you have little to lose.

WOMEN

Traveling alone as a woman in Guatemala can be tiring. Catcalling single females, especially foreign ones, is practically routine. The best reaction is to make like local women and ignore it. Going to a bar alone will be seen as an open invitation for attention.

Unfortunately, Guatemala has also been the site of some disturbing assaults on women. These have occurred on buses, usually late at night in remote areas, so avoid traveling alone at night. There's very little crime outside the major cities, but it does happen. Hiring a guide through the local tourist office or through a respectable tour agency can help to avoid such situations.

TAXES

Guatemala has an international departure tax of $30—check your air ticket carefully as it's sometimes included in the price—and a domestic departure tax of Q5. You also have to pay a Q20 airport security fee.

Most Guatemalan hotels and some tourist restaurants charge an additional 10% tourist tax. There is a 10% V.A.T. on most consumer products, but it is already included in the display price. There is no tax refund scheme for visitors.

TIME

Guatemala is six hours behind G.M.T., the same as U.S. Central Standard Time. Daylight saving time is usually not observed, although the government has occasionally instituted the system in recent years on a last-minute, as-needed basis, depending on the energy situation.

TIPPING

In Guatemala tipping is a question of rewarding good service rather than an obligation. Restaurant bills don't include gratuities; adding 10% is customary. Bellhops and maids expect tips only in the most expensive hotels. You should also give a small tip to tour guides, or to guards who show you around ruins. Rounding up taxi fares is a way of showing your appreciation to the driver, but it's not expected.

TOURS

Wildland Adventures prides itself on culturally and ecologically sensitive trips. It has three Guatemala tours, all of which emphasize learning about Mayan culture, one of which combines Belize. One of AdventureSmith Explorations' nine-day Guatemala trips focuses exclusively on El Petén, and another focuses on the highlands; others combine Tikal and Palenque or Tikal and Copán.

British-based Responsible Travel has many Guatemala trips: the range includes low-budget packages and combinations with other Central American countries. Small groups and low-impact touring are also an important part of Intrepid Travel's holidays. They have 13 Guatemala trips, all aimed at independent travelers, that include a 10-day mountain-biking holiday, ecotours, language programs, and multi-week volunteer opportunities.

Adventure Center's trips usually involve a little bit of action (rafting, hiking, or cycling), as well as more standard touring. Guatemala is often combined with Mexico,

Belize, and Costa Rica on their longer holidays. Canoe, foot, bike, and even zip-line are some of the modes of transport on The World Outdoors' Guatemala Multi-Sport holiday.

Overseas Adventure Travel takes pride in small groups and excellent guides. One of its tours combines Guatemala with Honduras, El Salvador, and Belize.

Recommended Companies Adventure Center (☎ *800/228-8747* 🌐 *www.adventurecenter.com*). **AdventureSmith** (☎ *800/728-2875* 🌐 *www.adventuresmithexplorations.com*). **Intrepid Travel** (☎ *800/970-7299* 🌐 *www.intrepidtravel.com*).**Overseas Adventure Travel** (☎ *800/493-6824* 🌐 *www.oattravel.com*). **Responsible Travel** (☎ *44/1273/600030 [UK]* 🌐 *www.responsibletravel.com*). **The World Outdoors** (☎ *800/488-8483* 🌐 *www.theworldoutdoors.com*). **Wildland Adventures** (☎ *800/345-4453* 🌐 *www.wildland.com*).

BIRD-WATCHING

Cayaya Birding is a Guatemalan company. Their six set-itinerary birding tours last from 4 to 16 days; they can also arrange personalized tours.

Contacts Cayaya Birding (☎ *502/5308-5160* 🌐 *www.cayaya-birding.com*).

CULTURE

Culture Xplorers' Guatemala trip focuses on grassroots culture, includes visits to indigenous communities and coffee-farmers, and introduces you to Mayan textiles.

Contacts Culture Xplorers (☎ *866/877-2507* 🌐 *www.culturexplorers.com*).

FISHING

The Great Sailfishing Company has a range of escorted fishing packages based at villas or resorts on Guatemala's Pacific coast.

Contacts The Great Sailfishing Company (☎ *877/763-0851* 🌐 *www.greatsailfishing.com*).

INSPIRATION

Great Reads. Two Nobel Priz... top the Guatemala reading list. *I, Rig... Menchú* and *Crossing Borders* are autobiographical works chronicling the life of indigenous activist Rigoberta Menchú, who won the 1992 Nobel Peace Prize. Miguel Angel Asturias won the 1967 Nobel Prize for Literature; his best-known novels are *The President* and *Men of Maize.*

On Screen. Mel Gibson's bloody Mayan epic *Apocalypto* was loved by critics and hated by Guatemalan Maya—no matter what you think, the scenery is fabulous.

VISITOR INFO

The Guatemala Tourist Commission, known as INGUAT, has offices in Guatemala City (city and airport), Antigua, Panajachel, Quetzaltenango, and Flores (city and airport). The Antigua and Panajachel offices are excellent; staff members at the others are helpful but have few resources beyond free maps to hand out. The offices can also put you in contact with the Tourist Police, who run free escort services to visit popular sights. The ubiquitous TOURIST INFORMATION signs you see around Antigua, Panajachel, Quetzaltenango, and Flores are private agencies looking to sell you their own tours rather than unbiased sources of information.

Tourist Information Guatemala Tourist Commission (INGUAT) (☎ *2421-2800* 🌐 *www.visitguatemala.com*).

ONLINE TRAVEL TOOLS

We're really proud of our Web site: Fodors.com is a great place to begin any journey. Scan "Travel News" for suggested itineraries, travel deals, restaurant and hotel openings, and other up-to-the-minute info. Check out "Today's Top Deals" to research prices and book plane tickets, hotel rooms, rental cars, and vacation packages. Head to "Travel Talk Forums" for on-the-ground pointers n travelers who frequent our message boards. You can also link to loads of other travel-related resources.

All About Guatemala **Guatemala Tourist Commission** (*www.visitguatemala.com*), Guatemala's official tourism site, has overviews of different destinations in Guatemala and is a useful pre-trip planning resource. **Guatemala-web** (*www.guatemalaweb.com*) is run by a local travel agent and has useful advice about Guatemala's different regions. **Latin American Network Information Center** (*lanic.utexas.edu*), based at the University of Texas, provides a wealth of tourism, arts, academic, cultural, business, and political links to Internet information about Guatemala and Latin America. **Turansa** (*www.turansa.com*) has general information about travel in Guatemala and some good maps.

Currency Conversion **Google** (*www.google.com*) does currency conversion. Just type in the amount you want to convert and an explanation of how you want it converted (e.g., "14 Guatemalan quetzals in dollars"), and then voilà. **Oanda.com** (*www.oanda.com*) also allows you to print out a handy table with the current day's conversion rates. **XE.com** (*www.xe.com*) is a good currency-conversion Web site.

Media **Prensa Libre** (*www.prensalibre.com*) is the country's most respected daily newspaper (in Spanish). **Revue Magazine** (*www.revuemag.com*), the online version of a monthly English-language magazine, has articles on travel as well as local news and culture. **Siglo XXI** (*www.sigloxxi.com*) is a Spanish-language daily newspaper.

Safety **Transportation Security Administration** (*TSA; www.tsa.gov*).

Time Zones **Timeanddate.com** (*www.timeanddate.com/worldclock*) can help you figure out the correct time anywhere.

Weather **Accuweather.com** (*www.accuweather.com*) is an independent weather-forecasting service with good coverage of hurricanes. **Weather.com** (*www.weather.com*) is the Web site for the Weather Channel.

Other Resources **The World Factbook** (*www.cia.gov/library/publications/the-world-factbook*), published by the CIA, has profiles of every country in the world. It's a good source if you need some quick facts and figures.

INDEX

PHOTO CREDITS

14, Bruno Morandi/age fotostock. 15, Danita Delimont/Alamy. 18, J Marshall-Tribaleye Images/Alamy. 19 (left), Inger Hogstrom/age fotostock. 19 (right), Rico S. Rostro/age fotostock. 20, Sylvain Grandadam/age fotostock. 21 (left), Ryan Fox/age fotostock. 22 (right), Robert Harding Picture Library Ltd/Alamy.

NOTES

NOTES

NOTES

ABOUT OUR WRITER

Central America–based freelance writer and pharmacist **Jeffrey Van Fleet** has spent the last 17 years enjoying the isthmus's long rainy seasons and Wisconsin's cold winters. (Most people would try to do it the other way around.) No matter what the time of year, he never passes up any chance to partake of the incredible variety that is Guatemala. Jeff is a regular contributor to Costa Rica's English-language newspaper *the Tico Times* and has written about Central America for United Airlines' inflight magazine *Hemispheres*. He has contributed to Fodor's guides to Costa Rica, Peru, Chile, Argentina, Panama, Los Cabos & Baja, and Central and South America.

Teresa Nicholas and **Gerard Helferich** are former book-publishing executives who left the fast lane in 2002 to become freelance writers. Since then, Teresa completed a memoir and is a contributor to *Delta* and *Mississippi* magazines, as well as a commentator on NPR's Opinion Page. Gerard is the author of two books, *Humboldt's Cosmos: Alexander von Humboldt and the Latin American Journey That Changed the Way We See the World*, and *High Cotton: Four Seasons in the Mississippi Delta*. They divide their time between San Miguel de Allende, Mexico, and Yazoo City, Mississippi. For this book they updated the Guatemala City and Las Verapaces chapters and wrote the Guatemalan regional cuisine feature.